SECURITY, STRATEGY, AND MILITARY DYNAMICS IN THE SOUTH CHINA SEA

Cross-National Perspectives

Edited by
Gordon Houlden, Scott N. Romaniuk,
and Nong Hong

With a Foreword by
Stein Tønnesson

BRISTOL
UNIVERSITY
PRESS

First published in Great Britain in 2021 by

Bristol University Press
1-9 Old Park Hill
Bristol
BS2 8BB
UK
t: +44 (0)117 954 5940

Details of international sales and distribution partners are available at bristoluniversitypress.co.uk

British Library Cataloguing in Publication Data
A catalogue record for this book is available from the British Library

ISBN 978-1-5292-1345-4 hardcover
ISBN 978-1-5292-1346-1 ePub
ISBN 978-1-5292-1347-8 ePdf

Cover design by Clifford Hayes
Front cover image: Alamy/dec925
Bristol University Press uses environmentally responsible print partners
Printed and bound in Great Britain by CPI Group (UK) Ltd,
Croydon, CR0 4YY

FSC
www.fsc.org
MIX
Paper from responsible sources
FSC® C013604

Contents

List of Tables

Notes on Contributors

Rommel C. Banlaoi is President of the Philippine Association for Chinese Studies, a member of the Management Board of the World Association for Chinese and a member of the Board of Directors of China-Southeast Asia Research Center on the South China Sea. He is Professorial Lecturer at the Department of International Studies at Miriam College, the Philippines and Chairman of the Philippine Institute for Peace, Violence and Terrorism Research (PIPVTR). He obtained his PhD in International Relations at Jinan University, China.

Tobias Burgers is a project assistant professor at the Keio Global Research Institute and at the Cyber Civilization Research Center at Keio University, Japan and a non-resident research fellow at the Taiwan Center for Security Studies, National Chengchi University. His research focuses on new technologies – AI, cyber and robotics – and their impact on international security and military relations, with a geographical focus on East Asia. He holds a doctorate from the Otto Suhr Institute, Free University Berlin.

Leszek Buszynski is Honorary Professor at the Strategic and Defence Studies Centre at the Australian National University. He was professor of International Relations in the Graduate School of International Relations at the International University of Japan. He has published widely on Asia-Pacific security issues and is co-editor of *The South China Sea: From Regional Maritime Dispute to Geostrategic Competition* (2020) and author of *The Geopolitics of the Western Pacific: China Japan and the United States* (2019).

John Callahan is Dean of the School of Graduate and Professional Studies, New England College, USA. He is also Director for Combined Online Military Programs in International Relations, Homeland Security, and Public Policy for New England College. He received a PhD in International Studies from Old Dominion University in 2015. His research focus is on foreign policy decision making, framing, and strategic communication. He is a Co-Convenor for the Political Science Association of the UK German

Studies Group, focusing on the rise of populism in Europe. Callahan served as deputy spokesman at the Office of the Director of National Intelligence and was honoured to be selected by the Department of Defense and the Department of State to serve as a public affairs officer at the American Embassy in Baghdad, Iraq. He has served on the Board of Directors of the International Ambassador Club since 2018.

Senia Febrica is the knowledge exchange associate of the One Ocean Hub, University of Strathclyde. She is also an honorary senior researcher at the American Studies Center, Universitas Indonesia. She received her PhD from the University of Glasgow. Her research on militarized civil society organizations in Indonesia was funded by the Gerda Henkel Stiftung (2015–2017). Her book, *Maritime Security and Indonesia: Cooperation, Interests and Strategies*, was published in 2017.

Sourabh Gupta is a senior Asia-Pacific international relations policy specialist with 15 years of Washington, DC-based experience in a think tank and political risk research and advisory capacity, and is Resident Senior Fellow at the Institute for China-America Studies. His areas of specialization include: analysis of key major power relationships in the Asia-Pacific region (China–USA, China–Japan, China–India, USA–Japan, USA–India, Japan–India relations); political, security, and economic risk evaluation of key states in the Asia-Pacific region; territorial disputes and maritime law-related developments in the Asia-Pacific region; analysis of developments in Asian economic regionalism; and World Trade Organization and Asia-Pacific-related trade policy, politics, and negotiations. He is a member of the United States Council for Security Cooperation in the Asia-Pacific and was a 2012 East Asia Forum Distinguished Fellow.

Đỗ Thanh Hải is Senior Fellow at the Diplomatic Academy of Vietnam. He obtained a doctorate from the Australian National University and a master's degree in Global Studies from the European Union's Erasmus Mundus Global Studies Program.

Joshua Hastey is Visiting Assistant Professor in the Robertson School of Government at Regent University and Adjunct Professor of Strategy at the United States Naval War College. He completed his PhD in International Studies at Regent University. He specializes in international security and grand strategy, with special interests in the politics of territorial disputes and United States–China relations. Ongoing research projects explore the politics of territorial disputes in the Arctic, the role of power shifts on interstate bargaining, and the effects of regime change on state foreign policymaking.

Nong Hong is Executive Director and Senior Fellow of the Institute for China-America Studies. She holds a PhD in the interdisciplinary study of international law and international relations from the University of Alberta, Canada and held a postdoctoral fellowship in the University's China Institute. She was ITLOS-Nippon Fellow for International Dispute Settlement (2008–2009) and Visiting Fellow at the Center of Oceans Law and Policy, University of Virginia (2009), at the Max Planck Institute for Comparative Public Law and International Law (2007), and at the Australia National Center for Ocean Resources and Security (2019). She is also a research fellow with the National Institute for South China Sea Studies, China, and the China Institute, University of Alberta, Canada. Her research takes an interdisciplinary approach to examining international relations and international law, with a focus on international relations and comparative politics in general, ocean governance in East Asia, law of the sea, international security, particularly non-traditional security, and international dispute settlement and conflict resolution. Her publications include *China's Role in the Arctic: Observing and Being Observed* (2020) and *UNCLOS and Ocean Dispute Settlement: Law and Politics in the South China Sea* (2012).

Gordon Houlden is Director Emeritus of the China Institute, Professor of Political Science and Adjunct Professor of the Alberta School of Business, Canada. He is also Adjunct Professor at the National Institute for South China Sea Studies. Houlden joined the Canadian Foreign Service in 1976 and was posted to Havana, Hong Kong (twice), Warsaw, Beijing (twice), and as Executive Director of the Canadian Trade Office in Taipei (2004–2006). Twenty-two of his years in the Canadian foreign service were spent working on Chinese affairs. Under Houlden's leadership, the China Institute has focused on contemporary China studies, with an emphasis on Canada's trade, investment, and energy linkages with China. He has been interviewed by many Canadian, Chinese, and other international media on Asian economic, trade, and investment issues.

Masafumi Iida is Senior Research Fellow, China Division, National Institute for Defense Studies (NIDS). He has held various positions within NIDS, and was assigned as senior staff to the Defense Policy Bureau within the Japanese Ministry of Defense. Additionally, he completed a term as Visiting Scholar with the Center for East Asian Studies at Stanford University in 2011 and with the China Maritime Studies Institute at the United States Naval War College in 2014. Iida has focused his research primarily on China's foreign and security policies and in particular the growing maritime implications of this relationship within East Asia. His publications in English include, "China's Foreign Strategy Causes Friction with the Existing World

Order," NIDS China Security Report (2019); "Japan's Reluctant Embrace of BRI?" Working Paper for BCAS (2018); and "China Establishing Regional Dominance," *Strategic Vision* (2014).

Alexander Korolev is Lecturer in Politics and International Relations in the School of Social Sciences, Faculty of Arts and Social Sciences, at the University of New South Wales, Sydney. His research interests include international relations theory and comparative politics with special reference to great power politics and China–Russia–United States relations in East and Southeast Asia. His recent articles appeared in various peer-reviewed journals, including *Foreign Policy Analysis*, *International Studies Review* and *Journal of Strategic Studies*.

YingHui Lee is Senior Analyst with the Maritime Security Programme at the S. Rajaratnam School of International Studies, Nanyang Technological University. She holds a BA (Hons) in international relations and economics from the University of Reading and a masters in international relations from Peking University. Her main research interests are in maritime security and cooperation in the Indo-Pacific, maritime trade and the blue economy, and Chinese foreign policy with particular focus on China's ocean policy.

Mingjiang Li is Associate Professor at S. Rajaratnam School of International Studies (RSIS), Nanyang Technological University, Singapore. He is also Coordinator of the China Programme at RSIS. He received his PhD in political science from Boston University. His main research interests include China–ASEAN relations, Sino-United States relations, Asia-Pacific security, and domestic sources of Chinese foreign policy. He is the author (including editor and co-editor) of 12 books. His recent books are *New Dynamics in US–China Relations: Contending for the Asia Pacific* (lead editor, 2014) and *Mao's China and the Sino-Soviet Split* (2012). He has published papers in various peer-reviewed journals including the *Journal of Strategic Studies*, *Global Governance*, *Cold War History* and *Journal of Contemporary China*. Li frequently participates in various track-two events on East Asian regional security.

Kun-Chin Lin is Lecturer in Politics and Deputy Director of the Forum on Geopolitics at the University of Cambridge. He graduated magna cum laude from Harvard College and obtained his PhD in political science from the University of California at Berkeley. He was a Leverhulme Postdoctoral Fellow at the University of Oxford and taught at King's College London and the National University of Singapore. His research projects include industrial policy and privatization of Chinese state-owned enterprises, energy security, transport infrastructure development, and the economic and security nexus in maritime governance in Asia. He is an editorial board member of *Business and Politics*, *Cambridge Review of International Affairs*, *Maritime Policy and Management*, and *Chinese (Taiwan) Yearbook of International Law and Affairs*.

Nguyễn Thị Linh is a research fellow at the Diplomatic Academy of Vietnam. She works on a wide range of maritime security topics including arms build-up, maritime strategies, and nautical politics.

Ian Park is a barrister in the Royal Navy and specializes in international law. He has been a legal adviser on operations to Afghanistan and, on many occasions, to the Middle East. Park is, or has been, a Mountbatten Fellow at Cambridge University, a Hudson Fellow at Oxford University, a Visiting Fellow at Harvard Law School, a First Sea Lord's Fellow, and a Freeman of the City of London. He has a doctorate in law from Balliol College, Oxford and is the author of *The Right to Life in Armed Conflict* (2018). In 2018, he was the winner of the outstanding performance by an HM Forces barrister at the United Kingdom Bar Awards.

Sumathy Permal is Fellow and Head of Centre for Straits of Malacca with the Maritime Institute of Malaysia. Permal's research areas are on geopolitics and geostrategies in the Asia-Pacific and maritime security issues in the Indo-Pacific. Permal is on the editorial board of the *Australian Journal of Maritime and Ocean Affairs Australia* and is Associate Member of the Corbett Centre for Maritime Policy Studies. Permal's publications include "Post SCS Arbitration Development and Issues Relating to Freedom of Navigation, Rights of Coastal States and Environmental Protection in the 'Area'" (2018) in *Asian Politics and Policy*, "The Straits of Malacca: A Critical Sea lanes in the Indian Ocean" (2016) in *Pentagon's Yearbook*, and "Malaysia's Diplomatic and Security Responses" (2016, *South China Sea Lawfare: Legal Perspectives and International Responses to the Philippines v China Arbitration Case, Geopolitics Trends in South China Sea 2013–2015*, eds Liu and Spangler).

Scott N. Romaniuk received his PhD in international studies from the University of Trento. He holds an MRes in political research, an MA in terrorism, crime and global security, and an MA in military studies (joint warfare). His teaching and research specializations include international relations, military and strategic studies, security studies, terrorism and political violence, and research methods. His current research explores China's global security and military roles, China's political, economic, and (cyber-)security policies in the surrounding region including the South China Sea, and the rise of security architectures in Asia, robotic systems in international security, and technology and the future of warfare.

Yann-huei Song is a research fellow in the Institute of European and American Studies, Academia Sinica, Taipei. He is also Global Fellow of the Peace Research Institute Oslo. Song received his masters in political science from Indiana State University and PhD in international relations from Kent State University, Ohio. He has broad academic interests covering ocean law and policy studies, international fisheries law, international environmental law, maritime security, and maritime disputes in the East and South China Seas. One of his most recent publications appears in the *International Journal of Ocean Development and International Law*, titled "The July 2016 Arbitral Award, Interpretation of Article 121(3) of the UNCLOS, and Selecting Examples of Inconsistent State Practices," (2018). Song is a member of the editorial boards of *Ocean Development*, *International Law*, and *Chinese (Taiwan) Yearbook of International Law and Affairs*.

Stein Tønnesson is a Norwegian peace researcher and historian. His doctoral thesis, defended at the University of Oslo in 1991, was on the international history of the Vietnamese Revolution in 1945. His main areas of research are Vietnam, nation building in Southeast Asia, and the disputes in the South China Sea. In the years 2011–16 he led a research programme at the University of Uppsala on "East Asia peace" since 1979. He is a frequent commentator in Norwegian and international media on issues of peace and conflict and writes regularly for the Norwegian weekly *Morgenbladet*. He has also worked on energy security and has served as a consultant to several Norwegian companies. Since 2007, he has served on the board of Norfund, a state-owned development finance institution.

Hui-Yi Katherine Tseng is Research Associate in the East Asian Institute, National University of Singapore. Trained as an international law scholar with trade dispute settlement experience (a member of the World Trade Organization dispute settlement team of Taiwan, 2003–2007), her research interests expand from international trade dispute resolutions to legal-political developments in East and Southeast Asia. She is studying regional legal and political issues using an interdisciplinary approach, touching upon international law, geopolitics, history, international relations, political theory, and sociology. Tseng hopes that her research and works can help solicit reconsiderations of the legal-political order in the post-World War II era in this region and help identify new directions and challenges amid the increasing uncertainties of this new era.

Veasna Var completed his PhD in international relations and political sciences at the University of New South Wales at the Australia Defence Force Academy in 2020. His thesis, "Assessing the Impact of China's Aid on

Sustainable Development in Cambodia: 1993–2018," examines the role of Chinese investment in the development process of Cambodia. His primary research pertains to development studies, Cambodian foreign and defence policy, Cambodian strategic partnerships, Chinese foreign policy, and the role of foreign aid in the Asia-Pacific region. He has published upwards of 30 articles in the field of political science. His professional career includes 30 years' experience in the public sector and the rank of Brigadier in the Royal Cambodian Armed Forces. He has also completed masters degrees in strategic studies (Deakin University and United States Army War College), security studies (National Defence Academy of Japan), and Human Resource Management (University of New South Wales, Sydney).

Li Yang is Assistant President of the National Institute for South China Sea Studies (NISCS). He is also Director of the NISCS Research Center for Maritime Economy. He graduated from the Law School of Wuhan University and got his masters law in 1996. He then became a diplomat in the Ministry of Foreign Affairs of China, working in the Department of Treaties and Law and the Department of Boundary and Ocean Affairs successively. Most of his jobs in the Ministry were focused on issues relating to the law of the sea as well as to the territorial and maritime jurisdiction disputes in the South China Sea and the East China Sea. His overseas posts include Counsellor of China's Permanent Mission to the United Nations. He joined the NISCS in 2017.

Sukjoon Yoon is a retired captain in the Republic of Korea Navy and is currently a senior fellow of the Korea Institute for Military Affairs. Yoon's more than 35 years of commissioned service included 13 years at sea as a principle surface warfare officer and several command and staff appointments. He holds a masters in Chinese politics from the National Defense University, Taiwan and a PhD in Chinese military affairs from Bristol University. His academic work focuses on military strategy, maritime/naval strategy, maritime security, and Chinese military modernization.

Foreword

Stein Tønnesson

For well over a hundred years, the South China Sea (SCS) has been a theatre for sovereignty disputes and naval rivalry. There are long-standing disputes among its surrounding states over sovereignty to islands, notably the Paracel and Spratly island groups, and Scarborough Shoal. Since the end of the Second World War, when states began to expand their territorial waters and demand rights to their continental shelf, there has also been conflict concerning overlapping claims to maritime zones. And naval power has shifted between China, Japan, Russia, European colonial empires, and the United States (US).

The stakes of the sovereignty disputes rose considerably in the 1970s, when oil discoveries were made, more islands were occupied or conquered, and the 3rd United Nations Convention on the Law of the Sea (UNCLOS 3) adopted the principle of a 200 nautical mile exclusive economic zone (EEZ). In its famously vague article 121.3, UNCLOS failed to resolve if very small islands, rocks or reefs can be used as basis for generating EEZ and continental shelf claims. In 2016, when an Arbitral Tribunal in the *Philippines v. China* case sought to resolve this issue, its ruling was not accepted by either Beijing or Taipei (Taiwan occupies the largest Spratly island, Yann-huei Song, Chapter 4).

Since UNCLOS 3 there is also a long-standing dispute over freedom of navigation, pitting some of the coastal states against the world's leading naval powers and small commercial states. While the latter group stands for a principle of total freedom for both civilian and military navigation in the EEZs of other states, seeing them as "international waters," the former group reserves a right in their national legislation to inhibit military reconnaissance and exercises in their EEZs.

Only a few of the SCS's boundary disputes have been resolved, and there is a constant risk that incidents related to fisheries, oil exploration or naval and aerial operations will escalate and lead to confrontation. This risk has most likely increased with the proliferation of weapons systems – precision-guided missiles, aircraft, naval surface vessels, submarines, drones (see Scott N. Romaniuk and Tobias Burgers, Chapter 2) – and also the expansion of coast guard and fishing fleets. As the first chapter in the present volume affirms, there are three main overlapping inter-state systems, within and between which conflict is played out: a US system of bilateral alliances; the Association of Southeast Asian Nations (ASEAN) and ASEAN Regional Forum (ARF); and the Sino-US rivalry.

Until 2010, when the US was still seen as a naval hegemon in East Asian waters, it preferred to remain aloof diplomatically, always emphasizing that it did not take a position in the legal disputes over sovereignty and sovereign rights. Since 2010, the US has continued to refrain from supporting particular national claims. Yet, in reaction to China's rising economic and military power, the US has more actively than before insisted on the principle of a rules-based order, with maritime zones being measured by distance from coasts, and with total freedom of navigation in international waters, including military reconnaissance and exercises. The US defines EEZs as "international waters" as far as navigation is concerned. To back up their understanding of international law, the US Navy (USN) as well as some other navies regularly demonstrate their navigational rights by conducting so-called Freedom of Navigation Operations (FONOPs). China sees the FONOPs as highly provocative, and has dramatically upped the ante by reclaiming huge amounts of land in the Spratlys, and building installations on seven islands or reefs, and deploying weapons and reconnaissance systems on them.

One positive aspect of the rising tensions in the SCS is the research and debates they have stimulated among analysts and scholars in the countries concerned, both in and outside the region. Most analysts are patriots. If they do not always argue in favour of their own nation's claims they at least do not seek to undermine them. So, to some extent, as can be seen in the present volume, their arguments are set out against each other. A trend is also visible, however, for scholars and quite a few policy makers to establish platforms for respectful and innovative discussions based on common values: peace and conflict avoidance, environmental protection, management of fish stocks, and a rules-based international order. The trend began in 1990–91, with the Managing Potential Conflict in the SCS workshops, organized annually by Indonesian Ambassador Hasjim Djalal and the late Professor Ian Townsend-Gault of the University of British Columbia, with Canadian funding. The trend was further stimulated by the Council for Security Cooperation in the Asia Pacific (CSCAP), which was established in 1993 by a number of regional think tanks. On the official level the trend manifested itself in the 2002 China-ASEAN Declaration on the Conduct of Parties and in the now still ongoing negotiations for a legally binding Code of Conduct (COC).

In the last decade, the trend towards more mutual understanding has been stimulated by a string of scholarly conferences in one country after the other, with China, Vietnam, and the US as the most active, and with Canada taking a constructive background role. At these conferences, the host nations have withstood the temptation to use them for propaganda. Scholars have been invited to express widely different views and perspectives, which have subsequently been reflected in a growing scholarly literature. The present book is an eminent example of that trend. Its 23 authors come from more than ten different countries. Readers of their texts will realize how many perspectives we need to apply if we want to achieve a comprehensive understanding of the conflicts in the SCS.

Introduction: Strategic Challenges and Escalating Power Rivalry in the South China Sea

Scott N. Romaniuk and Nong Hong

The South China Sea (SCS) dispute is regarded as the most complex and challenging ocean-related regional conflict in East Asia. The security in the SCS is a concern for both the regional countries (for example, China, Vietnam, the Philippines, Malaysia, and Brunei) and extra-regional countries (for example, the United States (US), Russia, Australia, India, and Japan), among others, due to their strategic and economic interests in this region. While many contend that competition and disputes over the region are principally concerned with its natural resources, others argue that the essence of the dispute is oriented toward China's expanding power and challenge to the status quo position of the US and its hegemonic power, though China has moved against other states in the region to enhance its own strategic position overall, amplifying existing tensions over the region's riches and bring states closer to conflict. China, often characterized as a revisionist power, however, is not the only state to project its intentions to defend its interests in the region. Among other states, the Philippines, Indonesia, and Vietnam also exhibit provocative pursuits and competing interests, potentially imperilling prospects for peace and dispute resolution as well as raising concerns about the increase of military confrontation between states.

State policies, driven in part by revisionist behaviour, have been formulated and implemented not only to support major geographic claims and politico-military positions but also to contain the growing military and economic power – notably that of China – and interests of competing states in the region. The US, with its self-claimed "Pivot to Asia" in 2010 and its "Free and Open Indo-Pacific Strategy" efforts to curb the economic and military interests of China and others, has contributed to the militarization of the SCS. China, for its part, has constructed military facilities on several features in the SCS. The US and other outside actors largely situate their concerns regarding the SCS in terms of preserving freedom of navigation (FON). This volume engages the geostrategic motivations, interests, and reactive measures of states concerning the SCS, and aims to present the most comprehensive and elucidating volume on states' policies and interests in the SCS and their system impact on the security architecture of the region.

This volume is comprised of 18 chapters, including two introductory chapters, across four parts that address the respective perspectives from (1) claimants of the contested SCS, (2) non-claimants in Southeast Asia, (3) Quadrilateral Security Dialogue (QSD) states, and (4) non-claimants in Europe and Eurasia. The volume's chapters present some level of engagement and interaction with one another whereby chapters reference the discussions and data presented. Chapter 1 explores various security structures of the SCS, both as context for ongoing competition between Washington, DC and Beijing, and as a complex system of states whose interests shape and constrain the behaviour of both major powers that vie for regional primacy. This chapter analyses the multiple security structures that exist as part of regions within a larger region, locates the sources of both diplomatic impasse between the major actors in the SCS region as well as the sources of potential military conflict, and identifies the key stressors to regional security from a systemic perspective. Chapter 2 argues that the recent development in the SCS, such as oil rigs, newly-built and militarized islands on coral reefs, have not only increased the political tensions in the region, but have also made it a test case for how the rest of East Asia will respond to the rise of China. The authors argue that the SCS region, which features China's salami-slicing tactics and strategy and has produced a miasma of heightened military tension and anxiety, serves as an "echo chamber" of China's aggressive and expansionistic policy elsewhere on its periphery. In examining China's evolving military policies and ("creeping") assertiveness,[1] the authors explain that the arising conflict, however, still appears to be politically controllable, due to means by which SCS states have sought to either expand or protect their claims.

Part I is composed of five chapters on major claimants of the contested SCS waters: mainland China, Taiwan, Vietnam, the Philippines, and Malaysia. Chapter 3 explores China's broad security interests in the SCS, including what the author refers to as a concern over territorial sovereignty and

[1] See, Ian James Storey, "Creeping Assertiveness: China, the Philippines and the South China Sea Dispute," *Contemporary Southeast Asia* 21, no. 1 (April 1999), 95–118.

maritime jurisdiction as well as growing appeal for overall strategic stability, homeland security, and sea routes safety. In addition, the author contends that China seeks to create and maintain a stable regional security order, conducive to managing disputes, and build cooperation to better deal with non-traditional maritime security threats.

Chapter 4 examines the development and content of Taiwan's SCS policy under the Tsai administration since May 2016, when Tsai Ing-wen was inaugurated as the 14th Republic of China (ROC) president. It is clear that the policy decision-making process and the implementation of Taiwan's SCS policy have been influenced by the US government's concerns and interests. As a result, Taiwan supports the US-led Indo-Pacific strategic alliances and partnerships and Washington's efforts to develop a multilateral joint patrolling force in the SCS. The Tsai administration avoids mentioning the "U-shaped line" and historic right claims in the SCS as a partial recognition of the ruling made by the Arbitral Tribunal in the arbitration case. In addition, cross-Strait dialogue on the SCS issue has become much more difficult, if not completely suspended.

Chapter 5 depicts how Vietnamese political elites often attached great importance to the maritime corridor and offshore territories on its eastern front. This domain has served not just as a medium to enhance national unity but also as a security buffer. Hanoi increasingly adopted the notion of comprehensive security and views an open, stable, and rules-based SCS would best serve its strategic interest. To this end, Vietnam built up just enough defence and stood firm to defend the existing legal order at sea while sparing no chance to improve its relations with any stakeholders in the SCS.

Chapter 6 examines the Philippines' foreign and security policy towards the SCS using the neorealist concept of security dilemma and the strategy of hedging. It is argued that President Rodrigo Duterte is not changing the Philippines' long-standing policy towards China and the SCS dispute. What Duterte has changed instead is the Philippine government's present attitude towards China and Manila's current approach in dealing with territorial conflicts in the SCS.

Chapter 7 explores Malaysia's approach and policies in the SCS and how they are evolving. Additionally, it examines the rules-based framework and the conduct of parties in promoting maritime cooperation in the SCS. The SCS debate presents a formidable mix of seemingly intractable issues, multi-nation manoeuvrings, and exceptional possibilities. Geo-strategic interests, military expansion, major-power relations, overlapping claims, and rules-based legal orders dominate maritime matters in the SCS. The multiple interests and multifaceted claims are further complicated by major external powers seeking to entrench their interests in this vital waterway.

Part II of this volume comprises four chapters on Southeast Asia non-claimants in the disputed waters of the SCS. Chapter 8 examines Indonesia's strategic interests and policies in the SCS, with attention given to the country's unique involvement in the dispute as a non-claimant state. Despite Indonesia's official status as a non-claimant, both the previous administration under Susilo Bambang Yudhoyonoand and Indonesia's current one under President Joko Widodo have maintained a delicate balance with respect to territorial waters and rights in the region. Indonesia's security posture in its immediate waters is predicated on two principal concerns: (1) Indonesia's ongoing war on foreign fishers and pirates, and (2) responding to the policies of other countries while maintaining a firm but moderating role through what Senia Febrica and Scott N. Romaniuk refer to as "soft-assertiveness."

Chapter 9 addresses Singapore's SCS portfolio by mainly addressing development-oriented issues. Singapore has re-postulated the SCS issue in the broader context of great-power wrestling and regional terrorist attack while preferring to maintain flexibility as much as possible in handling it. Yet, the overriding national interests would post daunting challenges to future ASEAN integration.

Chapter 10 contributes to the ongoing debates regarding Cambodia's position on the SCS dispute between China and ASEAN claimant states – in particular, the Philippines and Vietnam. Among the strategic challenges facing Cambodia, balancing between ASEAN, the West, and China on the contentious issue of the SCS is – and continues to be – the most significant strategic challenge for its foreign policy in the 21st century.

Chapter 11 asserts that the actions of the four ASEAN claimants in the SCS – and the other non-claimant ASEAN states – are fundamentally driven by their respective strategic national interest in the dispute, amid various historical narratives and legal arguments. The effort to maintain a balance of power in the region creates a dilemma for individual ASEAN countries as they attempt to navigate between the strategic dependence on the US and the economic opportunities presented by China. As the Sino-American strategic rivalry intensifies, ASEAN is likely to face even more challenges and constraints in playing a role in managing security in the SCS.

Part III of this volume is comprised of four chapters from the perspectives of Quadrilateral Security Dialogue (QSD) states (the US, Japan, Australia, and India). Chapter 12 discusses the perspective of the US in the SCS dispute. Combining diplomatic, information, military, and economic approaches, the US attempts to emphasize the cost to China of "unlawful" expansionism. Through US Pacific Command (USPACOM) and US Strategic Command (USSTRATCOM), Washington coordinates military responses to China that focus on efforts to keep sea lines of communications (SLOCs) open. Diplomatically, the US operates both bilaterally and through ASEAN in order to contain Chinese expansion while continuing to emphasize the US' long-established "hub and spoke" alliance system in the region.

Japan's strategic interest in the SCS is explored in Chapter 13. Japan holds responsibility for maintaining stability in the sea since sustainable development of the Japanese economy heavily relies on the safety of sea lines of communications (SLOCs) in the SCS. The SCS is an integral part of the "Free and Open Indo-Pacific" vision vigorously promoted by the Japanese government. The Japan Self Defence Forces (SDF) has gradually increased its presence and conducts a variety of military exercises by itself and with the regional and extra-regional countries for enhancing internationally shared rules and norms in the SCS as a responsible maritime power.

Australia's geopolitical concern, as is argued in Chapter 14, has been the security of the northern approaches, which is stressed by a series of defence white papers. Australian governments have emphasized the importance of a "rules-based order" in the Indo-Pacific and are disturbed by the Chinese activities in the SCS that undermine this order and create uncertainty to Australia's north. However, Australia faces a dilemma in dealing with this issue since China is its major trade partner and has contributed to Australia's economic growth.

India, as discussed in Chapter 15, has been a long-standing external stakeholder in Southeast Asia. Subsequently, while the Indian Navy has not been shy to show its flag in the SCS, India's engagement with the sub-region and the claimant states of the SCS has been relatively mundane. The breadth of activities notwithstanding, the depth of India's defence cooperation diplomacy and naval engagement with its Southeast Asian counterparts remains modest. It is instructive in this regard to note what New Delhi has *not* provided, conducted, cooperated with, or participated in vis-à-vis the SCS. Barring a paradigm-shift in the geopolitics of this waterway, India's cautious inclinations will not make a marked difference.

The perspectives of non-claimants in Europe and Eurasia are collected in Part IV of this volume. Chapter 16 explores the United Kingdom's (UK) policy commitment to establishing a regular naval presence in the SCS. This policy has received criticism as a political message in the trying times of "Brexit" and amid fiscal pressures on the Royal Navy which, if carried out in the form of "freedom of navigation" missions and naval bases in the region, will likely complicate its foreign policy – especially in relationship with China. The UK faces significant uncertainties in its international standing. It is also concerned with new sources of insecurity in more proximate waters and likely risks of military entanglement and threat of economic retaliation from Beijing. Such insecurities leave the realization of the UK's national security priorities in Asia largely contingent on political leadership at 10 Downing Street navigating within pressures from the US and European allies.

Chapter 17 argues that Russia remains demonstrably disengaged from the SCS dispute. However, its relationship of comprehensive strategic cooperation with both China and Vietnam reveals that Moscow has strategic interests that directly or indirectly affect the evolution of the dispute. This chapter demonstrates that Russia's behaviour towards the dispute is the result of two different – but intersecting – modes of great power behaviour: *systemic balancing* and *regional hedging*. These two different modes coexist in Russia's behaviour towards the SCS. Untangling them helps to shed light on the evolution of Russia's policies in the region and enhance understanding of how other great powers might react to regional disputes involving various stakeholders.

Chapter 18 examines the SCS dispute from the point of view of South Korea, arguing that while South Korea is far from the immediate region under analysis and in which tensions continue to rise, the implications of rivalry between China, the US, and other SCS claimant and non-claimant states alike have dangerous consequences on the peace and order of the broader area. The author illustrates South Korea's position as a regional middle power interested in "balanced and constructive policies" with the ultimate aim of de-escalating tension between those states that have brought all others closer to physical conflict.

As Stein Tønnesson points to in the Foreword, one positive aspect of the rising tensions in the SCS is the research and debates they have stimulated among analysts and scholars in the countries concerned, both inside and outside the region. This has been approved in the trend towards a more mutual understanding that is also supported by a string of scholarly conferences in a variety of countries. The present volume is an eminent example of that trend. This comprehensive volume brings together the expertise and knowledge of more than a dozen academics and professionals, all of whom are considered leading experts in their respective areas. Engaging with individual states and core themes, the chapters collectively present a robust and comprehensive outlook on the currently geography of security and potential conflict in the SCS.

1

Between Competition and War: Complex Security Overlay and the South China Sea

Joshua Hastey and Scott N. Romaniuk

Introduction

The South China Sea (SCS) has become the setting of one of the most intensive territorial and resource disputes in history. A myriad of small and medium states, together with the two greatest economic and military powers in the contemporary period, have laid claim to and contest states' alternative claims to large sections of the SCS. China, as a revisionist power, has made the most sweeping claim of all states, designating nearly the entire sea as its own. In addition to its extensive resources, the SCS is a vital strategic waterway and a strategic locale critical for future power projection by existing great and rising powers. This chapter unpacks the central components of the conflict in the SCS that has been steadily intensifying since states began staking claims over islands and zones within the SCS in the 1970s. In doing so, we refer to the SCS as a "system of systems" involving multi-dimensional security overlay based on political, economic, and military interests as well as power projections. We argue that the central challenge facing would-be defenders of the status quo is their decentralized organization, with the US, the Philippines, and Vietnam intersecting in various subsystems though not forming a cohesive cooperative security system with a unified, cohesive purpose. Concurrently, China has seen much more success in marshalling a coherent, focused (Sinocentrist) stratagem for its salami-slicing approach in the region, much to the detriment of the region's status quo actors, even in spite of internal competition and rivalry regarding China's grand strategy and geopolitical trajectory as a state.

Geography and national security in the South China Sea

Situated at the nexus of the Western Pacific and the Indian Ocean, the SCS is one of the world's busiest bodies of water. More than half of the world's yearly shipping by tonnage passes through the various straits – Malacca, Sunda, Lombok, and Makassar – that feed into the SCS, with more than six times as much oil passing through these straits each year than through the Suez Canal.[1] Beyond its importance as a shipping hub, the SCS itself is resource rich, with fisheries that provide a large portion of the nutrition for the inhabitants of the states around it and plentiful, largely untapped, hydrocarbon deposits under the seabed.[2] Apart from its inherent value in terms of resources and sea lines of communication (SLOCs), the SCS is a source of competition due to its location. Surrounded by maritime nations, the SCS is claimed in whole or in part by six different states: China, Taiwan,[3] the Philippines, Malaysia, Brunei, and Vietnam. Beyond the challenges that normally accompany territorial disputes, China's claim is problematic for the other claimants both because of the extent of its claimed territory and its ambiguity regarding the meaning of its claims.

China's claim – known as the "cow's tongue" or China's infamous "nine-dash line" after the nine dashes marking the territory on official Chinese maps – encompasses nearly the entire SCS, cutting down the coasts of both Vietnam and the Philippines before skimming the coast of Borneo. Vietnam claims both the Spratly and Paracel island chains in their entirety. These overlapping claims are further complicated by confusion over what rights are accorded within claimed territory. Furthermore, both China and the Philippines are able to assume new and drastically different trajectories through the course of their bilateral relations and communications over these features, though China's ongoing militarization efforts are indicative of the state's commitment to the islands and yet fail to present the inherent competition that lies within China over strategic moves into the SCS. In this vein, it is important to discharge the central state element from Beijing's state-level policy in the SCS, leaving the provincial interests in the People's

---

1 Robert D. Kaplan, "The South China Sea Is the Future of Conflict," *Foreign Policy* (2011), 80.

2 Ibid.

3 In this chapter, we recognize Taiwan as a sovereign state, distinct from the dictatorship currently ruling China.

Republic of China (PRC), which can stand at odds with one another, to be considered.

The United Nations Convention on the Law of the Seas (UNCLOS) recognizes three types of maritime territory: *territorial seas*, *contiguous zones*, and *exclusive economic zones* (EEZs). *Territorial seas* are recognized as extending up to 12 nautical miles from a state's coastal baseline and islands under its sovereignty. While all ships enjoy the right of innocent passage in these waters, a state enjoys full sovereignty in its territorial sea, including policing and development privileges. A *contiguous zone* extends 24 nautical miles from a state's coastal baseline and allows it to exercise control over enforcement of local laws and customs as it would on its landmass. Most countries (but not the PRC) hold that all aircraft and ships enjoy the same freedoms of passage that they would enjoy on the high seas. EEZs extend a coastal state's economic rights beyond its contiguous zone up to 200 nautical miles from its baseline. This designation grants economic rights, such as the right to exploit and regulate fishing and hydrocarbon resources, within the EEZ but does not grant sovereignty rights. Like territorial seas, EEZs can be extended by islands to which a state claims sovereignty, but EEZ rules stipulate that such islands must be habitable.[4]

As one Congressional Research Service (CRS) report indicates: "China has not clarified whether it is claiming sovereignty over the entire sea and seabed enclosed by the nine dash line, or is making a more limited set of claims … This ambiguity has been an important driver of tensions."[5] However, its actions appear to indicate an intent to exert control over both economic activity within the nine-dash line and, occasionally, to prevent the passage of naval vessels through waters claimed by the PRC. Against what the PRC describes as stabilization operations and an adherence to a self-proclaimed "peaceful development" and humanitarian undertakings – cynically pursing aggressive territorial acquisition consolidation under the COVID-19 global pandemic – in the SCS, China has crept forward during the course of diplomatic engagement over the region's assets, resorting at times to aggressive and violent behaviour at sea.[6] China, along with Vietnam and the Philippines, supports its maritime claims on the basis of historical presence in the region and UNCLOS regulations allowing habitable islands

[4] Ben Dolven, Shirley A. Kan, and Mark E. Manyin, "Maritime Territorial Disputes in East Asia: Issues for Congress," (Washington, DC: Congressional Research Service, 2013), 6.

[5] Ibid., 8.

[6] The State Council Information Office of the People's Republic of China, "The Development of China's Maritime Cause," (May, 1998); The State Council Information Office of the People's Republic of China, "China's Peaceful Development," (September 6, 2011).

to extend EEZ claims. Unlike China, however, Vietnamese and Filipino maritime claims specify most of their maritime claims as EEZ claims, and explicitly acknowledge the right of foreign naval and cargo vessels to innocent passage through their claimed waters. This places Chinese claims in conflict with its neighbours not only on the location of maritime boundaries, but also on the rules that would apply even if the boundaries themselves are agreed upon.

This uncertainty, coupled with the then upcoming establishment of the UNCLOS regime, led to a dash among SCS claimant states during the 1990s to establish a presence on islands in the Spratly and Paracel island chains. Currently, all of the Paracel Islands are under Chinese control, though Vietnam disputes the legitimacy of China's control of the islands. The Philippines administers 53 islands, reefs, and shoals in and around the Spratly chain, the Kalayaan islands (located between the Spratly Islands and the Philippine island of Palawan), and Scarborough Shoal, though China and Vietnam do not recognize its control over islands in the Spratly chain as legitimate.[7] For its part, Vietnam claims the entirety of the Spratly and Paracel island chains, but only controls 31 islands and reefs in the Spratlys and Western SCS. The US has not taken sides over the specifics of the disputed territories, voicing support for resolution of these disputes through UNCLOS arbitration, choosing to prioritize its insistence on continued freedom of navigation through the region's sea lines of communication (SLOCs), regardless of the actual territorial boundaries.

Also contributing to regional tensions are ongoing shifts in power distributions, including, as Leszek Buszynski explains in Chapter 14, the necessitation of "alliance relationships with stronger powers" and the drawing in of SCS states and external power, according to Senia Febrica and Scott N. Romaniuk (see Chapter 8). The US, the extant superpower, is rapidly being joined by the PRC as a great power in the region. China has made significant strides in expanding its economic and military strength in the past decade with notable new contributions to its military, and enhancements made to its military budget over the past few years. Economically, China is one of the most vibrant nations in the world, with a burgeoning middle-class and an unprecedented level of growth in GDP interrupted only by the ubiquitous effects of the coronavirus (COVID-19) that emerged out of Wuhan.[8] Its military, and particularly the People's Liberation Army Navy (PLAN), is showing signs of improving sophistication amid dramatic increases

[7] Ibid., 11–12.

[8] Richard Silk, "Plenty of Productivity Still in Store for China, Economist Says," *Wall Street Journal Online* (February 21, 2013).

in funding and the integration of new military technologies and their applications.[9] This new capacity has enabled China to become more assertive in pursuing its interests in the SCS, investing further military resources and making gains through a strategy of aggressive defence.

Fishing resources

The fishing areas throughout the SCS constitute a critical part of China's overall fisheries and fishing industry, thus placing both fishing and the SCS together at the forefront of Beijing's ambitions. The fishing industry, which is a key source of income specifically for China's coastal provinces, has been recast as a critical source of food supplies following the coronavirus outbreak, although the incomes of locals in Hainan, that are dependent on fishing, have not been affected by the coronavirus. Some have called attention to the issue of overfishing and depleted stocks in the SCS as the main driver behind the escalating dispute in the region. Adam Greer visited these issues in the context of Beijing's aggressive expansion in the SCS, stating that: "China's regional interests can be roughly lumped into the three "P's" – politics, petroleum, and proteins (fish). The last of these interests, competition over dwindling SCS fisheries, may be most consequential in driving competition, but has not received sufficient analytic attention."[10] Yearbook data indicate that, beyond these fisheries' role as a key source of nutrition in coastal provinces, the yearly value of saltwater fisheries production in Guangdong, Guangxi and Hainan alone exceeded US$1.5 billion.

With coastal fishery stocks diminishing, Chinese fishers are seeking their catches further into contested waters (as discussed further by Senia Febrica and Scott N. Romaniuk in Chapter 8), even pursuing their interest in waters that are well-insulated from territorial-administrational contestation, sparking competition over contested fishing areas with Vietnam and the Philippines.[11] The process on China's part has sought to incorporate created techniques and tactics, including a turn to hybrid warfare tactics, primarily through the mobilization of a vast fisher militia, occupying the roles of civilian fishers and security-resource pseudo-guarantors.[12] While these resources are of

---

9 Adam Liff and Andrew S. Erickson, "Demystifying China's Defence Spending: Less Mysterious in the Aggregate," *The China Quarterly*, 216 (2013), 4.

10 Adam Greer, "The South China Sea is Really a Fishery Dispute," *The Diplomat* (July 20, 2016).

11 Keyuan Zou, "The Sino-Vietnamese Agreement on Maritime Boundary Delimitation in the Gulf of Tonkin," *Ocean Development & International Law*, 36 (2005), 16–17.

12 Tobias Burgers and Scott N. Romaniuk, "Hybrid Warriors: China's Unmanned, Guerrilla-Style Warfare in Asia's Littorals," *The Diplomat* (February 16, 2017).

particular interest to the central government of the PRC, they are also of key interest to the provincial government of Hainan province. Following several shifts in the location and authority of the administration office established on Yongxing (Woody) Island in 1959,[13] and after the Hainan Administrative Region (which later became Hainan Province as well as a Special Economic Zone (SPZ) – a promotion from an administrative region under the governance of Guangdong Province) was granted administrative rights over many of the islets, reefs, and waters adjacent to Hainan.[14]

In late 2012, Hainan's People's Congress accepted a set of amendments to the security and borders measures in place that concern its coastal waters and territory as well as its jurisdictions that lie further out at sea. Hainan Province retains complete authority over security measures concerning the regulations (as per Article 5) and their associated territory. Hainan Province has emerged as a sub-national actor of sorts in the SCS dispute, seeking to secure its direct territorial and resources interests, which harmonize with Beijing's state-level interests. As Shahar Hameiri and Lee Jones write: "Hainan theoretically administers the entire nine-dashed-line area, which is 60 times larger than its own land surface. It thus has a strong interest in asserting maximalist territorial claims to promote its local fisheries industry."[15]

Like China, Vietnam depends on its fishing industry both for its economic value and as a key source of nutrition. Vietnam's annual net fishing exports exceed US$71 billion per year, accounting for 7 per cent of its annual export market. Equally importantly, Vietnam's saltwater catch provides half of the total protein intake for much of Vietnam's population. However, both countries' traditional fisheries are seeing decreased fish populations due to overfishing and ecologically damaging fishing methods.[16] Reports indicate that fishing grounds in the Gulf of Tonkin can sustain an annual catch of 600,000 tons, while total fishing in that area between Chinese and Vietnamese fishers has exceeded 1,000,000 tons since the early 2000s.[17] As

---

[13] Authority over the office was moved to Guangdong Province in 1969.

[14] These include: Paracel Islands (Xisha Islands) (Vietnam and Taiwan also claim these): Money Island, Rocky Island, Tree Island, Triton Island, Woody Island; Zhongsha Islands; Spratly Islands (Nansha Islands) (Vietnam, Taiwan, Malaysia, the Philippines, and Brunei also claim these): Spratly Island, Flat Island, Taiping Island, James Shoal, Loaita Island, Namyit Island, Nanshan Island, Sin Cowe Island, Thitu Island, West York Island, among many other maritime features of diverse description.

[15] Shahar Hameiri and Lee Jones, "Rising Powers and State Transformation: The Case of China," *European Journal of International Relations*, 22 no. 2 (2015), 88.

[16] Keyuan Zou, "The Sino-Vietnamese Agreement on Maritime Boundary Delimitation in the Gulf of Tonkin," *Ocean Development & International Law*, 36 (2005), 15–16.

[17] Ibid., 16.

we illustrate further on in this chapter, the perception and treatment of a zero-sum game in the SCS is driven by a measurable decrease in some of the region's vital resources, thus incorporating an element of diminishing time for those determined to acquire what wealth can be accessed in the SCS. Also, like China, Vietnam has responded to diminishing catches near its coast by encouraging its fishers to venture further from the coast.[18] This has increased the frequency of conflicts, such as those noted, over fisheries in contested waters. In addition to the incidents cited in the preceding section, the Vietnamese government reports that PRC forces seized at least 36 fishing boats and detained 468 fishers between 2009 and 2010.[19] These confrontations continued to escalate through 2011 and 2012, with China imposing a unilateral fishing ban, enforced by the PLAN and China Marine Surveillance (CMS), in disputed waters during Vietnam's peak fishing season.[20]

For the Philippines, like China and Vietnam, fishing is a crucial economic activity. This fact is compounded by the fact that the Spratly and Kalayaan chains comprise some of the world's richest fishing grounds. The area, over 150,000 square miles, is home to 314 species of fish, including 66 commercially profitable species. The area lies on the migratory route of yellowfin tuna, a particularly profitable species, and provides over 8 per cent of the world's fishing catch each year.[21] As in the overlapping Sino-Vietnamese fisheries, this has led to competition and increasingly frequent clashes between Chinese and Filipino fishers and patrol ships. In a typical case on February 25, 2011, a Chinese frigate confronted three Filipino fishing vessels operating near Jackson Atoll, 140 nautical miles west of the Philippine Island of Palawan, broadcasting, "I will shoot you," before firing three shots 500 metres from the lead fishing vessel.[22]

Energy resources

States around the periphery of the SCS are also increasingly pressed for energy resources. In 1990, the PRC was a petroleum exporter, exporting

---

18 "Stirring up the South China Sea (II): Regional Responses," (International Crisis Group, 2012), 16.

19 James Bellacqua, "The China Factor in US Vietnam Relations," (Washington, DC: Center for Naval Analysis, 2012), 15.

20 "Stirring up the South China Sea (II): Regional Responses," 17.

21 Christopher C. Joyner, "The Spratly Islands Dispute in the South China Sea: Problems, Policies and Prospects for Diplomatic Accommodation," *Investigating Confidence Building Measures in the Asia Pacific Region* (1999), 66.

22 Carlyle Thayer, "South China Sea Disputes: Asean and China," (2011), 3.

over 471 thousand barrels per day. By 1993, it had become a net petroleum importer, and in 2009 China imported over four million barrels.[23] China's oil consumption has steadily increased since 1990 and began accelerating at the turn of the millennium. By 2016, China's crude oil, which included base condensate imports, was five times what it was in 2000 and 50 per cent greater than what it was in 2010. By 2019, China's daily imports of crude oil exceeded 10 million barrels.[24] Chinese consumption of hydrocarbons has vastly outstripped its production in the past decade and a half. With China having entered into a relationship of consumption–supply imbalance, we see the emergence of an extreme and possibly unshakable dependence on nearby resources on which numerous other countries equally rely.

In 2000, China produced slightly more than three million barrels per day and consumed nearly five million, a gap of slightly more than one million barrels per day. By 2009, that gap had grown to over four million barrels per day.[25] Long-term projections place total Chinese energy needs up nearly 80 per cent by 2035 and China's natural gas needs increasing nearly 230 per cent in the same timeframe.[26] Such a desire for energy could permanently affix China to its current trajectory with respect to the SCS. As with fishing, expansion further into the SCS offers potential solutions to PRC policy makers concerned with China's energy shortage. While estimates of oil and natural gas deposits in the SCS vary, the US Energy Information Administration (USEIA) reports Chinese estimates of 213 billion barrels of oil and two quadrillion cubic feet of natural gas in the region. While the US agency's estimates are more conservative, 28 billion barrels of oil and four to six trillion cubic feet of natural gas, even the lower figures present a tempting prize for the energy-starved PRC.[27]

Vietnam has also seen a dramatic shift in its need for energy. From 1990 through 2009, Vietnam was an oil exporter. However, rising energy consumption in Vietnam caused its net exports to fall into sharp decline beginning in 2003; in 2010 Vietnam imported more oil than it exported for the first time since 1989.[28] The vast hydrocarbon deposits in the SCS offer a possible solution to Vietnam's energy crunch. However, as with fishing, Hanoi's attempts to exploit the SCS's hydrocarbon resources have led to increased tensions with Beijing.

---

[23] USEIA, "China."

[24] USEIA, "China's Crude Oil Imports Surpassed 10 Million Barrels Per Day in 2019," (March 23, 2020).

[25] Ibid.

[26] USEIA, International Energy Outlook.

[27] USEIA, "Country Analysis Briefs: South China Sea," 6.

[28] USEIA, "Vietnam."

The energy resources under the seabed near the southern end of the Spratlys are also an important interest to Filipino leaders. Unlike Vietnam and China, the Philippines has been a net energy importer since US Energy Information Agency (USEIA) records began in 1980. However, like its two maritime neighbours, Filipino demand for energy is growing. The Philippines currently must import over 270 thousand barrels of oil per day – up from 200 thousand barrels per day in 2000 and just over 250 thousand per day in 2010 – to meet domestic demand. The abundant oil and natural gas in the Spratlys – where the largest deposits in the SCS are thought to be located – present not only the possibility of ameliorating this shortfall, but sufficient deposits to turn the Philippines into a net energy exporter. Not surprisingly, however, disputes over access to these resources have been a source of conflict between the Philippines and China.

With all three parties in a pressure cooker, labouring to meet growing domestic energy demands, each has an interest in exploiting the oil and natural gas resources to be found in the SCS. However, these resources are limited and each country's claims are disputed by the others. In 2005, the three states agreed to a joint exploration scheme under which the three states would explore the seabed under disputed waters, sharing any information and resources gained with the others. However, this tripartite agreement fell apart in 2008 amid domestic accusations of corruption in the Philippines, and mutual suspicion among all three states has prevented a similar agreement from being attempted since.[29] Indeed, while the growing power of China has come into loggerheads with the US military presence and intention to remain active in the SCS region, we suggest the likeliness of both China and the US becoming embroiled in war to be rather low, though vastly exceeding the probability of entering into direct conflict as a result of action by a smaller claimant state in the SCS region.

Security imperatives

For Beijing, a further interest in the SCS is securing exclusive use of the area within its claimed nine-dash line for military patrols and exercises. The PRC's coastline, while productive and resource-rich, has also proven to be difficult to defend against outside intervention. One of China's highest priorities is to press the threat of invasion of its coastline and foreign acquisition of its most populous and rich cities as far away as possible.[30] Beijing's perception

[29] Stein Tønnesson, "China's Changing Role in the South China Sea: Reflections on a Scholars' Workshop," *Harvard Asia Quarterly* 12 no. 4 (2010), 26.

[30] Nan Li and Christopher Weuve, "China's Aircraft Carrier Ambitions: An Update," *Naval War College Review* 63 (2010), 19.

of its geopolitical positioning and hence vulnerability carries significant overtones of insecurity. Cognizant of the extreme buffer between the US and other powers, be they small, medium, or large, China has no such buffer to speak of. This point is not lost on the PRC leadership, which has seen the US Navy (USN) repeatedly intervene in its conflicts with Taiwan. In 1950 and again in 1996, the US responded to cross-Strait tensions by sending aircraft carriers to demonstrate its resolution in defending Taiwan – a show of force that for Beijing was too close to its own major industrial and financial centres on the eastern coast. In 2008, as Chen Shui Bian's Democratic Progressive Party (DPP)-led government was poised to oversee a referendum over Taiwanese independence, the US again dispatched two aircraft carriers to the waters just off Taiwan, implicitly indicating willingness to protect Taiwan from intervention from the mainland.[31] To an infuriated Chinese public, these were outrageous interventions in China's domestic affairs. To the People's Liberation Army (PLA), they were sober reminders of its need to secure its own coastline in addition to the inescapability of China's vulnerable geographical positioning.

To this end, the PLAN has begun to implement a forward defence strategy in the SCS in order to project its naval power further from its coastline and establish a military presence throughout the SCS. However, this forward defence plan is supplemented by the creation of "outposts" or the minor representations of Chinese military power and political determination that can be found well beyond the SCS proper. The existence of such "outposts" serves to blur the lines of territorial-power boundaries and areas of operation. In the event of an armed conflict, an established military presence and ability to control maritime activity beyond the immediate coastline would allow the PLAN to interdict hostile vessels in open water, decreasing the risk to its key coastal cities and ports.[32] While China has not made any public statements explicitly claiming exclusive rights to use the SCS, it has sought to develop means, both legal and military, to establish a level of control over the region that goes beyond what most states and legal scholars would recognize under UNCLOS.[33] Moreover, US officials have reported that their Chinese counterparts have referred to Chinese sovereignty in the SCS as a core interest, on a par with Tibet or Taiwan.[34]

---

31 Reuters "US Carriers Sent toward Taiwan before Election," *Reuters* (March 19, 2008), 1.

32 Li and Weuve, 17.

33 Ronald O'Rourke, "Maritime Territorial and Exclusive Economic Zone (EEZ) Disputes Involving China: Issues for Congress," (Washington, DC: Congressional Research Service, 2012), 4.

34 Edward Wong, "China Hedges over Whether South China Sea Is a 'Core Interest' Worth War," *New York Times* (March 30, 2011), 1.

CMS and the China Fishery Administration both have active and growing armed patrol fleets which have been used to police civilian fishing and hydrocarbon exploration within the nine-dash line, but well beyond what legal experts regard as China's coastal EEZ. The PLAN recently completed a new naval base on Hainan Island and is in the process of updating and upgrading the South Sea Fleet.[35] It has also conducted unprecedented military exercises in the region, including its largest ever military exercise in August 2010, which included "half of the vessels from all three Fleets, as well as bombers and anti-ship missiles."[36] This was followed in November by a live-fire exercise in which amphibious assault ships and tanks simulated an assault while countering electromagnetic interference.[37] Live-fire exercises and repositioning its littoral power vis-à-vis new naval bases represents only one element of how China's "power projects" deeper into the SCS.

The commissioning in 2012 of the PLAN's first aircraft carrier, the *Liaoning*, further evidences China's intent to strengthen its foothold in its maritime periphery through the development of a blue-water navy capable of projecting the Chinese Communist Party's (CCP) power well beyond the shores of the Chinese mainland.[38] Daniel Kostecka, Senior China Analyst for the US Department of the Navy, argues that in the short run, the primary mission of a Chinese aircraft carrier will be to secure its maritime claims in the SCS. Capable of launching conventional fixed-wing aircraft, such as the Su-33 and J-15, which perform both air superiority and air-to-ground operations, the *Liaoning* is well-suited for enforcing Chinese maritime claims throughout the SCS's 3.5 million km^2.[39] The development of Chinese aircraft carriers effectively enables the CCP to diffuse its power over the territory Beijing seeks to procure. However, as potential objectives and political ambitions driven by economic imperatives change through expansion, its aircraft carriers are the main components in pushing its protective coverage further outward. In fact, the development of the *Liaoning*, along with the overall modernization and expansion of the South Sea Fleet, has made forward defence a viable strategy for the PLAN.[40]

35 Carlyle Thayer, "South China Sea Disputes: Asean and China," paper presented at the East Asia Forum (July 14 2011), 2.

36 Stacy Pedrozo, "China's Active Defense Strategy and Its Regional Impact," (Washington, DC: Council on Foreign Relations, 2011), 3.

37 Ibid.

38 Kathrin Hille, "China's First Aircraft Carrier Takes to the Sea," *Financial Times* (August 10, 2011), 2.

39 Daniel Kostecka, "From the Sea: PLA Doctrine and the Employment of Sea-Based Airpower," *Naval War College Review* 64 (2011), 14–15.

40 Li and Weuve, 17.

Some describe China's increasing assertiveness in the SCS as a response to the US' 2012 "pivot" to Asia.[41] However, former Australian Prime Minister Kevin Rudd points out a key flaw in this argument, contending that, "[s]ome have criticized Washington's renewed vigor as the cause of increased tensions across East Asia. But this does not stand up to scrutiny, given that the proliferation of significant regional security incidents began more than half a decade ago."[42] An explanation that more compellingly captures the state of play in the SCS, specifically the change in China's SCS policies, is rooted in its enhanced and growing economic and military capacities. This increased capacity serves to bolster Beijing's assertiveness in two ways. First, an increased capacity allows China to pursue goals that were previously desirable but not feasible. Such goals include securing its coastline from outside military interference and securing access to profitable resources in and under China's adjacent seas.[43] Second, as China's capabilities have increased, its attempts to revise the regional status quo have grown correspondingly ambitious.

With Xi Jinping's continued consolidation of power within the CCP, this trend is unlikely to abate. Xi served as vice chair of the Central Military Commission, which oversees the nation's armed forces, from 2010 to 2012, when its assertive policies were beginning to escalate rapidly. In that position, Xi played a key role in the commission's "leading groups" on East China Sea and SCS policy and presided over PLAN policy during its incidents with Vietnam and the Philippines in the SCS over the course of those two years. This is key to understanding current Vietnamese and Filipino policies, as well as the slow but now shifting policies of other states in the region, as these incidents gave weight to the perception of China not only as a strong, proximate power, but also as an aggressive state playing by the rules of orthodox realism and adhering to (as least in part) the central tenets of Mearsheimer's offensive neorealism. Furthermore, Xi's role in presiding over these policies as chair of the Central Military Commission has caused some analysts to conclude that he is an "unapologetic hard-liner on national security policy."[44] With his position strengthened in the 19th Chinese Communist Party Congress in October 2017 and term of office extended to

41 Dolven et al, 23.

42 Kevin Rudd, "Beyond the Pivot: A New Road Map for US-Chinese Relations," *Foreign Affairs* 92 no. 2 (2013), 12.

43 Ronald O'Rourke, *China Naval Modernization: Implications for US Navy Capabilities 2012* (Washington DC: Congressional Research Service, 2012), 23. For the most recent and updated version of O'Rourke's report at the time of writing this chapter, see: Ronald O'Rourke, *China Naval Modernization: Implications for US Navy Capabilities 2012* (Washington DC: Congressional Research Service (May 21, 2020).

44 Rudd, 12.

an indefinite period in 2018, he is unlikely to face any domestic constraints, politically speaking, to continued revisions in the SCS and modifications to power-relations in the greater SCS region.

The South China Sea and grey zone operations

Do artificial islands lead to legitimate claims? Land reclamation is a central and driving mechanism in Beijing's SCS expansionist policy, especially when it comes to the Spratly Islands, where China has been pumping sand onto the disputed reefs. A policy that started in 2013, with three islands completed by November 2014, has since resulted in coral features becoming completely developed islands – seven in total as of December 2019.[45] The Philippines' and Vietnam's position on the issue remains clear: artificial islands are not islands. As UNCLOS makes clear, "a naturally formed area of land, surrounded by water, which is above water at high tide." Thus, China's island-building ventures in the SCS have legally resulted in no new island being created. The fact that artificial islands do not share the same legal status as that of natural islands, along with the maritime features and land reclamation taking place after the "critical date" that determines when the dispute officially began, became a matter of the international legal process. However, according to China, the maritime features currently in its possession and being fortified are islands. Additionally, the tension resulting from the convergence of what international law *is* and what China *does* has almost certainly worked in China's favour.

Emphasis of the grey zone environment and definitional ambiguity have leveraged China's overall position in the SCS, enabling the state to expand its control without direct provocation with states or warranting other states' use of kinetic force and military application. First, the grey zone of international law has provided China with ample room to navigate the tension in the SCS, avoiding direct military or kinetic exchange with states that have competing interests, and enabled Beijing to strengthen its presence. Second, the pace of international legal processes and debates within it are unable to keep up with developments in the field. This logic is in step with the strategy the US adhered to in pursuit of known and suspected terrorists using weaponized drones over Afghanistan and Pakistan. Russia has also pursued grey zone

---

[45] Jane Perlez, "China Said to Turn Reef into Airstrip in Disputed Water," *New York Times*, November 23, 2014; David Sanger and Rick Gladstone, "Piling Sand in a Disputed Sea, China Literally Gains Ground," *New York Times*, April 8, 2015; Ronald O'Rourke, "US-China Strategic Competition in South and East China Seas: Background and Issues for Congress," ed. Congressional Research Service (Washington, DC, May 1, 2020).

operations, and continues to do so, as part of its illegal acquisition and eventual annexation of Crimea in 2014. Third, Beijing frequently employs the language of restraint and agreement with its neighbours, notably through its foreign policy documents and white papers, while pursing stridently different courses of action in the SCS. Fourth, China has in a sense detached and distanced itself from its own actions in the SCS via fishing activities and fishers, who purportedly act of their own volition when operating in the waters off disputed islands and features. Such activity converges with depictions of depleted fishing grounds cultivating a non-traditional security threat as one posing an existential danger to millions of people who rely on regional fish stocks. These tactics need not be applied by a particularly weak state. Even a larger and very powerful state like China can employ these tactics and operate against weaker states to elicit a desired response (for example, aggressive or military) to frame that state as the aggressor. China is unlikely to pursue this type of action against an adversary of equal or greater strength, notably the US, due to the risk associated with coercive engagement with a superpower so directly.

Strategic competition

Over the past two decades, the PRC has developed the ability to project power – and threaten to deny access to the US in the event of a conflict – into the first island chain, which stretches from the Japanese archipelago through Taiwan to the Philippines. In doing so, it presents the impression of having also carved out a period, possibly temporarily, in which it enjoys relatively low costs of unilateral revisions to the territorial status quo in the SCS that can mature over time so as to produce the changes to the power statuses of competitors in the SCS that China has shown it seeks.

In terms of naval assets, China has spent the past two decades modernizing and expanding its surface and submarine fleets.[46] In 2016, for example, China commissioned 18 new surface ships with a total displacement of 150,000 tons, or about half the total displacement of the British Royal Navy.[47] Since 2000, China's surface and submarine fleet have transitioned from a small green-water fleet, comprised almost entirely of imported systems and vessels and restricted to its coastline, to a modern – albeit largely untested – and

---

[46] Toshi Yoshihara and James R. Holmes, *Red Star over the Pacific, Revised Edition: China's Rise and the Challenge to US Maritime Strategy* (Naval Institute Press, 2018); M. Taylor Fravel, "China's Strategy in the South China Sea," *Contemporary Southeast Asia* 33 no. 3 (2011); "Revising Deng's Foreign Policy," *The Diplomat* (January 17, 2012).

[47] Ronald O'Rourke, *China Naval Modernization: Implications for US Navy Capabilities 2018* (Washington DC: Congressional Research Service, 2018), 3.

domestically produced blue-water navy.[48] Over the same period, China has gone from possessing no aircraft carriers to one fully operational carrier with two more in production. Here too, one can observe evidence of developing internal capacity. China's first aircraft carrier, initially named the *Varyag* and later rechristened as the *Liaoning*, is a retrofitted former Ukrainian carrier from the Cold War era. Its second carrier was designed domestically and launched from the Dailan shipyard in Southern China in 2017. While not a state-of-the-art model, the *Shandong* demonstrates the extent to which Beijing's military infrastructure has grown and modernized over the past two decades. The PLAN's third carrier, however, features an electromagnetic catapult assisted take-off system similar to the US Ford Class carriers, and a large island that allows for rapid deployment of its more than 50 aircraft complement.[49] The first two carriers are ill-suited for long-range power projection missions but are perfectly configured to establish air dominance in conflicts within the first and second island chains, supplemented by China's evolving unmanned aerial vehicle fleet (UAV), which can undertake a variety of PLAN support roles. While the aircraft complements and accompanying capital ships cannot match the firepower of a US aircraft carrier battle group, there are more than sufficient to confront any of China's neighbours within the region. The third carrier, with its larger complement, more advanced communications and countermeasure systems, and modern catapult, is the PLAN's first step into long-range power projection capabilities and a critical part of the state legitimizing any view that China is becoming or has become a "great power."

In addition to its expanding carrier fleet, the PLAN is also adding new surface ships and submarines to its arsenal. Over the past 20 years, it has acquired 42 new conventional submarines with torpedo and anti-ship cruise missile capabilities. Of these, 12 were purchased from Russia with the remaining 30 produced domestically.[50] Its development of a nuclear submarine force is still more impressive, with the design and construction of 10 nuclear powered submarines – six nuclear powered attack submarines and four nuclear powered ballistic missile submarines.[51] The PLAN's

---

48 "The PLA Navy: New Capabilities and Missions for the 21st Century," Office of Naval Intelligence (Washington, DC: Defense Technical Information Center, 2015), 11.

49 Franz-Stefan Gady, "China Kicks Off Construction of New Supercarrier," *The Diplomat* (January 5, 2018); H. I. Sutton, "The Chinese Navy Is Building an Incredible Number of Warships," *Forbes* (December 15, 2019).

50 Center for Strategic and International Studies (CSIS), "How is China Modernizing its Navy?" (December 17, 2018).

51 "Military and Security Developments Involving the People's Republic of China 2018," (Office of the Secretary of Defense, 2018), 29.

growth in submarine assets has been matched by its surface fleets, with new, modernized corvettes, frigates, and guided missile destroyers entering service at a rapid rate over the past decade.[52] That China has built up the capacity to produce these sophisticated platforms domestically speaks to its technical advancements, while its rapid deployment of its new ships into the South and East China Seas demonstrates its interest in projecting power into the region while positioning the PRC to challenge US supremacy in the Western Pacific.[53]

Perhaps the most alarming development in China's force modernization has been the development of new anti-ship missile capabilities which threaten the US' ability to project power into the region via its carrier battle groups. These new capabilities threaten to overwhelm USN missile defence systems on multiple axes. Newly developed cruise missiles, along with ballistic missiles equipped with glide vehicles for re-entry, approach carriers from a low angle of attack, while new ballistic missiles with the capability to target moving ships present a threat from above. On the horizontal axis, China's new capabilities include the Russian SS-N-22 Sunburn and the SS-N-27 Sizzler cruise missiles, which are carried on Russian-made destroyers and submarines, respectively. These are complemented by the domestically produced YJ-83, a versatile system that can be launched from most Chinese ships and some strike fighters, and the YJ-62, and YJ-18 cruise missiles, which are delivered by surface ships and submarines, respectively.[54] Finally, China also recently completed operational testing on the DF-17, a ballistic missile equipped with a glide vehicle for low-angle, high-speed re-entry and approach. This long-range anti-ship ballistic missile (ASBM) is capable of approaching ships from a range of up to 1,300 nautical miles – well-beyond the 600 nautical mile range of US carrier sorties – and at speeds exceeding Mach two (twice the speed of sound, or approximately 1,534 miles per hour).[55]

On the vertical axis, China has developed a new version of its DF-21 medium-range ballistic missile, the DF-21D (CSS-5 MOD 5), with a range of 800 nautical miles and the ability to correct its trajectory during terminal approach to hit moving ships outside the effective strike range of a

[52] Lindsay Maizland, "China's Modernizing Military" (February 5, 2020).

[53] Scott N. Romaniuk and Tobias Burgers, "China's Next Phase of Militarization in the South China Sea," *The Diplomat* (March 20, 2019); Congressional Research Service (CRS), "China Naval Modernization: Implications for US Navy Capabilities – Background and Issues for Congress," (March 18, 2020).

[54] O'Rourke, *China Naval Modernization: Implications for US Navy Capabilities 2018.*

[55] Ankit Panda, "Introducing the DF-17: China's Newly Tested Ballistic Missile Armed with a Hypersonic Glide Vehicle," *The Diplomat* (December 28, 2017).

carrier's aircraft complement. Finally, with an even longer range, the DF-26 intermediate-range ballistic missile has the independent targeting capability of the DF-21D and an effective range of 2,100 nautical miles.[56] All of these newly developed cruise and ballistic missile capabilities are coordinated by an increasingly sophisticated satellite-based targeting network which, though still unproven against US countermeasures, appears to be a largely functional and effective system.[57] Finally, recent reporting has shown that the PLAN has been outpacing the USN in the production of modern destroyers and missile cruisers capable of intercepting aircraft and incoming missile sorties at a rate of nearly three to one.[58] Rather than posing a direct threat to USN vessels, these new warships increase the PLAN's Anti-Access/Area Denial (A2/AD) capabilities by threatening to deny access to ship-based aircraft and cruise missiles that may be used in a conflict scenario.

The increased power projection and A2/AD capabilities in Beijing's naval and missile forces have given Beijing room to consolidate its gains through the construction of fortified artificial islands. Over the course of the past seven years, China has dredged submarine features in the Spratlys into artificial islands on which it has placed soldiers, supply stores, airstrips, and other military infrastructure – essentially transforming barren islets into miniature fortifications.[59] While this is an example of the sort of revisionist behaviour we seek to emphasize, it is also an example of a feedback effect. Without the power projection capacity to act freely in the SCS, China would not have been able to develop these features into mini military bases. Yet, once established, these 11 outposts serve to consolidate China's power in the region and extend its projection capability throughout the first island chain and then to the second island chain. The radar stations on some of these features extend China's ability to surveil the region, coordinate long-distance strikes from its missile corps or aircraft, and disrupt the communications

[56] Because the DF-26 is also capable of hitting land-based targets, this also puts American bases as far away as Guam within its range.

[57] Andrew Erickson, "Chinese Anti-Ship Ballistic Missile Development and Counter-Intervention Efforts," (Washington, DC: US-China Economic and Security Review Commission, 2017).

[58] Sutton, "The Chinese Navy Is Building an Incredible Number of Warships." *Forbes*, December 15, 2019. https://www.forbes.com/sites/hisutton/2019/12/15/china-is-building-an-incredible-number-of-warships/#334756d069ac

[59] Harry Kazianis, "Face It, the Mighty US Aircraft Carrier Is Finished," *The American Conservative* (November 29, 2017); Victor Robert Lee, "Satellite Imagery: China Expands Land Filling at North Island in the Paracels," *The Diplomat* (March 7, 2016); Scott N. Romaniuk and Tobias Burgers, "China's Next Phase of Militarization in the South China Sea," *The Diplomat* (March 20, 2019).

systems of adversaries in the area.[60] The landing strips allow for extended surveillance or strike missions from the air that can pose a direct threat to international shipping, including foreign warships. Equally important here is that each artificial island serves as a fortified refuelling and refitting station for China's naval assets throughout the SCS.[61]

The combination of modernized non-carrier surface vessels, improved command and control capabilities through expanded radar stations interacting with space-based assets and anti-ship missiles, an expanding carrier fleet, and growing submarine capabilities have not only increased the lethality of PLAN forces, but have also broadened the vectors of attack available to the PLA as it seeks to increase the costs of US intervention in the region. As James Samuel Johnson writes:

> Notwithstanding the operational effectiveness of U.S. countermeasures, if ASBMs were employed by Beijing as part of integrated multi-axis A2/AD campaigns in the Western Pacific, the risks posed to U.S. surface fleets would increase substantially ... even if the U.S. were able to effectively exploit the existing operational weaknesses of China's ASBMs, this weapon would still create challenges ... by diverting or splitting the attention of its missile defenses during a combat scenario.[62]

These developments – in quantitative and qualitative terms over the course of a decade – have raised costs for US and US-partner intervention in the region while simultaneously making unilateral revisions an ever more accessible goal for the PLAN. This has not only disadvantaged the US materially, but also reputationally, and runs the risk of damaging the US' image among other claimants of the SCS and non-claimants with their own interests. As defence analyst Andrew Erickson stated in his 2017 congressional testimony, "Even the perception that China was on track to achieving parity [with the United States] would gravely harm America's standing and influence across the Asia-Pacific and around the world."[63]

---

60 David Brennan, "Beijing's South China Sea Military Bases Now Have Jammers That Can Block American Radar and Communications, US Claims," *Newsweek* (April 9, 2018).

61 Thomas Shugart, "China's Artificial Islands Are Bigger (and a Bigger Deal) Than You Think," *War on the Rocks* (September 21, 2016).

62 James Samuel Johnson, "China's 'Guam Express' and 'Carrier Killers': The Anti-Ship Asymmetric Challenge to the US in the Western Pacific," *Comparative Strategy* 36 no. 4 (2017), 323.

63 Erickson, "Chinese Anti-Ship Ballistic Missile Development and Counter-Intervention Efforts," 10.

Conclusion

This chapter has explored the various security structures of the SCS, both as context for ongoing competition between Washington and Beijing, and as a complex system of states whose interests shape and constrain the behaviour of both major powers vying for primacy in the region. This chapter has analysed the multiple security structures that exist as part of regions within a region, located the sources of impasse between the major actors in the SCS region as well as the sources of potential military conflict, and identified the key stressors to regional security from a systemic perspective. In terms of security dynamics, it is more helpful to think of the SCS as a system of systems rather than a single, monolithic security system, in which these states, as well as states not situated in the immediate SCS area, retain vested interests in maintaining a military presence and protecting what they perceive to be areas falling within their national boundaries. Among the most important subsystems at work in the region are the US' network of allies and security partners, some of which have outstanding internecine conflicts between each other, ASEAN and the larger ASEAN Regional Forum, and the dyadic great power competition between China and the US that permeates each subsystem throughout the region. China's spectacular economic growth, coupled with its newly developed soft power capabilities and renewed tensions with the United States, have fuelled speculation over a looming "Thucydides Trap," triggering an armed conflict between the United States and China, with the potential to drag multiple states into escalating conflict. While the concerns raised by Sino-US competition deserve attention, they do not exist in a vacuum. Each competitor's range of manoeuvre is shaped by the broader security structures in and around the SCS.

References

Bellacqua, James. "The China Factor in US Vietnam Relations." Washington, DC: Center for Naval Analysis, 2012. https://www.cna.org/cna_files/pdf/DRM-2012-U-000184-FINAL.pdf

Brennan, David. "Beijing's South China Sea Military Bases Now Have Jammers That Can Block American Radar and Communications, US Claims." *Newsweek*, April 9, 2018. https://www.newsweek.com/beijings-south-china-sea-military-bases-now-have-jammers-can-block-american-877604

Center for Strategic and International Studies (CSIS). "How Is China Modernizing Its Navy?" December 17, 2018. https://chinapower.csis.org/china-naval-modernization/

Congressional Research Service (CRS). "China Naval Modernization: Implications for US Navy Capabilities – Background and Issues for Congress," March 18, 2020. https://crsreports.congress.gov/product/pdf/RL/RL33153/233

Dolven, Ben, Shirley A. Kan, and Mark E. Manyin. "Maritime Territorial Disputes in East Asia: Issues for Congress." Washington, DC: Congressional Research Service, 2013. https://fas.org/sgp/crs/row/R42930.pdf

Erickson, Andrew. "Chinese Anti-Ship Ballistic Missile Development and Counter-Intervention Efforts." Washington, DC: US-China Economic and Security Review Commission, 2017. http://www.andrewerickson.com/2017/02/my-testimony-before-the-u-s-china-commission-chinese-anti-ship-ballistic-missile-development-and-counter-intervention-efforts-hearing-on-chinas-advanced-wea/

Fravel, M. Taylor. "China's Strategy in the South China Sea." *Contemporary Southeast Asia*, Vol. 32, No. 3 (2011), 292–319.

Fravel, M. Taylor. "Revising Deng's Foreign Policy." *The Diplomat*, January 17, 2012. https://thediplomat.com/2012/01/revising-dengs-foreign-policy-2/

Gady, Franz-Stefan. "China Kicks Off Construction of New Supercarrier." *The Diplomat*, January 5, 2018. https://thediplomat.com/2018/01/china-kicks-off-construction-of-new-supercarrier/

Greer, Adam. "The South China Sea Is Really a Fishery Dispute." *The Diplomat*, July 20, 2016. https://thediplomat.com/2016/07/the-south-china-sea-is-really-a-fishery-dispute/

Hameiri, Shahar and Lee Jones, "Rising Powers and State Transformation: The Case of China." *European Journal of International Relations*, Vol. 22, No. 2 (2015), 72–98.

Hille, Kathrin. "China's First Aircraft Carrier Takes to the Sea." *Financial Times*, August 10, 2011. http://www.ft.com/cms/s/0/6b20cdce-c300-11e0-8cc7-00144feabdc0.html

Johnson, James Samuel. "China's 'Guam Express' and 'Carrier Killers': The Anti-Ship Asymmetric Challenge to the US in the Western Pacific." *Comparative Strategy*, Vol. 36, No. 4 (2017), 319–32.

Joyner, Christopher C. "The Spratly Islands Dispute in the South China Sea: Problems, Policies and Prospects for Diplomatic Accommodation." *Investigating Confidence Building Measures in the Asia Pacific Region* (1999), 53–108.

Kaplan, Robert D. "The South China Sea Is the Future of Conflict." *Foreign Policy* (2011): http://www.foreignpolicy.com/articles/2011/08/15/the_south_china_sea_is_the_future_of_conflict?page=full

Kazianis, Harry. "Face It, the Mighty US Aircraft Carrier Is Finished." *The American Conservative*, November 29, 2017. https://www.theamericanconservative.com/articles/face-it-the-mighty-u-s-aircraft-carrier-is-dead/

Kostecka, Daniel. "From the Sea: PLA Doctrine and the Employment of Sea-Based Airpower." *Naval War College Review*, Vol. 64 (2011), 11–30.

Lee, Victor Robert. "Satellite Imagery: China Expands Land Filling at North Island in the Paracels." *The Diplomat*, March 7, 2016. https://thediplomat.com/2016/03/satellite-imagery-china-expands-land-filling-at-north-island-in-the-paracels/

Li, Nan, and Christopher Weuve. "China's Aircraft Carrier Ambitions: An Update." *Naval War College Review*, Vol. 63 (2010), 13–31.

Liff, Adam P., and Andrew S. Erickson. "Demystifying China's Defence Spending: Less Mysterious in the Aggregate." *The China Quarterly*, Vol. 216 (2013), 805–30.

Maizland, Lindsay. "China's Modernizing Military." February 5, 2020. https://www.cfr.org/backgrounder/chinas-modernizing-military

"Military and Security Developments Involving the People's Republic of China 2018." Office of the Secretary of Defense, 2018. https://fas.org/man/eprint/dod-china-2019.pdf

O'Rourke, Ronald. *China Naval Modernization: Implications for US Navy Capabilities – Background and Issues for Congress*. Washington, DC: Congressional Research Service, 2012. https://china.usc.edu/sites/default/files/legacy/AppImages/crs-2012-china-naval-modernization.pdf

O'Rourke, Ronald. "Maritime Territorial and Exclusive Economic Zone (EEZ) Disputes Involving China: Issues for Congress." Washington, DC: Congressional Research Service, 2012. https://www.hsdl.org/?view&did=811054

O'Rourke, Ronald. *China Naval Modernization: Implications for US Navy Capabilities 2018*. Washington, DC: Congressional Research Service, 2018. https://crsreports.congress.gov/product/pdf/RL/RL33153/222

O'Rourke, Ronald. *China Naval Modernization: Implications for US Navy Capabilities – Background and Issues for Congress*. Washington, DC: Congressional Research Service, May 21, 2020. https://crsreports.congress.gov/product/pdf/RL/RL33153/235

O'Rourke, Ronald. "US–China Strategic Competition in South and East China Seas: Background and Issues for Congress," ed. Congressional Research Service. Washington, DC, May 1, 2020. https://crsreports.congress.gov/product/pdf/R/R42784/105

Panda, Ankit. "Introducing the DF-17: China's Newly Tested Ballistic Missile Armed with a Hypersonic Glide Vehicle." *The Diplomat*, December 28, 2017. https://thediplomat.com/2017/12/introducing-the-df-17-chinas-newly-tested-ballistic-missile-armed-with-a-hypersonic-glide-vehicle/

Pedrozo, Stacy. "China's Active Defense Strategy and Its Regional Impact." Washington, DC: Council on Foreign Relations, 2011. https://www.uscc.gov/sites/default/files/1.27.11HPR.pdf

Perlez, Jane. "China Said to Turn Reef into Airstrip in Disputed Water." *The New York Times*, November 23, 2014. https://www.nytimes.com/2014/11/24/world/asia/china-said-to-be-building-airstrip-capable-area-in-disputed-waters.html

Romaniuk, Scott N. and Tobias Burgers. "China's Next Phase of Militarization in the South China Sea." *The Diplomat*, March 20, 2019. https://thediplomat.com/2019/03/chinas-next-phase-of-militarization-in-the-south-china-sea/

Rudd, Kevin. "Beyond the Pivot: A New Road Map for US–Chinese Relations." *Foreign Affairs*, Vol. 92, No. 2 (2013), 9–15.

Sanger, David and Rick Gladstone. "Piling Sand in a Disputed Sea, China Literally Gains Ground." *The New York Times*, April 8, 2015. https://www.nytimes.com/2015/04/09/world/asia/new-images-show-china-literally-gaining-ground-in-south-china-sea.html

Shugart, Thomas. "China's Artificial Islands Are Bigger (and a Bigger Deal) Than You Think." *War on the Rocks*, September 21, 2016. https://warontherocks.com/2016/09/chinas-artificial-islands-are-bigger-and-a-bigger-deal-than-you-think/

Silk, Richard. "Plenty of Productivity Still in Store for China, Economist Says." *Wall Street Journal Online*, February 21, 2013. https://blogs.wsj.com/chinarealtime/2013/02/21/plenty-of-productivity-still-in-store-for-china-economist-says/

"Stirring up the South China Sea (II): Regional Responses." International Crisis Group, 2012. https://www.crisisgroup.org/asia/south-east-asia/south-china-sea/stirring-south-china-sea-ii-regional-responses

Sutton, H. I. "The Chinese Navy Is Building an Incredible Number of Warships." *Forbes*, December 15, 2019. https://www.forbes.com/sites/hisutton/2019/12/15/china-is-building-an-incredible-number-of-warships/#334756d069ac

Thayer, Carlyle. "South China Sea Disputes: ASEAN and China." *East Asia Forum*, July 14, 2011. https://www.eastasiaforum.org/2011/07/14/south-china-sea-disputes-asean-and-china/

"The PLA Navy: New Capabilities and Missions for the 21st Century." Office of Naval Intelligence. Washington, DC: Defense Technical Information Center, 2015. https://fas.org/nuke/guide/china/plan-2015.pdf

The State Council Information Office of the People's Republic of China. "The Development of China's Maritime Cause." May 1998. http://www.scio.gov.cn/zfbps/ndhf/1998/Document/307963/307963.htm

The State Council Information Office of the People's Republic of China. "China's Peaceful Development." September 6, 2011. http://www.scio.gov.cn/zfbps/ndhf/2011/Document/1000031/1000031.htm

Tønnesson, Stein. "China's Changing Role in the South China Sea: Reflections on a Scholars' Workshop." *Harvard Asia Quarterly*, Vol. 12, No. 4 (2010), 18–30.

"US Carriers Sent toward Taiwan before Election." *Reuters*, March 19, 2008. https://www.reuters.com/article/us-usa-taiwan-crriers/u-s-carriers-sent-toward-taiwan-before-election-idUSN1934158120080319

US Energy Information Administration (USEIA). "China's Crude Oil Imports Surpassed 10 Million Barrels per Day in 2019." March 23, 2020. https://www.eia.gov/todayinenergy/detail.php?id=43216#

Wong, Edward. "China Hedges over Whether South China Sea Is a 'Core Interest' Worth War." *The New York Times*, March 30, 2011. https://www.nytimes.com/2011/03/31/world/asia/31beijing.html

Yoshihara, Toshi and James R. Holmes. *Red Star over the Pacific, Revised Edition: China's Rise and the Challenge to US Maritime Strategy*. Annapolis, MD: Naval Institute Press, 2018.

Zou, Keyuan. "The Sino-Vietnamese Agreement on Maritime Boundary Delimitation in the Gulf of Tonkin." *Ocean Development & International Law*, Vol. 36 (2005), 13–24.

2

The South China Sea as an Echo Chamber of Chinese Foreign and Security Policy

Scott N. Romaniuk and Tobias Burgers

Introduction

The South China Sea (SCS) has long been one of the primary security interests of the People's Republic of China's (PRC, hereafter China).[1] As early as 1958, through its "Declaration of the Government of the People's Republic of China on China's Territorial Sea," China claimed parts of the SCS through the infamous nine-dash line.[2] Throughout the ensuing decades, mostly minor hostilities occurred and China was unable to increase its power in the waters significantly. Instead, the SCS was something of a phoney, mainly diplomatic, conflict that only occasionally turned violent. The region featured conflicts based on limited escalation, though with significant pressure-potential for all actors engaged. However, over the past decade-and-a-half, foremost under the leadership of Xi Jinping, China has sought to abandon Deng's mantle of "hiding its strength and biding its time." China has, in the SCS at least, since 2009 when it declared its sovereignty over the seas, embarked on a tour de force, seeking political, economic,

1 Congressional Research Service, "US-China Strategic Competition in South and East China Seas: Background and Issues for Congress" (Rep.), June 23, 2020, 8.

2 People's Republic of China, *Declaration of the Government of the People's Republic of China on China's Territorial Sea* (Annex 2/5), 1958.

and military control over the strategic waterway.[3] China has been sought to achieve these goals almost entirely through the application "salami-slicing." Now widely applied by the Chinese military, paramilitary, and civil actors, salami-slicing is a "strategy that employs a series of incremental actions, none of which by itself is a casus belli, to gradually change the status quo in China's favor."[4] The SCS has remained a hotbed of this strategy and can be considered one, if not the core, area in which China has employed this approach the longest, most consistently, and efficiently. Through a strategy that appears to have been too successful, China has established a clear position of dominance and secured the upper hand vis-à-vis the other regional claimants, and has put non-regional actors, without a direct claim on the SCS, on the defensive.

Accordingly, the SCS has become one of the anchors, if not the leading anchor, of China's newly assertive foreign and security policy behaviour.[5] The combination of its importance, its longitude – running well over a decade – and its success, makes the SCS an ideal case study of its foreign and security policy, notably under Xi. It offers clues and lessons on Chinese tactics, strategies, methods of operations, political goals, and reactions to what the ruling party in China has called "interference" from other actors. These lessons are valuable for understanding Chinese intentions, and future goals regarding the SCS, and could help regional, and other actors, such as Australia, Japan, and the US, to understand and possibly counter Chinese activities. Simultaneously, the lessons learned from China's behaviour in the SCS can be applied beyond the maritime domain of the SCS. China also appears to be repeating its pattern of behaviour in other conflicts: its military, paramilitary, and civil forces have been using salami-slicing tactics in other regional conflicts. Over the years, China has intensified its efforts over the Senkaku/Diaoyutai/Diaoyu Islands, incrementally increasing its actions, but never to the level that has prompted Japan to respond with kinetic force.[6] Likewise, in its conflict with Taiwan, China – particularly since the outbreak of COVID-19 and the second term of Taiwanese president Tsai Ing-wen – presents the image of having decided to raise the temperature in the Sino-Taiwanese pressure pan. Yet, here too, rather than going from

[3] Derek Grossman, "China Just Botched a Monumental Opportunity With the Philippines," *The Diplomat* (June 18, 2020).

[4] Congressional Research Service, "US-China Strategic Competition in South and East China Seas: Background and Issues for Congress" (Rep.), June 23, 2020, 8.

[5] Patrick M. Cronin and Ryan Neuhard, "Total Competition China's Challenge in the South China Sea" (Rep.). Center for New American Security, January 8, 2020.

[6] Council on Foreign Relations, "Tensions in the East China Sea | Global Conflict Tracker," 2020.

lukewarm to boiling, China is adept at applying pressure incrementally and with sharp calculation, avoiding sudden surges.[7] Both cases illustrate how China is seeking to replicate its SCS tactics and strategies.

In this chapter we argue that the SCS serves as a case study and the echo chamber of Chinese foreign and security policy.[8] Lessons can be drawn from analysing and studying long(er) term PRC trends and developments in the SCS with which to establish a pattern of assertive behaviour that features salami-slicing at its core. It now seems apt to apply this pattern beyond the SCS. In the wake of the COVID-19 outbreak and subsequent spread, China has embarked on foreign and security policy that looks intent on flexing its muscles further and more than anything prior.[9] This has raised concern about China's behaviour in any near and long-term future conflict in which China could become active. China's behaviour in the SCS could serve as a possible blueprint for how its current leadership would likely conduct itself in other regional conflicts, such as the conflict between Taiwan and China, the East China Sea flashpoint, possible tensions with Australia, power competition between the US and China, as well as the Sino-Indian border conflict. Understanding the SCS conflict will therefore serve as an essential, and much needed, echo chamber that should allow other actors, regional and beyond, to develop possible countermeasures in other regional flashpoints where China is engaged, and is or could be applying its salami-slicing strategies. This echo chamber is not, however, an orbuculum that will present direct answers, as each of the other flashpoints in which China is engaged exhibits significantly different political, military, and security dynamics. Nevertheless, we argue that by analysing China's activities in the SCS, where the state has not deviated from a path of assertiveness and confrontational behaviour since the Xi-ization of China, we will be able to understand developments in other areas of strategic interest. The SCS, within this context, serves as an

---

7 Seth Cropsey, "China's Salami-Slicing Policy toward Taiwan," Hudson Institute, May 14, 2018.

8 Suisheng Zhao, "Foreign Policy Implications of Chinese Nationalism Revisited: The Strident Turn," *Journal of Contemporary China*, Vol. 22, No. 82 (2013): 535–53.

9 *Deutsche Welle*, "Is China Taking Advantage of COVID-19 to Pursue South China Sea Ambitions?" May 26, 2020; Robert A. Manning and Patrick M. Cronin, "Under Cover of Pandemic, China Steps Up Brinkmanship in South China Sea," *Foreign Policy*, May 14, 2020; Harsh Pant, "China's Salami Slicing Overdrive: It's Flexing Military Muscles at a Time When Covid Preoccupies the Rest of the World," May 13, 2020. https://timesofindia.indiatimes.com/blogs/toi-edit-page/chinas-salami-slicing-overdrive-its-flexing-military-muscles-at-a-time-when-covid-preoccupies-the-rest-of-the-world/

echo chamber for Chinese foreign and security policy – one that allows a vision for areas immediately adjacent and beyond the SCS.

We apply the lessons learned from this echo chamber to two other conflicts that have recently intensified due to Chinese actions. First, the Taiwan Strait conflict. As mentioned previously, China has, in the last few years and particularly since the beginning of 2020, engaged in aggressive actions that sought to challenge the Taiwanese position by means of salami-slicing. As such, China has already progressed beyond the initial stage of salami-slicing regarding Taiwan. Its current actions, such as incursions into Taiwanese air and maritime space, and aggressive naval operations around the island, are not the trademark of early salami-slicing strategies. Instead, these are examples of more forceful and escalatory tactics. This leaves the question of how China could progress its tactics in the ensuing months and years. Second, we briefly engage with the Indian-Sino border conflict, which has intensified during the first half of 2020, with deadly clashes on both sides. Here, we consider whether salami-slicing tactics have been used at all or to the same extent as with Taiwan. As China's actions and its intentions behind them with respect to its shared border with India are not clear-cut compared to the Taiwan Strait case, and we argue that the conflict, or least the current intensification, is still in its early phases of development. Therefore, comparing this conflict to the early stages of the events in and across the SCS is of considerable value in order to determine what, if any, lessons can be learned on how the conflict could further develop and possibly escalate. Logically, in order to compare both cases to the SCS conflict, a case study on the SCS itself is needed to identify critical patterns and tactics of salami-slicing. The following section will achieve this. Finally, following our comparative examination of both case studies, the following section ends with a concluding paragraph in which we discuss the extent to which the SCS salami-slicing strategies have been used, and to what extent the echo chamber of the SCS serves as a useful indicator and barometer of future Sino-foreign and security policy and behaviour.

The second section of this chapter will analyse Chinese behaviour in the SCS dating back to the 2000s. The aim is to illustrate and clarify the salami-slicing concept, through examples, and demonstrate how, through the appliance of this strategy, China has been able to increase its dominance, power, and establish quasi-control over the waters. The third paragraph of this section focuses on the Taiwan Strait conflict. The main focus will be on the conflict since the start of the Tsai Ing-wen presidency in 2016, and the aim is to identify and illustrate how early signs of salami-slicing can be established. Furthermore, and based on the conclusions of the prior SCS-focused section, it establishes a possible pattern of Chinese action, and raises the questions of what Taiwan could do to successfully counter the salami-slicing strategy, while ensuring the conflict does not reach boiling point.

China in the South China Sea

With the world's focus on urgent healthcare matters as a result of the COVID-19 outbreak and spread, China pursued a number of (escalatory) actions in its immediate vicinity and elsewhere along its borders and within its immediate periphery. China has even been accused of advancing its interests and influence through adjacent regions under the cover of the pandemic. Irrespective of any perceived cover, China's actions are far from novel and fit well in the framework of salami-slicing – a widely used tactic by the Chinese state to gradually raise the escalatory level. In 2012, Robert Haddick discussed salami-slicing tactics, defining the practice as "the slow accumulation of small actions, none of which is a casus belli, but which add up over time to a major strategic change."[10] Yet, what has changed since the emergence of COVID-19 is the pace with which China has been pursuing its interests vis-à-vis salami-slicing. Rather than slowly slicing miniature pieces of the larger salami, in recent months, China has begun slicing larger portions and at a faster rate. This is peculiar because it indicates a palpable shift from its established salami-slicing tactic, and can be regarded as a possible sign that China is increasingly intent on engaging in a more aggressive manner. Already, scholars have pointed to a dramatic rise in China's assertive behaviour. Questions subsequently arise if this increased pace of operations, as well their impact, are part of a larger strategy, seeking to escalate China's foreign and security policy. One postulation is that it could be part of a well-timed, and well-planned, tactical alteration that seeks to increase China's influence in the broader SCS region, expanding China's influence well beyond its shores and to distant locales, in stride with its military development and expansion, and potential changes in China's military strategy.

Taylor Fravel illuminates, in his work on the evolution of China's military strategy since the beginning of the CCP's state power, the Maoist (and still current) doctrine of Active Defence, describing a long process of change that has taken place over numerous decades.[11] Over that protracted length of time, a great deal of surface interpretation has been made about China's military strategies and how its defence policies connect with the world around China. Much of the West's interpretation has been wrought with misreading of the changes that had taken place within China over the evolution of and decision making regarding its military strategy.[12] The stages

[10] Robert Haddick, "Salami Slicing in the South China Sea," *Foreign Policy*, August 3, 2012.

[11] M. Taylor Fravel, *Active Defense: China's Military Strategy Since 1949*, 2019, Princeton: Princeton University Press.

[12] Ibid.

of Chinese military strategy that have unfolded since the 1950s paved the way for China to engage with newer and more modern forms of warfare, with initial concerns presiding over US invasion and dislodging of the CCP's relatively young power. Its military strategy was also guided by the "conduct of warfare [that] has occurred in the international system" and the coherence of CCP leadership across a decades-long thread.[13] Although China's military strategy hinged on positional warfare for some time, a significant change took place in 1993, when China looked past its borders and conceived of war-fighting on its periphery, especially with respect to conflict centring on issues of territory and sovereignty.[14] Fravel explains:

> A shift in the conduct of warfare creates a strong incentive for a state to adopt a new military strategy if the shift demonstrates that a gap exists between a state's current capabilities and the requirements of future wars. The effect of these shifts should be particularly salient for developing countries or late military modernizers such as China who are trying to improve their military capabilities.[15]

While Fravel argues that a major change in the CCP's military strategy should be expected as, "in response to a significant shift in the conduct of warfare that arises when the party is unified," we argue that the China military strategy can be understood as one undergoing moderate changes in spite of the CCP's tight coherence under Xi Jinping and against the absence of considerable change or shifts in the conduct of warfare in the world today.[16] Since 2013, Xi has signalled the potential for major change in China's armed forces and military strategy with the publication of the new *Science of Military Strategy* – China's official handbook disseminated by the Academy of Military Sciences, which explicates the national security strategy of China and war as a multi-faceted, multi-dimensional whole. It presents entire five-dimensional expanses constituting warfare as truly full spectrum. This major signal of change is supplemented by a second significant event, that came in the form of the CCP issuing the 10th Military Strategy White Paper.[17] As these internal changes took place, the Chinese military and its

---

13 Ibid., 271.
14 Ibid.
15 Ibid.
16 Ibid., 4.
17 中华人民共和国国务院 [State Council, PRC], "新时代的中国国防" ["China's National Defense in the New Era"], July 24, 2019.

various services continued along the path of modernization, augmentation, and preparation for defensive and offensive warfare.

The 2015 White Paper[18] goes beyond the intimation of improving military capabilities and, rather, calls for expanding and broadening the ambitions of PLA modernization, transforming it into a fighting force of a major world power with the ability to project its military power overseas, conduct joint operations, and function beyond its traditional security threats. China's 2017 White Paper[19] regarding policies on Asia-Pacific security cooperation, as well as its 2019 White Paper on national defence, stress the need to respond to rising non-traditional maritime threats, and that the Chinese homeland faces the threat of foreign national forces illegally entering Chinese waters and thus undermining China's national security. The US Defense Intelligence Agency's (DIA) 140-page report on China's military power and force modernization referred to Xi's efforts as part of extensive and comprehensive design to facilitate "Beijing's transition from peace to war."[20]

Since setting these major changes in motion and presenting its aims, China has established its military presence in distant regions and locales, exemplified by the construction of its first overseas and geostrategic base at Djibouti, which opened on July 11, 2017. This has, in part, been made possible by the ever-expanding and modernizing PLAN, which remains a crucial aspect of China's great-power rise, and interests and activities beyond-Chinese shores. China, thus, mirrors the rise of great powers of the past, espousing elements of Mahanian naval doctrine as did other great and aspiring powers such as Great Britain, Imperial Germany, and Imperial Japan, which adopted Mahanian concepts of sea power in the development of their respective war-fighting navies, facilitating their maritime aspirations.[21] In the case of the latter two, Mahanian doctrine underpinned the pursuit of war-fighting materials and capabilities to dislodge the power of existing hegemons and assume their position. These substantial reforms coincide with military redesigns to make room for newer forces and services, new command structures and

---

18 中华人民共和国国防部 [Ministry of National Defense, PRC], "中国的军事战略" ["China's Military Strategy"], May 26, 2015.

19 中华人民共和国国务院 [State Council, PRC], "中国的亚太安全合作政策" ["China's Policies on Asia-Pacific Security Cooperation"], 2017.

20 Defense Intelligence Agency, "China Military Power: Modernizing a Force to Fight and Win," 2019, 5.

21 See, James R. Holmes and Toshi Yoshihara, "The Influence of Mahan upon China's Maritime Strategy," *Comparative Strategy*, Vol. 24, No. 1 (2005): 23–51; James R. Holmes and Toshi Yoshihara, *Chinese Naval Strategy in the 21st Century: The Turn to Mahan*, 2008, Abingdon: Routledge; Toshi Yoshihara and James R. Holmes, *Red Star over the Pacific: China's Rise and the Challenge to US Maritime Strategy*, 2013, Annapolis: Naval Institute Press.

command theatres, and the integration of innovative military technologies so as to elevate the overall armed forces of China to a level commensurate with those of a (quasi-)superpower military.

Strategic interests in the South China Sea

The strategic value of the SCS, as a volatile security cauldron, is supported by a number of key factors ranging from geographically strategic importance, to economic imperatives (such as oil and liquefied natural gas (LNG), and fish stocks), to state-level interest asymmetry, principally between China and the US. Additionally, both elements of sovereignty and territorial integrity have remained salient features of the state interest in the region and competition between states over it, and this is likely to remain the case for decades to come. The added complexity of the SCS dispute can be attributed to the complexity inherently associated with addressing territoriality and territorial acquisition or disputes in a maritime context. As a result, the SCS has become one of the most hotly contested and militarized regions over the previous decades. The density of the SCS dispute can be traced back to the 1970s, with attention increasingly invested by several states in the region during the course of the 1980s and 1990s – this carries on into the new millennium, and into new frictious pursuits.

The strategic importance and significance of the SCS has been well documented, with its resource stocks receiving much attention. Initial estimates by the Russian Federation, which undertook a survey of resources in the SCS during the mid-1990s, estimated that the Spratlys alone occupied the site of approximately 6 billion barrels of oil – a figure Chinese authorities recalibrated to 150 billion barrels.[22] The American Geosciences Institute (AGI) shows that, for 2017, US oil consumption stood at approximately 7.2 billion barrels,[23] and that current US oil reserves stand at approximately 35.2 billion barrels, or five years of consumption at current consumption levels. To put this into perspective, Chinese specialists' estimations of the SCS oil stocks are five times the US' current reserves and would theoretically yield just over 20 years' worth of US oil consumption, assuming a constant rate of consumption.

Control of the SCS region refers, in addition to control of immense oil and gas reserves, command over the strategic waterway through which

22 Institute of Peace and Conflict Studies, "South China Sea: Emerging Security Architecture," August 1, 2012, http://www.ipcs.org/issue_select.php?recNo=479; Tim Daiss, "Why the South China Sea Has More Oil Than You Think," May 22, 2016.

23 American Geosciences Institute, "How Much Oil Is Consumed in the United States?" 2020.

pass more than three times the amount of oil and LNG than pass through the Suez Canal.[24] The SCS is also an economic and transport bottleneck for Japan, South Korea, Taiwan, and Indonesia – all states competing over the SCS' waters. Beyond its economic significance, the SCS accounts for a disproportionately large area of state coastlines, including Vietnam, Indonesia, Malaysia, the Philippines, and Taiwan. Thus, any single state controlling the SCS in its entirety would ultimately have direct access to the coastal waters of these states.

The pursuit of national interests and the introduction of salami-slicing

The dispute over territorial claims emerged in the 1970s, with prior attention given to ownership over reefs and islands largely ignored until that point. Marked by maritime resource exploration, and state interests in laying claim to projected assets beneath the waters, states clashed via official discourse and low-level military engagements (notably three cases of conflict centring on the Spratlys in 1988, 1992, and 1995).[25] The subsequent phase of the SCS dispute occupied the 1980s and 1990s in the form of a claims race as well as the reinforcement of those claims by means of physical territory occupation, or the occupation of small islands so as to deepen the credibility of respective claims. Intensification of claims and the deployment of military forces established a new pace of regional saturation with arms and equipment.

Among the parties taking part in complex claims on areas of the SCS, we focus in this chapter on those of China and China's efforts in pursuing its political and military interests in the broader region. With much of its claims having been made on the basis of historical grounds, much like those of other SCS claimants, China has set out to "correct" a series of territorial injustices through treaty folly. Reference has consistently been made to Chinese exploration, navigation, and visitations of the Spratlys (eventually known as the Paracel or Xisha Islands) dating back thousands of years to the Han Dynasty and the Ming Dynasty.[26] These claims laid the groundwork for the mapping of an SCS depicted as under Chinese control and the

---

[24] US Energy Information Administration, "The Suez Canal and SUMED Pipeline are Critical Chokepoints for Oil and Natural Gas Trade," July 23, 2019.

[25] See, Lam Peng Er, "Japan and the Spratlys Dispute: Aspirations and Limitations," *Asian Survey*, Vol. 36 No. 10 (1996): 995–1010; Xavier Furtado, "International Law and the Dispute over the Spratly Islands: Whither UNCLOS?" *Contemporary Southeast Asia*, Vol. 21, No. 3 (1999): 386–404.

[26] See, Teh-Kuang Chang, "China's Claim of Sovereignty over Spratly and Paracel Islands: A Historical and Legal Perspective," *Case Western Reserve Journal of International Law*, Vol. 23, No. 3 (1991): 399–420.

eventual creation of the "nine-dash line" through Zhou Enlai's revisions. China's claim was reinforced through military efforts against Vietnam in 1974, resulting in China's control of the Paracel Islands. Placing the islands under the ownership of Hainan Province was a bold and effective move that further solidified China's political and military control over its SCS assets. These efforts, notably political aspirations supported by hard military power capabilities and the reconfiguration of the Paracel Islands in 1988 to represent Chinese territory directly, constitute the extended and initial "soft" phase of China's salami-slicing in the SCS.

Developments in the SCS and treatments of the SCS – in terms of energy, maritime and military or national security, and territory as national security – elevated the SCS's importance and the emerging dispute from its non-conflict and pre-conflict phases to its current and protracted phase, which we call the "early low-intensity conflict period." The interrelation of complex security imperatives has greatly expanded the spectrum of resources that China has enlisted to secure its claims. A turn to both civilian and military resources, while pre-existing the Xi-era in China, has been exemplified following the Xi-ization of China and the country's development into a maritime power. Although other claimants have pursued the path of maritime military asset acquisition, efforts to offset or at least partially counter the maritime military growth and deployments of China have generally failed to produce conditions favourable to China's SCS competitors. China's military assertiveness in the SCS and the CCP's current policy of expansion have been consistently reinforced by the military power asymmetry between China and all other claimants. While the security and military forces of Indonesia, the Philippines, and Vietnam, for example, may be sufficient for policing maritime zones and EEZs, their size and military effectiveness are conspicuously insufficient for engaging with China's maritime and aerial forces.

The apparent force asymmetry between China and neighbouring countries, specifically other SCS claimants, has generated much deeper foreign connections and the inclusion of other states with fewer and even no direct geographical ties to the SCS. US involvement and deeper engagement has generally been a positive unfolding of events for the Philippines, which has, for many years, relied on both direct and indirect or implied defence and military support. Likewise, the involvement of Australia in the SCS dispute and growing conflict serves in part as a reflection of China's expansionist-driven policies in the region, which are strongly tied to the security of the Chinese mainland. Both the US and Australia, in addition to the United Kingdom (UK) as party to the Five Power Defence Arrangements (PDFA-1971), however, have reasoned that their engagement is concomitantly based on interests of defending international law and the freedom of navigation through strategically important waterways.[27] The subsequent investment of further military resources and military deployments in the SCS by both China and the US has raised the spectre that both major powers may not be able to avoid the Thucydides Trap.

China's South China Sea expansion before Xi

In the period leading up to Xi Jinping assuming power and redirecting China down new, more assertive and expansionist paths, several sources of continuity can be identified. These continuities transcend the pre-Xi Jinping period and that of his current leadership. First, China's rise as a major power has unearthed some of the most sensitive imperatives of a great power rising, in the form of energy shortages and reliance on energy sources found beyond China's state borders. In this regard, China's efforts to pursue new sources of energy and to secure those sources as well as the delicate lines of supply and communication with which they are intricately associated is not at all surprising. Second, as a still emerging and developing modern state, China's development of its military forces, has yet to reach a conclusive point. Its force development and growth, in stride with its evolving naval maritime plan and strategy, is a natural process associated with state growth. This often-overlooked and Mahanian-based strategy is a long-term one that extends across a period of four decades, taking China's military presence from its immediate coastal waters to near seas, to far seas or distant waters. Third, China's expansionist policies towards the SCS were well established and in turn established a vibrant framing for China's current and more elevated assertive expansionism to the south.

The question of sea power has gained significant attention in China, and from Chinese scholars and experts, who generally share the view that China's future great power status and continued rise in tandem with its expanding interests is predicated, at least in part, on the modernization and development of its navy into a "blue-water" force. Shared opinion on this point has played a significant role in redirecting the leadership's perception of the criticality of sea lines of communication (SLOCs), and the manner in which SLOCs figure in the state's overall security. This perspective also subscribes to the assumption that China's security on the mainland is inextricably tied to the security of its interests and its efforts in neighbouring waters suffused with important resources. Thus, the protection of China's maritime interest

[27] See, Andrew T. H. Tan, "The Five Power Defence Arrangements: The Continuing Relevance," *Contemporary Security Policy*, Vol. 29, No. 2 (2008): 285–302.

beyond its coastal waters, reaching out into the near seas and far seas, is fixed within China's core interests.

Prior to Xi's ascent to power, China began investing considerably in the development of a more sophisticated and advanced maritime force. Its maritime force development has been complemented by force advancement in other service branches as well, yielding military capabilities sufficient for protecting its core interest off the coast of China. Accordingly, China's PLAN and military complements have become the primary guarantor of Chinese security in its maritime environs and is the main feature of Beijing's recently developed "Far Sea Defence" strategy and the view to deploying forces capable of exorcizing foreign military forces from its interest areas. But the need to turn to its military power as instruments of kinetic force has never fully materialized, and instead, China has remained committed to brandishing its military might as a flexing mechanism in its approach to the region and other nations' interests with respect to it. China has remained dedicated to the dictate of Sun Tzu, who argued that, "[t]he supreme art of war is to subdue the enemy without fighting."[28] That same dedication has undergone modification, interweaving elements of soft power and incentivizing, with coercive policy and bullying,[29] along with shows of force, bold moves of occupation, redrawing maps, and military manoeuvres within the sovereign territorial waters of other states. Such a change in tenor may be attributed to a constricting of legal options for China, particularly after China lost the 2016 Arbitral Tribunal in international court.

Under Xi: China's renewal of "divide (and isolate) and conquer"

China's SCS policy under Xi's management has assumed new levels of expansion and military assertiveness. Often referred to as a significant turning point in the trajectory of China's SCS policy and pursuits, China's expansion in the SCS since 2012 shows that the SCS is now at the furthest point in the exponential pressure curve, and has moved well past previous apex points noted by specialists on the topic. China's activities in the SCS since Xi's ascension to power also illustrate that China has made notable gains over much of the region under the framework of salami-slicing. Under the fixed leadership of Xi, China has amplified its efforts of constructing military bases on artificial islands, placed further pressure on other claimant-states through the presence

[28] Sun Tzu, *The Art of War* (Trans. Lionel Giles).

[29] Sumathy Permal, Senia Febrica and Scott N. Romaniuk, Mingjiang Li and YingHui Lee, and John Callahan, in particular, either mention or discuss China's multi-layered coercive tactics and strategies in their respective chapters.

of military maritime forces, and frequently confronted US warships using threatening manoeuvring tactics, provoking US warships by triggering targeting radars, and intercepting US aircraft and flying over US fleets. Additionally, the heavily militarized SCS has simultaneously been nuclearized, currently playing host to both US nuclear ballistic missile submarines (SSBNs) as well as China's Type 094A Jin-class SSBNs put on public display in the SCS in 2018. Satellite imagery is evidence of the near-constant presence of China's SSBNs at strategic bases in the SCS in addition to advanced warships of various types. Bases at which the PLAN's warships dock have been equipped with submarine-hunting technology. A noteworthy development in this context is the military nuclearization of the region by China, which is now capable of launching nuclear attacks or undertaking nuclear-based defensive measures and response from SSBNs in the depths of the SCS and from base facilities.

China's announcement of new administrative districts in the SCS on April 19 – related to management of the Spratly and Paracel Islands – was one of Xi's most recent exploitative moves, taking advantage of the COVID-19 pandemic and large-scale state distraction through lockdowns as well as political and economic obligations in their domestic domains. Beijing has laid claim to an even larger body of water, and by extension to its resources. Vietnam protested China's establishment of the administrative zones, citing a patent violation of its state sovereignty. China's State Council's announcement that it has established two new administrative districts in the SCS has had several immediate effects. Immediately and initially strengthening China's resolution in claiming nearly all of the SCS as its own, the second effect is to demonstrate the leadership's intention to maintain its expansionary momentum during a temporary reduction in US naval presence and operations. The pandemic-stricken *USS Theodore Roosevelt* (CVN-71), a Nimitz-class nuclear-powered aircraft carrier, was withdrawn from operations in early 2020 after reporting approximately 1,000 COVID-19 cases.[30] While the *USS Harry Truman* was redeployed from the Middle East to the Indo-Pacific region as a replacement aircraft carrier, the shuffling of two aircraft carriers required time, resulting in a gap in US naval and air cover. The US also suspended its "Continuous Bomber Presence Mission" out of Anderson Air Force Base in Guam, where strategic bombers have been undertaking routine rotations since 2004.[31] This change, however, did not signal a withdrawal of US strategic bombers'

[30] Centers for Disease Control and Prevention, "SARS-CoV-2 Infections and Serologic Responses from a Sample of US Navy Service Members – USS Theodore Roosevelt, April 2020," June 12, 2020.

[31] Joseph Trevithick, "The Air Force Abruptly Ends Its Continuous Bomber Presence On Guam After 16 Years," *The Drive*, April 17, 2020.

routine operations and flights in the broader region, though it did contribute to a series of abrupt and unexpected changes to the US security tempo that together provided China with an opportune occasion for reasserting its maritime claims and ambitions in the SCS.

Another aspect of China's salami-slicing was observed in early 2020, when Beijing applied the tactic of "claiming-by-naming" in which it named 80 different features in the SCS. The move received swift responses from competing claimants and other states as a breach of international law, in which it was asserted that China does not have the authority to unilaterally and arbitrarily name what it does not own. Associate professor at the University of the Philippines College of Law and Director of the University's Institute for Maritime Affairs and Law of the Sea, Jay Batongbacal explained that, "[t]he act of surveying and naming underwater features as part of a marine scientific research activity cannot be made the basis of any claim to any part of the marine environment or any of its resources."[32] In such a case, however, ownership can be easily defined by possession. While Beijing's incendiary actions fail to enrich the code of conduct in the disputes waterway that it demanded others follow, it is unlikely that any state would either have the requisite military force and political willingness to exercise that force to dislodge a Chinese presence on any one of the artificial features. Chinese physical presence represents more than a tiger without teeth. Many of its artificial features have seen the construction military and industrial bases with significant military presence either within or in the adjacent waters that are ready to defend them on a moment's notice.

Tensions have developed further as a result of Beijing announcing a fishing ban (effective from May 1 to August 16, 2020) in the disputed waters. China would enforce the ban in the waters it claims above the 12th parallel.[33] The original policy was announced in 2018 and is an ongoing annual policy, covering seas near China, including the SCS. The date changes slightly every year but typically applies to the period from May to late August or early September. The ban has spawned protests from other claimants, with suspicion about whether Beijing would be likely to follow measures to conserve fish stocks. The COVID-19 pandemic has magnified the need to draw on fish stocks in the area due to food shortages with the UN World

32 *South China Morning Post*, "Beijing Could Face ASEAN's Wrath over 'Naming and Claiming' of South China Sea Features, Observers Say," April 25, 2020.

33 中华人民共和国农业农村部 [Ministry of Agriculture and Rural Affairs of the People's Republic of China], "农业部关于调整海洋伏季休渔制度的通告农业部通告〔2018〕1号" ["Announcement of the Ministry of Agriculture and Rural Affairs on the Adjustment of the Summer Fishing Moratorium System, Ministry of Agriculture Notice (2018) No. 1"], March 20, 2018; *The Korea Times*, "Beijing's South China Sea Fishing Ban Threatens to Raise Tensions," May 9, 2020.

Food Programme (WFP) having warned in late April of "acute food insecurity."[34] Protestors in the Philippines referred to the ban as "China's bullying" and information confirming that the pandemic has resulted in a loss of income, food, or food shortages for locals in Hainan is lacking.

Any misstep could elevate the probability of confrontation in the disputed waters of the SCS. While Stashwick, writing in *Foreign Policy*, argued that China's SCS militarization has peaked, we see that its salami-slicing campaign has neither peaked nor will remain limited to the SCS waterway.[35] Since the outbreak of COVID-19 and its rise to pandemic status, and indeed for years preceding its outbreak, Beijing has repeatedly and intentionally made decisions and undertaken measures in the SCS that have incrementally brought states closer to confrontation, simultaneously testing the determination of individual states in the region and their willingness to embrace solidarity against China's moves. At the same time, China has made incremental but collectively significant steps in its SCS expansion. Instances of violent clashes have already been seen, and Beijing's turn to hybrid warfare serves as a strong indication of its commitment to its expansionist policies to the south, in the East China Sea and the Indo-Pacific region more broadly.

Echo chamber in the Taiwan Strait: midway in the exponential pressure curve

Taiwan has long been among China's core security issues.[36] Zeng et al argue that the Taiwan issue, from a Chinese perspective, is separated from any of the other territorial issues: whereas the SCS, and the East China Sea as well Chinese claims along the Indian border, are considered territorial disputes, Taiwan is not considered part of the territorial issue, and is instead a matter of undisputed unity of the mainland.[37] In a more recent article, Zhou quoted former Australian Prime Minister and noted China-hand, Kevin Rudd, who reaffirms the position Taiwan holds for the CCP. Rudd argues that "China's core interests include seven aspects: … (ii) keeping national unity of mainland China and Tibet, Xinjiang, Inner Mongolia, and Taiwan."[38]

---

[34] World Food Programme, "COVID-19 Will Double Number of People Facing Food Crises Unless Swift Action Is Taken," April 21, 2020.

[35] Steven Stashwick, "China's South China Sea Militarization Has Peaked," *Foreign Policy*, August 19, 2019.

[36] Jinghan Zeng, Yuefan Xiao, and Shaun Breslin, "Securing China's Core Interests: The State of the Debate in China," *International Affairs*, Vol. 91, No. 2 (2015): 250 and 253.

[37] Ibid., 257.

[38] Jinghao Zhou, "China's Core Interests and Dilemma in Foreign Policy Practice," *Pacific Focus,* Vol. 34, No. 1 (2019): 34.

This illustrates the importance and sensitivity of the Taiwan issue for the CCP and can be witnessed throughout Sino-Taiwanese relations. During the 1949 war, the CCP sought to capture Kinmen, only to be defeated. Subsequent unsuccessful attempts were made in 1950, 1954–55 (first Taiwan Strait crisis), and 1958 (second Taiwan Strait crisis).[39] As a result of these failed attempts, a military and political stalemate emerged, in which both sides fought a low-intensity conflict that lasted until 1979 when China and the US established official diplomatic relations. In the wake of this, the conflict transformed into one of a political nature. A notable exception here would be the third Taiwan Strait crisis, during which China conducted a series of missile tests aimed (unsuccessfully) at influencing voter behaviour in the 1996 Taiwanese presidential elections. Nevertheless, we can conclude that despite diplomatic flares and strong language, much of the Taiwan conflict was primarily political in nature, somewhat stable, and neither side sought or pursued major escalatory action. Given the importance of Taiwan and national unity for the CCP as its core missions, and with reunification as a strongly stated objective, it was merely a matter of time before China would depart from the military stalemate and political ease.

An example of just how vital Taiwan's issue and its reunification are for China is the Anti-Succession law of 2005. In this law, the CCP outlines its policies towards Taiwan, including the controversial clause that it holds the right to reunite the island by "non-peaceful means" if it seeks official independence. However, it was not until a decade later, at the start of Xi Jinping's chairmanship (2012) and presidency (2013), that China sought to increase pressure on Taiwan. Initial diplomatic relations between the nations were positive at the start of Xi Jinping's chairmanship. During the first two years, under the Kuomintang (KMT) government led by Ma Ying-jeou, cross-Strait diplomatic and economic relations warmed, and cooperation was indeed sought by both sides. However, with the election victory of Tsai Ing-wen, and the Democratic Progressive Party (DPP), in 2016, relations between the nations soured. As opposed to the KMT's pro-China stance, Tsai and the DPP are pro-Taiwan parties that strongly oppose unification with China, and seek to move the nation away from Chinese influence and dominance initiatives such as the New Southbound Policy (NSP). At the onset of the Tsai presidency, China initiated its pressure campaign and started an ongoing campaign of what Cropsey refers to as "a series of small encroachments."[40] Whereas these encroachments were primarily

[39] See, Morton H. Halperin, "The 1958 Taiwan Straits Crisis: A Documented History," December 1966.

[40] Seth Cropsey, "China's Salami-Slicing Policy toward Taiwan," Hudson Institute, May 14, 2018.

military in the SCS, China sought to encroach on a multitude of fronts in the case of Taiwan. We draw attention to the existence of a series of pressure operations within a pressure campaign: not only was each encroachment within a domain a minor escalation, but encroachments throughout the domains also illustrate an escalatory pattern.

The start of China's salami-slicing campaign was modest, at least compared to its later actions in the SCS. In the wake of Tsai's election, and her unwillingness to take the 1992 consensus as a starting point, China cut back on tourist groups visiting Taiwan.[41] Under the previous Ma government, China had allowed an increasing number of Chinese tourists to visit the island, making them a primary source of revenue for Taiwan's tourist sector. Cutting a significant revenue source was China's first attempt to pressure the island into changing its policies. In 2019, the Chinese government added further economic pressure by banning individual tourism to the island, thus cutting another important revenue source for Taiwan.[42] The tourist ban illustrates how China is slowly increasing pressure on the economic front. Further economic pressure points included the Chinese government's order to global aircraft carriers to list Taiwan, as Taiwan, China, if these carriers sought to keep flying to China. And more recently, China has engaged in banning and punishing companies that conduct sensitive business with Taiwan, such as Lockheed Martin.[43]

Simultaneously to this economic pressure campaign, China engaged in a cyber campaign. In the wake of Tsai's election victory, her Facebook page was spammed with pro-China commentaries.[44] While not a state-sanctioned action, given the full control China exerts over its cyberspace, the spam campaign was at least tacitly approved by its government. In the wake of this, as Lin notes, China engaged in increasingly assertive and significant forms of digital political warfare, seeking to influence Taiwan's public opinion and its 2018 local elections.[45] While digital, it was a visible and high-impact

---

41 Nick Aspinwall, "Taiwan Slams China's Decision to Freeze Individual Travel to Taiwan," August 3, 2019;

David Santoro, "Beijing's South China Sea Aggression Is a Warning to Taiwan," September 16, 2019.

42 Nick Aspinwall, "Taiwan Slams China's Decision to Freeze Individual Travel to Taiwan," August 3, 2019.

43 Katie Hunt, "China's ramping up pressure on Taiwan," May 29, 2018; Sui-Lee Wee, "Giving In to China, US Airlines Drop Taiwan (in Name at Least)," July 25, 2018; Anna Fifield, "China Sanctions Lockheed Martin Over Taiwan Arms Sales, but Impact is Minimal," July 15, 2020.

44 *BBC*, "Pro-China Posts Spam Taiwan President-Elect Tsai's Facebook," January 21, 2016.

45 Ying Yu Lin, "China's Hybrid Warfare and Taiwan," *The Diplomat*, January 13, 2018.

illustration of how China sought to increase pressure over the island. A well-known example of this would be the *Want Want China Times* media group, which, quite openly, coordinates its actions with China's Taiwan Affairs Office. In the cyber and cyber information domain, an escalatory pattern can be witnessed. While Lin outlines an initial digital political warfare campaign, this grew in earnest during the last election in Taiwan, which took place in January 2020. Before and during the election campaign, digital Chinese influence operations reached an all-time high, seeking to promote the position of Kaohsiung's mayor Han Kuo-yu. Examples of Chinese influence operations are legion. Kurlantzick, Zhong, and Aspinwall all outline how China engaged in political warfare campaigns, seeking to influence the 2020 elections.[46] What stands out in these analyses is the brazenness with which China has engaged in these practices. What started as hidden outlines in the early stages of this digital information warfare campaign became a sharply visible affair in the end. Once more, we notice that China is increasing the scope and pressure of its tactics in the digital political warfare domain. During the same period, it actively sought pro-China business tycoons to increase (financial) control over Taiwan's media landscape by buying-up newspapers, television stations, and other news information services.[47] Notable in this is how China initially began an economic pressure campaign, now entitled a (domestic) political element, illustrating to the Taiwanese government that the CCP was increasingly able to control or hurt parts of Taiwan's essential infrastructure.

On the diplomatic front too, China sought to increase pressure on Taiwan. China started chipping away at Taiwan's already limited diplomatic allies from the start of the Tsai presidency. Under the Ma presidency, a so-called diplomatic truce was respected by both sides, meaning that neither side would actively try to lure nations' diplomatic allies away from one another. With the start of the Tsai presidency, that truce ended when The Gambia officially aligned itself with China. Once more, we can see an escalatory pattern unfolding. In the first year of her presidency, the number of nations switching remained limited.[48] In the ensuing two years, China was able to

---

[46] Joshua Kurlantzick, "How China Is Interfering in Taiwan's Election," Council on Foreign Relations, November 7, 2019; Ryamong Zhong, "Awash in Disinformation Before Vote, Taiwan Points Finger at China," *The New York Times*, January 6, 2020; Nick Aspinwall, "Taiwan's War on Fake News Is Hitting the Wrong Targets," *Foreign Policy*, January 10, 2020.

[47] Joshua Kurlantzick, "How China Is Interfering in Taiwan's Election," Council on Foreign Relations, November 7, 2019.

[48] Thomas J. Shattuck, "The Race to Zero?: China's Poaching of Taiwan's Diplomatic Allies. *Orbis,* Vol. 64, No. 2 (2020): 334–52.

convince six nations to switch sides – a quarter of Taiwan's existing allies. The CCP's *The People's Daily* went even further and proclaimed in the run-up to the 2020 Taiwanese elections that Taiwan was on the way to zero allies if it re-elected Tsai.[49] While Taiwan still has allies, partly the result of US law that imposes sanctions on nations switching sides, it illustrates clearly how increased Chinese diplomatic pressure is working out by sending an unmistakable signal to Taiwan.

Finally, in the military domain, China ramped up the pressure as well. However, whereas in the non-military domains, China quickly sought to apply pressure tactics, and increase the quantity and quality of these, it was notably slower to apply pressure in the military domain. Nevertheless, within the spectrum of possible pressure points, clearly, the military, and actions within this domain, are most escalatory. As such, and fitting in the broader cross-spectrum salami-slicing, it seems logical that increased military pressure would be at the end of the exponential pressure campaign. During much of Tsai's first year in office, military tensions were low. During the first two years of her presidency, when the non-military salami-slicing tactics were accelerating, aircraft of the People's Liberation Army Air Force (PLAAF) skirted Taiwan air zones ten times. At the turn of the year 2016, its aircraft carrier also sailed around the island.[50] However, in the final two years of her first presidency, China significantly increased its military pressure. Fly-bys increased in frequency and Chinese naval operations more assertive.[51] In April 2018 alone, four aerial operations took place.[52] Akin to patterns noticed in the SCS, not only the number of operations increased, so did the quality. As described earlier in China's efforts to militarize the SCS, it slowly increased the scope and depth of its military resources in the region. In its operations vis-à-vis Taiwan, it is doing likewise: the makeup of its naval forces conducting live-fire exercises around Taiwan has increased, as has the formation of its aerial patrols. Both now regularly feature large offensive platforms, such as destroyers with missile capacities, and bombers, such as the H-6, with long-range strike capabilities. Since the second election victory of Tsai, fly-bys have become intrusions into Taiwanese airspace, signalling further escalation within the military domain.

Such increased escalation patterns are now playing out in the naval domain too: on March 16, 2020, ships of Taiwan's Coast Guard Administration's

---

49 Ibid.

50 Ralph Jennings, "China's Military Flybys Raise Alarm in Taiwan," *VOA News*, December 25, 2017.

51 Liu Zhen, "Military Pressure on Taipei 'Will Continue' after Xi's Call for Unification," *South China Morning Post*, January 4, 2019.

52 Ibid.

(CGA) 9th Offshore Flotilla were targeted by more than 10 Chinese speedboats near the Kinmen Islands, not far from the coast of the Chinese mainland.[53] The site, which regularly attracts illegal fishers from China, was the setting of coordinated provocation and physical ramming of Taiwan's maritime vessels. Those aboard the Chinese boats also reportedly threw objects at CGA ships, which responded to the aggressive behaviour with non-lethal means. The Chinese ships eventually retreated. The use of actual force, even though non-lethal, follows a similar pattern to that of Sino operations in the SCS. Beijing has frequently employed "little blue men" as part of its state-sanctioned "maritime militia" operations against others in the vast SCS region. Beijing's partiality for this particular type of hybrid warfare, using in part what we refer to as Beijing's "little grey (un)men" allows it to harass the armed forces of its weaker neighbour without directly committing its military forces in an aggressive form.[54] Akin to the other domains, once more, we notice a growing, exponential pressure campaign. What started in one military domain now entails all military domains, with the exception of outer space. Furthermore, the scope and depth of these pressure operations have increased throughout the year. Now Chinese military aerial incursions and aggressive naval operations around the entire island, and even within the territory, are fast becoming the new normal. We are witnessing established expectation patterns akin to Chinese policy practices in the SCS.

As the sum of these examples attempts to illustrate, China has been applying salami-slicing tactics throughout the entire spectrum of possible pressure points. These included tactics in the diplomatic, economic, legal, and military domains. This process has started with the election of Tsai in 2016 but has seen exponential increase in the last few years, with a peak following the 2020 Taiwanese elections. China's Taiwan policy bears a strong resemblance to its policies of the SCS, with the Taiwan conflict now becoming an echo chamber of the SCS, and conversely. Yet, and in what is a fundamental difference, the timeframe in which China is increasing the pressure is significantly shorter than in the SCS. In a span of just four years, it has conducted a non-military salami-slicing campaign, that was increased by a military-focused, salami-slicing sub-campaign that increased the depth of its operations rapidly over the course of 2019. Given this echo chamber, it raises the question: what will be the future of Sino-Taiwan relations in the

[53] Keoni Everington, "10 Chinese Speedboats Attack Taiwan Coast Guard Cutters," *Taiwan Times*, March 20, 2020.

[54] Tobias Burgers and Scott N. Romaniuk, "Hybrid Warfare in the South China Sea: The United States' 'Little Grey (Un)Men,'" *The Diplomat*, December 31, 2016.

coming years? Tsai has only recently begun her new term and – with the political dominance of the DPP in Taiwan, as well the increased aversion against China within Taiwan's population and the growing assertiveness of being Taiwanese – the unlikelihood of a pro-China government arising in Taiwan in the near future is difficult to ignore. Given this, and studying prior and current patterns in the SCS, the expectation is that the Taiwan Strait conflict will see an increase in escalation within the civil and the military domains. Furthermore, given the prominence of "unity" for the CCP, and Xi Jinping's focus on this, it is highly unlikely that China would de-escalate and retreat from its current position.

Salami-slicing at high altitudes: the Indian-Sino border clash(es)

Following the 2017 standoff between India and China at Doklam, Narendra Modi and Xi Jinping met to restore peaceful toleration of one another's presence at the shared border. While the 2018 Wuhan summit provided an illusion of a modest peaceful co-existence, it only lasted for a short period. The tranquillity at the Sino-Indian border was eventually shattered by scuffles and skirmishes that began in May 2020. Transgressions have co-occurred at Pangong Tso, Galwan Nalah and Demchok in Ladakh and at Naku La in Sikkim (India).[55] Thousands of troops from both sides have descended to assume defensive positions in the Himalaya's Ladakh region. The deadly clashes at the borders have been the first of their kind in more than four decades. Attempts to de-escalate the standoff failed when clashes broke out on June 15, 2020, resulting in more than 20 deaths on the Indian side. The non-demarcated border (also, Line of Actual Control, LAC) facilitated competing interpretations of where the actual border lies and where it should be. Aksai Chin – an area claimed by India but occupied by China since 1962 – is part of the complex dispute in and around Ladakh. Kashmir's divisions are equally complex, with territory ceded to China by Pakistan in 1963, though India never formally recognized the cession of territory.[56]

The ambiguity of territory demarcation and non-recognized ownership and occupation of territory has served as main drivers of the ongoing border tension and disputes. From the Indian side, China has engaged in both provocative and premeditated action, dissatisfied with India's efforts to govern its territory in the area, and to undertake development projects in the

---

55 Prakash Katoch, "Ladakh Standoff – Keep the Powder Dry," *Indian Defence Review*, June 2, 2020.

56 Akhilesh Pillalamarri, "What India Gets Wrong About China," *The Diplomat*, June 7, 2014.

form of infrastructure that challenged the status quo that China previously tolerated. Chinese military forces breached the LAC in the Galwan Valley, where Indian troops moved in and were eventually again confronted by a larger group of Chinese soldiers. This appears to be the initial attempt by the Chinese military to test the resolve of the Indian forces stationed there. China reported casualties in the amount of 30 or more soldiers without having provided any evidence to support the claim.[57] Zhao Lijian, China's spokesperson with the Chinese foreign ministry placed the blame solely on India, citing "deliberate provocation."[58]

While Modi has faced bouts of pressure from military hawks in India to push back against Chinese aggression, in all calculations, India has played its cards well, avoiding provocation and resisting temptations to push against the Chinese forces stationed along the disputed border. China's perception of the dispute, however, differs considerably from this narrative, claiming that India has incited Chinese forces to act against Indian aggression along China's south-western border. As China's Ministry of Foreign Affairs (FMPRC, 2020) publicly stated on June 24: "First, it is the Indian border troops who crossed the line first. ... Second, it is the Indian side that violated bilateral consensus and started provocations first. ... Third, it is the India side that violated international rules and attacked the Chinese side first." As a new pressure point, China's attempts at salami-slicing along this border assume both military and diplomatic form, with tactics unfolding in the economic as well.

Chinese political-military behaviour with India has also been interpreted by analysts within India and elsewhere in the Western world as efforts to counterbalance the economic impacts of COVID-19 in China, to punish India for having cosied up to the US and its Western allies, and to send signals to India regarding China's military capabilities and presence. China's enigmatic Xi, however, has not been under pressure to compose the events along the border, in our estimation, in an effort to redirect attention away from China's domestic affairs and the CCP as Xi has achieved a remarkable accomplishment in concentrating power to himself alone in less than a decade, rendering himself a leader of absolute and unprecedented power in China, last seen in 1949. Kuldip Singh writes:

---

57 At the time of writing this chapter the number of casualties remained unclear, with media sources citing between 30 and 40, although no evidence was provided as of mid-July, 2020 to substantiate China's claim.

58 中华人民共和国外交部 [Ministry of Foreign Affairs of the People's Republic of China], "2020年6月24日外交部发言人赵立坚主持例行记者会" ["Foreign Ministry Spokesperson Zhao Lijian's Regular Press Conference on June 24, 2020"], June 24, 2020.

> To begin with, there's a need to dispel this popular "urban legend" that President Xi Jinping orchestrated this intrusion in order to distract domestic attention away from his problems at home. The reality is different – Xi Jinping is neither an elected leader of a democracy nor coming up for re-election, nor is he facing any threat internally. Since assuming power in 2012, President Xi has consolidated his control both as president and head of the Chinese Communist Party (CPC), and placed his confidantes in both political and military positions.[59]

These factors alone point to Chinese efforts to salami-slice in an area situated far from the SCS, where China's behaviour would benefit from less attention, and likewise in its conduct with Taiwan. Thus, deeper concentration in geographical locales and on political issues other than the SCS are of considerable value to Beijing's practices in the SCS. Increased tension between the two most populated and nuclear states has gained international attention and the focus of the United Nations (UN), which strongly urged both states to exercise restraint.

China's recent actions against India along the LAC failed to produce any significant gains for the time being but have been tactically beneficial, leaving India with looming challenges. In this regard, China's minimal moves have facilitated favourable conditions for further steps to secure its position and territory at key points along the LAC. China has since occupied new territory that remains disputed, with increased military deployments, suggesting China will be consolidating its recent, if minor, territorial acquisitions. This also raises the question of subsequent salami-slicing tactics and operations along its border with India. To supplement China's modest gains in terms of territory, including its tactical and operational positions, China has sliced at the political relationships in the region. India's arch-rival Pakistan, has received a great deal of Chinese assistance, resulting in Chinese-supported development in disputed Kashmir region.[60] Nepal, which has maintained positive relations with India so far, released on May 20, 2020, its new political and administrative map that includes territory currently part of India.[61] Thus,

[59] Kuldip Singh, "Why Disengagement and De-Escalation Have Been Stalled at Ladakh," *The Quint*, July 26, 2020.

[60] Parjanya Bhatt, "Revisiting China's Kashmir Policy," Observer Research Foundation, November 26, 2019; For comprehensive coverage of China's policies towards the Kashmir dispute see, John W. Garver, "China's Kashmir Policies," *India Review*, Vol. 3, No. 2 (January 2004): 1–24.

[61] *The Kathmandu Post*, "With Release of New Map, Nepal and India Enter a State of 'Cartographic War,' Experts Say," May 21, 2020.

China has achieved a degree of success in isolating India from two of its key neighbours with respect to the LAC and the adjacent territory.

As discussed in the preceding sections, China's initial efforts at salami-slicing can be seen as slow and incremental but gaining momentum over time. Slicing in one domain has typically been supplemented by slicing in others, yielding significant territorial, diplomatic, economic, legal, and military gains over time. What has begun as small-scale slicing at high altitudes along the Sino-Indian border may become a more multi-faceted and complex campaign of salami-slicing, similar to those observed with Taiwan and in the SCS.

Conclusion

China's approach of increasing the pressure through salami-slicing has worked to its benefit, enabling China to realize significant gains and extend its influence in the SCS, apply greater pressure on Taiwan, and make moderate tactical rewards along its shared border with India. In the span of eight years and through the use of salami-slicing, China has managed to establish what we deem to be near-military dominance in the SCS region, even though its political claims to much of the SCS remain disputed. Given the success of its approach, it is logical that it seeks to apply the same approach elsewhere. The two case studies on Taiwan and the India-Sino border conflict illustrate that China has sought to copy its tactics and strategies beyond the SCS conflict. In both conflicts, a noticeable increase in pressure can be observed. However, whereas in the SCS China adopted and remained committed to a gradual approach, and narrow approach focused on military issues, it has broadened its scope of pressure operations in these two conflicts and shortened the timeframe in which it has sought to increase the pressure. In both conflicts, rather than focusing on the military domain, we find that China under the current leadership of Xi Jinping has extended beyond the military spectrum. It now includes pressure operations in the diplomatic, economic, legal, and military domains. It also seems plausible that China has used the COVID-19 pandemic as a cover for continued salami-slicing in all three conflicts. Employing the SCS case as an echo chamber of Chinese foreign and security policy, we can further understand what China's approach will be in the other two conflicts. We conclude that China is seeking to increase its exponential pressure curve by significant margining. Given the exponential curve model, it seems evident that we might expect that both the Taiwan Strait issue as well as the Sino-Indian border conflict will see a considerable increase in pressure, and consequently political and military tension.

References

American Geosciences Institute. "How Much Oil Is Consumed in the United States?" 2020. https://www.americangeosciences.org/critical-issues/faq/how-much-oil-consumed-united-states#:~:text=In%202017%2C%20the%20United%20States,19.96%20million%20barrels%20per%20day.&text=EIA%20uses%20product%20supplied%20as%20a%20proxy%20for%20U.S.%20petroleum%20consumption

Aspinwall, Nick. "Taiwan Slams China's Decision to Freeze Individual Travel to Taiwan." *The Diplomat*, August 3, 2019. https://thediplomat.com/2019/08/taiwan-slams-chinas-decision-to-freeze-individual-travel-to-taiwan/

Aspinwall, Nick. "Taiwan's War on Fake News Is Hitting the Wrong Targets." *Foreign Policy* January 10, 2020. https://foreignpolicy.com/2020/01/10/taiwan-election-tsai-disinformation-china-war-fake-news-hitting-wrong-targets/

BBC (British Broadcasting Corporation). "Pro-China Posts Spam Taiwan President-Elect Tsai's Facebook." January 21, 2016. https://www.bbc.com/news/world-asia-china-35368930

Bhatt, Parjanya. "Revisiting China's Kashmir Policy." Observer Research Foundation, November 26, 2019. https://www.orfonline.org/research/revisiting-chinas-kashmir-policy-58128/

Burgers, Tobias and Romaniuk, Scott N. "Hybrid Warfare in the South China Sea: The United States' 'Little Grey (Un)Men.'" *The Diplomat*, December 31, 2016. https://thediplomat.com/2016/12/hybrid-warfare-in-the-south-china-sea-the-united-states-little-grey-unmen/

Centers for Disease Control and Prevention. "SARS-CoV-2 Infections and Serologic Responses from a Sample of US Navy Service Members – USS Theodore Roosevelt, April 2020." June 12, 2020. cdc.gov/mmwr/volumes/69/wr/mm6923e4.htm

Chang, Teh-Kuang. "China's Claim of Sovereignty over Spratly and Paracel Islands: A Historical and Legal Perspective." *Case Western Reserve Journal of International Law*, Vol. 23, No. 3 (1991), 399–420.

Congressional Research Service. "US-China Strategic Competition in South and East China Seas: Background and Issues for Congress (Rep.)." June 23, 2020. https://fas.org/sgp/crs/row/R42784.pdf

Council on Foreign Relations. "Tensions in the East China Sea | Global Conflict Tracker." 2020. https://www.cfr.org/global-conflict-tracker/conflict/tensions-east-china-sea

Cronin, Patrick M. and Neuhard, Ryan. "Total Competition China's Challenge in the South China Sea (Rep.)." Center for New American Security, January 8, 2020. https://www.cnas.org/publications/reports/total-competition

Cropsey, Seth. "China's Salami-Slicing Policy toward Taiwan." Hudson Institute, May 14, 2018. https://www.hudson.org/research/14327-china-s-salami-slicing-policy-toward-taiwan

Daiss, Tim. "Why the South China Sea Has More Oil Than You Think." May 22, 2016. https://www.forbes.com/sites/timdaiss/2016/05/22/why-the-south-china-sea-has-more-oil-than-you-think/#5d39e5ecdd8f

Defense Intelligence Agency. "China Military Power: Modernizing a Force to Fight and Win." 2019. https://www.dia.mil/Portals/27/Documents/News/Military%20Power%20Publications/China_Military_Power_FINAL_5MB_20190103.pdf

Deutsche Welle. "Is China Taking Advantage of COVID-19 to Pursue South China Sea Ambitions?" May 26, 2020. https://www.dw.com/en/is-china-taking-advantage-of-covid-19-to-pursue-south-china-sea-ambitions/a-53573918

Er, Lam Peng. "Japan and the Spratlys Dispute: Aspirations and Limitations." *Asian Survey*, Vol. 36, No. 10 (1996), 995–1010.

Everington, Keoni. "10 Chinese Speedboats Attack Taiwan Coast Guard Cutters." *Taiwan News*, March 20, 2020. https://www.taiwannews.com.tw/en/news/3901015

Fifield, Anna. "China Sanctions Lockheed Martin over Taiwan Arms Sales, but Impact Is Minimal." *The Washington Post*, July 15, 2020. https://www.washingtonpost.com/world/asia_pacific/china-sanctions-lockheed-martin-over-taiwan-arms-sales-but-impact-is-minimal/2020/07/14/3658b412-c5b7-11ea-a825-8722004e4150_story.html

Fravel, M. Taylor. *Active Defense: China's Military Strategy since 1949*. Princeton, NJ: Princeton University Press, 2019.

Furtado, Xavier. "International Law and the Dispute over the Spratly Islands: Whither UNCLOS?" *Contemporary Southeast Asia*, Vol. 21, No. 3 (1999), 386–404.

Garver, John W. "China's Kashmir Policies." *India Review*, Vol. 3, No. 2 (January 2004), 1–24.

Grossman, Derek. "China Just Botched a Monumental Opportunity with the Philippines." *The Diplomat*, June 18, 2020. https://thediplomat.com/2020/06/china-just-botched-a-monumental-opportunity-with-the-philippines/

Haddick, Robert. "Salami Slicing in the South China Sea." *Foreign Policy*, August 3, 2020. https://foreignpolicy.com/2012/08/03/salami-slicing-in-the-south-china-sea/

Holmes, James R. and Yoshihara, Toshi. "The Influence of Mahan upon China's Maritime Strategy." *Comparative Strategy*, Vol. 24, No. 1 (2005), 23–51.

Holmes, James R. and Yoshihara, Toshi. *Chinese Naval Strategy in the 21st Century: The Turn to Mahan*. Abingdon: Routledge, 2008.

Hunt, Katie. "China's Ramping Up Pressure on Taiwan." *CNN*, May 29, 2018. https://edition.cnn.com/2018/05/28/asia/taiwan-china-explainer-intl/index.html

Institute of Peace and Conflict Studies. "South China Sea: Emerging Security Architecture." August 1, 2012. http://www.ipcs.org/issue_select.php?recNo=479

Jennings, Ralph. "China's Military Flybys Raise Alarm in Taiwan." *VOA News*, December 25, 2017. https://www.voanews.com/east-asia-pacific/chinas-military-flybys-raise-alarm-taiwan

Katoch, Prakash. "Ladakh Standoff – Keep the Powder Dry." *Indian Defence Review*, June 2, 2020. www.indiandefencereview.com/news/ladakh-standoff-keep-the-powder-dry/

Kurlantzick, Joshua. "How China Is Interfering in Taiwan's Election." *Council on Foreign Relations*, November 7, 2019. https://www.cfr.org/in-brief/how-china-interfering-taiwans-election

Lin, Ying Yu. "China's Hybrid Warfare and Taiwan." *The Diplomat*, January 13, 2018. https://thediplomat.com/2018/01/chinas-hybrid-warfare-and-taiwan/

Manning, Robert. A. and Cronin, Patrick M. "Under Cover of Pandemic, China Steps Up Brinkmanship in South China Sea." *Foreign Policy*, May 14, 2020. https://foreignpolicy.com/2020/05/14/south-china-sea-dispute-accelerated-by-coronavirus/

Pant, Harsh. "China's Salami Slicing Overdrive: It's Flexing Military Muscles at a Time When Covid Preoccupies the Rest of the World." *The Times of India*, May 13, 2020. https://timesofindia.indiatimes.com/blogs/toi-edit-page/chinas-salami-slicing-overdrive-its-flexing-military-muscles-at-a-time-when-covid-preoccupies-the-rest-of-the-world/

People's Republic of China. *Declaration of the Government of the People's Republic of China on China's Territorial Sea* (Annex 2/5), 1958.

Pillalamarri, Akhilesh. "What India Gets Wrong about China." *The Diplomat*, June 7, 2014. https://thediplomat.com/2014/06/what-india-gets-wrong-about-china/

Santoro, David. "Beijing's South China Sea Aggression Is a Warning to Taiwan." *Foreign Policy*, September 16, 2019. https://foreignpolicy.com/2019/09/16/beijings-south-china-sea-aggression-is-a-warning-to-taiwan/

Shattuck, Thomas. J. "The Race to Zero? China's Poaching of Taiwan's Diplomatic Allies." *Orbis*, Vol. 64, No. 2 (2020), 334–52. doi:10.1016/j.orbis.2020.02.003

Singh, Kuldip. "Why Disengagement and De-Escalation Have Been Stalled at Ladakh." *The Quint*, July 26, 2020. thequint.com/voices/opinion/india-china-standoff-why-disengagement-and-de-escalation-stalled-at-ladakh

South China Morning Post. "Beijing Could Face ASEAN's Wrath over 'Naming and Claiming' of South China Sea Features, Observers Say." April 25, 2020. https://today.line.me/id/pc/article/Beijing+could+face+Asean+s+wrath+over+naming+and+claiming+of+South+China+Sea+features+observers+say-E9e2Pk

Stashwick, Steven. "China's South China Sea Militarization Has Peaked." *Foreign Policy*, August 19, 2019. https://foreignpolicy.com/2019/08/19/chinas-south-china-sea-militarization-has-peaked/

Tan, Andrew T. H. "The Five Power Defence Arrangements: The Continuing Relevance." *Contemporary Security Policy*, Vol. 29, No. 2 (2008), 285–302.

The Kathmandu Post. "With Release of New Map, Nepal and India Enter a State of 'Cartographic War,' Experts Say." May 21, 2020. https://kathmandupost.com/national/2020/05/21/with-release-of-new-map-nepal-and-india-enter-a-state-of-cartographic-war-experts-say

The Korea Times. "Beijing's South China Sea Fishing Ban Threatens to Raise Tensions." May 9, 2020. https://m.koreatimes.co.kr/pages/article.asp?newsIdx=289251

Trevithick, Joseph. "The Air Force Abruptly Ends Its Continuous Bomber Presence On Guam After 16 Years." *The Drive*, April 17, 2020. www.thedrive.com/the-war-zone/33057/the-continuous-strategic-bomber-presence-mission-to-guam-has-abruptly-ended-after-16-years

Tzu, Sun. *The Art of War.* (Trans. Lionel Giles). http://classics.mit.edu/Tzu/artwar.html

US Energy Information Administration. "The Suez Canal and SUMED Pipeline are Critical Chokepoints for Oil and Natural Gas Trade." July 23, 2019. https://www.eia.gov/todayinenergy/detail.php?id=40152

Wee, Sui-Lee. "Giving in to China, US Airlines Drop Taiwan (in Name at Least)." *The New York Times*, July 25, 2018. https://www.nytimes.com/2018/07/25/business/taiwan-american-airlines-china.html

World Food Programme. "COVID-19 Will Double Number of People Facing Food Crises Unless Swift Action Is Taken." April 21, 2020. www.wfp.org/news/covid-19-will-double-number-people-facing-food-crises-unless-swift-action-taken

Yoshihara, Toshi. and Holmes, James R. *Red Star over the Pacific: China's Rise and the Challenge to US Maritime Strategy*. Annapolis, MD: Naval Institute Press, 2013.

Zeng, Jinghan, Xiao, Yuefan, and Breslin, Shaun. "Securing China's Core Interests: The State of the Debate in China." *International Affairs*, Vol. 91, No. 2 (2015), 245–66. doi:10.1111/1468-2346.12233

Zhao, Suisheng. "Foreign Policy Implications of Chinese Nationalism Revisited: The Strident Turn." *Journal of Contemporary China*, Vol. 22, No. 82 (2013), 535–53.

Zhen, Liu. "Military Pressure on Taipei 'Will Continue' after Xi's Call for Unification." *South China Morning Post*, January 4, 2019. https://www.scmp.com/news/china/military/article/2180653/beijing-will-keep-military-pressure-taiwan-after-xi-jinpings

Zhong, Raymond. "Awash in Disinformation before Vote, Taiwan Points Finger at China." *The New York Times*, January 6, 2020. https://www.nytimes.com/2020/01/06/technology/taiwan-election-china-disinformation.html

Zhou, Jinghao. "China's Core Interests and Dilemma in Foreign Policy Practice." *Pacific Focus*, Vol. 34, No. 1 (2019), 31–54. doi:10.1111/pafo.12131

中华人民共和国农业农村部 [Ministry of Agriculture and Rural Affairs of the People's Republic of China]. "农业部关于调整海洋伏季休渔制度的通告农业部通告〔2018〕1号" ["Announcement of the Ministry of Agriculture and Rural Affairs on the Adjustment of the Summer Fishing Moratorium System, Ministry of Agriculture Notice (2018) No. 1"], March 20, 2018. http://www.moa.gov.cn/nybgb/2018/201803/201805/t20180528_6143235.htm

中华人民共和国国务院 [State Council, PRC]. "中国的亚太安全合作政策" ["China's Policies on Asia-Pacific Security Cooperation"], January 11, 2017. http://www.gov.cn/zhengce/2017-01/11/content_5158864.htm

中华人民共和国国务院 [State Council, PRC]. "新时代的中国国防" ["China's National Defence in the New Era"], July 24, 2019. http://www.gov.cn/zhengce/2019-07/24/content_5414325.htm

中华人民共和国国防部 [Ministry of National Defence, PRC]. "中国的军事战略" ["China's Military Strategy"], May 26, 2015. http://www.scio.gov.cn/zfbps/ndhf/2015/Document/1435159/1435159.htm

中华人民共和国外交部 [Ministry of Foreign Affairs of the People's Republic of China]. "2020年6月24日外交部发言人赵立坚主持例行记者会" ["Foreign Ministry Spokesperson Zhao Lijian's Regular Press Conference on June 24, 2020"], June 24, 2020. https://www.fmprc.gov.cn/web/fyrbt_673021/t1792042.shtml

PART I

Claimants of the Contested South China Sea

3

China's Security Interests and Strategies in the South China Sea

Li Yang

Introduction

The South China Sea (SCS) is at the strategic crossroads connecting Northeast and Southeast Asia on one hand and the Pacific and the Indian Ocean on the other. China is one of the countries bordering the SCS. China also claims sovereignty over four archipelagos in the SCS, including the Spratlys and Paracels (which China refers to as the Nansha and Xisha Islands respectively). Some of the claims are currently contested to different extents by other coastal states of the SCS.

According to official statistics from China, a total of 42 Spratly features have been successively occupied by other countries.[1] In January 1974, as the result of a military clash at sea, China gained effective control over the entirety of the Paracels by defeating South Vietnamese troops stationed on some of the features. In March 1988, China again took control of six features of the Spratlys after a naval conflict with Vietnam. In 1994, China built facilities on Mischief Reef (Meiji Jiao) of the Spratlys, followed by protests from the Philippines.

With regard to China's maritime rights and jurisdiction in the SCS, China claims that, under the 1982 United Nations Convention on the Law of the

[1] Wang Yi, *A Developing China and Chinese Diplomacy*, Speech at Center for Strategic and International Studies, February 26, 2016, https://www.fmprc.gov.cn/web/wjbz_673089/zyjh_673099/t1343410.shtml

Sea (UNCLOS), it is entitled to a 200 nautical mile exclusive economic zone (EEZ) and continental shelf in this area, where China also claims historical rights. China's maritime claims in the SCS also overlap with those of other coastal states.

China's holistic approach to national security

A study of China's official statements reveals that China's perceptions of its security interests in the SCS are multi-faceted. Since 2014, the Chinese leadership has adopted a holistic approach toward its national security, for which China will establish a national security team to safeguard its political and social system, its territory, military, economy, culture, scientific, and technological development, environment, natural resources, and nuclear programmes.[2]

As a result, as far as China is concerned, the term "security" might not be understood in its narrow sense, but rather be connected with interests in other fields. For example, China's security interests in the SCS may have a close connection with its territorial and maritime claims in this area. Against the backdrop of China's past century of "national humiliation," a term used by many Chinese people to describe the period from 1840s to 1940s, when the country ceded or lost large portions of territories to other states as a result of military defeats against other countries, there is a deep-rooted nationalistic sentiment among the Chinese population about the bond between its territorial sovereignty and its national security. Therefore, issues on territorial sovereignty and maritime rights always possess a domestic sensitivity, the mishandling of which might lead to political and social instability, which triggers the security concerns of the country.

China's perceived security interests in the South China Sea

China made many official statements concerning the SCS in the past, and most of them were territorial in nature.[3] In the face of escalation of the SCS disputes and the growing military presence of the United States (US) in this

[2] National Security, *China Daily*, online report, April 18, 2014, http://www.chinadaily.com.cn/opinion/2014-04/18/content_17443364.htm

[3] For example, the Ministry of Foreign Affairs (MFA) of China published a document in 1980 entitled "China's Sovereignty over Xisha and Nansha Islands is Indisputable." The State Council Information Office of China published a white paper in 2016 entitled "China Adheres to the Position of Settling Through Negotiation the Relevant Disputes Between China and the Philippines in the South China Sea." There is a copious amount of public statements on the SCS issue made by Chinese leaders and by the spokespersons of the MFA of China.

area during the past decade, China has become more articulate in its security interests in the SCS parallel to the appeal on territorial sovereignty. From the assessments of the security situation in China's periphery by its official documents in recent years, one may get a glimpse of how China views its security interests in the SCS.

A 2015 government white paper on China's military strategy outlines the security challenges faced by China, including in the SCS: the US is carrying on its "rebalancing" strategy and continues enhancing its military presence and its military alliances in the Asia-Pacific region. Japan is sparing no effort to dodge the post-war mechanism, overhauling its military and security policies. On the issues concerning China's territorial sovereignty and maritime rights and interests, some of its offshore neighbours take provocative actions and reinforce their military presence on China's reefs and islands that they have illegally occupied. Some external countries are also busy meddling in SCS affairs; a tiny few maintain constant close-in air and sea surveillance and reconnaissance against China.[4]

In 2017, a white paper on China's policies on Asia-Pacific security cooperation makes similar observations and points out that non-traditional maritime security threats are on the rise.[5] In 2019, China's white paper on national defence asserts that China's homeland security still faces threats – in particular, countries from outside the region illegally enter China's territorial waters and the waters and airspace near China's islands and reefs, undermining China's national security.[6] This is in fact China's official narrative on the freedom of navigation operations (FONOPs) conducted by the US in the SCS since 2015.

In Chinese scholars' research on the subject, Wu Shicun interprets China's interests in the SCS as having three types: priority interest, extended interests, and interests by nature. The priority interest refers to China's sovereignty, sovereign rights, and historical rights over the four archipelagos and their adjacent waters. The extended interests are mainly resource and energy related. The interests by nature mean that the SCS gives China, a geographically disadvantaged state whose maritime space is blocked by chains of outlying islands, a potential space to expand its sea power, plus a protection zone shielding China from any security threats from the southwest

[4] The State Council Information Office, PRC, *China's Military Strategy*, May 26, 2015, http://www.scio.gov.cn/zfbps/ndhf/2015/Document/1435159/1435159.htm

[5] The State Council Information Office, PRC, *China's Policies on Asia-Pacific Security Cooperation*, January 11, 2017, http://www.scio.gov.cn/zfbps/ndhf/36088/Document/1539910/1539910.htm

[6] The State Council Information Office, PRC, *China's National Defense in the New Era*, July 24, 2019, http://www.scio.gov.cn/zfbps/ndhf/39911/Document/1660528/1660528.htm

direction as well as a major sea route for its foreign trade and energy imports. And China certainly cares about the security of this strategic space and the safety of the sea lanes.[7]

Another Chinese scholar, Nie Wenjuan, classifies China's perception on its national interests in the SCS into territorial appeal, energy and resource demand, and national security concern. She says that 80 per cent of China's crude oil imports are transported through the SCS region and the importance of the security of sea lines of communication (SLOCs) to China will keep rising. She also quotes other specialists by saying that the SCS consists of a forward position for China's strategic defence and a protective shield for China's southern mainland, that it is also a significant location where China breaks out of its near sea and goes to the Pacific and transforms itself from a land power to a maritime power.[8]

Peter Dutton of the US points out that China is pursuing three main objectives in the SCS Sea and Southeast Asia: regional integration, resource control, and enhanced security. By enhanced security, he refers to China's objective to enhance its control over the SCS in order to create a maritime security buffer zone that protects the major population centres, industry, and rich cultural sites of China's developed eastern coastal area.[9]

In this chapter, I summarize China's perceptions on its security interests in the SCS under the following headings.

Territorial sovereignty and maritime rights and jurisdiction

Although China is confronted with divergent types of security threats, territorial sovereignty and the maritime rights are still its top priority in the SCS. Part of the reason is China's historical experience as well as the existing territorial and maritime disputes between China and other claimants.

During the past decade China was repeatedly asked to clarify the actual extent of its maritime claims in the SCS. China has not given a clear-cut response. However, reacting to a 2016 award by an ad hoc tribunal set-up under the arbitral proceedings instituted by the Philippines against China on the SCS disputes, China released a declaration presenting the most detailed

[7] Wu Shicun and Chen Xiangmiao, Great Game Between China and the United States in the South China Sea: Interests, Conflicts, Causes and Countermeasures, *Asia Pacific Security & Maritime Affairs*, No.6, 2019, pp 46–7.

[8] Nie Wenjuan, China's Identity and Understanding of National Interest in the South China Sea, *Journal of Contemporary Asia-Pacific Studies*, No. 1, 2017, pp 141–3.

[9] Peter Dutton, *Three Disputes and Three Objectives: China and the South China Sea*, Naval War College Review, Vol. 64, No. 4 (Autumn 2011), US Naval War College Press, pp 42–67.

description of its claims in the SCS so far. According to the document, China has territorial sovereignty and maritime rights and interests in the SCS, including, inter alia:

1. China has sovereignty over Nanhai Zhudao, consisting of Dongsha Qundao (the Pratas), Xisha Qundao (the Paracels), Zhongsha Qundao (the Macclesfield Bank) and Nansha Qundao (the Spratlys);
2. China has internal waters, territorial sea and contiguous zone, based on Nanhai Zhudao;
3. China has exclusive economic zone and continental shelf, based on Nanhai Zhudao;
4. China has historic rights in the South China Sea.[10]

China does not elaborate further on its historical rights in the document, and the famous SCS U-shaped line is not mentioned, either. However, some relevant remarks could be found in a Chinese foreign ministry spokesperson's statement earlier that the Chinese government had published the Nine-Dash Line in the SCS (China's official name for the U-shaped line) back in 1948 and that China's sovereignty and related claims had been established gradually in the long course of history, which had sufficient legal grounds and had been upheld by successive Chinese governments.[11]

The following observation could be made through an analysis of China's official statements and practice: the U-shaped line is in essence a historical claim of China. The line was officially published in 1948, but its origin might far predate that time. The implication is that the delineation of the line was rather a reflection or reaffirmation of China's sovereignty and other maritime rights and interests exercised by China through history. Such a historical claim is deemed not to be necessarily in conflict with but a supplement to China's maritime entitlement under the UNCLOS.

Overall external environment

China attaches importance to an external environment that is favourable to the country's survival and development. The SCS is considered part

[10] *Statement of the Government of the People's Republic of China on China's Territorial Sovereignty and Maritime Rights and Interests in the South China Sea*, website of China's MFA, July 12, 2016, https://www.fmprc.gov.cn/nanhai/eng/snhwtlcwj_1/t1379493.htm

[11] MFA responded to Vietnam's objection to China's Dotted Line Claim in the South China Sea, online report, www.people.cn, December 12, 2014, http://js.people.com.cn/n/2014/1212/c360300-23196285.html

of that overall environment. Since China proclaims that it adheres to a national objective of peaceful development, efforts are required to ensure a generally secure and friendly external environment conducive to such development.

Making sure that the SCS is free from any wars or chaos is part of China's strategic objective in maintaining a peaceful and stable external environment, which implies that China is supposed to keep generally amicable and cooperative relations with its neighbours. Although there are divergent views within Chinese strategic circles about China's policies toward the SCS, it seems that a general consensus exists around such an objective.

The stated peaceful intention of China is doubted by politicians and scholars of other countries. They believe that China is becoming more assertive in recent years in its external relations, including its SCS policies. This issue is examined in the following section of the chapter.

Homeland security

The SCS also possesses an important security value for China's mainland. Its large expanse creates an ideal buffer zone for China to defend its mainland against any foreign invasion or attack from the sea. Leszek Buszynski (see also Chapter 14 in this volume) asserts that the SCS may play the role of a protective sanctuary required by the Chinese navy against pre-emptive attack and harassment by submarines or aircraft.[12] Since China claims sovereignty over the four archipelagos in the SCS, it also takes the defence of these archipelagic territories, particularly those currently under the control of China, as part of its homeland security.

As a result, China is sensitive to the military build-up of other countries, especially those of major world powers, in the SCS region. As the US started to implement its "pivot to Asia" under the Obama administration and to strengthen its military deployment around the Indo-Pacific region under the current Trump administration (with, in particular, high-frequency and high-profile military operations, including the FONOPs conducted in close vicinity of the Spratly features, the Paracels and Scarborough Shoal under China's control), China grows more alert against US intervention in the SCS, which is viewed as a major threat against China's homeland security and the strategic stability in its periphery.

---

[12] Leszek Buszynski, *Chinese Naval Strategy, the United States, ASEAN and the South China Sea*, Security Challenges, Vol. 8, No. 2 (Winter 2012), p 22.

Security and safety of sea routes of communication and trade

China has become the world's second largest economy. Along with its increasing engagement with global business and trade, China is making more public statements about the country and its people's desire to "go out." The protection of the country's extending overseas interests therefore becomes a major mission for China's government and its military, especially the navy.

The Chinese government views the SCS as home to a number of important sea lanes, which are among the main navigation routes for China's foreign trade and energy imports. The region is also described as a bridge of communication and a bond between China and its neighbours,[13] and also considered as part of "the strategic fulcrum" of the 21st Century Maritime Silk Road, one of the two wings of China's Belt and Road Initiative (BRI).

As a result, the security of the SCS assumes a special role in the protection of China's overseas interests. This is especially the case given the ever-mounting non-traditional security threats and concerns for the safety of vessels with their crews passing through these sea routes.

Testing ground for maritime power building

Since 2012, China has fixed a national target of establishing itself as a maritime power. The rationale behind this strategy is that China is not only a country with a large area of landmass, but also a big maritime country. China's mainland coastline is more than 18,000 km long. It also has more than 5,000 islands each with an area of more than 500 square metres.[14] In the meantime China is still in a developing phase in terms of maritime affairs, in comparison with other traditional and developed maritime powers. This situation might be partly due to a tradition of "land outweighing sea," which had been dominating Chinese policy making for a long period of time in history. The building of maritime power is supposed to be an effort to break away from that tradition and turn China into a real maritime power commensurate with its natural conditions.

The SCS is the biggest marginal sea China is adjacent to. Its political, military, and natural environment is all very complicated. It may be assumed that if China is capable of managing this marine space properly, including

[13] *Statement of the Government of the People's Republic of China on China's Territorial Sovereignty and Maritime Rights and Interests in the South China Sea*, website of China's MFA, July 12, 2016, https://www.fmprc.gov.cn/nanhai/eng/snhwtlcwj_1/t1379493.htm

[14] The State Council Information Office, PRC, *The Development of China's Maritime Cause*, May 1998, http://www.scio.gov.cn/zfbps/ndhf/1998/Document/307963/307963.htm

maintaining its security and order, with positive interactions with other coastal states and outside powers, it would provide useful experience for China to fulfil the goals of its overall maritime strategy and to participate more effectively in global ocean governance.

China's South China Sea strategies

The Chinese government acknowledges the existence of territorial disputes over part of the Spratlys and of sea boundary delimitation issues with other SCS coastal states, and is committed to settle the disputes peacefully through direct talks with other claimants directly. This commitment has been observed by China since the 1990s, although there have been a number of incidents or clashes involving law enforcement and civilian vessels at sea between China and other claimants. Prior to that, China did enter into military conflicts with South Vietnam and the unified Vietnam in 1974 and in 1988 over the Paracels and the Spratlys respectively. Those conflicts happened under a bigger picture of the Cold War, when the two sides belonged to rival camps.

The interpretations of China's current strategy toward the SCS are divergent. A report made by the US Congressional Research Service (CRS) points out that observers frequently characterize China's approach to the SCS as a "salami-slicing" strategy that employs a series of incremental actions, none of which by itself is a casus belli, to gradually change the status quo in China's favour. The report also says that other observers have referred to China's strategy as "gray zone operations" (that is, operations that reside in a grey zone between peace and war).[15]

Another argument holds that China is pursuing a new "grand Strategy," which is changing from a soft- to a hard-power approach, by using military aggression as well as military and political coercion in order to change the balance of power in the Asian Pacific.[16]

Leszek Buszynski contends that, despite China's public statements, what China wants to do is not so easily identified. China's intentions are closely linked to the opportunities created by its activities in the area, as undertaken by the Chinese navy, provincial authorities, and maritime surveillance agencies. These activities, which include harassment tactics and low-level confrontation, are the instruments of Chinese policy, and China's objectives

---

[15] Congressional Research Service, *US-China Strategic Competition in South and East China Seas: Background and Issues for Congress*, updated April 24, 2020, p 8.

[16] Thomas Engelbert, *The South China Sea Conflict: Analyses and Perspectives. An Introduction to the Topic*, The South China Sea Conflict after the Arbitration of July 12, 2016, Analyses and Perspectives, Thomas Engelbert (ed), published by Internationaler Verlag der Wissenschaften, Berlin, 2019, p 20.

would expand according to their success, or could be curtailed if significant dangers were revealed.[17]

Eric Hyer was quoted as saying that popular nationalism has contributed to a more assertive PRC attitude, which complicates conflict resolution. However, he thinks that there are no signs that China seeks territorial expansion in the waters surrounding it, especially in the SCS.[18]

Peter Kreuzer suggests that the interpretation that China is a ruthless Goliath tends to link the starting-points for cycles of conflict to assertive acts by China and to ignore similar acts by other claimants which, from the Chinese perspective, have triggered Chinese "defensive assertiveness." It also assumes without proof that Chinese past and present assertiveness is part and parcel of an overarching long-term salami-slicing strategy that also includes periods of reassurance that only serve to calm resistance periodically.[19]

Mingjiang Li, by conducting interviews with over 50 Chinese officials in charge of maritime affairs and analysts close to policy making, observes that the changing Chinese posture towards assertiveness is a reflection of its growing discontent with the actions of other regional states, its desire to benefit economically, and the growth of its capabilities and power, and that there are significant constraints that could limit China's muscle-flexing, with a dilemma on how to maintain a balance between protecting its sovereignty and other maritime interests in the SCS and sustaining a peaceful and stable relationship with Southeast Asian countries. He concludes that, in this larger strategic context, Beijing has pursued, and is likely to continue to pursue, a more or less moderate policy in the SCS.[20]

Feng Zhang questions whether China has a coherent strategy toward the SCS and explores China's domestic debates on this subject. He identifies three schools of thought currently dominating relevant debates within China, namely the pragmatists, the moderates, and the hardliners.[21] He concludes that China's actual policy towards the SCS has reflected the influence of these different approaches at different times.[22]

---

[17] Leszek Buszynski, *The South China Sea Maritime Dispute: Legality, Power, and Conflict Prevention*, Asian Journal of Peacebuilding, Vol. 1, No. 1 (2013), pp 57–8.

[18] Thomas Engelbert, p 28.

[19] Peter Kreuzer, *From Hostile Goliath to Partner in Development: Philippine Perceptions and Strategies for Dealing with China*, The South China Sea Conflict after the Arbitration of July 12, 2016, Analyses and Perspectives, Thomas Engelbert (ed), published by Internationaler Verlag der Wissenschaften, Berlin, 2019, p 79.

[20] Mingjiang Li, *Reconciling Assertiveness and Cooperation? China's Changing Approach to the South China Sea Dispute*, Security Challenges, Vol. 6, No. 2 (Winter 2010), pp 49, 58, 62.

[21] Feng Zhang, *Chinese Thinking on the South China Sea and the Future of Regional Security*, Political Science Quarterly, Vol. 132, No. 3 (2017), pp 435–6.

[22] Ibid., pp 464–5.

Li and Zhang's researches both capture a feature of China's SCS strategy, that is, keeping a proper balance between the two goals of "defending sovereignty and maritime interests" and "maintaining an overall peaceful and stable external environment."

In China's official documents, "striking a balance between rights protection and stability maintenance" and "making overall planning for both" are placed as guiding principles for the Chinese armed forces to uphold.[23]

A commentator associated with the Department of Boundary & Ocean Affairs of the Chinese Ministry of Foreign Affairs (MFA) considers the adoption of a balanced approach toward "safeguarding rights" and "maintaining stability" as one of the successful experiences for China's diplomacy on land border and ocean affairs, and describes how China has been appropriately managing the "dialectical relations" between these two goals in handling land boundary and maritime disputes.[24]

It has been often questioned that whether the SCS falls within China's perceived "core interests." There have been concerns among international observers that China takes the SCS as one of its core interests and would risk a war to defend it.

Alistair Iain Johnston suggested, as a result of his research, that it was likely that the source for the story about China's definition of the SCS as its core interest was wrong, although he noticed that the SCS was perhaps the only example where China's diplomatic rhetoric and practice did shift fairly sharply towards a more hardline direction at that time.[25]

In order to shed more light on this core-interest question, it might be helpful to look at the Chinese official description in a 2011 government white paper, in which China's core interests are defined as "state sovereignty, national security, territorial integrity and national reunification, China's political system established by the Constitution and overall social stability, and the basic safeguards for ensuring sustainable economic and social development."[26]

The reference to state sovereignty, national security, and territorial integrity testifies that the SCS, because of its connection to all three items, does have something to do with China's core interests. However, the conclusion that

---

[23] The State Council Information Office, PRC: *China's Military Strategy,* May 26, 2015, http://www.scio.gov.cn/zfbps/ndhf/2015/Document/1435159/1435159.htm

[24] Hai Min, *China's Foreign Policy on Boundary & Ocean Affairs with Its Characteristics,* Journal of Boundary & Ocean Studies, Vol. 3, No. 6 (2018), p 14.

[25] Alistair Iain Johnston, *How New and Assertive Is China's New Assertiveness?,* International Security, Vol. 37, No. 4 (Spring 2013), p 19.

[26] The State Council Information Office, PRC, *China's Peaceful Development,* September 6, 2011, http://www.scio.gov.cn/zfbps/ndhf/2011/Document/1000031/1000031.htm

the SCS *is* China's core interest seems to be an exaggerated interpretation of China's intentions. The proper reading might be that China *has* certain core interests in the SCS, but it is not in China's long-term strategic interest and also beyond its capacity to turn the entire SCS into a "Chinese lake."

Even if the SCS does contain China's core interests, it does not mean that China will necessarily resort to war to protect them. Studying the pattern of China's behaviour in the SCS since the start of the territorial and maritime disputes therein, China's SCS strategies may contain four elements.

First of all, try to keep the disputes as they are. It is generally acknowledged that the SCS disputes will not be settled in a foreseeable period of time. Under such circumstances, China's demand, as one of the claimants, is to keep the occupied features under dispute in order to ensure that the occupation of them by other countries will not be legitimized, no more features are taken, and the disputes will not be expanded to the undisputed areas. China is also interested in preventing its positions regarding territorial sovereignty and maritime entitlements in the SCS from being jeopardized or weakened before final settlements of the disputes are reached. In other words, any moves of other claimants triggering China's concerns will set off corresponding responses from China.

For example, when Vietnam and Malaysia made their submissions in 2009 of continental shelves beyond 200 nautical miles in the SCS to the Commission on the Limits of Continental Shelf (CLCS) established under the UNCLOS, the action was considered by China as a challenge toward its sovereignty and maritime rights, and the latter adopted the countermeasure of sending a note verbale, attaching a map containing the U-shaped line, to the UN Secretary General for the purpose of fulfilling necessary procedures to prevent the submission from being considered by CLCS. In 2012, a naval vessel from the Philippines tried to detain some Chinese fishing boats in the waters of Scarborough Shoal, which is claimed by China.[27] That incident triggered a standoff between China and the Philippines for almost three months and resulted in regular patrols by Chinese coast guard vessels in this area. In 2019, China sent a scientific research vessel to the disputed waters between China and Vietnam in the southwest of the SCS, allegedly in response to Vietnam's oil drilling activities in the waters around the Vanguard Bank (Wan'an Tan), where the national oil company of China has an oil contract dated back to 1992 whose operation has been suspended because of the dispute.

[27] Spokesperson of Ministry of Foreign Affairs, *China Asked the Philippines to Stop Provocation*, online report, www.people.cn, May 24, 2012, http://world.people.com.cn/GB/8212/191617/9491/237724/17979902.html

The mindset and corresponding behavioural pattern of China seem to suggest that China's strategies toward the SCS disputes are generally reactive in nature. The growing assertiveness might be a result of the increasing provocations from other claimants perceived by China. Chinese decision makers reveal that it is imperative to make strong reactions and forestall further provocations by changing the opponents' calculation on cost and benefits. "Gaining mastery by striking only after the enemy has struck" toward the actions of other claimants, which challenges China's core interests and breaks its bottom line, is referred to by Hai Min as one of the successful experiences of China's maritime diplomacy.[28]

Second, practice a dual-track approach, a diplomatic initiative held on to by both ASEAN countries and China aiming at solving the disputes and managing them in parallel through bilateral means and regional institutions.

China insists that the territorial and maritime disputes in the SCS must be settled through negotiations by the countries directly concerned, that is, the claimant states. China has been engaging itself with setting up bilateral consultation mechanisms with other claimants, in hopes that the ongoing talks could help bridge the differences gradually, explore provisional arrangements such as joint development of the resources, or for the time being may serve at least as a long-standing channel of communication between the parties to help put the situation under control. There are quite a few bilateral mechanisms between China and Vietnam on maritime issues. The bilateral consultations between China and the Philippines were disrupted by the 2013–2016 SCS arbitration and came back on track after the Duterte administration took office in 2016, with a formal bilateral consultation mechanism established subsequently. A similar mechanism between China and Malaysia was declared in 2019.

China also takes part in regional multilateral institutions as a collective effort to *manage* the South China Sea disputes. In 2002, the ten ASEAN member states and China signed the Declaration on the Conduct of Parties in the SCS (DOC), a confidence-building measure to keep peace and stability and to promote cooperation in the region. In 2013, the eleven signatories to DOC started talks on a code of conduct (COC) in the South China Sea. The COC process is part of the efforts of the parties involved to establish a rules-based order in the SCS. China's participation in this process seems to demonstrate its awareness of the role of rules-making in achieving its policy objectives in the SCS. China is also active in pushing regional maritime cooperation. A concrete proposal of a South China Sea coastal states cooperation mechanism, on the basis of the provisions of the

[28] Hai Min, p 15.

UNCLOS regarding cooperation in close or semi-enclosed seas, was put forward by a senior official of the Chinese MFA.[29]

Third, manage differences with the US. The SCS is increasingly described by many observers as an arena for strategic competition between the US and China. China views this situation as a potential threat against its national security as well as the overall external environment for its development.

On one hand, China tries to keep the US from "meddling" into the disputes between itself and its neighbours, worrying that this might complicate the situation. China has also stated its willingness to maintain open dialogue with the US in order to reduce misunderstandings between the two countries. There is a general understanding between the US and China that any unintended clashes must be avoided, and certain arrangements have been made for that purpose. A vision of positive interaction between the US and China in Asia-Pacific also used to be frequently repeated by Chinese leaders, diplomats and scholars.

On the other hand, China has to prepare for any worst-case scenarios against its security in the SCS. China's military deployment in the SCS is mainly intended to create a favourable strategic posture against the mounting strategic pressure from the United States and the US-led military alliance around China's periphery. The objectives of China's armed forces in the SCS are described as maintaining military presence, handling maritime and air situations, and responding to security threats, infringements, and provocations on the sea, strengthening military preparedness with emphasis on the sea.[30] China's military facility installations on the Spratly features under its control can be seen to some extent as part of such overall strategic schemes, although this presence has some implications on the territorial disputes in the SCS.

Fourth, enforce a transformation of its naval strategies. In conformity with the demand from its extending overseas interests and rising non-traditional security threats, China's PLAN is gradually shifting its focus from "offshore waters defence" to the "combination of offshore waters defence with open seas protection." The South Sea also serves as a theatre for Chinese military to build its "far seas forces."[31]

---

[29] Liu Zhenmin, *The Future of East Asia, Remarks on Regional cooperation in Asia*, The Commercial Press (H.K.), March 2020, pp 195–9.

[30] *China's Military Strategy*, http://www.scio.gov.cn/zfbps/ndhf/2015/Document/1435159/1435159.htm

China's National Defense in the New Era, http://www.scio.gov.cn/zfbps/ndhf/39911/Document/1660528/1660528.htm

[31] Ibid.

Conclusion

China's strategies toward the SCS security are not static, but rather dynamic. It may be seen that geography and history are two important factors shaping China's perceptions of its security interests in the SCS, and the strategies it adopts to protect those interests. In addition, other dynamics also have a growing influence on the evolution of such perceptions and strategies, including the maritime power-building process of China and its increasing participation in global maritime affairs, and the interactions between China with the ASEAN countries and the US. For instance, when China is developing into a maritime power and "going global," it is even less likely to adopt the doctrine of "mare clausum" in the SCS.

References

Alistair Iain Johnston, How New and Assertive Is China's New Assertiveness?, *International Security*, Vol. 37, No. 4, Spring 2013.

Congressional Research Service, *US–China Strategic Competition in South and East China Seas: Background and Issues for Congress*, April 24, 2020.

Feng Zhang, Chinese Thinking on the South China Sea and the Future of Regional Security, *Political Science Quarterly*, Vol. 132, No. 3, 2017.

Hai Min, China's Foreign Policy on Boundary & Ocean Affairs with Its Characteristics, *Journal of Boundary & Ocean Studies*, Vol. 3, No. 6, 2018.

Leszek Buszynski, Chinese Naval Strategy, the United States, ASEAN and the South China Sea, *Security Challenges*, Vol. 8, No. 2, Winter 2012.

Leszek Buszynski, The South China Sea Maritime Dispute: Legality, Power, and Conflict Prevention, *Asian Journal of Peacebuilding*, Vol. 1, No. 1, 2013.

Liu Zhenmin, *The Future of East Asia, Liu Zhenmin on Asia Regional Cooperation*, Haikou: Hainan Publishing House, August, 2018.

MFA responded to Vietnam's objection to China's Dotted Line Claim in the South China Sea, Report, www.people.cn, December 12, 2014, http://js.people.com.cn/n/2014/1212/c360300-23196285.html

Mingjiang Li, *China Debates Its South China Sea Policy, Navigating the Indo-Pacific Arc*, edited by Euan Graham and Henrick Z. Tsjeng, Singapore: S. Rajaratnam School of International Studies, 2014.

Mingjiang Li, Reconciling Assertiveness and Cooperation? China's Changing Approach to the South China Sea Dispute, *Security Challenges*, Vol. 6, No. 2, Winter 2010.

National Security, *China Daily*, Report, April 18, 2014, http://www.chinadaily.com.cn/opinion/2014-04/18/content_17443364.htm

Nie Wenjuan, China's Identity and Understanding of National Interest in the South China Sea, *Journal of Contemporary Asia-Pacific Studies*, Vol. 1, 2017.

Peter Dutton, Three Disputes and Three Objectives: China and the South China Sea, *Naval War College Review*, Vol. 64, No. 4, Autumn 2011, US Naval War College Press.

Peter Kreuzer, From Hostile Goliath to Partner in Development: Philippine Perceptions and Strategies for Dealing with China, in *The South China Sea Conflict after the Arbitration of July 12, 2016, Analyses and Perspectives*, edited by Thomas Engelbert, Berlin: Internationaler Verlag der Wissenschaften, 2019.

Spokesperson of Ministry of Foreign Affairs, *China Asked the Philippines to Stop Provocation*, Report, www.people.cn, May 24, 2012, http://world.people.com.cn/GB/8212/191617/9491/237724/17979902.html

Statement of the Government of the People's Republic of China on China's Territorial Sovereignty and Maritime Rights and Interests in the South China Sea, China's MFA, July 12, 2016, https://www.fmprc.gov.cn/nanhai/eng/snhwtlcwj_1/t1379493.htm

The State Council Information Office, PRC, *China's Military Strategy*, May 26, 2015, http://www.scio.gov.cn/zfbps/ndhf/2015/Document/1435159/1435159.htm

The State Council Information Office, PRC, *China's National Defense in the New Era*, July 24, 2019, http://www.scio.gov.cn/zfbps/ndhf/39911/Document/1660528/1660528.htm

The State Council Information Office, PRC, *China's Peaceful Development*, September 6, 2011, http://www.scio.gov.cn/zfbps/ndhf/2011/Document/1000031/1000031.htm

The State Council Information Office, PRC, *China's Policies on Asia-Pacific Security Cooperation*, January 11, 2017, http://www.scio.gov.cn/zfbps/ndhf/36088/Document/1539910/1539910.htm

The State Council Information Office, PRC, *The Development of China's Maritime Cause*, May, 1998, http://www.scio.gov.cn/zfbps/ndhf/1998/Document/307963/307963.htm

Thomas Engelbert, The South China Sea Conflict: Analyses and Perspectives. An Introduction to the Topic, in *The South China Sea Conflict after the Arbitration of July 12, 2016, Analyses and Perspectives*, edited by Thomas Engelbert, New York: Peter Lang, 2019.

Wang Yi, *A Developing China and Chinese Diplomacy*, Speech at Center for Strategic and International Studies, February 26, 2016, https://www.fmprc.gov.cn/web/wjbz_673089/zyjh_673099/t1343410.sht

4

Taiwan's South China Sea Policy under the Tsai Administration

Yann-huei Song

Introduction

In January 2016, Tsai Ing-wen, the candidate for the Democratic Progress Party (DPP), won in Taiwan's presidential election and was inaugurated as the 14th-term president of the Republic of China ("ROC") in May of the same year. The new Tsai government adopted a foreign policy position of "cutting off Mainland China, following the United States [US] and Japan, and catering to ASEAN,"[1] which affects the planning and development of Taiwan's South China Sea (SCS) policy under the Tsai administration. In July 2016, Taiwan announced that the award rendered by the Tribunal that heard the *Philippines v. China* SCS arbitration case is completely unacceptable because, inter alia, in the award, the ROC is referred to as the "Taiwan Authority of China."[2]

On July 19, 2016, President Tsai put forth four principles and five actions pertaining to the SCS issues. One of the policy principles is concerned about the obligation to uphold the freedom of navigation and overflight in the SCS region, which is also one of the main policy concerns of the US

[1] Chieh Ko Talu, Chui Sui Mei Jih, and Ying Ho Tung Hsieh, 「蔡藉南海挺台獨 惡化兩岸關係」，旺報，2017年11月11日，https://www.chinatimes.com/newspapers/20171111000714-260309?chdtv

[2] "ROC position on the South China Sea Arbitration," Ministry of Foreign Affairs, Republic of China (Taiwan), *Statements*, July 12, 2016, https://www.mofa.gov.tw/en/News_Content.aspx?n=0E7B91A8FBEC4A94&sms=220E98D761D34A9A&s=5B5A9134709EB875

government.[3] In January 2019, asked by *The Sunday Telegraph* if she would support a British presence in the SCS, President Tsai signalled that Taiwan would welcome: "any actions that will be helpful towards maintaining peace in the SCS, as well as maintaining freedom of passage."[4] The Tsai government is also taking actions to promote closer Taiwan–Japan security cooperation in line with the development of the US Indo-Pacific strategy. In March 2017, it was reported that Taiwan's Ministry of Defence was taking a very low-profile attitude in response to Japan's sending warships to the SCS.[5]

Currently, Taiwan's main SCS policy actions focus on the promotion of scientific collaboration and developing Taiping Island as a centre of humanitarian assistance and rescue as well as a base for logistic supply. In June 2019, an international conference on the Pratas Islands was organized by the newly established Ocean Affairs Council (OAC).[6] International scholars were invited to visit the Pratas Islands and make presentations on a variety of issues regarding ocean law, policy, and security. However, it should be noted that President Tsai herself, as the head of the National Security Council (NSC), together with senior national security advisors of the Council, is in charge of the government's SCS policy making, not the OAC. At the time of writing, it remains to be seen if Tsai would disregard the opposition from the Trump administration and decide to pay a visit to Taiping Island in the Spratly archipelago during her second term of presidency (2020–23) after she again won Taiwan's presidential election in January 2020.

This chapter examines a number of important issues in relation to the development and implementation of Taiwan's SCS policy since May 2016 when Tsai Ing-wen was inaugurated as the 14th-term ROC president, which include: (1) the new government's response to the arbitral award issued by the Tribunal that heard the South China Sea arbitration case in July 2016; (2) the elaboration of principles and action plans that guide the implementation of Taiwan's SCS policy in July 2016; (3) implementation

---

3 "South China Sea Issue," Press Room, Ministry of Foreign Affairs, Republic of China (Taiwan), https://www.mofa.gov.tw/en/theme.aspx?n=E5A0D5E2432C234D&s=83376F561B7165E6&sms=BCDE19B435833080

4 Nicola Smith, "Taiwan president signals support for UK base in South China Sea," *The Sunday Telegraph*, January 5, 2019, https://www.telegraph.co.uk/news/2019/01/05/taiwan-president-calls-international-support-defend-democracy/

5 "Japanese Warships Entering the SCS, a Very Low Profile Attitude taken by Taiwan's Military," *China Review News*, March 16, 2017 (in Chinese), http://hk.crntt.com/doc/1046/1/3/1/104613149.html?coluid=93&kindid=4030&docid=104613149

6 Lin Chia-nan, "Dongsha meeting urges conservation, cooperation," *Taipei Times*, June 15, 2019, http://www.taipeitimes.com/News/taiwan/archives/2019/06/15/2003716964

of the Tsai administration's SCS policy since July 2016; and (4) US factor in the implementation of Taiwan's SCS policy.

Responses of the Tsai administration to the South China Sea arbitration award

Less than two months after the inauguration of the new government in Taiwan, President Tsai was forced to respond to the final award announced by the Arbitral Tribunal constituted under Annex VII to the United Nations Convention on the Law of the Sea (UNCLOS) in the dispute between the Philippines and People's Republic of China (PRC) over maritime claims in the SCS on July 12, 2016.[7] Among other things, the Tribunal concluded that: "none of the high-tide features in the Spratly Islands are capable of sustaining human habitation or an economic life of their own within the meaning of those terms in Article 121(3) of the Convention,"[8] and that: "[a]ll of the high-tide features in the Spratly Islands are therefore legally rocks for purposes of Article 121(3) and do not generate entitlements to an exclusive economic zone or continental shelf."[9] According to this ruling, Taiping Island is considered a rock and therefore Taiwan does not have the right to claim the exclusive economic zone (EEZ) or the continental shelf. The Tribunal also ruled that the Chinese nine-dash line had no basis under international law.

Taiwan is not a party to the SCS arbitration case and therefore bound by the Tribunal's ruling in accordance with Article 296(2) of UNCLOS, which provides that, "[a]ny such decision [by the Arbitral Tribunal] shall have no binding force except between the parties and in respect of that particular dispute." Because the SCS arbitration case is filed by the Philippines against the PRC and the Tsai administration does not accept the "One China" principle or the "92 consensus," Taiwan states that it is not bound by the award. On the same day that the Tribunal announced its final award, the Tsai administration issued a statement, explaining why Taiwan is not bound by the ruling. It also provided the government's official position on the territorial sovereignty and relevant maritime rights in the SCS. The statement issued by Taiwan's Ministry of Foreign Affairs (MOFA) provides that:

[7] Arbitration Between the Philippines and the People's Republic of China, PCA Case No. 2013–19, Award (July 12, 2016), on the website of the Permanent Court of Arbitration, https://pca-cpa.org/en/cases/7/

[8] Ibid., para. 646, 260.

[9] Ibid., para. 646, 260.

1. In the text of the award, the ROC is referred to as "Taiwan Authority of China." This inappropriate designation is demeaning to the status of the ROC as a sovereign state.
2. Taiping Island was not originally included in the Philippines' submissions for arbitration. However, the tribunal took it upon itself to expand its authority, declaring ROC-governed Taiping Island, and other features in the Nansha (Spratly) Islands occupied by Vietnam, the Philippines, and Malaysia, all to be rocks that "do not generate an exclusive economic zone." This decision severely jeopardizes the legal status of the South China Sea Islands, over which the ROC exercises sovereignty, and their relevant maritime rights.[10]

Consistent with the previous Ma administration's position, the new government here claims that Taiping Island should be considered as a fully-fledged island and therefore is entitled to the right to generate a 200 nautical mile EEZ and continental shelf. In addition, the statement says that, "the ROC is entitled to all rights over the SCS Islands and their relevant waters in accordance with international law and the law of the sea."[11] It adds that the award has no legally binding force on the ROC because the Tribunal did not formally invite Taipei to participate in the arbitral proceedings.[12] The Tsai administration also followed the previous ROC government's SCS position on territorial sovereignty, reiterating that the SCS islands are part of the ROC territory and that the government will take resolute action to safeguard the country's territory and relevant maritime rights.[13] Moreover, President Tsai followed the policy position of the previous government, urging that disputes in the SCS be settled peacefully through multilateral negotiations, in the spirit of setting aside differences and promoting joint development, and that the ROC is willing, through negotiations conducted on the basis of equality, to work with all states concerned to advance peace and stability in the SCS.[14]

Based on Taiwan's official statements, it can be argued that the new Tsai administration did not change or revise the ROC SCS policy. However, it should be noted that the new government did not mention the U-shaped

[10] ROC position on the South China Sea Arbitration, *Statements*, Ministry of Foreign Affairs, the Republic of China (Taiwan), July 12, 2016, https://www.mofa.gov.tw/en/News_Content.aspx?n=0E7B91A8FBEC4A94&sms=220E98D761D34A9A&s=5B5A913470 9EB875

[11] Ibid.

[12] Ibid.

[13] Ibid.

[14] Ibid.

line in all of the statements it issued in response to the Tribunal's ruling that rejected the PRC's nine-dash line and historic rights claims.

The Tsai Administration's South China Sea policy principles and action plans

On July 13, 2016, the day following the announcement of the award, President Tsai boarded a Kang Ding-class frigate at the naval port in Kaohsiung ahead of its patrol mission to Taiping Island, where she encouraged the crew to "defend Taiwan's national interest" in the SCS.[15] Cabinet spokesman Tung Chen-yuan also said that Taiwan's coast guard would step up patrols in the SCS.[16] This was followed by a joint statement issued by Taiwan's Legislative Yuan on July 15, 2016, which expressed its support for the government's position on rejecting the Tribunal's ruling and its territorial and maritime right claims in the SCS.[17]

In response to the rising national sentiment on the issue, Taiwanese legislators and fishers announced respectively their plans to visit Taiping Island to demonstrate their determination to protect Taiwan's rights in the SCS.[18] At the same time, it was voiced that President Tsai should visit Taiping Island for the purpose of defending Taiwan's sovereignty and maritime rights. Former President Ma considered Tsai's visit positive because Taiwan's important SCS policy, to be announced on the island, would attract the world's attention. However, Taiwan's Foreign Minister David Lee, in responding to a question from a DPP legislator on whether Tsai planned to visit Taiping Island, stated that there were no current plans for the President to visit the island, but the possibility would not be ruled out for the future.[19]

Ma offered the following ten policy suggestions for President Tsai's reference if she were to visit Taiping Island:

---

[15] Stacy Hsu, "Tsai Ing-wen visits frigate, vows that the nation will safeguard its interests," *Taipei Times*, July 14, 2016, http://www.taipeitimes.com/News/front/archives/2016/07/14/2003650986

[16] "Taiwan stepping up Coast Guard patrols in South China Sea," *Focus Taiwan News Channel*, July 13, 2016, http://focustaiwan.tw/news/aipl/201607130018.aspx

[17] Alison Hsiao, "Legislature rejects S China Sea ruling," *Taipei Times*, July 16, 2016, http://www.taipeitimes.com/News/front/archives/2016/07/16/2003651126

[18] Minnie Chan, "South China Sea: Taiwanese lawmakers land on Taiping Island in sovereignty, fishing rights push" *South China Morning Post*, July 20, 2016, https://www.scmp.com/news/china/diplomacy-defence/article/1992173/south-china-sea-taiwanese-lawmakers-land-taiping-island

[19] Joseph Yeh, "Government won't rule out Tsai visit to Taiping," *The China Post*, July 13, 2016, https://chinapost.nownews.com/20160713-13986

1. Reaffirming Taiwan's sovereignty over Taiping Island and its legal status as an "island," as well as not accepting the Tribunal's wrong judgement in the SCS arbitration case.
2. Quickly marking and announcing the base points, baselines, territorial sea, contiguous zone, and 200 nautical mile EEZ surrounding Taiping Island.
3. Conveying to the government of the Philippines Taiwan's desire in negotiating the overlapping EEZs in the SCS, and asking Taiwan's Coast Guard Administration to protect fishermen operating within the zones before any talks begin.
4. Continuing the second phase of the project that aims to enhance Taiwan's law enforcement capability in the air and at sea, and increase the patrolling capability in the SCS.
5. Extending the existing 1,200-metre runway on Taiping Island so that it can accommodate small passenger aircraft.
6. Running ads in leading world media to explain the status of Taiping Island and why the Tribunal's ruling was erroneous.
7. Ministry of Education (MOE) adding the history and geography of Taiping Island and the island's current situation to the textbook guidelines used by elementary and junior high schools; Ministry of Defence (MND) expanding the Spratly Studying Camp in Summer for college students; the goal is to enrich the knowledge about Taiping Island for the next generation.
8. Ministries of Economic Affairs (MOEA), Ministries of Transportation and Communications (MOTC), Ministry of Science and Technology (MOST), and the Environmental Protection Administration (EPA) gradually developing the industries on Taiping Island, including bottled waters, tourism, low carbon economy, scientific research, environmental research, and so on.
9. Ministry of the Interior (MOI) encouraging the increase of household register on Taiping Island and planning on the use of land.
10. Inviting allies and international friends to visit Taiping Island, expanding publicity, as December 12, 2016 marks the 70th anniversary of the recovery of Taiping Island.

The US government considers the visit by national leaders of the SCS claimant countries to the disputed islands in the SCS as unhelpful and therefore discourages this kind of move. Taiwan has been informed by US officials about the US' position on the issue. Former President Ma cancelled his trip to Taiping Island in December 2015 mainly because of opposition from Washington. As such, President Tsai disregarded the domestic call and decided not to visit Taiping Island. Seven days after the announcement of the

Tribunal's ruling, however, she convened the first National Security Council meeting, discussing Taiwan's response to the award in the SCS arbitration case and how the new government should handle the SCS issues. The meeting came out with the four principles that guide the future development of Taiwan's SCS policy and five plans of action that implement the policy.

The four principles are:

- Disputes in the SCS should be settled peacefully in accordance with international law and the law of the sea, including the UNCLOS;
- Taiwan should be included in multilateral mechanisms aimed at resolving disputes;
- States concerned have an obligation to safeguard freedom of navigation and overflight in the region; and
- Disputes should be resolved by setting aside differences and promoting joint development. Through negotiations conducted on the basis of equality, the ROC is willing to work with other States concerned to advance peace and stability, as well as protect and develop resources, in the region.[20]

These principles are considered consistent with the previous Taiwan governments' SCS policy. The five action plans are:

- *Protection of fishing rights*: The ROC government shall strengthen its capabilities to ensure the safety of fishermen and fishing operations.
- *Multilateral consultations*: The MOFA shall enhance dialogue and communication with the States concerned, so as to reach consensus on cooperation.
- *Scientific collaboration*: The MOST shall increase quotas for international experts invited by related government agencies to travel to Taiping Island to conduct scientific research on ecological, geological, seismological, meteorological, and climate change matters.
- *Humanitarian assistance and rescue*: The MOFA shall work with relevant international and nongovernmental organizations to make Taiping Island a centre of humanitarian assistance and rescue operations, as well as a supply base.
- *Cultivation of experts on the law of the sea*: The ROC government shall strengthen its ability to deal with issues pertaining to international law.[21]

---

[20] "South China Sea Issue," Press Room, Topics, Ministry of Foreign Affairs Republic of China (Taiwan), https://www.mofa.gov.tw/en/theme.aspx?n=E5A0D5E2432C234D&s=83376F561B7165E6&sms=BCDE19B435833080

[21] Ibid.

Based on this policy planning, Taiwan's Minister of the Interior Yeh Jiunn-rong led a team of officials and researchers to Taiping Island on August 16, 2016. The main purpose of the visit was to reaffirm Taiwan's sovereignty claim that the SCS islands are an inherent part of the nation's territory. As stated by the minister, "The ROC maintains all rights over the South China Sea islands and their surrounding waters in accordance with international law and the U.N. Convention on the Law of the Sea."[22] "While we will not assert excessive claims, we will also not give up any rights," he added.[23] In addition to this goal, the trip was taken as part of preparations to transform the island into a hub of marine scientific research, including climate change and marine ecology, and a humanitarian and rescue centre. Moreover, it was also a part of the new government's plans to hold a special exhibition to commemorate the 70th anniversary of Taiping Island's recovery by the ROC government on December 12, 1946.[24]

On December 9, 2016, an exhibition commemorating the 70th anniversary of the recovery of the SCS islands, jointly organized by the Ministry of Interior and Academia Historica, was opened to the public. The exhibition, focusing on the three themes of "Historical Development," "Key to the Southern Territories," and "Sustainable Peace," featured presentations of documents, artefacts, graphics, and audiovisuals so as to recreate the government's important policy decisions and history of governance in recovering the SCS islands, in particular, Taiping Island. President Tsai delivered a speech at the opening ceremony of the exhibition, in which she reaffirmed that the government will firmly safeguard the nation's territorial sovereignty in the SCS and claim rights in the maritime zones that belong to Taiwan in accordance with international law and the law of the sea. Taiwan will renounce neither sovereignty nor the legitimate rights, she said.[25] In addition, she elaborated on the initial results and progress made on the "four principles" and "five actions" for the implementation of her government's SCS policy as set out at the first National Security Council meeting on July 19, 2016.[26] Actions taken by the Tsai administration to implement its

---

22 "Interior minister visits Taiping Island, reasserts ROC sovereignty," *Taiwan Today*, August 17, 2016, https://taiwantoday.tw/news.php?unit=2,6,10,15,18&post=102355

23 Ibid.

24 Ibid.

25 President Tsai attends exhibition commemorating 70th anniversary of recovery of South China Sea Islands, News & activities, Office of the President, Republic of China, December 9, 2016, https://english.president.gov.tw/NEWS/5036/South%20China%20Sea

26 Ibid.

SCS policy in accordance with the "four principles" and "five actions" are examined next.

Safeguarding territorial sovereignty and maritime (fishing) rights

The first category of actions taken by the government is related to the efforts that aim to safeguard the country's territorial sovereignty claim and maritime rights in the SCS as well as to strengthen Taiwan's national defence and law enforcement capabilities. In April 2017, for example, the MOFA responded to the visit by the Philippine Defence Secretary Delfin Lorenzana to one of the disputed islands in the SCS, namely Thitu Island (Pagasa), that is occupied by the Philippines, but also claimed by Taiwan as part of its territory. The Ministry reiterated Taiwan's sovereignty over the SCS islands and urged all parties to refrain from action that could escalate tensions in the region.[27] The same response was seen in August 2017 when the PRC and the ASEAN member states adopted a negotiating framework for a Code of Conduct in the SCS,[28] and in February 2019 when the government of the Philippines conducted land reclamation activities on Thitu Island.[29] However, these responses are considered low-key as no official statements can be found in the website of Taiwan's MOFA.

Actions have also been taken by the MND and the Coast Guard Administration (CGA) that aim to safeguard Taiwan's sovereignty and maritime rights claims in the SCS. In September 2016, Taiwan had already begun building anti-aircraft defences on Taiping Island. The CGA stepped up protection of Taiwanese fishers who conducted fishing activities in the areas near the Pratas Islands and Spratly Islands. It increased the frequency and duration of patrols and strengthened law enforcement against foreign fishing boats that illegally operate in the relevant waters of the SCS islands. The Tsai administration formulated a comprehensive plan to boost Taiwan's defensive ability on the island, which is the largest naturally formed marine feature in the Spratly archipelago. In April 2017, the MND made a 17-point proposal to the CGA, which included the deployment of advanced

[27] Elaine Hou, "Taiwan reiterates sovereignty over South China Sea Islands," *FOCUS TAIWAN News Channel*, April 22, 2017, http://focustaiwan.tw/news/aipl/201704220016.aspx

[28] Ku Chuan and Y. F. Low, "Taiwan reiterates sovereignty over South China Sea," *FOCUS TAIWAN News Channel*, August 7, 2017, http://focustaiwan.tw/news/aipl/201708070031.aspx

[29] See Press Briefing Summary, the Ministry of Foreign Affairs, Republic of China, February 12, 2019 (in Chinese), https://www.mofa.gov.tw/News_Content_M_2.aspx?n=70BCE89F4594745D&sms=700DE7A3F880BAE6&s=E43941BB47062B8E

high-tech weapons on Taiping Island.[30] The CGA also performed live-fire drills on Taiping Island in August 2017, March 2018, and November 2018, respectively, which triggered protest from Vietnam, which names the island "Ba Binh."[31] In response to Hanoi's accusation of "a serious violation" of Vietnam's sovereignty over the Spratly Islands, Taiwan's foreign minister said in a statement that "Taiping Island is part of our country's territory" and "[w]e have the right to conduct routine drills on the island."[32]

Participating in regional dialogue and multilateral negotiations

Probably the most unsuccessful implementation of President Tsai's SCS policy falls in the second category of actions undertaken by Taiwan's government, which aims to increase Taipei's participation in regional dialogue and multilateral negotiations on the SCS issues. Although the Taiwan government has expressed to the international community its position on "setting aside differences and promoting joint development," its participation in regional multilateral dialogue processes remains very difficult, if not totally unlikely.

In March 2017, Lin Cheng-yi, First Deputy Minister for Mainland China Affairs, expressed the hope that Taiwan would be included in dialogues concerning maritime and international affairs.[33] Two months later, President Tsai expressed disappointment that Taiwan had been excluded in the discussions on the SCS row. She reiterated the government's position that, "Taiwan had to take part in all discussions on the South China Sea because it claimed one of the largest islands in the contested territory."[34] In August 2017, after the PRC and ASEAN member states adopted the negotiating framework for a Code of Conduct in the SCS, Taiwan's MOFA urged in a statement that, "Taiwan should not be excluded from relevant multilateral

30 Hsieh Chia-chen and S. C. Chang, "Taiwan has 'overall plan' to boost defense of Taiping Island," *FOCUS TAIWAN News Channel*, April 17, 2017, http://focustaiwan.tw/news/aipl/201704170018.aspx

31 Huyen Le, "Vietnam denounces Taiwan's live-fire drill in South China Sea," *VnExpress International*, March 22, 2019, https://e.vnexpress.net/news/news/vietnam-denounces-taiwan-s-live-fire-drill-in-south-china-sea-3898274.html

32 Elaine Hou and Y. F. Low, "Taiwan reiterates sovereignty over Taiping Island," *FOCUS TAIWAN News Channel*, August 25, 2017, http://focustaiwan.tw/news/aipl/201708250011.aspx

33 Jhesset O. Enano, "Taiwan seeks seat in dialogue on South China Sea dispute," *INQUIRER.NET*, March 12, 2017, https://globalnation.inquirer.net/153247/taiwan-seeks-seat-dialogues-south-china-sea-disputes

34 Germelina Lacorte, "Taiwan seeks inclusion in South China Sea talks," *INQUIRER.NET*, May 8, 2017, https://globalnation.inquirer.net/156213/taiwan-seeks-inclusion-south-china-sea-talks

dialogues and peaceful settlement of dispute mechanisms."[35] On July 31, 2019, Chinese Foreign Minister, Wang Yi, announced that the PRC and ASEAN member states had completed the first reading of the text to negotiate the Code of Conduct (COC) ahead of schedule.[36] There is no provision contained in the draft text that could allow Taiwan to sign or accede to the COC after it is adopted. As the cross-Strait relations continue to stay in a very difficult stage, there is no hope at all for Taiwan to be included in the COC negotiating process or other multilateral consultation mechanisms that aim to manage potential conflicts or develop cooperative projects in the SCS.

While having such difficulties, however, Taiwan and the Philippines reached consensus on issues relating to law enforcement cooperation in fisheries. In February 2019, the 5th Fisheries Technical Working Group meeting between Taiwan and the Philippines was held in Quezon City. The two sides agreed to share information on fishery inspection, and to improve management of Davao port and the environment for Taiwanese fishing vessels to unload their catches. In addition, Taiwan reiterated that, as close neighbours, fisheries cooperation is an important foundation for the deepening of bilateral relations, hoping to sustain Taiwan–Philippines fishery cooperation under the "New Southbound Policy."[37] In addition, Taiwan, together with the PRC, continued to participate in an Informal Workshop on Managing Potential Conflicts in the SCS. 2020 marked the 30th anniversary of the SCS workshop.[38]

Promoting scientific research and international cooperation

The third category of actions is related to the efforts to promote international scientific cooperation in the SCS. In November 2016, Taiwan's MOST established the South China Sea Science Research Platform, which

---

35 "The ROC Government's Position on the adoption of the Framework for the SCS Code of Conduct at ASEAN-Mainland China Foreign Ministerial Meeting," *Press Release* No. 135, August 7, 2017 (in Chinese), https://www.mofa.gov.tw/News_Content.aspx?n=8742DCE7A2A28761&s=52DF0241ACFC272A

36 Jitsiree Thongnoi, "'Major progress' on South China Sea code of conduct talks even as Beijing warns other countries against 'sowing distrust,'" *South China Morning Post*, July 31, 2019, https://www.scmp.com/news/asia/southeast-asia/article/3020838/major-progress-south-china-sea-code-conduct-chinese

37 "Taiwan, Philippines agree to improve Davao port management," *Taiwan News*, March 1, 2019, https://www.taiwannews.com.tw/en/news/3648915

38 See, Yann-huei Song, "Maritime cooperation in the South China Sea: Three possible ways to help achieve the goal of making the SCS a 'sea of peace, friendship and cooperation,'" China-Southeast Asia Research Center on the South China Sea, Haikou, China.

integrates the SCS-related research projects commissioned by the MOST, the MOI, the COA, and the MOTC. In September 2017, MOST organized an international science forum on the SCS in Taipei. The participating international scientists were invited to visit Taiping Island.[39] In November 2018, the OAC led a delegation of representatives from the MOTC, the MND, the MOST, and the Ministry of Health and Welfare (MOHW) visited Taiping Island for policy inspection purpose.[40] In June 2019, OAC organized an international conference on the Pratas Islands in Kaohsiung. The participating experts from Belgium, Canada, Indonesia, India, Japan, Malaysia, the Philippines, UK, US, and Vietnam were invited to visit Pratas Islands.[41] In August 2019, a delegation from OAC visited the Philippines to discuss and exchange views on possible marine cooperation.[42]

Transforming Taiping Island into a humanitarian assistance and rescue centre

Humanitarian assistance and rescue drills conducted by the CGA, MND, and other government agencies are included in the fourth category of actions that were undertaken to implement the Tsai administration's SCS policy. President Tsai directed the CGA to establish Taiping Island as a "humanitarian search and rescue center." As such, the CGA collaborated with the MND and other government agencies, and performed humanitarian assistance and rescue exercises, entitled "Operation Nanyuan," in the relevant waters of Taiping Island and Pratas Islands. Operation Nanyuan No. 1 was conducted in November 2016[43] and No. 4 in May 2019.[44] It is the government's goal

[39] International Science Forum on the South China Sea, September 4–5, 2017. For more information about the forum, visit the web site of MOST at https://www.most.gov.tw/folksonomy/detail?subSite=&l=ch&article_uid=5ba72107-92d2-4205-abfa-2f0a625b6f38&menu_id=282751fe-6008-4911-879f-449084d17d47&content_type=P&view_mode=listView

[40] "Cross-ministerial joint inspection of Taiping Island to review progress in South China Sea," *News Release*, Ocean Affairs Council, November 14, 2018, https://www.oac.gov.tw/GipOpen/wSite/ct?xItem=126982&ctNode=10435&mp=oac

[41] Lin Chia-nan, "Dongsha meeting urges conservation, cooperation," *Taipei Times*, June 15, 2019, http://www.taipeitimes.com/News/taiwan/archives/2019/06/15/2003716964

[42] Taiwan OAC representatives witness signing of TW-PH MOU for ocean industries cooperation, News Release, Ocean Affairs Council, August 21, 2019, https://www.oac.gov.tw/GipOpen/wSite/lp?ctNode=10435&mp=oac&nowPage=1&pagesize=15

[43] "Rescue exercise staged near Itu Aba," *Taipei Times*, November 30, 2016, http://www.taipeitimes.com/News/taiwan/archives/2016/11/30/2003660279

[44] "Taiwan conducts humanitarian rescue drill near Taiping Island," *FOCUS TAIWAN News Channel*, May 21, 2019, http://focustaiwan.tw/news/aipl/201905210018.aspx

to demonstrate to the international community that Taiping Island is fully capable of serving as a base for humanitarian assistance and supply in the SCS. Because the exercises were conducted near Taiping Island, Vietnam lodged a protest as it also claims sovereignty over the island.

Nurturing and encountering research talent in the law of the sea

This is the first time Taiwan's government has included cultivation of research talent in the law of the sea as part of action plans to implement its SCS policy. The goal is to reinforce Taiwan's capacity to respond to international legal issues. The Ministry of the Interior and other relevant agencies have already organized workshops on the law of the sea, and are actively cultivating specialists on maritime issues. In August 2019, the OAC and the National Sun Yat-sen University signed a cooperation memorandum to help personnel become more knowledgeable of international laws and policies at sea and more capable of international negotiation.[45] This was followed by a study trip led by the OAC Deputy Minister, Chuang Ching-ta, to visit Paris for the purpose of learning more about issues related to marine pollution.

The US factor in the implementation of Taiwan's South China Sea policy

US concern, and its resulting policy, has been one of the important factors affecting the implementation of the Taiwan government's SCS policy. The Trump administration's talk about upgrading US–Taiwan security defence cooperation and including Taipei in the US-led Indo-Pacific strategic partnerships can be seen in the 2017 *National Security Strategy of the United States of America*,[46] the Defense Department's 2018 *Summary of National Defense Strategy*,[47] and the same Department's 2019 *Indo-Pacific Strategy Report*.[48] Under the Trump administration, Washington intended

45 Ocean Affairs Council and National Sun Yat-sen University Signed Cooperation Memorandum for Ocean Talents, News Release, Ocean Affairs Council, August 12, 2019, https://www.oac.gov.tw/GipOpen/wSite/ct?xItem=127757&ctNode=10435&mp=oac

46 The report is available on the website of the US White House at https://www.whitehouse.gov/wp-content/uploads/2017/12/NSS-Final-12-18-2017-0905.pdf

47 The summary of the Defense Department's report is available on the website of the US Department of Defense at https://dod.defense.gov/Portals/1/Documents/pubs/2018-National-Defense-Strategy-Summary.pdf

48 The report is available on the website of the US Department of Defense at https://media.defense.gov/2019/Jul/01/2002152311/-1/-1/1/DEPARTMENT-OF-DEFENSE-INDO-PACIFIC-STRATEGY-REPORT-2019.PDF

to maintain strong ties with Taiwan in accordance with the "One China" policy of the US, including its commitments under the 1979 Taiwan Relations Act (TRA) to provide for Taiwan's legitimate defence needs and deter coercion.[49] The US government will take actions to strengthen US–Taiwan partnerships into a networked security architecture capable of deterring aggression, maintaining stability, and ensuring free access to common domains in the Indo-Pacific region.[50] As stated in the 2019 Indo-Pacific Strategy Report, the objective of the US defence engagement with Taiwan "is to ensure that Taiwan remains secure, confident, free from coercion, and able to peacefully and productively engage the mainland on its own terms."[51] Accordingly, the US government is committed to providing Taiwan with defence weapons and services, "in such quantity as may be necessary to enable Taiwan to maintain a sufficient self-defense capability."[52]

In addition to the actions taken by the executive branch, the US Congress also passed a number of legislations that urged the Trump administration to deepen its relations with Taiwan. In March 2018, for instance, the US Congress passed the Taiwan Travel Act (TTA), which became the US Public Law No. 115–135. The law urges the US government to encourage visits between the United States and Taiwan at all levels.[53] In August 2018, the Congress passed the National Defense Authorization Act for Fiscal Year 2019, which became law on August 13, 2018.[54] Under this law, the US Defense Secretary should, in consultation with appropriate counterparts in Taiwan, conduct a comprehensive assessment of Taiwan's military forces, particularly Taiwan's reserves.[55] It is the sense of the Congress that the United States and Taiwan should expand cooperation in humanitarian assistance and disaster relief and the Defense Secretary should consider supporting the visit of a US hospital ship to Taiwan as part of the annual "Pacific Partnership" mission, in order to improve disaster response planning and preparedness as well as to strengthen cooperation between the US and Taiwan.[56] On

[49] The 2017 National Security Strategy of the United States of America, supra note 46, 47.

[50] The Defense Department's 2018 Summary of National Defense Strategy, supra note 47, 8–9.

[51] The 2019 Indo-Pacific Strategy Report, supra note 48, 31.

[52] Ibid.

[53] H.R. 535 became Public Law No. 115–135 on March 16, 2018. For the text of the law, visit: https://www.congress.gov/bill/115th-congress/house-bill/535/text

[54] H.R. 5515 became Public Law No. 115–232 on August 13, 2018. For the text of the law, visit https://www.congress.gov/bill/115th-congress/house-bill/5515/text

[55] Sec. 1257(a), Strengthening Taiwan's Force Readiness, Ibid.

[56] Sec. 1258, Sense of Congress on Taiwan, Ibid.

December 31, 2018, the Asia Reassurance Initiative Act of 2018 became US Public Law No. 115–409.[57]

Under the law, the US President should conduct regular transfers of defence articles to Taiwan that are tailored to meet the existing and likely future threats from the PRC, including supporting the efforts of Taiwan to develop and integrate asymmetric capabilities, as appropriate, including mobile, survivable, and cost-effective capabilities, into its military forces. In addition, the President should encourage the travel of high-level US officials to Taiwan, in accordance with the TTA.

In March 2019, the US and Taiwan launched a series of consultations called "Indo-Pacific Democratic Governance Consultations."[58] This was followed by a meeting between NSC director Lee and US national security advisor Bolton in May 2019. In July 2019, the US Department of State approved the potential sale to Taiwan of US$2.2 billion in arms, including Abrams tanks and Stinger missiles.[59] In August 2019, the US government announced an US$8 billion sale of 66 F-16 fighter jets to Taiwan.[60]

As far as US–Taiwan cooperation in the SCS is concerned, there had been reports of Taiwan's receiving "assistance and training" from the US in October 2015.[61] In November 2016, in response to a report on the US role in Taiwan's humanitarian assistance and rescue exercises, Taiwan's CGA, in a press release, denied local reports that the US would send observers to join the drills conducted in the waters around Taiping Island.[62] In March 2017, in response to a question raised by Taiwan's legislator about the plan to lease Taiping Island to the US, Taiwan's Defence Minister, Feng Shih-kuan, replied

[57] S.2736 - Asia Reassurance Initiative Act of 2018 became Public Law No. 115–409 on December 31, 2018. For the text of the law, visit: https://www.congress.gov/bill/115th-congress/senate-bill/2736/text

[58] "The United States and Taiwan to launch Indo-Pacific democratic governance consultations," American Institute in Taiwan, Press Release #: PR-1906, March 19, 2019, https://www.ait.org.tw/the-united-states-and-taiwan-to-launch-indo-pacific-democratic-governance-consultations/

[59] "US approves potential sale of $2.2bn in arms to Taiwan, stoking China's anger," *The Guardian*, July 9, 2019, https://www.theguardian.com/world/2019/jul/09/us-approves-potential-sale-of-22bn-in-arms-to-taiwan-stoking-chinas-anger

[60] Edward Wong, "Trump administration approves F-16 fighter jet sales to Taiwan," *The New York Times*, August 16, 2019, https://www.nytimes.com/2019/08/16/world/asia/taiwan-f16.html

[61] Ankit Panda, "US to support Taiwan in South China Sea per 2016 Defense Budget Bill," *The Diplomat*, October 4, 2015, https://thediplomat.com/2015/10/us-to-support-taiwan-in-south-china-sea-per-2016-defense-budget-bill/

[62] You Kai-hsiang and Bear Lee, "No US role in humanitarian rescue drill in South China Sea: CGA," *FOCUS TAIWAN News Channel*, November 20, 2016, http://focustaiwan.tw/news/aipl/201611200019.aspx

that it was non-reliable news and, "I will absolutely disapprove it."[63] In June 2018, Taiwan's MOFA denied a report on the government's plan to lease the island to the US. MOFA spokesperson, Andrew Lee, stated that, "The government has no plans to lease Taiping Island to any other country" and that neither the US nor any other country had made such a request.[64] In October 2018, the US Navy (USN) research vessel, *Thomas G. Thompson*, docked in Taiwan's southern port city Kaohsiung. There has been speculation in some quarters that the vessel's port call in Taiwan could be part of US plans for a global show of force directed at PRC, because the ship belongs to the USN Office of Naval Research (ONR).[65] In November 2018, there was speculation about Taiwan's intention to join the US military exercises conducted in the SCS and that Taiwan was considering hosting US warships on Taiping Island for regional security.[66]

It is clear that that both the decision-making process and implementation of Taiwan's SCS policy have been influenced by the US government's concerns and policy. As a result, Taiwan supports the US-led Indo-Pacific strategic alliances and partnerships and Washington's efforts to develop a multilateral joint patrolling force in the SCS. Not only does Taiwan support the activities conducted by the US military under the name of freedom of navigation or overflight in the SCS, but also the actions taken by its allies, such as the United Kingdom and Japan. The Tsai administration avoids mentioning the U-shaped line and historic right claim in the SCS as a partial recognition of the ruling made by the Arbitral Tribunal in the SCS arbitration case. In addition, cross-Strait dialogue on the SCS issue has become much more difficult, if not completely suspended.

Conclusion

The SCS issue has never been put at the top of Taiwan's foreign policy agenda. The sovereignty dispute between Taipei and Beijing and PRC's insistence on the "One China" principle has made it unlikely that Taiwan

---

63 "Never lease Taiping Dao 馮世寬 guts Reply," *China Times*, March 2, 2017 (in Chinese), https://www.chinatimes.com/realtimenews/20170302005101-260407?chdtv

64 Ku Chuan and Flor Wang, "Taiwan denies rumors about leasing Taiping Island to US," *China Post*, June 11, 2018, https://chinapost.nownews.com/20180611-350448

65 Cheng Chi-feng and Chi Jo-yao, "US vessel docked in Kaohsiung delays departure for Australia," *FOCUS TAIWAN News Channel*, October 19, 2018, http://focustaiwan.tw/news/aipl/201810190014.aspx

66 Lawrence Chung, "Taiwan 'will consider' hosting US warships on Taiping Island for regional security," *South China Morning Post*, November 5, 2018, https://www.scmp.com/news/china/military/article/2171756/taiwan-will-consider-hosting-us-warships-spratly-island

will be included in the SCS dialogue processes. The previous governments of Taiwan and the current Tsai administrations have taken similar low-key approaches in dealing with the SCS issue. Without a strong policy determination and in the absence of new ideas or approaches, it is likely we will see Taiwan become further marginalized and excluded from the regional efforts to manage the potential conflicts in the SCS.

The Tsai administration will continue to follow the four principles and five action plans. During the 2020 presidential campaign, the SCS issue was not mentioned in the debates of the presidential candidates. Unless serious conflicts or developments occur in the SCS, we are unlikely to hear a demand from the Taiwanese people for President Tsai to visit Taiping Island to safeguard its claims to territorial sovereignty and maritime rights. As President Tsai won Taiwan's 2020 presidential election, it is believed that Taiwan's SCS policy will remain the same for some time. However, it cannot be totally ruled out that the new Tsai administration, for the purpose of improving the cross-Strait relations, might adopt a different approach to deal with the SCS issue. As such, it is possible to see actions taken by President Tsai to call for the resumption of the cross-Strait dialogue process and promote cooperation on the SCS issue with mainland China. However, the US concerns and Washington's SCS policy will continue to play a role in influencing the approach adopted by Taiwan to handle the SCS issue. The re-election of President Trump in 2020 would have likely brought about further ambiguity in Taiwan's SCS policy with regard to historic rights and U-shaped line claims. It is also likely that, with Trump's re-election, there would have been a renewal of statements issued and actions undertaken by Taiwan in line with the US Indo-Pacific strategy and SCS policy. However, with Biden elected US President, what remains to be seen is if the new administration will pursue many of the same policies as its predecessor.

References

2017 National Security Strategy of the United States of America, US White House, https://www.whitehouse.gov/wp-content/uploads/2017/12/NSS-Final-12-18-2017-0905.pdf

2018 Summary of National Defense Strategy, US Department of Defense, https://dod.defense.gov/Portals/1/Documents/pubs/2018-National-Defense-Strategy-Summary.pdf

2019 Indo-Pacific Strategy Report, US Department of Defense, https://media.defense.gov/2019/Jul/01/2002152311/-1/-1/1/DEPARTMENT-OF-DEFENSE-INDO-PACIFIC-STRATEGY-REPORT-2019.PDF

Alison Hsiao, "Legislature rejects S China Sea ruling," *Taipei Times*, July 16, 2016, http://www.taipeitimes.com/News/front/archives/2016/07/16/2003651126

Ankit Panda, "US to support Taiwan in South China Sea per 2016 Defense Budget Bill," *The Diplomat*, October 4, 2015, https://thediplomat.com/2015/10/us-to-support-taiwan-in-south-china-sea-per-2016-defense-budget-bill/

Arbitration Between the Philippines and the People's Republic of China, PCA Case No. 2013-19, Award (July 12, 2016), the Permanent Court of Arbitration, https://pca-cpa.org/en/cases/7/

Asia Reassurance Initiative Act of 2018, https://www.congress.gov/bill/115th-congress/senate-bill/2736/text

Cheng Chi-feng and Chi Jo-yao, "US vessel docked in Kaohsiung delays departure for Australia," *FOCUS TAIWAN News Channel*, October 19, 2018, http://focustaiwan.tw/news/aipl/201810190014.aspx

"Cross-ministerial joint inspection of Taiping Island to review progress in South China Sea," *News Release*, Ocean Affairs Council, November 14, 2018, https://www.oac.gov.tw/GipOpen/wSite/ct?xItem=126982&ctNode=10435&mp=oac

"Duterte to 'raise the Philippine flag' in South China Sea," *Deutsche Welle*, April 6, 2017, https://www.dw.com/en/duterte-to-raise-the-philippine-flag-in-south-china-sea/a-38320961

Edward Wong, "Trump Administration approves F-16 fighter jet sales to Taiwan," *The New York Times*, August 16, 2019, https://www.nytimes.com/2019/08/16/world/asia/taiwan-f16.html

Elaine Hou, "Taiwan reiterates sovereignty over South China Sea Islands," *FOCUS TAIWAN News Channel*, April 22, 2017, http://focustaiwan.tw/news/aipl/201704220016.aspx

Elaine Hou and Y. F. Low, "Taiwan reiterates sovereignty over Taiping Island," *FOCUS TAIWAN News Channel*, August 25, 2017, http://focustaiwan.tw/news/aipl/201708250011.aspx

"Former president suggests ways to uphold Taiping Island rights," *Focus Taiwan News Channel*, July 16, 2016, http://focustaiwan.tw/news/aipl/201607160009.aspx

Germelina Lacorte, "Taiwan seeks inclusion in South China Sea talks," *INQUIRER.NET*, May 8, 2017, https://globalnation.inquirer.net/156213/taiwan-seeks-inclusion-south-china-sea-talks

"Government won't cooperate with any party on South China Sea issue: mainland council," *The China Post*, July 16, 2016, http://www.chinapost.com.tw/print/472442.htm

Hsieh Chia-chen and S. C. Chang, "Taiwan has 'overall plan' to boost defense of Taiping Island," *FOCUS TAIWAN News Channel*, April 17, 2017, http://focustaiwan.tw/news/aipl/201704170018.aspx

Huyen Le, "Vietnam denounces Taiwan's live-fire drill in South China Sea," *VnExpress International*, March 22, 2019, https://e.vnexpress.net/news/news/vietnam-denounces-taiwan-s-live-fire-drill-in-south-china-sea-3898274.html

"If Tsai Ing-wen visits Taiping Island, Ma Ying-jeou: it should be positive," *ETtoday*, July 14, 2016 (in Chinese), https://www.ettoday.net/news/20160714/735170.htm

"Interior minister visits Taiping Island, reasserts ROC sovereignty," *Taiwan Today*, August 17, 2016, https://taiwantoday.tw/news.php?unit=2,6,10,15,18&post=102355

International Science Forum on the South China Sea, Ministry of Science and Technology, Republic of China, September 4–5, 2017, https://www.most.gov.tw/folksonomy/detail?subSite=&l=ch&article_uid=5ba72107-92d2-4205-abfa-2f0a625b6f38&menu_id=282751fe-6008-4911-879f-449084d17d47&content_type=P&view_mode=listView

"Japanese warships entering the SCS, a very low profile attitude taken by Taiwan's military," *China Review News*, March 16, 2017 (in Chinese), http://hk.crntt.com/doc/1046/1/3/1/104613149.html?coluid=93&kindid=4030&docid=104613149

Jhesset O. Enano, "Taiwan seeks seat in dialogue on South China Sea dispute," *INQUIRER.NET*, March 12, 2017, https://globalnation.inquirer.net/153247/taiwan-seeks-seat-dialogues-south-china-sea-disputes

Jitsiree Thongnoi, " 'Major progress' on South China Sea code of conduct talks even as Beijing warns other countries against 'sowing distrust,' " *South China Morning Post*, July 31, 2019, https://www.scmp.com/news/asia/southeast-asia/article/3020838/major-progress-south-china-sea-code-conduct-chinese

Joseph Yeh, "Government won't rule out Tsai visit to Taiping," *The China Post*, July 13, 2016, https://chinapost.nownews.com/20160713-13986

Ko Shu-ling, "Chen Shui-bian defends his visit to Taiping Island," *Taipei Times*, February 4, 2008, http://www.taipeitimes.com/News/taiwan/archives/2008/02/04/2003400181

Ku Chuan and Flor Wang, "Taiwan denies rumors about leasing Taiping Island to US," *China Post*, June 11, 2018, https://chinapost.nownews.com/20180611-350448

Ku Chuan and Y. F. Low, "Taiwan reiterates sovereignty over South China Sea," *FOCUS TAIWAN News Channel*, August 7, 2017, http://focustaiwan.tw/news/aipl/201708070031.aspx

Lawrence Chung, "Taiwan 'will consider' hosting US warships on Taiping Island for regional security," *South China Morning Post*, November 5, 2018, https://www.scmp.com/news/china/military/article/2171756/taiwan-will-consider-hosting-us-warships-spratly-island

Lin Chia-nan, "Dongsha meeting urges conservation, cooperation," *Taipei Times*, June 15, 2019, http://www.taipeitimes.com/News/taiwan/archives/2019/06/15/2003716964

"Ma Ying-jeou mentioning Taiping Island 10 suggestions, Tsai Ing-wen's office: no comments," *Wen Wei Po*, July 17, 2016, http://news.wenweipo.com/2016/07/17/IN1607170028.htm (in Chinese)

Minnie Chan, "South China Sea: Taiwanese lawmakers land on Taiping Island in sovereignty, fishing rights push" *South China Morning Post*, July 20, 2016, https://www.scmp.com/news/china/diplomacy-defence/article/1992173/south-china-sea-taiwanese-lawmakers-land-taiping-island

National Defense Authorization Act for Fiscal Year 2019, https://www.congress.gov/bill/115th-congress/house-bill/5515/text

"Never lease Taiping Dao 馮世寬 guts Reply," *China Times*, March 2, 2017 (in Chinese), https://www.chinatimes.com/realtimenews/20170302005101-260407?chdtv

Nicola Smith, "Taiwan president signals support for UK base in South China Sea," *The Telegraph*, January 5, 2019, https://www.telegraph.co.uk/news/2019/01/05/taiwan-president-calls-international-support-defend-democracy/

Ocean Affairs Council and National Sun Yat-sen University Signed Cooperation Memorandum for Ocean Talents, News Release, Ocean Affairs Council, August 12, 2019, https://www.oac.gov.tw/GipOpen/wSite/ct?xItem=127757&ctNode=10435&mp=oac

President Tsai attends exhibition commemorating 70th anniversary of recovery of South China Sea Islands, News & activities, Office of the President, Republic of China, December 9, 2016, https://english.president.gov.tw/NEWS/5036/South%20China%20Sea

Press Briefing Summary, the Ministry of Foreign Affairs, Republic of China, February 12, 2019 (in Chinese), https://www.mofa.gov.tw/News_Content_M_2.aspx?n=70BCE89F4594745D&sms=700DE7A3F880BAE6&s=E43941BB47062B8E

"Rescue exercise staged near Itu Aba," *Taipei Times*, November 30, 2016, http://www.taipeitimes.com/News/taiwan/archives/2016/11/30/2003660279

"ROC position on the South China Sea Arbitration," Ministry of Foreign Affairs, Republic of China (Taiwan), *Statements*, July 12, 2016, https://www.mofa.gov.tw/en/News_Content.aspx?n=0E7B91A8FBEC4A94&sms=220E98D761D34A9A&s=5B5A9134709EB875

Song, Yann-huei. "Maritime cooperation in the South China Sea: Three possible ways to help achieve the goal of making the SCS a 'sea of peace, friendship and cooperation,'" China-Southeast Asia Research Center on the South China Sea, Haikou, China. www.csarc.org.cn/yann-huei-song-maritime-cooperation-in-the-south-china-sea-three-possible-ways-to-help-achieve-the-goal-of-making-the-scs-a-sea-of-peace-friendship-and-cooperation/

"South China Sea Issue," Press Room, Ministry of Foreign Affairs, Republic of China (Taiwan), https://www.mofa.gov.tw/en/theme.aspx?n=E5A0D5E2432C234D&s=83376F561B7165E6&sms=BCDE19B435833080

Stacy Hsu, "Ma's visit is 'unhelpful,' AIT says," *Taipei Times*, January 28, 2016, http://www.taipeitimes.com/News/front/archives/2016/01/28/2003638226

Stacy Hsu, "Tsai Ing-wen visits frigate, vows that the nation will safeguard its interests," *Taipei Times*, July 14, 2016, http://www.taipeitimes.com/News/front/archives/2016/07/14/2003650986

Stephanie Chao, "Ma encourages Tsai to visit Taiping," *The China Post*, July 15, 2016, https://chinapost.nownews.com/20160715-13626

"Taiwan conducts humanitarian rescue drill near Taiping Island," *FOCUS TAIWAN News Channel*, May 21, 2019, http://focustaiwan.tw/news/aipl/201905210018.aspx

Taiwan OAC representatives witness signing of TW-PH MOU for ocean industries cooperation, News Release, Ocean Affairs Council, August 21, 2019, https://www.oac.gov.tw/GipOpen/wSite/lp?ctNode=10435&mp=oac&nowPage=1&pagesize=15

"Taiwan, Philippines agree to improve Davao port management," *Taiwan News*, March 1, 2019, https://www.taiwannews.com.tw/en/news/3648915

"Taiwan stepping up Coast Guard patrols in South China Sea," *Focus Taiwan News Channel*, July 13, 2016, http://focustaiwan.tw/news/aipl/201607130018.aspx

Taiwan Travel Act, https://www.congress.gov/bill/115th-congress/house-bill/535/text

"The government of the Republic of China (Taiwan) reiterates its sovereignty over the Nansha Islands and surrounding waters," News and Events, Ministry of Foreign Affairs, Republic of China, March 11, 2009

"The ROC Government's Position on the adoption of the Framework for the SCS Code of Conduct at ASEAN-Mainland China Foreign Ministerial Meeting," *Press Release* No. 135, August 7, 2017 (in Chinese), https://www.mofa.gov.tw/News_Content.aspx?n=8742DCE7A2A28761&s=52DF0241ACFC272A

"The United States and Taiwan to launch Indo-Pacific democratic governance consultations," American Institute in Taiwan, Press Release #: PR-1906, March 19, 2019, https://www.ait.org.tw/the-united-states-and-taiwan-to-launch-indo-pacific-democratic-governance-consultations/

"US approves potential sale of $2.2bn in arms to Taiwan, stoking China's anger," *The Guardian*, July 9, 2019, https://www.theguardian.com/world/2019/jul/09/us-approves-potential-sale-of-22bn-in-arms-to-taiwan-stoking-chinas-anger

Wu Shicun, "Where is the road for cross-Strait SCS cooperation?" *Phoenix Weekly*, No. 14, 2016, http://www.nanhai.org.cn/review_c/159.html

You Kai-hsiang and Bear Lee, "No US role in humanitarian rescue drill in South China Sea: CGA," *FOCUS TAIWAN News Channel*, November 20, 2016, http://focustaiwan.tw/news/aipl/201611200019.aspx「蔡藉南海挺台獨 惡化兩岸關係」，旺報，2017年11月11日，https://www.chinatimes.com/newspapers/20171111000714-260309?chdtv

5

Vietnam and the East Sea in Its Strategic Thinking

Đỗ Thanh Hải and Nguyễn Thị Linh

Vietnam is a coastal state and a disputing party in the South China Sea (SCS), which is called the East Sea in Vietnam due to its location vis-à-vis its mainland.[1] Within the framework of this chapter, these two terms are used interchangeably. There, Vietnam claims sovereignty over the land features in the Paracels and Spratlys, and over a suite of maritime zones as stipulated by the United Nations Convention on the Law of the Sea (UNCLOS), which overlap wholly and partly with those of its neighbours. The country has been well-known as one of the claimants which has stood firmly in a series of stand-offs with its giant neighbour, China. It is a big puzzle for many why Hanoi would risk antagonizing Beijing, its most important neighbour, for a bunch of remote, barren and tiny features in the middle of the sea and for the waters off its coast. This chapter builds on the existing literature of Vietnam's maritime activities and its statecraft to map and identify the importance of the East Sea in the Vietnamese perspective throughout the course of history. It should be noted that the SCS and the offshore islets have not only been incorporated into Vietnam's political geography since at least the 17th century but also into its strategic thinking. In other words, the sea and islands serve as a layer of defence that increases the country's strategic depth.

[1] Disclaimer: The views in this chapter are the authors' own, not necessarily reflecting those of the government of Vietnam or any other institutions.

Lack of strategic depth and insecurity

Vietnam's strategic thinking is conditioned by history and geography. The combination of the asymmetry of power and geographical proximity created a permanent concern among Vietnamese political elites about the Northern threat. History textbooks remind schoolchildren about the bitter experience of King An Dương Vương in trusting Chinese General Zhao Tuo (magistrate of Nanhai Province), which resulted in the fall of the Âu Lạc Dynasty in 179BCE and a longue durée of Chinese suzerainty. Consequently, such a dark time under the Chinese yoke, or "a millennium of grievance," created a deep sense of insecurity and served as an undying reminder of the danger from the North.

Geographically speaking, Vietnam's most dominant feature is the lack of strategic depth. The concept broadly refers to the distance between the frontline and the country's core areas, including the capital and main industrial cities. In the case of Vietnam, it is defined as the vulnerability of its key centres of population to the source of threat in terms of distance and exposure, and also the breadth of its hinterland to serve as sanctuaries to resist invasions. As the Southeast Asian country most exposed to the Chinese empire by land and by sea, Vietnam was aware of the vulnerability of and accessibility to its imperial cities. Even in the feudal time, it took just a couple of days for the Chinese army marching from Guangxi to reach the imperial citadel of Thăng Long (now Hanoi), the capital city for Đại Việt, a name for the land ruled by the Vietnamese between the 11th and 14th centuries.

More often than not, Đại Việt's forces could not afford decisive front-on battles against Chinese cavalries and infantries at the beginning. Neither were strong fortifications, such as rounds of defensive walls built by the Âu Lạc and Hồng Bàng dynasties (1400–16), sufficient to hold against massive Chinese legions. Most of the time, the Vietnamese armies had to retreat from Thăng Long to fight an attrition war. As a result, the depth of the hinterland was very important. In the 13th century, the Trần emperor and his armies narrowly escaped from a pincer of a strong Yuan army storming through the northern defences and its massive fleet sailing through the Gulf of Tonkin and penetrating through riverine landscape. At times, Đại Việt faced invasions from Champa, which was the kingdom in the central part of today's Vietnam. Therefore, the Vietnamese rulers of Đại Việt had strong incentives to expand southward to increase its strategic depth vis-à-vis the threat from the North and neutralize the challenge from the South. Đại Việt's resistance to the North and the gradual expansions into the South from the 11th century to the 18th century essentially created the elongated shape of current Vietnam's territory.

While such an expansion made the centre of Vietnam further away from the Chinese empire, the country's broadened contact with Biển Đông (East

Sea), a large swathe of waters to its East rendered it more vulnerable to seaborne invasions.[2] By the end of the 17th century, the Việt settlers set foot in the Mekong region, giving the mainland an S-shape with an elongated coastline of nearly 2,000 miles. However, Vietnam's eastern façade lacks hinterland. The country's East-West width varies from as little as 33 miles (in the central region) to 300 miles. The Red River Delta in the North and Mekong River Delta in the South are riverine landscape, which are penetrated by navigable waterways. From the North to the South, the terrain is also divided by rivers and mountain ranges. As a result, the maritime corridor along the mainland serves a fluid medium to keep the North and the South together. However, the arrival of the European traders and iron warships with powerful cannons became a new source of threat to the land for the Vietnamese rulers.

Offshore islands as new frontiers

The conquest and incorporation of Champa by the Lê Dynasty in the 15th century made Đại Việt a regional maritime power. The Cham people were Hindu maritime people, who crisscrossed the SCS and beyond as fishers, traders, and even pirates for centuries. The kingdom of Champa was a maritime trading empire before all its territories were annexed by Đại Việt.[3] It is reported that the Nguyễn Lords, the rulers of the southern realms, built upon Đại Việt's naval use and Cham's maritime tradition to make the region an *entrepôt* for international commerce. In the early 16th century, commerce thrived in the South, while the North remained an agrarian society. Traders from China, Japan, India, Indonesia, and Europe made frequent visits to Hội An and Thuận Hóa to buy porcelain, silks, and peppers while selling sugar and rare wood.[4] It is reported that a ruler, Nguyễn Hoàng, also sent a big ship with 1,200 passengers to Japan to establish relations with Tokugawa shogunate.[5]

However, the more Đại Việt expanded, the more divisive it was. Ben Kiernan convincingly observed, "As its territory expanded, the country divided into two kingdoms, whose geographic variety fostered further diversification into three distinct economic regions."[6] By being open to commerce, Đàng Trong (Inner Region, the South) became more prosperous

---

[2] Spencer C. Tucker, *Vietnam*, London: Routledge 1998, p.8.

[3] David Hatcher Childress, *The Lost World of Cham*, Illinois: Adventures Unlimited Press, 2017, Chapter 1.

[4] Ben Kiernan, *Việt Nam*, New York: Oxford University Press, 2017, pp.230–3.

[5] Ben Kiernan, *Việt Nam*, p.230.

[6] Ibid., p.254.

and powerful than Đàng Ngoài (Outer Region, the North). By 1620, the Nguyễn Lords of the South refused to pay taxes to Lê-Trịnh masters in Thăng Long, and civil war broke out between Đàng Trong and Đàng Ngoài. Đàng Trong was reportedly strong in naval power, at one time possessing 230 "*thuyền*" (naval galleys, boats), "each equipped with a cannon and two artillery pieces manned by sixty four rowers and mariners."[7] Historian Li Tana contended that thuyền were central to Nguyễn's military power.[8] Such force build-up was sensible given the natural terrain of the central and the southern realm, largely divided by rivers and connected by the sea. In this case, boats were reasonably efficient for coastal transport and troop mobility.

It was also in this period that the southern rulers were interested in the offshore atoll chains of the Paracels, or Hoàng Sa (Golden Sandbank), and the Spratlys, or Trường Sa. These archipelagos, which were reached by a voyage of "three days and three nights" from the coast, were incorporated into the political geography. In a note attached to the map of Quảng Ngãi Province in *Thiên Nam Tứ chí lộ đồ thư* [Handbook of the South's road map atlas], Đỗ Bá noted that, "In the middle of the sea, facing the coastline between the harbor of Đại Chiêm and the harbor of Sa Vinh lies a long sandbank, called "Bãi Cát Vàng" (golden sandbank), which is 400 *lý*[9] long and 2000 *lý* wide."[10] These areas were also described in *Phủ biên tạp lục* [Miscellany Records of the Pacification of the Frontiers] by Lê Quý Đôn, a mandarin sent by the Trịnh Lords to govern the provinces of Thuận Hóa and Quảng Nam.[11] It was well-noted in many historical records that the Nguyễn Lords established two maritime militia detachments, Hoàng Sa and Bắc Hải, to do regular patrols and visits to these areas:

> Hoang Sa militia, consisted of 70 persons selected from An Vinh villages, took turn to go to the Paracel Islands to dive and search for the area's own flora and fauna. Every year, a team departed in the third month, bringing with them 6-months' food supply, arriving in the islands after a voyage of three days and three nights.[12]

---

7 Li Tana, *Nguyễn Cochinchina: Southern Vietnam in the Seventeenth and Eighteenth Centuries*, Ithaca: Cornell University Press, 1998, p.41.

8 Ibid.

9 *Lý* is the Vietnamese traditional length-measuring unit. One *lý* equals 500 metres.

10 Ministry of Foreign Affairs (Socialist Republic of Vietnam), *The Hoàng Sa and Trường Sa Archipelagoes*, Hanoi, 1981, p.19.

11 Đỗ Thanh Hải, *Vietnam and the South China Sea*, New York: Routledge, 2017, p.31.

12 Requoted from Hãn Nguyên Nguyễn Nhã, *Vietnam, Territoriality and the South China Sea*, London and New York: Routledge, 2019 [Translated by Vinh-The Lam], p.8.

Perhaps the Vietnamese initial interests in the scattered offshore territories were mostly shaped by economic benefits. As Lê Quý Đôn also mentioned, the mission of the Hoàng Sa flotilla was "to collect things from shipwrecks: bronze swords, bronze horses, flower-shaped silver, silver coins, circle-shaped silver, bronze items, tin blocks, lead blocks, rifles, ivory tusks, beeswax, ceramics, and other items." He went on, "They also searched for sea turtle shells, sea cucumbers, and striped cochlea grains. They came back in the 8th month, going directly through Eo estuary to the capital city of Phú Xuân to deliver all collected items."[13] It was clear that the Vietnamese seamen knew that the Paracels and Spratlys were "dangerous grounds" for navigation, and the Hoàng Sa and Bắc Hải militia were designed for the lucrative business of ship salvage to finance the costs of the civil war. Such practices came to a halt when the Tây Sơn brothers[14] led an uprising to defeat both the Nguyễn Lords in the South and the Trịnh rulers in the North.

The Hoàng Sa and Trường Sa became formally part of national consciousness in the early 19th century when the civil war ended. Nguyễn Ánh defeated the Tây Sơn forces and proclaimed himself as the emperor with title of Gia Long[15] of the unified kingdom of An Nam (pacified South) in 1802. Unlike other dynasties, he chose Huế City, in the central part of Vietnam, as the capital. Reportedly, he ordered a stocktake of all the lands in the kingdom and the resumption of the operations of the Hoàng Sa and Bắc Hải companies. In 1816, Gia Long formally claimed Hoàng Sa and Trường Sa as part of his kingdom territory.[16] In the same year, he assigned the Royal Navy and the Hoàng Sa flotilla to the Paracel area to do surveys and mapping of the sea routes. His successors kept on such state-sponsored practice of maintaining the annual patrolling and visits to the offshore islands. While the search for economic benefits continued, such operations also bore security significance. It was observed that the islands were considered as outer outposts of national defence.

Such thinking was evident in the archive of imperial court decrees. Emperor Minh Mạng's court recognized the offshore territories as "critical territorial frontiers" [*cương vực hiểm yếu*],[17] therefore the Royal Navy had been

---

13 Requoted from Ibid., p.9.

14 Three brothers were Nguyễn Ánh, Nguyễn Huệ and Nguyễn Lữ. Nguyễn Huệ later gained the throne to declare himself the King of An Nam with the title of *An Nam Quốc Vương*.

15 His title of Gia Long was the combination of the names "Gia Định" (the main city in the South) and "Thăng Long" (the capital city of Đại Việt), which reflected national unity.

16 Đỗ Thanh Hải, *Vietnam and the South China Sea,* p.31.

17 Hãn Nguyên Nguyễn Nhã, *Vietnam, Territoriality and the South China Sea.*

annually and continuously involved in the exploiting, surveying, planting of border makers, erecting of sovereignty steles, and other activities in the Paracels and Spratly archipelagos. For example, in the 17th Year of Minh Mạng (1836), the Ministry of Public Works reported the exploration mission of the Royal Navy Commander Phạm Hữu Nhật, together with Emperor Minh Mạng's following correction: "Order the Province of Quảng Ngãi to implement immediately and have him [Phạm Hữu Nhật] acknowledge receipt of the order." Emperor Minh Mạng also commented: "Anywhere any boat can reach, border markers should be planted." It was Emperor Minh Mạng who closely supervised these missions to the Paracel Islands, together with issuing decrees for reward or punishment. This fact revealed the utmost importance of this "special task force," as well as the state's willingness in exercising sovereignty.

The anxieties about maritime security were reasonable in the context the Nguyễn court anxiously observing the expansions of European powers across the region and the presence of their gunboats in its waters. In 1819, the British occupied Singapore and set up colonial government there. In 1840, they forced the Qing to open China's ports through the Opium War. China gradually made a series of concessions to both the European powers and the United States. When diplomacy did not bring assurance, Minh Mạng proceeded with a ban on Christianity in Vietnam and executed a number of priests who defied the order. In 1847, French warships went into the Hàn River and bombarded Đà Nẵng to place pressure for the release of Bishop Lefebvre, captured by the Thiệu Trị court. In 1858, after its demands for establishment of a consulate and a trading post in Đà Nẵng were refused by Emperor, a flotilla of twelve French warships opened fire on Đà Nẵng and captured the two maritime ports of An Hải and Điện Hải.[18] The war broke out, but it was clear that Vietnam's Royal Navy and coastal defensive systems were overwhelmed by the powerful cannons of the advanced French warships. In 1859, the French attacked and occupied Gia Định. In 1861, Mỹ Tho, Biên Hòa and Bà Rịa fell to the French control. In 1873, French armies launched an assault to take over Hanoi. It was clear that to modern Vietnam, the biggest threat no longer came from the North or the South, but the East, where it had a large swathe of maritime domain but no capacity to control it. The lack of hinterland coupled with the long coastline made the country extremely exposed to seaborne attacks.

18 Vũ Hồng Liên and Peter D. Sharrock, *Descending Dragon, Rising Tiger*, London: Reaktion Books, pp.153–75.

The contest for Hoàng Sa and Trường Sa

By 1885, the French expeditionary forces managed to defeat all Vietnamese resistance and set up its colonial rule across Vietnam. In 1884, France and the Nguyễn Dynasty entered into the Treaty of French Protectorate, in which the French were in charge of defending and governing all of the Indochinese region, including Cambodia, Laos, and Vietnam. For the matter of divide and rule, France split Vietnam into three regions. The South, or Nam Kỳ, was named Cochinchina and was considered as a French overseas territory. The North, or Bắc Bộ, was named Tonkin in French and was regarded as a protectorate. The central region, or Trung Kỳ, was called Annam and was governed by the Vietnamese emperor with direction of the French authority. Though these regions carried different administrative status, they were all run by French-appointed officials, called the *Résident-Supérieur*. In 1897, the whole of Indochina was administered by a civil administration under a Governor General.[19]

In the early stage of its rule over Indochina, the French administration did not pay much attention to the offshore islands governed by Annam. A couple of times, the Annam court appealed to the French authority to pay more attention to such territories. The requests often fell on deaf ears, perhaps because the French rulers were busy with fighting revolts from one place to another. Additionally, the French were by and large in entire control of Indochina and the nearby waters; the remote, uninhabited islets did not have much value to their rule. As the areas were considered hazardous for navigation, the Indochinese Governor General Paul Doumer gave an order to build a lighthouse on the Paracels in 1899.[20] However, the plan was later abandoned, mostly due to the lack of funds. The rulers of Indochina were seemingly not aware that the area was later surveyed by an expedition of Kwangtung Province led by Admiral Li Chun in 1909.

Perhaps the increased presence of the Japanese navy in the SCS prompted French Indochina to pay more attention to the offshore territories. Researchers from the Oceanographic Institute in Nha Trang were sent to the Paracels in 1925 and the Spratlys in 1927.[21] On December 4, 1931, the French government stated its claim over the Paracels in a protest against China's permit for guano mining in the area.[22] France claimed the Paracels

[19] Vũ Hồng Liên and Peter D. Sharrock, *Descending Dragon, Rising Tiger*, pp. 176–77.

[20] Gerard Sasges, "Absent Maps, Marine Science, and the Reimagination of the South China Sea, 1922–1939," *The Journal of Asian Studies*, vol.75, No.1, 2016, p.164.

[21] Marwyn Samuels, *Contest for the South China Sea*, New York: Methuen, 1982, p.60.

[22] Gerard Sasges, "Absent Maps, Marine Science, and the Reimagination of the South China Sea, 1922–1939," p.164.

as part of Indochina on the record of the Gia Long Emperor's assertion in 1816 and Annam's construction of a temple and a stone tablet on one islet in 1835.[23] In June 1932, the French authority in Indochina renamed the Paracel Islands the *Delegation des Paracels*, and included the islands administratively within Thừa Thiên-Huế, Annam.

The French were also worried about the Spratlys. In 1925, the French authority over Cochinchina put the Spratlys under the administration of Bà Rịa province. When the Japanese expressed interest in the islands and reefs off the west of the Philippines, France was worried about Japanese penetration into the area.[24] In April 1930, the French warship *Malicieuse* was dispatched to the area, and it was reported that its commander declared French sovereignty over the Spratly Islands and adjacent features. France took another step forward, proclaiming an annexation of six islands, namely Spratly, Amboyna Cay, Itu Aba, Les Deux Iles, Loaita and Thi Tu, in the *Journal Officiel* of July 26, 1933. It was clear that France's claims over the Paracels and Spratlys were not unchallenged. Over the Paracels, French Indochina's assertion met with Chinese protests. On the Spratlys, French incorporation was disputed by the Chinese and Japanese, though initially the Chinese mistook them as the Paracels. Though the British also claimed sovereignty over the Spratlys and Amboyna Cay, they did not issue formal protests.[25]

Historical evidence shows that the French viewed the Paracel and Spratly archipelagos from a security and strategic point of view. A report of 1937 came to an observation that these islets had little commercial value, but they could be used as a springboard for Japanese advancement into the South.[26] In the run-up to the Second World War, the Japanese were increasingly interested in establishing footholds in the SCS. As the tensions built up between China and Japan, French Indochina decided to take actions to forestall Japanese occupation by establishing a more permanent presence over the uninhabited rocks and islets. In June 1938, French Indochina worked out a plan to build a meteorological mission in Itu Aba. At the same time, it sent a task force to construct lighthouses and weather stations in the Woody and Pattle Islands of the Paracels. A Franco-Annamite military detachment of was stationed in these two islands. Reportedly, while Pattle Island hosted only Franco-Vietnamese detachments, Woody Island became a shared place

[23] Stein Tønnesson, "The South China Sea in the Age of European Decline," *Modern Asia Studies*, Vol.40, No.1, 2006, p.4.

[24] Ibid.

[25] Ibid., p.6.

[26] Ibid., p.9.

between the Indochinese and Japanese. In the Spratly area, the Indochinese and Japanese also co-existed on the Itu Aba and Spratly Islands.

During the Second World War, the SCS and all Indochina were basically under Japanese control. French Indochina effectively was governed by the Japanese expeditionary forces. After the war ended, France sought to revive its colonial rule over Indochina and its claimed offshore territories. In January 1947, the warship *Le Tonkinois* was sent to the Paracels and a garrison was established on Pattle Island. The French tried to persuade Chiang Kai-shek's troops to withdraw from Woody Island but without success. In 1946, the warship *Chevreud* made a visit to Spratly Island and Itu Aba Island. By October 1950, the administration of the Paracels was handed over to the South Vietnamese authority. It should be noted that, by 1956, Vietnam was actually split into two states, the Democratic Republic of Vietnam in the North and the Republic of Vietnam in the South, in short South Vietnam. In April 1956, when the French withdrew from Indochina under the provisions of the Geneva Accord, the South Vietnamese took over the Spratly Islands and sent a detachment there to guard the area. However, the conflicts dragged on in Vietnam, and the involvement of great powers in the region prompted special interests in the remote, barren rocks in the middle of the sea. The contest over the islands became fiercer. In 1974, the Chinese launched an military attack to expel the South Vietnamese from the Crescent Group in the Paracels. In 1988, a short conflict broke out, and the Chinese established its first presence in the Spratlys.

Chinese expansion into the Paracels and Spratlys in the 1970s and 1980s also reflected opportune geopolitical calculations in Beijing. By 1956, the Paracels were divided into two parts. The People's Republic of China occupied the eastern side; the Amphitrite Group fell under the control of the Republic of Vietnam. Between 1956 and 1973, there were no clashes between the two sides. However, when the US decided to withdraw its troops from Vietnamese battlefields, and it looked more likely that Hanoi would win over Saigon, China saw a window of opportunity to take over the Crescent Group. It was also a move to pre-empt the takeover of the islands by the North Vietnamese. It seemed that China rightly predicted that the US would abandon its ailing South Vietnamese ally. The then Nixon administration sought the support of China to "have an honorable end to the war in Vietnam."[27] In Vietnamese eyes, the US colluded with China, allowing the PLAN to take on its South Vietnamese ally in the Paracels.[28]

---

[27] Robert J. McMahon, Thomas W. Zeiler (eds), *Guide to US Foreign Policy: A Diplomatic History*, Los Angeles: CQ Press, 2012, p.628.

[28] Bộ Ngoại giao, *Sự thật về quan hệ Việt-Trung trong 30 năm qua [The Truth of Vietnam-China Relations over the last 30 years]*, Hanoi: Sự Thật Publisher, 1979, p.69

The Chinese communists' move to occupy the entire Paracels surprised the North Vietnamese leaders, and triggered concerns on their part. The latter, who had already been resentful of Beijing's rapprochement with Washington, rushed to take over the South Vietnamese positions in the Spratlys right after the final campaign to liberate Saigon in April 1975. The unified Vietnam inherited South Vietnamese claims over the Paracel and Spratly archipelagos, which were considered as part of its national sovereignty. In the early 1980s, in fear of Chinese expansions, Vietnam quickly moved to take over unoccupied islets in the Spratlys.[29] Not only did China/Taiwan have competing claims with Vietnam over the offshore territories, but the Philippines, Malaysia, and Brunei also joined the scramble for the Spratlys.

The main factor behind these countries' increased interest in these far-off, barren rocks and shoals of little economic value was perhaps the emergence of the new legal order of the oceans, when the law of the sea was being negotiated within the framework of the United Nations. The negotiation at UNCLOS 3 between 1973 and 1982 gave rise to the exclusive economic zone (EEZ) regime, which might give any tiny islet vast maritime entitlements if it is considered to qualify as a fully-fledged island.[30] Furthermore, the energy crisis in 1973 and 1979 prompted countries to look for hydrocarbon reservoirs to ensure their energy security. Under these circumstances, China made the move to occupy the Spratlys at the expense of Vietnam. In March 1988, the Chinese engaged in a brief skirmish with the Vietnamese to occupy six reefs: Fiery Cross, Cuarteron, Johnson South, Hughes, Subi and Gaven. Crippled by its involvement in the Cambodia conflicts and handicapped by international political isolation, Vietnam was reluctant to escalate the conflicts, and chose to express its protests through diplomatic channels and at the United Nations.

Maritime zones as security buffers

Though stepping out from the war as the victor, the leadership of the unified Vietnam did not feel safe. In fact, Vietnam quickly fell into fighting on three fronts. In the North, tensions over the land border with China quickly built up, resulting in a number of skirmishes. In the West, its relations with Pol Pot's regime in Cambodia also deteriorated quickly. The Khmer Rouge forces raided Vietnamese villages near the border more frequently, causing thousands of civilian deaths. Worrying about

[29] Đỗ Thanh Hải, *Vietnam and the South China Sea*, p.50.

[30] Under UNCLOS 1982, the fully-fledged island is a feature which is capable of sustaining inhabitation and having its own economic life.

the collusion between China and the Khmer Rouge, Vietnam invoked the right to self-defence to send troops to Cambodia. In the East, the Vietnamese were highly suspicious of China's ambition in its East Sea. The white book on Vietnam–China relations published in 1979 referred to a map of the nine-dash line in the Atlas of China published in 1973 as an indication of Chinese maritime expansionism.[31]

Unified Vietnam observably exhibited a strong desire to extend its sovereignty and jurisdiction beyond the shoreline. Right after the war, Lê Duẩn, Secretary General of the Communist Party of Vietnam, approached the chief of the Chinese Communist Party (CCP) to raise the issue of the Paracels and Spratlys.[32] As mentioned earlier, Vietnam's People's Navy were rushing to take over the South Vietnamese outposts in the Spratlys right after taking over Saigon. It quickly expanded occupation in the Spratlys in order to pre-empt any incursions from other claimants. On May 12, 1977, two years after unification, in light of the negotiation on the law of sea, Vietnam issued a statement on the territorial sea, contiguous zone, exclusive economic zone, and continental shelf (later referred to as the 1977 Statement). This statement staked a unilateral claim for the full range of maritime zones possible not only for the mainland, but also for its offshore islands. Shortly before the signature of the law of the sea convention (UNCLOS), Hanoi published a Declaration on the Baseline of the Territorial Waters of the Socialist Republic of Vietnam on November 12, 1982 (later referred to as the 1982 Declaration).

The rush to delineate boundaries for the waters under its sovereignty, sovereign rights, and jurisdiction were indicative of Vietnam's strong desire to expand eastward in the name of international law. It should be noted that the 1977 Statement followed closely the letters and the spirit of the Revised Single Negotiating Text, which came out after the fourth UNCLOS negotiation session in 1976. Some scholars argued that such claims reflected "maximalist interpretation" of UNCLOS provisions in three areas. First, Vietnam's claim to the full set of maritime zones for the offshore islets might not be justified, as the barren and tiny features in the Paracels and Spratlys were not suitable for living. Second, the straight baselines delineated in the 1982 Declaration might contain some inappropriate basepoints, especially those on the islands far off the coast. Third, the proposed application of

[31] Bộ Ngoại giao, *Sự thật về quan hệ Việt-Trung trong 30 năm qua,* p.17.

[32] Duy Chiến, "Con đường dẫn đến sự kiện đảo Gạc Ma" [Pathway to Johnson South Reef Skirmish], *Vietnamnet,* 16 June 2014. https://vietnamnet.vn/vn/tuanvietnam/con-duong-dan-den-su-kien-dao-gac-ma-181110.html.

historic waters to the Gulf of Tonkin and the Gulf of Thailand was also quite controversial.

It should be noted that excessive maritime claims were quite common, as countries always wanted to maximize their access to maritime resources. However, the case of Vietnam reflected not only narrowly defined concepts of interests but also excessive concerns about national security. The fresh memories of the wars against France and the US understandably shaped the revolutionary leaders' inclination to draw up a security bubble around its borders, either on land or at sea. The desire to control the sea beyond the country's coastline was strong, as the national history of Vietnam showed that, "ten out of fourteen invasions into the country were sea-borne inroads."[33] As security concerns dictated Vietnamese thinking, international law was no more than an instrument for the Vietnamese leaders to address existing challenges. In other words, Vietnam attempted to make full use of the new maritime order under UNCLOS to limit the navigation of the Western warships near its coast, while facilitating the country's eastward expansion into the sea.

Multi-layer defence

As the Cold War receded, Vietnam's view of international law, particularly UNCLOS, has also changed significantly. It is observed that Hanoi gradually came to the realization that peaceful settlement of existing disputes is a must, and reliance on international law is the best way to serve its interests. As a result, Vietnam actively sought negotiations with its neighbours to settle the sovereignty and maritime boundary disputes. It gradually aligned its maritime claims to the letters and the spirit of UNCLOS, abolishing excessive claims, to facilitate negotiations with other disputing parties. Just within a span of less than two decades, Vietnam managed to settle a number of outstanding disputes, such as disputes over land border and maritime boundary in the Gulf of Tonkin with China (1999 and 2000 respectively), disputes over maritime boundary with Thailand in the Gulf of Tonkin (1997), and continental shelf delimitation with Indonesia (2003).[34]

Yet, Vietnam's unease about its maritime façade persisted. Despite much efforts put on bilateral and multilateral engagements, the disputes in the South

---

[33] Nguyễn Trang, "Tuyên truyền về biển đảo cho ngư dân Quảng Ngãi [Information Session on the Sea and Islands for Quang Ngai's Fishermen]," *Sài Gòn Giải Phóng*, 21 June 2017.

[34] See Ramses Amer and Nguyễn Hồng Thao, "The management of Vietnam's border disputes: What Impact on its Sovereignty and Regional Integration?" *Contemporary Southeast Asia*, Vol.27, No.3, 2005.

China Sea proved to be intractable. Clearly, the reliance on international law, particularly UNCLOS 1982, and ASEAN multilateralism have not resulted in satisfactory outcomes. It is quite interesting that the concern about lack of strategic depth has come up in public discussion. One commentator raised a point that: "Due to its elongated S-shaped mainland and its narrow width (600 kilometers at the widest and 50 kilometers at the narrowest), our country is strategically shallow. Almost all our political, economic and social centres are not far from the coast, therefore vulnerable to sea-borne bombardments."[35] As a result, it is argued that, "Vietnam's sea and islands play an important role in national building and defence, adding to the country's strategic depth." The sea and islands can be considered as "many rounds of fences and barriers which form a multi-layer defensive system to defend the country's sky and waters." In these systems, the offshore features in the Spratlys were viewed as "furthermost outposts" to guard the maritime façade of the mainland.[36] It is contended that: "Therefore, building up bases, shelters, and logistic facilities for the Vietnam People's Navy and other forces would help increase defensive depth for our country."[37] Together with this multi-layer system, Vietnam has also developed a network of four-dimensional firepower, including land-based, submarine-based, subsurface-based, and air-based platforms.

Conclusion

Throughout the course of history, the sea and offshore territories in its East Sea have always been important to Vietnam. The lack of strategic depth and the nature of the riverine terrain have made the Vietnamese susceptible to possibilities of being attacked by powerful foreigners. In feudal times, Vietnam was under pressures from both the North and the South. Therefore, while resisting the expansions of the Chinese empire, Vietnam expanded southward at the expense of Champa and Khmer Kingdoms to increase the strategic depth vis-à-vis China. However, the more the Vietnamese march south, the more important the maritime domain to the east of Vietnam was to the country. The new geopolitical configuration prompted the Vietnamese rulers to place an eye on the offshore islets, which had been considered as "dangerous ground" for navigation, for both security and economic benefits.

[35] Hoàng Thanh, "Biển đảo quan trọng thế nào trong bảo vệ an ninh quốc phòng [How are the sea and islands important in national security and defence]," *Infornet*, 23 November 2017.

[36] Ibid.

[37] Ibid.

During colonial times, French Indochina, on behalf of Vietnam, maintained a claim over the Paracels and annexed the Spratlys, which resulted in its disputes with China and Japan. After the Second World War, the contest for these two island chains continued, and armed conflicts occurred on at least two occasions, and the Vietnamese lost control of the Paracels and some reefs in the Spratlys in 1974 and 1988 respectively. It is clear that, after the war with the United States and its South Vietnamese ally, unified Vietnam saw the East Sea more as the function of a security zone rather than a medium for connecting with its neighbours. Consequently, it made a couple of unilateral claims, which were seen as extreme interpretations of the UNCLOS provisions, in a bid to extend jurisdiction further from shore. As Vietnam opened up and integrated into the world community, Hanoi increasingly realized that aligning with international law, particularly UNCLOS, is in its interests. However, international law is not sufficient. As security concerns persisted, Vietnamese leaders opted for a multi-layer defensive system and a range of advanced weapon systems to compensate for the natural deficiency of strategic depth.

References

Amer, Ramses and Nguyễn, Hồng Thao. "The Management of Vietnam's Border Disputes: What Impact on Its Sovereignty and Regional Integration?" *Contemporary Southeast Asia*, Vol. 27, No.3, 2005.

Bộ Ngoại giao. *Sự thật về quan hệ Việt-Trung trong 30 năm qua [The Truth of Vietnam-China Relations over the last 30 years]*. Hanoi: Su That Publisher, 1979.

Childress, David Hatcher. *The Lost World of Cham*. Kempton: Adventures Unlimited Press, 2017, Chapter 1.

Đỗ, Thanh Hải. *Vietnam and the South China Sea*. New York: Routledge, 2017.

Duy Chiến. "Con đường dẫn đến sự kiện đảo Gạc Ma" [Pathway to Johnson South Reef Skirmish.] *Vietnamnet*, 16 June 2014. https://vietnamnet.vn/vn/tuanvietnam/con-duong-dan-den-su-kien-dao-gac-ma-181110.html

Hãn Nguyên, Nguyễn Nhã. *Vietnam, Territoriality and the South China Sea*. London: Routledge, 2019.

Hoàng, Thanh. "Biển đảo quan trọng thế nào trong bảo vệ an ninh quốc phòng [How are the sea and islands important in national security and defence?]" *Infornet*, 23 November 2017.

Kiernan, Ben. *Việt Nam: A History from Earliest Times to the Present*. New York: Oxford University Press, 2017.

McMahon, Robert J. and W. Zeiler, Thomas (eds). *Guide to US Foreign Policy: A Diplomatic History*. Los Angeles: CQ Press, 2012.

Ministry of Foreign Affairs (Socialist Republic of Vietnam). *The Hoang Sa and Truong Sa Archipelagoes*. Hanoi, 1981.

Nguyễn, Li Tana. *Cochinchina: Southern Vietnam in the Seventeenth and Eighteenth Centuries*. Ithaca: Cornell University Press, 1998.

Nguyễn, Trang. "Tuyên truyền về biển đảo cho ngư dân Quảng Ngãi [Information Session on the Sea and Islands for Quang Ngai's Fishermen]." *Sài Gòn Giải Phóng*, 21 June 2017.

Samuels, Marwyn. *Contest for the South China Sea*. New York: Methuen, 1982.

Sasges, Gerard. "Absent Maps, Marine Science, and the Reimagination of the South China Sea, 1922–1939." *The journal of Asian Studies*, Vol.75, No.1, 2016, 164.

Tucker, Spencer C. *Vietnam*. London: Routledge, 1998.

Tønnesson, Stein. "The South China Sea in the Age of European Decline." *Modern Asia Studies*, Vol.40, No.1, 2006, 4.

Vũ, Hồng Liên and Sharrock, Peter D. *Descending Dragon, Rising Tiger*. London: Reaktion Books.

6

The Philippines and the South China Sea Dispute: Duterte's Hedging Approach with China and the United States

Rommel C. Banlaoi

Introduction

When President Rodrigo Roa Duterte visited China for the fifth time on August 28 to September 1, 2019, the United States (US) Navy had conducted more Freedom of Navigation Operations (FONOPs) in 2019 than in any year during the same period, to challenge China's position in the South China Sea (SCS). Duterte's fifth visit to China provided him with opportunities to meet President Xi Jinping for the eighth time, amid increasing US–China rivalry in the SCS.

Duterte set a historic record for having the most meetings by a Filipino president with a Chinese counterpart during a mid-term in office, notwithstanding Manila's long-time security alliance with the US. Duterte's visits to China strongly demonstrated his ardent commitment to befriend and comprehensively engage with China on many pragmatic economic and political considerations, with a high expectation that this kind of appeasement could lead to the peaceful management of disputes in the SCS, a vital issue touching the core of Philippine national security interest.

One important outcome of Duterte's 2019 visit to China was the landmark implementation of the November 2018 Memorandum of Understanding (MOU) entered into by the Philippines and China to facilitate their joint cooperation on the development of oil and gas resources in the SCS, particularly in areas being claimed by the Philippines called the West Philippine Sea (WPS), located mainly in the Spratlys. The Philippines and China agreed to move to the next step of joint cooperation by creating steering committees tasked to supervise the process.

With the idea of joint cooperation in the SCS, opposition forces in the Philippines strongly criticized Duterte for being pro-China. Duterte's decision to terminate the US–Philippines Visiting Forces Agreement (VFA) in February 2020 also convinced critics that his administration has become really pro-China. But Philippine Defence Secretary Delfin Lorenzana, who served as Philippine defence attaché to the United States, asserted that Duterte "is pro-Filipino, not pro-China" in his foreign and security policy.[1]

A more nuanced analysis of Duterte's actions in the SCS, however, reveals his apparent pragmatism in dealing with China and the US. Though this pragmatism seemingly displays a pro-China position at the surface, it is arguably not changing the Philippines' long-standing policy towards China, the US and the SCS dispute. Like his predecessors, Duterte pursues the usual Philippine policy towards China of pursuing friendly diplomatic relations and peaceful settlement of disputes while maintaining good relations with the US. What Duterte has changed is his personal attitude towards China and the US and his official approach in dealing with the SCS dispute. Neorealist theory of international relations offers some explanations to this kind of foreign policy attitude.

Neorealism: balancing, bandwagoning, and hedging

Neorealism challenges the classical realist understanding of international systems. While classical realism regards states as the main unit of analysis in international relations, neorealism regards the international structure as the main analytical unit.[2] International anarchy is the main source of security dilemma for sovereign states. Security dilemma can drive states to go to war, though they do not want that situation to really occur.[3] John

1 Delfin Lorenzana, "Duterte is Pro-Filipino, Not Pro-China, Lorenzana," *Philippine Daily Inquirer* (20 June 2019).

2 Robert C. Art and Robert Jervis. *International Politics: Enduring Concepts and Contemporary Issues*, 4th edition (New York: Harper-Collins College Publishers, 1996).

3 Herbert Butterfield, *History and Human Relations*. London: Collins, 1951. Also see Shiping Tang, "The Security Dilemma: A Conceptual Analysis," *Security Studies*, 18:3, 2009: 587–623.

Herz popularized the concept of security dilemma to describe a situation of anarchy where states constantly aspire for power to address their security anxieties.[4] The structure of international anarchy defines the overall security situation in the SCS.[5]

Neorealism agrees with classical realism that states are all equal in terms of national interest, which is state survival in the international situation of anarchy. States are also equal in terms of their sovereign status in the international community. But neorealism strongly differs with classical realism by arguing that states are not equal in terms of their powers and capabilities. Factual recognition of unequal powers and capabilities between the Philippines and China deeply affects Duterte's attitude towards China. This attitude, in turn, greatly defines Duterte's pragmatic approach in dealing with the SCS dispute. Duterte recognizes the reality that China is a big power that is ascending to become a global power. On the other hand, the Philippines, like the majority of states in the international system, remains a small and developing state with fewer capabilities to fend for themselves. In facing the China challenge to Philippine foreign and security policy, Duterte refuses to behave like a major power. He prefers the Philippines to behave like other small states in dealing with major powers.

To overcome state vulnerability and to strengthen state resilience in the midst of international anarchy, diplomacies of small states inform Duterte's pragmatic foreign policy towards China and the SCS disputes.[6] Neorealism provides useful perspectives to understand the diplomacies of small states and to appreciate the role of weak states in international relations.[7]

Balancing is a strategic option that compels states to increase their powers and capabilities against more powerful and threatening states. Balancing is normally undertaken by a major power to match or even surpass the other major power. In the midst of major power rivalry, small states take the

---

4 John Herz, *International Politics in the Atomic Age* (New York: Columbia University Press, 1961) and John Herz, *Political Realism and Political Idealism: A Study in Theories and Realities* (Chicago: University of Chicago Press, 1961).

5 Rommel C. Banlaoi, "The State of Anarchy and Security Situation in the SCS: Difficulties in Passing a Code of Conduct After the Scarborough Standoff" in Teresita Ang See and Chito Sta. Romana, eds, *Philippines-China Relations: Sailing Beyond Disputed Waters*. (Quezon City: Philippine Association for Chinese Studies, 2013).

6 Andrew F. Cooper and Timothy M. Shaw, *The Diplomacies of Small States: Between Vulnerability and Resilience* (New York: Palgrave Macmillan, 2009).

7 Samir Hanna Kassab, *Weak States in International Relations Theory: The Cases of Armenia, Lebanon and Cambodia* (New York: Palgrave Macmillan, 2005).

balancing option by joining the established and dominant power against a rising power.[8]

Bandwagoning is considered to be the antithesis of balancing. It pursues an option taken by smaller and weaker states to join rather than balance a stronger and adversarial power.[9] Bandwagoning extends from the assumption that balancing a stronger power is costly and risky. Bandwagoning offers more benefits by reducing the cost and risk of balancing. In the context of major power rivalry, smaller states can join rather than oppose a rising power for pragmatic considerations. Small states are bandwagoning to avoid costly and unnecessary conflict with the rising power.[10]

Hedging offers the third strategic option for small states to survive in international anarchy where major power rivalry occurs. Rather than pursue balancing or bandwagoning acts, hedging offers the middle ground of neither balancing nor bandwagoning. Hedging encourages small states to take two sides rather choose from these sides. Small states hedge to compensate for their smallness and to overcome their lack of hard power to advance their national interests.[11] In fact, hedging has become the primary response of most states in the Asia-Pacific to address many strategic uncertainties unleashed by increasing competition between China and the US on key regional security issues.[12]

The Philippines' long-standing policy towards China and the South China Sea dispute

The Philippines established diplomatic relations with China on June 9, 1975. Since then, Philippine-China diplomatic relations have become one of the most important bilateral relations the Philippines has with foreign countries, next to the US.[13] Since then, Philippines-China relations have evolved to become comprehensive and multi-faceted.

---

8 G. John Ikenberry, "From Hegemony to the Balance of Power: The Rise of China and American Grand Strategy in East Asia," *International Journal of Korean Unification Studies*, Volume 23, Number 2 (2004): 41–63.

9 Kenneth Waltz, *Theory of International Politics* (New York: Random House, 1979). Also see Wright, Quincy. *The Study of War* (Chicago and London: University of Chicago Press, 1942).

10 Charles Chonghan Wu, "Hierarchy and Bandwagoning in Asia: The Rise of China and its Grand Strategy in the Post-Cold War Era" (Columbia: University of South Carolina, 2009).

11 Leah Sheerwood, "Small States' Strategic Hedging for Security and Interest," *Trends Research and Advisory* (14 September 2016).

12 Elena Atanassova-Cornelis, "Strategic concerns of the US and China, Regional Hedging and the Evolving Security Order in the Asia-Pacific." *ISA Asia-Pacific Conference* (City University of Hong Kong, 15–27 June 2016).

13 Rommel C. Banlaoi, *Defense and Military Cooperation Between the Philippines and China: Broadening Bilateral Ties in the Post-9/11 Era.* (Taipei: Chinese Council of Advanced Policy Studies, 2007).

From 1975 to 1995, Philippines-China relations enjoyed a period of normalization. However, normal diplomatic ties became troubled in 1995 when China asserted its sovereign control of the Mischief Reef. This encouraged the Philippine military to strongly push for the passage of the Armed Forces of the Philippines (AFP) Modernization Law to increase its capability to defend its national territory against external threats. The Philippine government also solicited the support of the members of the ASEAN Regional Forum (ARF) to deal with China. The Philippine government even sponsored the drafting of a regional code of conduct in the SCS to prohibit the building of any structures on the disputed islands. China, however, objected to the "internationalization" of the SCS dispute and opposed the effort to pass a regional code of conduct. China considered the South China dispute a bilateral concern.[14] Since the Mischief Reef incident, the SCS dispute has become a major thorny issue in Philippines-China relations.

Bilateral relations turned sourer in 2012 during the Scarborough Shoal standoff. The situation encouraged the Philippine government, under then President Benigno Aquino III, to submit its claims before international arbitration in 2013. But China vehemently rejected and ignored the arbitration. Because of the case, Philippines-China relations suffered the lowest moment in both countries' bilateral history.

Amid the SCS disputes, the Philippines pursues a policy of maintaining friendly ties with China, a policy established by former President Marcos (1975–86), sustained by former President Corazon Aquino (1986–92), peacefully managed by former President Fidel V. Ramos (1992–98) and former President Joseph Estrada (1998–2001), and enhanced by former President Arroyo (2001–10). It was during the administration of President Arroyo that the Philippines and China enjoyed the "golden age" of their bilateral relations. In 2005, then Chinese President Hu Jintao visited the Philippines. During this visit, the Philippines and China decided to set aside the SCS dispute in order to pursue joint development, leading to the adoption in 2005 of the Joint Marine Seismic Understanding (JMSU) in the SCS by China, the Philippines and Vietnam.

However, the Philippines stopped the implementation of JMSU because of domestic controversies. Under President Arroyo, the Philippine government pursued the bandwagoning policy with China after the US became lukewarm with Arroyo when Manila withdrew its troops from Iraq in 2004. Philippines-China relations severely deteriorated under President Benigno Aquino III (2010–16). The Scarborough Shoal standoff in 2012 and subsequent filing

[14] Ibid.

of an arbitration case by the Philippines against China in 2013 led to the rapid deterioration of their bilateral ties under the Aquino III administration. President Aquino III pursued the balancing policy against China when Manila solidified its security alliance with the US, through the signing of the Enhanced Defense Cooperation Agreement (EDCA) in 2014.

Duterte's hedging approach with the US

The Philippines under Duterte is pursuing the hedging approach in order to deal with the US and China in the SCS. With hedging, Duterte is, in fact, reaffirming rather than changing the Philippines' long-standing policy on the SCS. If there is any change in Duterte's actions towards the US, China and the SCS dispute, the change, apparently, is in the approach and not in the policy itself. Duterte's hedging approach is vividly found in his various speeches and two major official documents: *National Security Policy 2017–2022* (NSP) and the *National Security Strategy 2018* (NSS).

Duterte underscores that the NSP is in line "with our constitutional mandate to serve and protect the people."[15] This alone indicates that Duterte is not changing state policy but upholding it. Duterte contends that the NSP "embodies our efforts to address all threats to our nation's survival and way of life."[16] One major external security issue that the NSP identifies is the situation in the West Philippine Sea (WPS). The NSP says that the territorial dispute in the WPS "remains to be the foremost security challenge to the Philippines' sovereignty and territorial integrity."[17]

By citing the ruling of the Tribunal, the NSP is upholding and not abandoning the decision. This is contrary to the perception that Duterte has totally neglected the Arbitral verdict just to accommodate China. Duterte decided not to flaunt the ruling because of his intention to promote friendly ties with China. In stark contrast with Aquino III, Duterte is pursuing a security strategy that is cautious, pragmatic, and reconciliatory towards China.[18]

---

15 *National Security Policy 2017–2022* (Office of the President Malacanang Palace, Manila, 2017).

16 Ibid.

17 Ibid.

18 Rommel C. Banlaoi, "Post-Arbitration SCS: Philippines' Security Policy Options and Future Prospects" in Fu-Kuo Liu, Keyuan Zou, Shicun Wu and Jonathan Spangler, eds. *SCS Lawfare: Post-Arbitration Policy Options and Future Prospects*. (Taipei: SCS Think Tank and Taiwan Center for Security Studies, 2017): 99–110. Also see Rodrigo Roa Duterte, Speech delivered during his First Cabinet Meeting (Manila: Malacanang Palace, 30 June 2016).

The Philippines under Duterte is not bandwagoning to China, as the country continues to maintain its strong security alliance with the US. Though critical of American security policy, Duterte recognizes the strategic value of a Philippine-US alliance. His NSS even asserts, "The Philippines will work closely with the US on a whole range of issues, including shared security and economic concerns."[19]

Despite Duterte's rapprochement with China, he maintains the security alliance with the US, which for the Pentagon is America's oldest security alliance in the Indo-Pacific. During his visit to the Philippines in November 2017, President Donald Trump even declared, "We have a very, very strong relationship with the Philippines, which is really important – less so for trade, in this case, than for military purposes."[20]

On July 15–16, 2019, the Philippines and the US held their 8th Bilateral Strategic Dialogue (BSD). The BSD is the principal forum for discussing the full range of political, security, and economic cooperation between the Philippines and the United States. Aside from the BSD, Filipino and American defence officials hold regular meetings of the Mutual Defense Board (MDB) and the Security Engagement Board (SEB). The MDB tackles vital issues pertaining to the implementation of the Mutual Defense Treaty (MDT) covering traditional security issues of mutual military protection in case of armed attacks. The SEB, on the other hand, covers non-traditional security issues covered by EDCA, like international terrorism, transnational crimes, maritime domain awareness, and humanitarian assistance and disaster response, among others.

In other words, the Philippine government continues to maintain good relations with the US while strengthening friendly ties with China. Although Duterte maintains Philippine relations with the US, he is not strictly balancing China as he continues to value his friendship with China. Duterte is, in fact, hedging with the two major powers. Duterte calls it an independent foreign policy. Duterte's decision to terminate the VFA is part of the pursuance of an independent Philippine foreign policy.[21] Despite the VFA termination, the Philippine government still eyes continued military ties with the US.[22]

---

[19] *National Security Strategy* (Office of the President: Malacanang Palace Manila, 2018). Also see Rodrigo Roa Duterte, Remarks during the Courtesy Call of US Secretary Rex Tillerson (Manila: Malacanang Palace, 7 August 2017).

[20] Donald Trump, Remarks during his Meeting with President Rodrigo Duterte at the sideline of the East Asia Summit. (Manila: International Convention Center, 13 November 2017).

[21] "Duterte defends VFA termination: Territory of the Americans or a province of China?," *The Filipino Times* (26 February 2020).

[22] "US, PH eye continued military ties after VFA," *Philippine Daily Inquirer* (19 February 2020).

Duterte's hedging approach with China

As part of his hedging approach in the SCS, Duterte pursues friendly ties with China while strengthening security alliance with the US. An outcome of Duterte's friendly relations with China is the creation of the Philippines-China Bilateral Consultative Mechanism in the SCS (BCM).

The Philippines and China established the BCM after Duterte's state visit to China in 2016. One important result of the Duterte-Xi meeting was the resumption of fishing activities of Filipino fishers in the Scarborough Shoal. In their Joint Statement issued in October 2016, "Both sides agree to continue discussions on confidence-building measures to increase mutual trust and confidence and to exercise self-restraint in the conduct of activities in the SCS that would complicate or escalate disputes and affect peace and stability."[23]

As a result, the Philippines and China held their First BCM in Guiyang, Guizhou Province, China on May 19, 2017. It was during this period that security experts, particularly from Vietnam, raised serious concerns on China's "expansive" construction activities on Fiery Cross, Subi, and Mischief Reefs in the Spratly Islands and on North, Tree, and Triton Islands in the Paracel Islands.[24] But the BCM, as a pioneering bilateral mechanism, contributed enormously to the warming of friendly relations between the Philippines and China, which in turn helped in calming the overall security situation in the SCS under the first year of the Duterte presidency. The First BCM was a milestone in Philippines-China relations as it opened practical channels of communication between the two countries in dealing with many issues in the SCS.[25]

On February 13, 2018, both countries held the Second BCM in Manila, amid international criticism of China's increased "militarization" in the SCS. But during the meeting, the Philippines and China levelled up the nature of their agenda by discussing "ways to manage and prevent incidents at sea, promote dialogue and cooperation on maritime issues, and enhance mutual trust and confidence." They also discussed "ways to strengthen cooperation

---

[23] *Joint Statement of the Republic of the Philippines and the People's Republic of China*. Beijing (21 October 2016).

[24] Hong Thao Nguyen and Binh Ton-Nu Thanh. "Perspectives on the South China Sea Disputes in 2018," Analysis from Maritime Awareness Project (National Bureau of Asian Research, March 2018).

[25] *Joint Press Release for the First Meeting of the Philippines-China Bilateral Consultative Mechanism on the SCS* (Guizhou, China, 19 May 2017).

in areas such as marine environmental protection, fisheries, marine scientific research, and oil and gas, without prejudice to their respective positions on sovereignty, sovereign rights, and jurisdiction."[26]

On October 18, 2018, the Philippines and China held the Third BCM in Beijing despite reports of China's "continuing militarization" in the SCS, such as the landing of China military transport planes on Mischief Reef, deployment of advanced jamming equipment in Fiery Cross Reef, and installation of surface air missiles and anti-ship cruise missiles in the Spratlys.[27] Thus, during this meeting, the Philippines and China reiterated the need to promote "cooperation on joint exploration and development of maritime oil and gas" in the SCS. Both countries also:

> reaffirmed their commitment to the principles of freedom of navigation in and over flight above the SCS, freedom of international commerce and other peaceful uses of the sea, addressing territorial and jurisdictional disputes by peaceful means, without resorting to the threat or directly concerned and the exercise of self-restraint, in accordance with universally recognized principles of international law, including the Charter of the United Nations and the 1982 United Nations Convention on the Law of the Sea.[28]

Results of the Second and Third BCMs provided meaningful inputs to the MOU in oil and gas development in the SCS signed by the two countries during the state visit to Manila of President Xi in November 2018. The MOU was a breakthrough in their bilateral ties as it demonstrated the two countries' serious efforts to promote practical cooperation through joint development, which has been viewed as the way ahead in the SCS.[29] Though opposition groups in the Philippines criticized the MOU, both parties

[26] *Joint Press Release for the Second Meeting of the Philippines-China Bilateral Consultative Mechanism on the SCS* (Manila, Philippines, 13 February 2018).

[27] Office of the Secretary of Defense. *Military and Security Developments Involving the People's Republic of China 2018*. Annual Report to Congress (16 March 2018).

[28] *Joint Press Release for the Third Meeting of the Philippines-China Bilateral Consultative Mechanism on the SCS* (Beijing, China, 18 October 2018).

[29] Rommel C. Banlaoi, "Functional Cooperation and Joint Development: A Way Ahead in the SCS" in Schicun Wu and Nong Hong, eds. *Recent Developments in the South China Sea Dispute: The Prospect of a Joint Development Regime* (London and New York: Routledge, 2014).

assured their public that the signing of the MOU is "without prejudice to the respective legal positions of both governments."[30]

On April 2–3, 2019, the two countries held the Fourth BCM in Manila amid controversies pertaining to the alleged strong presence of Chinese maritime militias near Pag-Asa Island. During the meeting, the Philippines and China "reaffirmed their commitment to cooperate and to continue to find ways forward to strengthen mutual trust and confidence."[31] Both parties reiterated, "that the relevant differences between China and the Philippines in the SCS is only part of the bilateral ties and should not affect the mutually beneficial cooperation in other fields." They also reaffirmed, "the importance of maintaining and promoting regional peace and stability, freedom of navigation in and over-flight above the SCS." More importantly, both parties reaffirmed, "their commitment to address their territorial and jurisdictional disputes by peaceful means, without resorting to or threatening with force, through friendly consultations and negotiations by sovereign states directly concerned."[32]

To sustain the achievements of the BCM, the Philippines and China held the Fifth BCM on October 28, 2019 in Beijing. They held the BCM while China and Vietnam were having a standoff in the Paracels over the issue of oilrigs in the area. During the Fifth BCM, both parties reaffirmed "the importance of the BCM as a platform for regular dialogue that can play a significant role in the enhanced and stable development of bilateral relations and peace and stability in the South China Sea."[33] An important outcome of the Fifth BCM was the creation of the Working Group on Political Security, Fisheries Cooperation, and the Working Group on Marine Scientific Research and Marine Environmental Protection. These two working groups are deemed important for the strict implementation of the DOC and the immediate conclusion of COC.

Through the BCM, the Philippine government was able to deal directly with China on the SCS. The BCM allowed both countries to discuss with each other their existing differences as well as their common interests on the SCS. The BCM provides greater clarity and transparency on some details of their respective national positions that are made known candidly

---

30 *Memorandum of Understanding (MOU) on Cooperation on Oil and Gas Development between the Government of the People's Republic of China and the Government of the Republic of the Philippines* (Manila, Philippines, 20 November 2018).

31 *Joint Press Release for the Fourth Meeting of the Philippines-China Bilateral Consultative Mechanism on the SCS* (Manila, Philippines, 2–3 April 2019).

32 Ibid.

33 *Joint Press Release for the Fifth Meeting of the Philippines-China Bilateral Consultative Mechanism on the SCS* (Manila, Philippines, 28 October 2019).

to each other, unlike before where details of their national positions were deliberately kept secret away from each other.

The benefits of Duterte's hedging approach

Benefits of hedging with China

By pursuing friendly relations with China, Duterte reached a mutual personal and official understanding with Xi to deliberately avoid conflicts in the SCS. As a result of this understanding between the two leaders, Filipinos were able to resume their fishing activities in the Scarborough Shoal while the Armed Forces of the Philippines (AFP) was able to resume their regular supply and personnel rotation missions in the Kalayaan Island Group (KIG). More importantly, the AFP was able to improve its facilities in Pag-Asa Island by repairing its runway and constructing a pier for effective docking of Philippine ships.

By calming the SCS dispute with China, Duterte was able to get huge economic assistance from Beijing to support its national development programmes under its pet Build Build Build Programme. Because of his friendly ties with China, the Philippines under Duterte has become an integral part of China's Belt and Road Initiative (BRI). Through the BRI, China agrees to fund a total of 12 big-ticket infrastructure projects in the Philippines, worth a total of US$167 billion. Through the BRI, China is also funding the New Centennial Water Source Kaliwa Water Dam Project, worth US$211 million. China has also started construction of the Chico River Irrigation Project, worth US$186 million. This project can irrigate more than 8,700 hectares of agricultural land in Kalinga and Cagayan provinces of Northern Philippines.

China supports major Philippine infrastructure projects nationwide from Luzon, Visayas, and Mindanao including major industrial park projects in Clark, Subic, and Cagayan Valley. In fact, during the visit of President Xi to the Philippines in November 2018, he signed 29 agreements aiming to achieve *comprehensive strategic cooperation* between the Philippines and China. Areas of cooperation include oil and gas exploration, agricultural modernization, education, information technology, humanitarian assistance, and of course infrastructures. During the 2nd BRI Forum in Beijing on April 25–27, 2019, China and the Philippines signed five additional agreements covering cooperation in education, anti-corruption, and drug rehabilitation. During his fifth visit to China in August 2019, Duterte signed six bilateral agreements covering cooperation in higher education, science and technology, mutual assistance on custom matters, general customs administration, container inspections, and utilization of concessional loans.

During the Marawi Siege, China immediately provided the Philippines with counterterrorism assistance of RMB50 million (US$7 million) covering the delivery of 3,000 assault rifles and RMB6 million (US$1 million) worth rounds of ammunition to support the Philippine military in its urban battle against ISIS (Da'esh) fighters. The Marawi Siege demonstrated the importance of counterterrorism cooperation to improve overall bilateral relations between the Philippines and China.[34]

However, there are fears that the Philippines is in danger of falling into a China debt trap. Though President Xi Jinping has already dismissed this fear in his speech to the 2nd BRI Forum, it continues to create anxieties for some Filipinos because of domestic oppositions. Groups and personalities opposed to President Duterte are using the debt trap issue to challenge the current achievements in Philippines–China relations.

Moreover, Duterte's conciliation with Beijing resulted in the influx of Chinese nationals in the Philippines to enjoy tourism, conduct business, or seek employment. As of the end of 2018, the Department of Tourism reported that 1.25 million Chinese nationals have entered the Philippines with tourist visas. By the end of 2019, it is expected that arrivals of Chinese nationals to the Philippines will reach 1.5 million, making China the number one source of foreign tourists to the Philippines, generating P3.2 billion (US$630 million) of revenues to the Philippine government.

Benefits of hedging with the US

While strengthening friendship with China, Duterte is also maintaining good relations with the US. Despite his anti-American rhetoric and his termination of the VFA, Duterte continues to value Philippine relationship with the US, considering cultural familiarities, common historical experiences, and strong economic ties.

Despite strong US criticism of Duterte's "war on drugs," the US gave the Philippines a US$32 million worth of assistance to the Philippine National Police (PNP) to improve policing standards, particularly in counterterrorism. At the height of the Marawi Siege in 2017, the US provided the Philippines with counterterrorism assistance in terms of intelligence training, military technical support, and ground tactical advice by US military Special Forces.

[34] Rommel C. Banlaoi, "Marawi City Siege and Its Aftermath: Opportunities and Challenges in Counterterrorism Cooperation" in Rommel C. Banlaoi, ed. *Philippines-China Relations: Geopolitics, Economics and Counterterrorism* (Quezon City: Philippine Association for Chinese Studies, 2019).

The US also donated an initial amount of US$14.7 million in aid to help residents forced out of their homes during the siege.

In the aftermath of the Marawi Siege, in 2018 the Philippines received from the US four OV-10B planes. The AFP also received a donation of US$15 million to develop the Philippine military's surveillance and reconnaissance system. Overall, the Philippines received from the US a total of US$193.5 million in military aid in 2018, aside from arms sales.

Despite Duterte's earlier statement about rejecting US military weapons sales to the Philippines, the Pentagon delivered 10 M-107 .50 calibre sniper rifles to the AFP on July 17, 2019. By the end of 2019, the Philippines was due to have received a total of US$145.6 million in military aid from the US. The US Embassy in the Philippines even claimed that the Philippines was receiving US$250 million worth of annual assistance from the US in the areas of security, military equipment, and exchange programmes.[35] Though the termination of the VFA could affect future deliveries of this military assistance, the US is open to negotiating with the Philippines to come out with an agreement similar to the VFA where the Philippines can enjoy better deals.

Since Duterte assumed office in 2016, the US has conducted more than 200 small-to-medium sized joint military and training exercises with the Philippines. For 2020, the Philippines and the US planned to conduct more than 300 joint military exercises. The largest of these military exercises is the Balikatan ("Shoulder-to-Shoulder"), which is being held annually. In April 2019, the US and the Philippines held the Balikatan 2019, involving 4,000 Filipino, 3,500 American, and 50 Australian soldiers. So far, this was the largest Balikatan exercise in the history of both countries' bilateral relations. The Balikatan 2019 involved counterterrorism training, amphibious operations, live-fire training, urban operations training, aviation operations, and bilateral planning.[36]

Most importantly, the Philippine government never hampered nor criticized America's freedom of navigation operations (FONOPs) in the SCS. When the *USS Preble* of the US 7th Fleet conducted FONOPs within 12 nautical miles of the Scarborough Shoal on May 20, 2019, to challenge China's "excessive claims" in the SCS, Duterte simply commented that the US was just enjoying the right of innocent passage.

In short, the Philippine-American alliance has been solid since Duterte assumed the presidency in 2016 until the termination of the VFA in February

[35] US Embassy in the Philippines. "8th Philippines-United States Bilateral Strategic Dialogue (BSD) Joint Statement" (Manila, Philippines, 17 July 2019).

[36] Armed Forces of the Philippines. *Balikatan 2019 Reference Folder* (1 April 2019).

2020. Duterte has been utilizing the Philippine security alliance with the US as a fallback position if his current approach to China fails to achieve its intended goals. Though the termination of the VFA has placed this security alliance at the crossroads, there have been efforts to rescue it from breaking because of security uncertainties associated with the resurgence of China as an Asian power.

Conclusion

Duterte's approach to the SCS dispute fervently exhibits the neorealist logic of hedging. Duterte's cautious hedging with China and with the US intends to get the best of both worlds. Duterte strengthens his friendship with China in order to calm the security situation in the SCS and to get the needed financial support for his national economic development. Duterte has economic needs that China is expected to provide.

But Duterte also has real security needs in the SCS that the US is expected to guarantee. China's activities in the SCS continue to create security anxieties in the Philippines despite Duterte's efforts not to overreact when controversial incidents occur on the issue. Thus, Duterte plays the US card to meet the Philippines' security requirements. Though the use of the US card is now in doubt with the VFA termination, the Philippine government is open to use other options to deal with China in the SCS. Building an autonomous defence is one of the options.

As the Philippines attempts to be independent and aspires to pursue autonomous defence, there is no doubt that the Philippines still benefits from the US security umbrella in Asia and the wider Indo-Pacific region. The US also serves as a security fallback for the Philippines and as political leverage in dealing with China.

It is still premature to assess the long-term repercussions of Duterte's hedging approach to Philippine security. There are indications for Duterte in sustaining this approach until the end of his term in 2022. Whether the next Philippine administration will pursue the same approach remains to be seen.

There is neither guarantee nor certainty that the next Philippine administration will follow the Duterte approach towards China and the SCS. What is certain at the moment is Duterte's resolve to maintain his strong-willed pragmatism in pursuing an independent Philippine foreign and security policy that is viewed to be expedient in promoting Philippine national interests in the SCS. It is also very certain that the Philippines cannot peacefully manage the SCS dispute without a friendly relationship with and the full cooperation of China.

References

Armed Forces of the Philippines. *Balikatan 2019 Reference Folder.* April 1, 2019.

Art, Robert C. and Robert Jervis. *International Politics: Enduring Concepts and Contemporary Issues*, 4th edition. New York: Harper-Collins College Publishers, 1996.

Atanassova-Cornelis, Elena. "Strategic concerns of the US and China, Regional Hedging and the Evolving Security Order in the Asia-Pacific." ISA Asia-Pacific Conference, City University of Hong Kong, June 15–27, 2016.

Banlaoi, Rommel C. *Defense and Military Cooperation Between the Philippines and China: Broadening Bilateral Ties in the Post-9/11 Era.* Taipei: Chinese Council of Advanced Policy Studies, 2007.

Banlaoi, Rommel C. *Drivers of Philippine Foreign and Security Policy Towards SCS Disputes Under President Aquino III: Current Conflicts and Prospects for Cooperation in Philippine Relations with China.* PhD Dissertation: Jinan University, China, 2015.

Banlaoi, Rommel C. "Functional Cooperation and Joint Development: A Way Ahead in the SCS" in Wu Schicun and Nong Hong, eds. *Recent Developments in the SCS Dispute: The Prospect of a Joint Development Regime.* London: Routledge, 2014: 228–40.

Banlaoi, Rommel C., "Marawi City Siege and Its Aftermath: Opportunities and Challenges in Counterterrorism Cooperation" in Rommel Banlaoi, ed. *Philippines-China Relations: Geopolitics, Economics and Counterterrorism.* Quezon City: Philippine Association for Chinese Studies, 2019.

Banlaoi, Rommel C. "Post-Arbitration SCS: Philippines' Security Policy Options and Future Prospects" in Fu-Kuo Liu, Keyuan Zou, Shicun Wu and Jonathan Spangler, eds. *SCS Lawfare: Post-Arbitration Policy Options and Future Prospects.* Taipei: SCS Think Tank and Taiwan Center for Security Studies, 2017.

Banlaoi, Rommel C. "The State of Anarchy and Security Situation in the SCS: Difficulties in Passing a Code of Conduct After the Scarborough Standoff" in Teresita Ang See and Chito Sta. Romana, eds. *Philippines-China Relations: Sailing Beyond Disputed Waters.* Quezon City: Philippine Association for Chinese Studies, 2013.

Butterfield, Herbert. *History and Human Relations.* London: Collins, 1951.

Cooper, Andrew F. and Timothy M. Shaw. *The Diplomacies of Small States: Between Vulnerability and Resilience.* New York: Palgrave Macmillan, 2009.

Duterte, Rodrigo Roa. "4th State of the Nation Address," 22 July 2019.

Duterte, Rodrigo Roa. Remarks during the Courtesy Call of US Secretary Rex Tillerson. Manila: Malacanang Palace, 7 August 2017.

Duterte, Rodrigo Roa. Speech delivered during his First Cabinet Meeting. Manila: Malacanang Palace, 30 June 2016.

Herz, John. *International Politics in the Atomic Age*. New York: Columbia University Press, 1961.

Herz, John. *Political Realism and Political Idealism: A Study in Theories and Realities.* Chicago: University of Chicago Press, 1961.

Ikenberry, G. John. "From Hegemony to the Balance of Power: The Rise of China and American Grand Strategy in East Asia," *International Journal of Korean Unification Studies*, Volume 23, Number 2 (2004): 41–63.

Joint Press Release for the Fifth Meeting of the Philippines-China Bilateral Consultative Mechanism on the SCS. Manila, 28 October 2019.

Joint Press Release for the First Meeting of the Philippines-China Bilateral Consultative Mechanism on the SCS. Guizhou, 19 May 2017.

Joint Press Release for the Fourth Meeting of the Philippines-China Bilateral Consultative Mechanism on the SCS. Manila, 2–3 April 2019.

Joint Press Release for the Second Meeting of the Philippines-China Bilateral Consultative Mechanism on the SCS. Manila, 13 February 2018.

Joint Press Release for the Third Meeting of the Philippines-China Bilateral Consultative Mechanism on the SCS. Beijing, 18 October 2018.

Joint Statement of the Republic of the Philippines and the People's Republic of China. Beijing, 21 October 2016.

Kassab, Samir Hanna. *Weak States in International Relations Theory: The Cases of Armenia, Lebanon and Cambodia.* New York: Palgrave Macmillan, 2005.

Lorenzana, Delfin. "Duterte is Pro-Filipino, Not Pro-China, Lorenzana," *Philippine Daily Inquirer*, 20 June 2019.

Memorandum of Understanding (MOU) on Cooperation on Oil and Gas Development between the Government of the People's Republic of China and the Government of the Republic of the Philippines. Manila, 20 November 2018.

National Security Policy 2017–2022. Office of the President, Malacanang Palace, Manila, 2017.

National Security Strategy. Malacanang Palace, Manila: Office of the President, 2018.

Nguyen, Hong Thao and Binh Ton-Nu Thanh. "Perspectives on the South China Sea Disputes in 2018," Analysis from Maritime Awareness Project, National Bureau of Asian Research, March 2018.

Office of the Secretary of Defense. *Military and Security Developments Involving the People's Republic of China 2018*. Annual Report to Congress. 16 March 2018.

Sherwood, Leah. "Small States' Strategic Hedging for Security and Interest." *Trends Research and Advisory*, 14 September 2016.

Tang, Shiping. "The Security Dilemma: A Conceptual Analysis," *Security Studies*, 18:3, 2009.

The West Philippine Sea: The Territorial and Maritime Jurisdiction Disputes from a Filipino Perspective, A Primer. 2013. Quezon City: The Asian Center and the Institute for Maritime Affairs and the Law of the Sea, University of the Philippines, April.

Trump, Donald. Remarks during his Meeting with President Rodrigo Duterte at the sideline of the East Asia Summit. Manila: International Convention Center, 13 November 2017.

US Embassy in the Philippines. "8th Philippines-United States Bilateral Strategic Dialogue (BSD) Joint Statement." Manila, 17 July 2019.

US Embassy in the Philippines. "US Embassy Reminds Duterte: We give $250 M a year in military, education aid," 31 May 2019.

Waltz, Kenneth. *Theory of International Politics*. New York: Random House, 1979.

Wright, Quincy. *The Study of War*. Chicago: University of Chicago Press, 1942.

Wu, Charles Chonghan. "Hierarchy and Bandwagoning in Asia: The Rise of China and its Grand Strategy in the Post-Cold War Era." Columbia: University of South Carolina, 2009.

Wu, Schicun and Nong Hong, eds. *Recent Developments in the South China Sea Dispute: The Prospect of a Joint Development Regime*. London: Routledge, 2014

7

Competition, Contention, and Cooperation in the South China Sea: The Malaysian Perspective

Sumathy Permal

Introduction

The South China Sea (SCS) is one of the most geostrategically contested maritime spaces. The long-standing overlapping territorial disputes among claimants including Brunei, China, Malaysia, Philippines, Taiwan, and Vietnam are complicated by the added element of US-Sino relations and their respective policies and strategies. China's emergence as a major economic power, the growth in military spending by Asian countries led by China, and the increasing attention by European nations in the SCS present a volatile mix that provides opportunities as well as posing threats to be negotiated. The almost 4 million square kilometres of the SCS provides regional states and the international community with a strategically important maritime highway for the transportation of goods and energy supplies, and forms a critical link between trading hubs and ports in Europe, South and Southeast Asia, and Northeast Asia.[1] The SCS figures prominently as a link in the management of the world's energy

[1] Joshua Hastey and Scott N. Romaniuk identify the SCS not only as a vital waterway for the movements of goods and equipment but also as a multi-faceted "system of systems" and an instrument "for future power projection by existing great and rising powers" (see Chapter 1).

supply network of marine routes that facilitate the economic, commercial, and strategic interests of many nations.[2]

Apart from shipping, the SCS also forms a large portion of the area where international communication traffic is routed to facilitate commerce and other activities so essential for the world today. The use of the sea for these purposes must be well managed to check any untoward impact on the environment, marine biodiversity, and ecosystems. There is much need for prudent conservation and protection of these systems to ensure sustainable management and use of the sea and its resources. The conventional hydrocarbons are located in undisputed areas while most of the discovered fields are clustered in the uncontested parts, close to the shorelines of various countries. Among the claimant countries, Vietnam, Malaysia, and Brunei Darussalam have the highest oil and gas reserves in the sea.

Background to states' territorial and maritime claims

Malaysia's maritime area is supported by all rights as provided by international law, particularly as set out under the United Nations Convention on the Law of Sea (UNCLOS). Malaysia's geographical areas of interest, as encapsulated in the Peta Baru Malaysia 1979, include rights to internal waters, territorial sea, continental shelf, exclusive economic zone (EEZ), and the airspace over applicable maritime zones. The maritime areas of Malaysia feature busy shipping sea lines of communication, such as the Straits of Malacca (SOM), the South China Sea (SCS), Sulu Sea and the Celebes Sea, and the Andaman Sea. These maritime areas act as gateways for the nation's trade and are rich in living and non-living resources which contributing significantly to the Malaysian economy. The EEZ and continental shelf surrounding the South China Sea also fall within Malaysia's offshore economic interests. Upon ratification of UNCLOS in 1996, Malaysia submitted a statement of declaration,[3] as allowed for under the convention.

Malaysia's National Defence Policy (NDP) establishes the country's geographical areas of vital interests that are protected from external threats and aggression by its armed forces. The Straits of Malacca and the Sea Lines of Communication (SLOCs) into the SCS, and the relevant areas of airspace above, are strategic areas critical to the nation's lifeline and for the security and

[2] See Sumathy Permal, Implementation of Declaration on the Conduct of Parties in the South China Sea and the Code of Conduct, Paper Presented at the Seminar-Workshop on Implementation 2002 ASEAN China Declaration on the Conduct of Parties in the South China Sea, 14 May 2015, Manila.

[3] See http://www.un.org/depts/los/convention_agreements/convention_declarations.htm

defence of the country. Malaysia deploys naval assets to provide constabulary support for law enforcement in Malaysian waters, including in the SCS.

Formal discourse and state behaviour

In September 2019, Malaysia's Ministry of Foreign Affairs published its Foreign Policy Framework of the New Malaysia, themed *Change in Continuity*.[4] The document establishes the nation's foreign policy priorities and direction, especially in regard to its sovereignty, independence, and territorial integrity. It highlights that issues relating to the SCS are based on close cooperation with ASEAN member states and the major powers, and on having a voice and position on emerging international matters including security in the SCS. Malaysia has identified the SCS as a potential flashpoint if not handled carefully. SCS disputes should be settled through peaceful means using a rules-based approach and universally recognized principles of international law, such as UNCLOS, and international arbitration.[5] Thus far, Malaysia's formal discourse and conduct have been consistent in urging parties to disputes to avoid the use of force, intimidation, or coercion, and to exercise restraint. Malaysia seeks non-militarization of the South China Sea and for it to be an area of peace, friendship, and trade.[6]

Malaysia has also continuously called for the full implementation of the 2002 Declaration on the Conduct of Parties (DOC) in the SCS and the expeditious conclusion of a Code of Conduct (COC) in the SCS as the way forward to managing issues there. The ASEAN-China endorsement of the Framework for the Code of Conduct is a step in the right direction and welcomed by Malaysia as a means to achieve the COC.

Malaysia's SCS discourse is based on the spirit of cooperation between ASEAN and China and reiterates the importance of an ASEAN-led process such as the ASEAN Regional Forum (ARF) and the ASEAN–China Dialogue as the primary forums for addressing common political and security

---

4 Foreign Policy Framework of the New Malaysia, Change in Continuity, Ministry of Foreign Affairs, 18 September 2019. https://www.kln.gov.my/foreign-policy-framework/files/assets/common/downloads/Foreign%20Policy%20Framework.pdf

5 Joint Statement Between Malaysia and Vietnam in Conjunction with Official Visit of HE Tun Dr. Mahathir Mohamad, Prime Minister of Malaysia to Socialist Republic of Vietnam, 28 August 2019. https://www.kln.gov.my/web/guest/-/press-release-joint-statement-between-malaysia-and-viet-nam-in-conjuction-with-the-official-visit-of-h-e-tun-dr-mahathir-mohamad-prime-minister-of-mal

6 Foreign Policy Framework of the New Malaysia, Change in Continuity, Ministry of Foreign Affairs, 18 September 2019. https://www.kln.gov.my/foreign-policy-framework/files/assets/common/downloads/Foreign%20Policy%20Framework.pdf

issues. The enhanced importance of maritime Southeast Asia and its related economic, security, safety, and environmental preservation issues require a strengthening of mechanisms, including the ASEAN Maritime Forum, ASEAN Regional Forum, and ASEAN Transport Ministers' Meeting.

Malaysia supports the establishment of a rules-based framework with a set of norms to guide the conduct of parties and promote maritime cooperation in the SCS. The DOC advocates self-restraint and promotes possible areas for cooperative activities. In this regard, there are several recommendatory and non-obligatory legal and agreed frameworks currently existing. They include the application of the Code for Unplanned Encounters at Sea (CUES) and the Declaration for a Decade of Coastal and Marine Environmental Protection in the South China Sea (2017–2027).[7]

Military build-up, organization, and application in the South China Sea

Apart from China and five other claimants, the SCS region remains an area of growing strategic interest for a number of other countries, including the US, Japan, Australia, and Europe. While the maritime strategic environment in the SCS seems to revolve around US–China relations, there has been increased attention by Japan, the United Kingdom (UK), France, and Russia. In particular, issues of Freedom of Navigation Operations (FONOPs) and military developments have generated much strategic concern. For instance, Florence Parly, Defence Minister of France's Armed Forces at the Shangri-La Dialogue, suggested that growing strategic competition in the region requires France to contribute to regional stability through multilateral security cooperation.[8]

According to SIPRI Military Database, 2019,[9] the US and China were among the top five in terms of military spending in 2018, with an increase of 4.6 per cent since 2010 by the US. On the other hand, Chinese military spending was lower by 5.0 per cent compared to previous years, although still accounting for 14 per cent of the global total. Such militarization complicates matters in the management of SCS issues by China and ASEAN. While

7 ASEAN China Strategic Partnership Vision 2030. https://asean.org/storage/2018/11/ASEAN-China-Strategic-Partnership-Vision-2030.pdf

8 Florence Parly, Minister of Armed Forces France, 18th Asia Security Summit, IISS Shangri-La Dialogue, 1 June 2019. file:///C:/Users/Sumathy/Downloads/Plenary%203%20-%20Florence%20Parly%20Minister%20of%20the%20Armed%20Forces%20France.pdf

9 Nan tian, Aude Fleurant, Alexandra Kuimova, Pieter D. Wezeman and Siemon T. Wezeman, Trends in World Military Spending, 2018, SIPRI Fact Sheet. https://www.sipri.org/sites/default/files/2019-04/fs_1904_milex_2018.pdf

China's recent actions seem to be a reaction to the US presence in the SCS, its military build-up and strongly worded statements show an increasingly strident position and the sending of assertive signals not just to the external powers but to all claimants including Vietnam, the Philippines, Malaysia, and Brunei. This strong position by China is an impediment to ASEAN–China cooperation in the SCS.

China's assertive actions and the responses from other claimants have been consistent and continue to create instability in the SCS and uncertainty in Asia. Of the claimants, the Philippines and Vietnam have confronted the Chinese in military and diplomatic rows and in legal battles. Malaysia too is confronted with the illegal presence and regular intrusions by the Chinese in its EEZ in addition to the 24/7 illegal patrolling of Chinese Coast Guard vessels around the Luconia Breakers since September 11, 2013. China and Vietnam have faced off due to the presence of Chinese survey vessels and their Chinese Coast Guard escort-ships near the Vietnamese-controlled Vanguard Bank[10] in the Spratlys in July 2019 and in 2014. The Philippines has also encountered Chinese vessels off Thitu Island in the Pagasa in August 2019, as well as in Reed Bank in June 2019.[11]

Apart from China, which has almost completed military outposts and airstrips on Fiery Cross Reef, Subi Reef, and South Johnson Reef, Indonesia had also developed a military base in Natuna Besar as a deterrence for potential threats primarily from China as well as a "flashpoint defense" base.[12] In December 2018, the Philippines called on the US to review its 1951 Mutual Defense Treaty. The US State Department assured, in March 2019, that "the US would defend the Philippines should there be any armed attack in the South China Sea,"[13] which stoked China's diplomatic opposition.

Japan, a non-claimant in the SCS, approved a security bill allowing the country to participate in any military venture for the first time since the Second World War. Though the new bill is not directly targeted at the SCS,

---

[10] Zhuang Pinghui, Vietnam Calls for Chinese Vessels to Leave Vanguard Bank. https://www.scmp.com/news/china/diplomacy/article/3019449/vietnam-calls chinese-vessels-leave-vanguard-bank-south-china, 20 July 2019

[11] Philippines Fishing Boat Hit by Chinese Ship, The Philippines Star, 13 June 2019. https://www.philstar.com/headlines/2019/06/13/1926016/philippine-fishing-boat-hit-china-ship-sinks

[12] Indonesia Opens Military Base Near Disputed South China Sea, Kyodo News, 19 December 2018. https://news.abs-cbn.com/overseas/12/19/18/indonesia-opens-military-base-near-disputed-south-china-sea

[13] Malcolm Cook, The Philippines Alliances Problem with the USA, Perspective, ISEAS Yusof Institute, Issues 29. No. 48, 13 June 2019. https://www.iseas.edu.sg/images/pdf/ISEAS_Perspective_2019_48.pdf

it has Japan–China maritime issues in mind, including in the East China Sea. Further, Japan has pledged to support the United States and other allies should there be a conflict in the SCS.

For Malaysia, the Straits of Malacca, the SLOCs adjoining the South China Sea, and the airspaces above are strategic areas critical to the nation's lifeline over which it has to maintain its presence and assert sovereignty. In addition, its territorial seas and EEZ need to be defended against external threats and aggression, and to deter or deny any hostile acts towards these interests.

Protecting and safeguarding interests

While China and the United States are Malaysia's major trading partners, Malaysia also values its relations with other nations such as Russia and India, and the EU as a supranational entity. Malaysia, as well other ASEAN member states, shares the values and aspirations of major powers in the 21st century. Malaysia's stand is not to take sides in its relations with the major powers in the context of the Asia-Pacific or in Asia. Malaysia is cognizant that issues on the overlapping claims in the South China Sea and the security of the Straits of Malacca will converge in the Indo-Pacific region.

Malaysia maintains naval stations on Layang Layang, Terumbu Mantanani, Terumbu Ubi, Terumbu Siput, and Terumbu Peninjau, and continues to have a presence around all other features within its EEZ and continental shelf (CS). Malaysia also has a law enforcement presence in Gugusan Betin Patinggi Ali (South Luconia), Betin Serupai (James Shoal), Gugusan Betin Raja Jarum (North Shoal), and Hempasan Betin (Luconia Breakers). While maintaining its presence in the SCS the Royal Malaysian Navy (RMN) also monitors movements of any foreign vessels into its area. Any incursions or sighting of illegal vessels are recorded, and action such as escorting them out are normally practised. The RMN's Eastern Command has stepped up its presence and attention on foreign vessel intrusions into Malaysia waters within the SCS.[14]

Malaysia also has a navigational beacon and a marine and scientific station in Layang Layang which is also being developed into a diving resort. Efforts have been undertaken to acquire national research vessels for hydrology and geology research on the mineral deposits in Malaysia's EEZ and CS in the SCS.

Militarily, Malaysia does not seek or have the inclination to challenge any country. It is, however, concerned with the issues of regional security

[14] No Chinese Navy Ship in Malaysian Waters, Bernama News, 24 June 2019. https://www.theedgemarkets.com/article/no-chinese-navy-ship-msian-waters-%E2%80%94-rmn

such as developments in the SCS. Besides, observations on the naval and air enhancements, modernization of weapon systems and force structures, and maritime doctrines of its neighbours, such as Singapore, Indonesia, Vietnam, and China, suggest that Malaysia needs to respond to the security risks in the region.

Geostrategic competition between the US and China as well increasing interest from Japan and other players, such as Australia, the UK, and Europe, are inevitable. In this regard, the management of security is aimed towards preventing either the resident or the emerging powers from exploiting or blocking the critical Straits of Malacca – a vulnerable choke point that extends into the SCS – in the event of a conflict between those powers. As such, Malaysia is keen to enhance its sea power in all aspects, including surveillance, deterrence, and defence capability.

The primary role of the RMN is to safeguard Malaysian waters in peacetime and to show a presence in both war and peacetime.[15] The RMN's core objectives are to have operational readiness and ensure a credible force. In the view of this writer, RMN's strategic objectives in the current geostrategic environment of the region are threefold: prevent conflict in Malaysian waters; protect the nation's maritime interests; and preserve and enhance navy-navy relations with major powers and regional countries.

The Malaysian Maritime Enforcement Agency (MMEA) and its areas of responsibility are governed by the MMEA Act.[16] Its role is to maintain law and order, and to preserve peace, safety, and security under its jurisdiction. This is done through the prevention and detection of crime, apprehension and prosecution of offenders, and gathering of security intelligence.

The SCS is a geostrategic flashpoint where Malaysia's military and law enforcement agencies need to be vigilant in safeguarding its interests. Encroachments are usually from foreign coast guards and occasionally military ships. It has been publicly reported[17] that Chinese Coast Guard vessels regularly encroach into Malaysia's EEZ despite sustained diplomatic protests from Malaysia. Such encroachments pose operational issues for the RMN, especially where it involves areas in which the RMN and MMEA conduct regular patrols and surveillance. Malaysia also faces the threat of illegal fishing

[15] Mohd Haffizuddin Md Damiri, Naval Capability Based Acquisition Reform: An Analysis of the Royal Malaysian Navy Transformation Program. https://www.academia.edu/31669231/Naval_Capability-Based_Acquisition_Reform_An_Analysis_of_the_Royal_Malaysian_Navy_Transformation_Program

[16] MMEA's Background. https://www.mmea.gov.my/eng/index.php/en/mengenai-kami/latar-belakang

[17] Chief of Navy, Malaysia, Top Brass Interview, Asian Defence Journal, June 2015

from foreign fishers, in addition to issues of vessels being "cloned," all of which contribute to illegal, unregulated, and unreported fishing.

Malaysia deploys naval assets in order to provide constabulary support for law enforcement by the MMEA. The RMN is also required to be constantly present in areas of interest. Other options that Malaysia should consider applying is a mix of private-public partnership to be the eyes and ears of the agencies. Deep-sea fishing vessels, private maritime security companies, and existing offshore stations can collectively help mitigate risks or deploy resources to report foreign vessels and assist agencies in deterring and addressing intrusions and encroachments.

Competing trends and tactics

The SCS is a transit point and an operating area for navies and air forces in Asia and the Indian Ocean and Persian Gulf areas. From a wider perspective, non-claimant or user-states depend on freedom of navigation in the conduct of their activities in the SCS. The naval activities of non-claimant states aimed at ensuring freedom of navigation, if not properly communicated or coordinated, could potentially create mistrust among parties to the disputes. Second, the area is of major interest to naval powers because it offers the shortest route from the Pacific to the Indian Ocean and facilitates the movement of naval fleets either for global strategic reasons or for mutual cooperation with allies in the region.

The maritime strategic environment in the region seems to revolve around US–China relations in the SCS. In particular, the issues of FONOPs and military developments have generated much strategic mistrust. There are two major reasons for US involvement in the SCS. First is to safeguard freedom of navigation which the US promotes for military activities. Second, the US has always been interested in the area as it offers the shortest route from the Pacific to the Indian Ocean and because it is essential for the movement of commercial shipping, that is estimated to account for 60 per cent of global maritime trade.

China has a unilateral nine-dashed line claiming the entire SCS basin.[18] China's advanced naval capability, including the use of asymmetric capabilities, electronic and cyber warfare, ballistic and cruise missiles, advanced air defences, mining, and other methods, pose serious challenges to US naval movements in the Pacific. Besides, China has deployed a range of military hardware, anti-ship and surface-to-air missiles, and electronic jammers in the area, as well as built islets and converted maritime features into hardened military facilities.

---

[18] People's Republic of China, Note Verbale CML/18/2009, 7 May 2009.

The United States Navy (USN) has been conducting regular Freedom of Navigation Operation (FONOPs) in the South China Sea since 2015. Prior to this, USN survey ships and Chinese Navy frigates had encounters in the Yellow Sea in March 2001, and in 2009 involving the US naval ship *Impeccable* surveillance ship with Chinese government vessels.[19] The main contentious issue lies with regard to operations by the USN challenging China's claims to its territorial sea. The US Department of Defense National Security Strategy (NSS) 2019 affirms that the USN will continue to sail, fly, and operate wherever international law allows. The US also encourages its allies and partners to conduct FONOPs.

The primary reason for the US naval ship to conduct FONOPs is to challenge the extended Chinese facilities and military outposts in the SCS. By doing so, the US seems to be endangering the free flow of trade, threatening the sovereignty of other nations, and undermining regional stability. China's activities in the SCS are directed towards militarization of the features in the SCS and having firm control over its sea lines of communication (SLOCs).

This development seems to be in line with China's aspiration to gain geopolitical mileage in the new world order. The US also views China as having pursued extraordinary military modernization aimed at minimizing US presence in the region and to give China unencumbered freedom to act. Prior to the 2018 Security Strategy document, the US administration had warned China of severe consequences if reclamation continues. In this regard, FONOPs is used as an instrument to reinforce its position on freedom of the seas and a component in dealing with China in the SCS.

If such developments are not contained, freedom of navigation in the SCS for the US, and its allies in particular, will be challenged. Safety of navigation, overflight, and the freedom of sea lines of communication are of critical strategic interests to the US, which uses the SCS as a transit point and an operating area for the USN and the United States Air Force (USAF) between military bases in Asia and the Indian Ocean and Persian Gulf areas.

The Chinese, on the other hand, firmly oppose US FONOPs. At the Shangri-La Dialogue China's Minister of National Defence and State Councillor reaffirmed their opposition stating, "We hold different views with the US side on several issues regarding the wrong words and actions of the US on Taiwan and the South China Sea. We express our firm opposition."[20] What's interesting is that one of the responses from China's

[19] Captain Raul Pedroza, Close Encounters at Sea, The USN Impeccable Incident, Naval War College Review, 2009. https://apps.dtic.mil/dtic/tr/fulltext/u2/a519335.pdf

[20] General Wei Fanghe, Minister of National Defence and State Councillor, 18 Asia Security Summit, The IISS Shangri-La Dialogue, 2 June 2019.

Ministry of National Defence was to call on the US not to waste its time creating tension in Asia; however, it warned the US military not to threaten peace and stability by conducting FONOPs in the SCS. The more important question is also whether the US FONOPs are a threat to peace and stability as stated by China or contribute to the maintenance of peace in the SCS.

In recent geopolitical developments, the SCS features prominently within the Indo-Pacific, which the US views as a "single consequential region" that connects the Pacific and the Indian Oceans.[21]

From the strategic point of view, the Indo-Pacific may complicate the existing order since it encompasses the interests of China and India and the continued strategic presence of the US in Asia. The Indo-Pacific/Free and Open Indo-Pacific (IP/FOIP) is seen as a framework in response to China's rise not only in SCS matters but also in Asia. Should ASEAN countries subscribe to the Indo-Pacific vision, their policies may appear more aligned towards the "strategic partnership" of the US, India and other middle powers to balance the rise of China in Asia. Being small nation states in a large power play theatre, ASEAN cannot afford to adopt that concept, at least until individual countries are assured that the converging and expanding interests of major powers will not destabilize the region. As it stands, this is too far a reach for smaller nations. SCS issues are best resolved through consultation by the parties concerned, mainly China and the claimant countries with the support of ASEAN.

Strategic competition between the US and China has further complicated new strategy and policy guidance on Indo-Pacific issues among the concerned countries. As suggested in *The Indian Ocean: A Future of Uncertainty (Looking out to 2020)*,[22] the interrelations of great power and possible rivalry between the three major powers of India (Sourabh Gupta labels India an "extra-regional 'leading power'" in Chapter 15), China and the US will continue to evolve in complexity, heightened by the possible rise of India and China, and a perceived decline of US power in the region.

Many countries in the Indo-Pacific region, including the US, Japan, Australia, and India, have, in some way, integrated the concept of the Indo-Pacific into their official strategic planning. Statements from official documents and scholars show a move away from reference to the Asia-Pacific to the Indo-Pacific (IP). The positions of the US and China have complicated efforts by many Southeast Asian countries to define and develop strategic

---

21 The Department of Defense Indo-Pacific Strategy Report, Preparedness, Partnership and Promoting Network Region, 1 June 2019

22 Leighton G. Luke and Tas Luttrell, Indian Ocean: A Sea of Uncertain Future Directions International, Future Directions International, 2012.

and security directions based on the new changing situation. Southeast Asian countries are divided and unclear on the IP concept although debate on it has been going on since the last decade. Currently, the IP policy and strategy is at the conceptual level in Southeast Asia and has not been adopted into foreign policy guidelines with the exception of Indonesia. Nevertheless, ASEAN adopted an *Outlook on Indo-Pacific* at the Senior Official Meeting on 23 June 2019 in Bangkok.[23] The Outlook provides that the Indo-Pacific dynamic is of interest to ASEAN and that it should remain central as it evolves. ASEAN acknowledges that the Indian and the Pacific Oceans should be closely integrated and interconnected and the Indo-Pacific Outlook should serve as a guide for cooperation as well to promote a peaceful environment.

Conclusion

The SCS is an area of dispute; however, ASEAN and China have endeavoured to find common grounds for cooperation. The China factor seems to be a key determinant in the strategic direction of the SCS geostrategic discourse. China's influence on economic, cultural, political, and security planning as well its firm position in the SCS have changed the entire game in this region. Strategic competition and contestation have moved the Asian-centric Asia-Pacific into larger multilateral security region, and the Indo-Pacific is expected to increasingly dominate the geosecurity environment in the mid- to long-terms. Malaysia is strategically located in the centre of Southeast Asia and an emerging middle power in terms of influence and governance; it has been a major influencer in the Southeast Asian political and leadership landscape. In this regard, the rise of Chinese influence and its growing economy should benefit the region especially in promoting peaceful management of the SCS.

Malaysia sees ASEAN as central to SCS issues. The DOC, one of the most important initiatives by ASEAN in managing disputes in the South China Sea, emphasizes "the necessity to resolve all sovereignty and jurisdictional issues pertaining to the SCS by peaceful means, without resort to force." Apart from addressing the six areas of cooperation, namely conservation of the marine environment, emergency and search and rescue assistance, joint search and rescue exercises, full and effective implementation of the DOC, enhancing maritime practical cooperation, and speeding up consultation on the COC, the DOC should address more pressing issues, such as the use of force and reclamation activities, and build on trust among claimants. Efforts

[23] ASEAN Outlook on Indo-Pacific, https.//asean.org/asean-outlook-indo-pacific,23 June 2019

and initiatives to enhance confidence building among the claimant states need to be seriously explored. Such initiatives will foster better understanding and hopefully enable negotiations to take place towards enhancing the confidence-building process.

References

Association of Southeast Asian Nations (ASEAN). *ASEAN-China Strategic Partnership Vision 2030*, 2019. https://asean.org/storage/2018/11/ASEAN-China-Strategic-Partnership-Vision-2030.pdf

Association of Southeast Asian Nations (ASEAN). *ASEAN Outlook on Indo-Pacific*, 2019. https://asean.org/storage/2019/06/ASEAN-Outlook-on-the-Indo-Pacific_FINAL_22062019.pdf

Bhatia, R. K., and Sakhuja, V. *Indo Pacific Region: Political and Strategic Prospects*. Vij Books India, 2014.

Chen, D., and Zhang, C. (eds). *China Quarterly of International Strategic Studies* (Vol. 2). Hackensack, NJ: World Century Publishing Corporation, 2016.

Chief of Navy. Top Brass Interview. *Asian Defence Journal*, Malaysia, June 2015.

Damiri. M. H. M. *Naval Capability Based Acquisition Reform: An Analysis of the Royal Malaysian Navy Transformation Program*, 2016. https://www.academia.edu/31669231/Naval_Capability-Based_Acquisition_Reform_An_Analysis_of_the_Royal_Malaysian_Navy_Transformation_Program

Department of Defense, USA. *The Indo-Pacific Strategy Report, Preparedness, Partnership and Promoting Network Region*, 2019. https://media.defense.gov/2019/Jul/01/2002152311/-1/-1/1/DEPARTMENT-OF-DEFENSE-INDO-PACIFIC-STRATEGY-REPORT-2019.PDF

Ho, K. L., and He, G. *Ensuring Interests: Dynamics of China-Taiwan Relations and Southeast Asia*. Institute of China Studies, University of Malaya, 2006.

International Institute for Strategic Studies (IISS). General Wei Fanghe, Minister of National Defence and State Councillor, 18 Asia Security Summit, The IISS Shangri-La Dialogue, 2 June 2019. https://www.iiss.org/press/2019/china-mindef-wei-fenghe-shangri-la-dialogue-2019%20

International Strategic Studies. *China Institute for International Strategic Studies*. 134 (3), 2019.

Keay, J. *China: A History*. London: Hachette UK, 2009.

Luke, L. G., and Luttrell, T. (eds). *Indian Ocean: A Sea of Uncertain*. Perth: Future Directions International, 2012.

Malaysian Maritime Enforcement Agency. MMEA's Background, n.d. https://www.mmea.gov.my/eng/index.php/en/mengenai-kami/latar-belakang

Ministry of Foreign Affairs (MOFA), Malaysia. Foreign Policy Framework of the New Malaysia. *Change in Continuity*, 2019. https://www.kln.gov.my/foreign-policy-framework/files/assets/common/downloads/Foreign%20Policy%20Framework.pdf

Nan tian, Aude Fleurant, Alexandra Kuimova, Pieter D. Wezeman and Siemon T. Wezeman. *Trends in World Military Expenditure*, SIPRI Fact Sheet, 2018. https://www.sipri.org/sites/default/files/2019-04/fs_1904_milex_2018.pdf.

Ngeow, C. B. (ed). *International Journal of China Studies*, 9(1/2). Kuala Lumpur: University Malaya Press, 2018.

Parly, F. Minister of the Armed Forces' Speech at the Security Summit, IISS Shangri-La Dialogue, 2019. https://www.defense.gouv.fr/salle-de-presse/discours/discours-de-florence-parly/discours-de-florence-parly-ministre-des-armees_allocution-au-shangri-la-dialogue.

Pedroza, R. Close Encounters at Sea, The USN Impeccable Incident. *Naval War College Review*, 62 (3), 2009.

People's Republic of China. Note Verbale. Law of the Sea. United Nations, May, 2009.

Philippines Fishing Boat Hit by Chinese Ship, The Philippines Star, 13 June 2019. https://www.philstar.com/headlines/2019/06/13/1926016/philippine-fishing-boat-hit-china-ship-sinks

Scobell, A., and Wortzel, L. *Civil-military Change in China: Elites, Institutes, and Ideas after the 16th Party Congress*. Army War Coll Strategic Studies Inst Carlisle Barracks, PA, 2004.

South China Morning Post. *Indonesia Opens Military Base on Edge of South China Sea to "Deter Security Threats,"* 2018. https://www.scmp.com/news/asia/southeast-asia/article/2178741/indonesia-opens-military-base-edge-south-china-sea-deter#

Sumathy Permal. *Implementation of Declaration on the Conduct of Parties in the South China Sea and the Code of Conduct, Paper Presented at the Seminar-Workshop on Implementation 2002 ASEAN China Declaration on the Conduct of Parties in the South China Sea*. Manila: Department of Foreign Affairs, May 2015.

Thuy, T. T., Weifield, J. B., and Trang, L. T. *Building a Normative Order in the South China Sea, Evolving Disputes, Expanding Options*. Cheltenham: Edward Elgar Publishing, 2019..

United Nations Law of the Sea (UNCLOS). *Declarations and Statements*, 2019. https://www.un.org/depts/los/convention_agreements/convention_declarations.htm

Vitug, M. D. *Rock Solid: How the Philippines Won Its Maritime Case Against China*. Manila: Ateneo de Manila University Press, 2018.

Zhuang P. Vietnam Calls for Chinese Vessels to Leave Vanguard Bank. *South China Sea Morning Post*, July 2019.

PART II

Non-Claimants in Southeast Asia

8

A Wary Warrior: Indonesia's "Soft-Assertiveness" in the South China Sea

Senia Febrica and Scott N. Romaniuk

Introduction

The South China Sea (SCS) – a semi-enclosed sea[1] – is one of the world's key shipping routes and richest fishing grounds. Shared by China, Vietnam, Malaysia, Singapore, Indonesia, Brunei, and the Philippines, the SCS also sees one third of global trade pass through its waters.[2] The SCS is also known for its high economic value. It is rich with high value marine life, particularly demersal fish and tuna, and significant deposits of hydrocarbons trapped beneath the Kalayaan Island Group's (KIG) seabed. The overarching maritime dispute in this highly strategic locale involves six claimant states including China, Taiwan, the Philippines, Vietnam, Malaysia, and Brunei, with China representing the strongest of these countries in terms of its military capabilities. Although Indonesia is not a claimant state, as one of the coastal states of the SCS Indonesia has played and will almost certainly continue to occupy a central role in efforts to manage the conflict. Through its ongoing efforts to diffuse the conflict, Indonesia has engaged parties to

---

1 Pakjuta Khemakorn, "Sustainable Management of Pelagic Fisheries in the South China Sea Region," United Nations, New York, United States, November 2006.

2 Jane Perlez, "Alarm as China Issues Rules for Disputed Area," *The New York Times*, December 2, 2012.

the disputes primarily through the ASEAN-China Joint Working Group[3] on the Implementation of the Declaration on the Conduct of Parties in the South China Sea[4] and the Track 2 approach, namely the Workshop on Managing Potential Conflict in the South China Sea[5] that Jakarta has organized since 1990.

In recent years the development of the multi-faceted dispute in SCS has raised serious concern among states about the potential escalation of the conflict, with experts assessing the possibility and probability that the dispute could turn into a hot war. Zheng Hao expressed that, "[a] close look at recent US military activities and China-US military relations would indicate that the SCS situation is moving towards the brink of conflict."[6] Oliana Skylar Mastro asserts that, "[i]t would be wrong to assume that China is satisfied with the gains it has made or that it would refrain from using more aggressive tactics in the future."[7] Referring to the Cold War and the improbability of war between the two superpowers starting in Central Europe, John Mearsheimer explained, "contrast that with the situation in East Asia, which is the central flash point between United States and China, the three places where you could possibly have a war involve the South China Sea, Taiwan and the East China Sea." Not only did Mearsheimer state that, "it's possible to imagine a limited conventional war breaking out in one of those three areas," he also explained that, "it's possible to think in terms of a 'limited nuclear war,' with limited nuclear use."[8]

In the past few years tensions between China and other Southeast Asian states, in particular Vietnam and the Philippines, have escalated significantly, creating a sense of regional crisis that has drawn in the Association of the Southeast Asian Nations (ASEAN) and external powers including the US and Japan. This concern is not without bases. The Hague Arbitral Tribunal

---

3 See, ASEAN, "Terms of Reference of the ASEAN-China Joint Working Group on the Implementation of the Declaration on the Conduct of Parties in the South China Sea," May 14, 2012.

4 Hồng Thao Nguyễn, "The 2002 Declaration on the Conduct of Parties in the South China Sea: A Note," *Ocean Development & International Law* 34, no. 3–4, 2002, 279–85.

5 Yann-huei Song, "The South China Sea Workshop Process and Taiwan's Participation," *Ocean Development & International Law* 41, no. 3, 2010, 253–69.

6 Zheng Hao, "Could China-US Tensions in the South China Sea Escalate Into a Hot War?," *Think China*, July 29, 2020. thinkchina.sg/could-china-us-tensions-south-china-sea-escalate-hot-war

7 Oliana Skylar Mastro, "Military Confrontation in the South China Sea," Contingency Planning Memorandum No. 36, Council on Foreign Relations, New York, United States, May 21, 2020. https://www.cfr.org/report/military-confrontation-south-china-sea

8 Kenji Minemura, "INTERVIEW/John Mearsheimer: US-China Rift Runs Real Risk of Escalating into a Nuclear War," *The Asahi Shimbun*, August 17, 2020. http://www.asahi.com/ajw/articles/13629071

issued their award on jurisdiction and admissibility on October 29, 2015, announcing that, "it is presently able to decide that it does have jurisdiction with respect to the matters raised in … the Philippines' submissions against China."[9] The July 2016 Hague Tribunal ruling on the SCS dispute was overwhelmingly opposed to China's claim of historic rights to resources in this area.[10] Despite the recent legal development, in a number of incidents China's increasing coordination and physical support between its maritime agencies and fishers in the SCS has led to considerable friction with the major states in Southeast Asia, including Indonesia.[11]

This chapter describes and examines how the SCS dispute is presented in the Indonesian government and media discourses. It provides a comprehensive analysis of Indonesia's diplomatic and military strategies for managing any potential conflict in the SCS, particularly involving China. Like that of other SCS claimant states and states in the region, Indonesia's policy in the SCS carries its own unique characteristics and can be understood through the state's geographical and strategic position, population, resources, and economy. As ASEAN's largest member, Indonesia has its own aspirations for regional leadership and has played a key role in the regional process to find a solution to the overall maritime dispute. Indeed, Indonesia has long been recognized as a natural leader in ASEAN and the region.[12] Indonesia is one of the founding members of the regional intergovernmental organization and has played a central role in shaping the regional architecture.[13] Indonesia proposed the concept of the ASEAN Security Community, actively sought

9 Permanent Court of Arbitration, "Arbitration between the Republic of the Philippines and the People's Republic of China: Tribunal Renders Award Jurisdiction and Admissibility; Will Hold Further Hearings," PCA Case No. 2013-19, October 29, 2015; Senia Febrica, "Philippines v. China Arbitration Case: Indonesia's Diplomatic and Security Responses," in Fu-Kuo Liu and Jonathan Spangler (eds), *South China Sea Lawfare: Legal Perspectives and International Responses to the Philippines v. China Arbitration Case*. Taiwan: South China Sea Think Tank and Taiwan Center for Security Studies, 2016, 101–110; Alfredo C. Robles, Jr., *Endangered Species and Fragile Ecosystems in the South China Sea: The Philippines v. China Arbitration*. London: Palgrave Macmillan, 2020.

10 *The Guardian*, "Beijing Rejects Tribunal's Ruling in South China Sea Case," July 12, 2016.

11 Lucio Blanco Pitlo, "Fishing Wars: Competition for South China Sea's Fishery Resources," Center for Security Studies, ETH Zürich, Switzerland, July 10, 2013.

12 Ralf Emmers, "Indonesia's Role in ASEAN: A Case of Incomplete and Sectorial Leadership," *The Pacific Review* 27, no. 4, 2014, 543–62.

13 Senia Febrica, *Maritime Security and Indonesia: Cooperation, Interests and* Strategies, Abingdon, Routledge, 131; Aileen Baviera, "Preventing War, Building A Rules-Based Order: Challenges Facing the ASEAN Political–Security Community," ASEAN@50 4, "Building ASEAN Community: Political-Security and Socio-Cultural Reflections," 5.

to conduct conflict mediation efforts in the Vietnam-Cambodia conflict and the South China Sea disputes, developed regional mechanisms to promote democracy and human rights, and initiated the development of the ASEAN Maritime Forum.[14] These roles and achievements have not gone unrecognized. There have been concerted efforts carried out by Indonesia and other ASEAN member states to draw China into regional processes.[15] Each of the ASEAN multilateral dialogues, such as the South China Sea Workshops, the ASEAN+3 and the Expanded ASEAN Maritime Forum, to name a few, includes China.[16] These arrangements provide opportunities for China to offer transparency regarding its state interests and aspirations in the region, and redefine its relations with ASEAN.[17]

This chapter is divided into four sections. The second section explains the representation of the SCS maritime dispute in the Indonesian government and media narratives. Drawing on interviews with the government officials and the analysis of primary and secondary literature, we explain how the dispute is depicted by the Indonesian government. The third section expounds Indonesia's diplomatic and military strategies in the SCS, with a focus on Indonesia's diplomatic and military efforts following the tribunal award regarding the arbitration between the Philippines and China in 2015 to 2020. The final section highlights key points to take away from this chapter. While Indonesia has its own strategic interests in the SCS, we argue that Jakarta remains an active player in the broader dispute with nested interests in its immediate maritime territory. Moreover, what we refer to as Indonesia's "soft-assertiveness," is the product of balancing between its own immediate interest and refraining from antagonizing an assertive China operating through an increasingly aggressive and volatile foreign policy specifically in the SCS region.

Locating the South China Sea in the Indonesian government's narrative

Indonesia has always reiterated its position as a non-claimant state in the SCS maritime dispute with no intentions of laying claim to any of the

[14] Shoji Tomotaka, "ASEAN Security Community: An Initiative for Peace and Stability," *NIDS Security Reports* 3, no. 4, 2008, Tokyo, Japan: The National Institute for Defense Studies, 17–34; Henning Borchers, "ASEAN's Environmental Challenges and Nontraditional Security Cooperation: Towards a Regional Peacekeeping Force?," *ASEAS – Austrian Journal of South-East Asian Studies* 7, no. 1, 2014, 5–20.

[15] Alice D. Ba, "China and ASEAN: Renavigating Relations for a 21st-Century Asia," *Asian Survey* 43, no. 4, 2003, 622–47.

[16] Ibid.

[17] Ibid.

region's maritime features. As part of Indonesia's official position, the government does not recognize China's infamous "nine-dash line" that serves as the basis of China's territorial claims in the SCS nor has Indonesia shown interest in holding bilateral talks with China over its claims. Therefore, in the SCS, Indonesia does not view China as a neighbour with whom it has to settle maritime boundaries.[18] As far as the Indonesian government is concerned, when it comes to maritime entitlements in the SCS, it only considers Malaysia and Vietnam as neighbouring countries.[19] As an Indonesian senior official from the Maritime Security Board pointed out in an interview:

> "We do not have shared boundaries with China. We do, however, share maritime boundaries with Vietnam ..."[20] A senior official from the Indonesian Ministry of Defence further asserted that "We have to be careful in looking at situations that I deem as sensitive ... In this region we focus on the South China Sea. Our focus, the Ministry of Defence's focus is to build peace in the region. We have a strong interest there because if the region becomes unstable, we will automatically be affected. With regards to the South China Sea dispute we are not a claimant state. Although there are people that pointed out that [China's] nine-dash-line cut through parts of Indonesia we until now still maintain our position as a non-claimant state This is a very sensitive [issue]. In diplomacy we still say that we are a non-claimant state. Yes, not a claimant."[21]

Despite not sharing maritime boundaries with China, as a leading country in the region, the Indonesian government has expressed the need to maintain an active role in an effort to improve US-China relations and interactions in the context of the SCS dispute resolution.[22]

During President Jokowi's administration, the reduction of inter-states tension to resolve maritime boundary disputes features as one the key

[18] Andi Arsana, "Is China A Neighbour to Indonesia?" *The Jakarta Post*, August 8, 2011.

[19] Ibid.

[20] Interview with a senior official from the Indonesian Maritime Security Board (Jakarta, August 26, 2015).

[21] Interview with a senior official at the Indonesian Ministry of Defence (Jakarta, August 24, 2015).

[22] Interview with a senior official at the Indonesian Ministry of Defence (Jakarta, August 24, 2015); Interviews with two officials at the Indonesian Ministry of Foreign Affairs (Jakarta, August 21, 2015).

components of the Indonesian Maritime Fulcrum Initiative. Since the resignation of President Suharto in 1998, Indonesia has been led by five Presidents: Habibie, Abdurrahman Wahid, Megawati, Yudhoyono, and most recently, Joko Widodo (known as Jokowi). Of these five, Jokowi is the only president to announce Indonesia's commitment to making maritime security concerns a national priority, a commitment made soon after he assumed office on October 20, 2014.

Jokowi announced the concept of Indonesia as the World Maritime Fulcrum in his speech during the 9th East Asia Summit in Myanmar in 2014.[23] Indonesia's Maritime Fulcrum concept is built upon five pillars including: the redevelopment of Indonesia's maritime culture; conservation of marine resources; the development of maritime infrastructure and connectivity by building up deep-seaports, ship industry and maritime tourism, for example; the implementation of maritime diplomacy to resolve various sources of inter-state tensions including boundary disputes, illegal fishing, and marine pollution; and the development of maritime defence power.[24]

During our interviews, Indonesian government officials frequently asserted that due to the proximity of Natuna to the disputed area, and the absence of China's clarification on whether or not its claims encompass Indonesia's exclusive economic zone, the growing tension in the SCS does indeed pose a serious threat to Indonesia.[25] Indonesian government officials used the word "threat" to describe Sino-Indonesian interactions in the SCS, drawing attention to the potential for escalation and a looming danger presented indirectly by China's interests and assertive practice, and directly through its official rhetoric about the region. Although Indonesian officials acknowledge the existing problems between Indonesia and other claimants of the SCS, such as Vietnam, China is perceived to be more aggressive than any other claimant state. To quote an Indonesian senior official during an interview in 2015:

---

[23] Aaron J. Connelly, "Sovereignty and the Sea: President Joko Widodo's Foreign Policy Challenges," *Contemporary Southeast Asia* 37, no. 1, 2015, 1–28.

[24] Indonesian Presidential Office. "Indonesia Sebagai Poros Maritim Dunia," November 13, 2015.

[25] Interviews with two officials from the Indonesian Maritime Security Board (Jakarta, August 26, 2015, an official from the Indonesian Coordinating Ministry for Political, Legal and Security Affairs (Jakarta, August 21, 2015), and an official from the Indonesian Ministry of Defence (Jakarta, August 24, 2015); Febrica, Senia and Suzia Sudarman, "Analysing Indonesian Media and Government Representation of China," *British Journal of Chinese Studies* 8, no. 2, 2018, 104.

> military standoff between Indonesian and China maritime authorities had taken place three times [in the South China Sea] … China's naval patrol vessel had provided protection to Chinese fishing vessels. In 2010 two incidents took place, and another one happened in 2014. China's patrol vessel forced the Indonesian authorities to release Chinese fishing vessels that were being arrested … The main challenge is to guard the Natuna Sea. It is an area with busy maritime traffic and rich in resources. This is our problem not only with China but also with Vietnam. China is, however, more aggressive. It has expanded its power not only in Asia but also Africa.[26]

The view expressed by Indonesian officials parallels the media's portrayal of China's policy in the SCS as a threat to Indonesia as an individual and sovereign state and to Southeast Asia as a region. The word "threat" was used by the two leading national newspapers, *Kompas* and *The Jakarta Post*, to describe China's engagement in the SCS in a negative manner. The words "South China Sea" (Laut *China* Selatan/*Laut Tiongkok Selatan*) appeared 92 times in *Kompas* and no less than 278 times in *The Jakarta Post* articles published between January 1, 2008 to October 1, 2019 (see Table 8.1). Both were searched with the keywords: "Indonesia and China." The negative representation of China in articles published by *Kompas* and *The Jakarta Post* that mentioned "South China Sea" was mainly due to China's military build-up in the area and as a result of illegal fishing activities by Chinese fishers in Indonesian waters. From 2008 to 2010, there was no depiction of China's involvement in the South China Sea disputes as a "threat" to Indonesia and the region, either in *The Jakarta Post* or in *Kompas*. This began to change in 2011 due to China's deployment of nuclear submarines and sundry other warships in addition to a network of underground tunnels at the Sanya base on the southern tip of Hainan Island.[27] From 2013 to 2017, the Indonesian media consistently portray China's engagement in the SCS as a "threat" due to China's military build-up, and its policy measures to restrict the fishing activities of foreign vessels, impose a naval blockade, include part of Indonesia's Natuna waters in its map, construct artificial islands in the area, and protect Chinese fishers conducting illegal fishing in Indonesian Natuna waters.

From January 1, 2018 to October 1, 2019, the words "South China Sea" were not mentioned in articles published by *Kompas* or *The Jakarta Post* on

[26] Interview with a senior official from the Indonesian Maritime Security Board (Jakarta, August 26, 2015).

[27] Senia Febrica and Suzia Sudarman, "Analysing Indonesian Media and Government Representation of China," *British Journal of Chinese Studies* 8, no. 2 (2018), 109.

Table 8.1: The frequency of the words "South China Sea" in Indonesian newspapers, and negative representation of China in the dispute (January 1, 2008–October 1, 2019)

Year	*The Jakarta Post*	*Kompas*	Corresponding major political event(s)
2008	0	0	---
2009	1	0	Chinese President Hu Jintao's state visit to Singapore in November 2009 and Lee Kwan Yew's warning about China's military build-up in the SCS.
2010	6	0	US Defense Minister Robert Gates' visit to Indonesia.
2011	45	1	China's military build-up in the SCS, including the placement of Chinese nuclear submarines, warships, and a network of underground tunnels at the Sanya base on the southern tip of Hainan Island.
2012	62	35	Military standoff between the Philippines and China maritime authorities in the Scarborough Shoal over fishing activities in the areas; the 45th ASEAN Ministerial Meeting in July, 2012; the deployment of four of China's State Oceanic Administration vessels to Huayang Reef, an area close to the Spratly Islands that Vietnam had declared as a territory under its authority; Indonesia's drafting and communicating the COC for the SCS dispute settlement effort in September, 2012; ASEAN Summit in Phnom Penh, Cambodia, in November, 2012.
2013	27	10	The 12th International Institute for Strategic Studies Asia Security Summit, the Shangri-La Dialogue in Singapore in June, 2013; the International Maritime Security Symposium in Jakarta in December, 2013; and the signing of Indonesia-China comprehensive strategic partnership.
2014	66	7	China's fishing restrictions in the SCS; the establishment of Air Defence in the East China Sea; a naval blockade around Second Thomas Shoal; and inclusion of part of Indonesia's Natuna Islands waters in China's territorial map.
2015	8	22	The 2015 ASEAN Summit in Kuala Lumpur, Malaysia; China's rapid progress in building an airstrip suitable for military use in the Spratly Islands; and the signing of the AIIB Articles of Agreement in June, 2015.
2016	52	11	Military standoff between the Indonesian Navy and the Chinese Coast Guard in Natuna waters following the arrest of a Chinese fishing vessel *Han Tan Cou* 19308 in June, 2016; Indonesian President, Jokowi, visited Natuna on warship.

Table 8.1: The frequency of the words "South China Sea" in Indonesian newspapers, and negative representation of China in the dispute (January 1, 2008–October 1, 2019) (continued)

Year	*The Jakarta Post*	*Kompas*	Corresponding major political event(s)
2017	11	6	The naming of Indonesian waters adjacent to the SCS as the North Natuna Sea and China's protest over the name; the inaugural summit of China's Belt and Road Initiative (BRI) in Beijing in May, 2017; and ASEAN's 50th Anniversary.
2018	0	0	---
2019	0	0	---

Source: Updated from Febrica and Sudarman, 2018

"Indonesia and China." The articles found using "Indonesia and China" keywords from January 2018 to October 2019 were focusing on cooperation between the two countries in the economic sector. In these articles, China was predominantly portrayed as a strategic and beneficial partner. A change in tone in the Indonesian government and media discourse on China took place just before the end of 2019. The act of illegal fishing in Indonesia's Natuna Sea conducted by Chinese fishing vessels from December 2019 to January 2020 and the presence of Chinese Coast Guard ships in protecting them have led Indonesian officials and the media to depict China in a far more negative light. From the third week of December 2019 until the second week of January 2020, the Indonesian Maritime Security Board had detected a sustained spate of illegal fishing activities by Chinese fishing vessels under the protection of the Chinese Coast Guard in Indonesia's North Natuna Sea.[28] The Indonesian Maritime Security Board reported that 50 Chinese fishing vessels had entered Indonesian waters on December 19, 2019 and left the next day.[29] On December 24, 2019, however, more fishing vessels under heavy guard by Chinese Coast Guard vessels returned to Natuna Sea.[30] The presence of government warships provides stark evidence that the Chinese regime sanctions the activity of illegal fishing as well as the violation of sovereign maritime territory of another state.

[28] *CNN Indonesia*. "China Ngotot Punya Hak dan Kedaulatan di Laut Natuna," January 4, 2020.

[29] *The Jakarta Post*, "Indonesia Lodges Strong Protest Against China for Trespassing, Poaching in Natunas," January 1, 2020.

[30] Ibid.

Additionally, the presence of the warships serves as a strong indication that China is prepared to escalate tensions with other states, whose waters it violates. Finally, in our estimation, the presence of Chinese warships can be seen as a litmus test for other states' willingness and capacity to respond to any maritime territorial intrusion and aggression. This final point, alongside the preceding ones, depletes the pro-harmony, good-friendship, and peaceful development rhetoric often present in China's official papers on its activities in the SCS of any value.

The Indonesian Ministry of Foreign Affairs summoned China's Ambassador, Xiao Qian, to Indonesia, to lodge a diplomatic protest over China's violation of Indonesia's sovereign rights in the Natuna Sea.[31] The Indonesian Foreign Minister, Retno L. Marsudi reiterated Indonesia's official position in the SCS dispute to provide clarity regarding Indonesia's sovereign rights in the Natuna Sea. As Marsudi asserted on January 3, 2020, "Indonesia will never recognise nine dash lines, unilateral claims made by China that do not have legal reasons recognized by international law, especially UNCLOS 1982."[32] Responding to the row over ownership claims of the Natuna Sea between Indonesia and China, President Jokowi made a bold statement to the domestic and international audience when he stressed, "there is no compromise in maintaining Indonesian sovereignty."[33] Despite his firm stance, Jokowi claimed that the government has continued to prioritize a peaceful diplomatic solution with China to resolve the conflict in the Natuna Sea.[34] Therefore, Indonesia has reiterated its role as a regional leader in the SCS dispute, but at the same time concretized Indonesia's soft-assertive position that no comprises or negotiations over Indonesian sovereignty would happen.

The Indonesian government decision to publicly protest China's violation of Indonesia's sovereign rights in the North Natuna Sea in 2020 indicates the government's growing assertiveness in dealing with China. From 2007 to 2015 the Indonesian maritime agencies had arrested 31 China-flagged vessels.[35] In 2010, a Chinese naval vessel confronted an Indonesian patrol boat and demanded the release of a Chinese trawler that fished illegally in Natuna waters. This incident was widely reported by the media. An Indonesian official claimed that at least three such incidents between Indonesia's maritime authorities and its Chinese counterparts occurred

31 Ibid.

32 *CNN Indonesia*, "China Ngotot Punya Hak dan Kedaulatan di Laut Natuna," January 4, 2020; *CNN Indonesia*, "Jokowi soal Kapal China di Natuna: Tak Ada Kompromi," January 4, 2020.

33 Ibid.

34 Ibid.

35 Indonesian Ministry of Marine Affairs and Fisheries, March 19, 2015.

in 2010 alone.[36] In 2013, armed Chinese vessels compelled an Indonesian maritime and fisheries ministry patrol boat to release Chinese fishers apprehended in Natuna waters.[37] This move is tantamount to a coercive military rescue operation and the counter-acquisition of citizens who were in clear violation of fishing regulations. Despite these incidents, the Indonesian government did not react strongly in the public eye against the Chinese government. Past incidents were resolved through closed-bilateral negotiation between the Indonesian defence agencies and the Chinese diplomatic mission in Jakarta.[38] This situation began to change in early 2016 when Indonesia started to assert itself in its relations with China. In March 2016, Marsudi announced that the government sent a note of protest to the Chinese government over the move of *MV Kwang Fey* 10078, a Chinese-flagged fishing vessel, and a Chinese Coast Guard vessel that entered Indonesian waters adjacent to Natuna.[39] In June 2016, the Indonesian Coordinating Minister for Political, Legal and Security Affairs, Luhut Pandjaitan, stated that the Indonesian government would ignore a letter of protest conveyed by the government of China following the shooting and arrest of a fishing vessel, registered under China's flag, by the Indonesian Navy in Natuna.[40] In early August 2016, the Indonesian government declared its plan to sink 71 foreign vessels to mark the country's 71 years of independence, including Chinese flagged vessels.[41] This decision was made following multiple military stand-off incidents involving the Indonesian and Chinese maritime authorities in Indonesian Natuna Sea.

As an act of resistance of China's unilateral claims in the SCS less than a year later in July 2017 Indonesia renamed the northern most part of its exclusive economic zone (EEZ) in the SCS as the North Natuna Sea.[42] A senior official

---

[36] See, Senia Febrica, "Indonesia's Diplomatic and Security Responses," in *South China Sea Lawfare: Legal Perspectives and International Responses to the Philippines v. China Arbitration Case*. South China Sea Think Tank and Taiwan Center for Security Studies, Taipei, Taiwan, 2016, 101–110.

[37] Fergus Jensen and Bernadette Christina Munthe, "Indonesia Says it Feels Peace Efforts on South China Sea 'Sabotaged,'" *Reuters*, March 21, 2016; Senia Febrica. *Maritime Security and Indonesia: Cooperation, Interests and Strategies*. Abingdon, Routledge, 170.

[38] Senia Febrica and Suzie Sudarman, "Indonesia's Perception of China's Leadership in Southeast Asia," Presentation paper for the Joint East Asian Studies Conference in September 2016 at SOAS, University of London, United Kingdom, 2016.

[39] *The Jakarta Post*, "Indonesia Protests Against China in South China Sea Fishing Dispute," March 21, 2016.

[40] *Kompas*, "Luhut: RI Tidak Perlu Tanggapi Protes China soal Penembakan Kapal di Natuna," June 20, 2016.

[41] *Kompas*, "17 Agustus Nanti, Menteri Susi Siap Tenggelamkan 71 Kapal," August 1, 2016.

[42] Prashanth Parameswaran, "Why Did Indonesia Just Rename Its Part of the South China Sea?," *The Diplomat*, July 17, 2017; Leo Suryadinata, "What Does Indonesia's Renaming

at the Indonesian Coordinating Ministry of Maritime Affairs, Arif Havas Oegroseno, noted that the northern side of its EEZ was the site of oil and gas activity and explained that Indonesia wanted to "update the naming of the sea [and] we gave a new name in line with the usual practice: the North Natuna Sea."[43] Responding to Indonesia's decision and action, the Chinese Foreign Ministry spokesman, Geng Shuang, criticized the policy move, stating that, "certain countries' so-called renaming is totally meaningless ... We hope the relevant country can meet China halfway and properly maintain the present good situation in the South China Sea region, which has not come easily."[44] The Indonesian Minister of Marine and Fisheries Affairs, Susi Pudjiastuti, rebuked China's criticism, further stating that Indonesia has the right to name its own waterway. As she put it: "Why not? It is our North Natuna Sea."[45] Indonesia continues to refer to the area in question as the North Natuna Sea.

As China is increasingly seen as a threat to Indonesia in the SCS, the Indonesian government officials and media began to view the US' growing influence in Southeast Asia as a positive development. In the context of the SCS dispute, the national media portrayed the US as a strategic partner of Indonesia in creating rules-based order in the Indo-Pacific region, fostering peaceful cooperation in Southeast Asia, and dealing with shared diplomatic and security.[46] As a senior official from the Indonesian Coordinating Ministry for Political, Legal, and Security Affairs claimed: "the US pivot to Asia does not pose such a big threat ... I think it brings plenty of advantages, benefits. Especially, when it comes to providing [us] with global political support ... We have to play between those two elephants [China and the US]."[47]

Indonesia's diplomatic and military strategies

Indonesia's diplomatic course of actions to help find peaceful settlement in the SCS maritime dispute are carried out primarily through ASEAN cooperation forums, including the ASEAN-China Joint Working Group

of Part of the South China Sea Signify?," ISEAS – Yusof Ishak Institute, August 18, 2017, Singapore.

43 *Reuters*. "Asserting Sovereignty, Indonesia Renames Part of South China Sea." July 14, 2017.

44 Ibid.

45 *Kompas*, "Menteri Susi Heran China Protes Penamaan Laut Natuna Utara," July 18, 2017.

46 See, for example, *The Jakarta Post*, "US Envoy Reaffirms Religious Tolerance amid Trump Ban," February 8, 2017; Stephen Smith and Hugo Seymour, "Australia Looks to Indonesia in an Era of Uncertainty," *The Jakarta Post*, August 19, 2019.

47 Interview with an official from the Indonesian Coordinating Ministry for Political, Legal, and Security Affairs (Jakarta, August 21, 2015).

on the Implementation of the Declaration on the Conduct of Parties in the South China Sea, the ASEAN+3, the ASEAN Defence Ministerial Meeting, the ASEAN Institute for Peace and Reconciliation, and the ASEAN Workshop on the South China Sea.

Indonesia has consistently expressed its willingness to play an active role as a facilitator in the dispute settlement negotiations with all concerned parties. Since the signing of the Declaration on the Conduct of Parties in the South China Sea in November 2002 by ASEAN member states and China, Indonesia has pushed for the formulation of a legally binding COC. In 2012 when Indonesia took the chairmanship of ASEAN, the Indonesian Ministry of Foreign Affairs initiated and circulated a draft of COC – that included the elements of conflict-prevention and management if a crisis arises – to ASEAN foreign ministers.[48] ASEAN member states were expected to discuss the draft before the ASEAN Summit in November 2012, prior to negotiations with China.[49] The deliberation on the draft has not led to a legally binding code, as China was not enthusiastic about the prospect of negotiating the terms and conditions of the COC in the ASEAN 10 plus 1 format.[50] On October 9, 2013, at the 16th China-ASEAN meeting in Brunei Darussalam, China agreed to take part in formal consultations on the COC and proposed the establishment of an Eminent Persons and Experts Group (EPEG), also known as Track 1.5, to consult on the COC draft.[51]

Indonesia's willingness to be a facilitator in mediating dispute resolution in the SCS has not always met with great enthusiasm by China. After the Hague Arbitral Tribunal issued its award in October 2015 on the jurisdiction and admissibility in the arbitration initiated by the Philippines against China, for example, a spokesperson for the Chinese Embassy in Washington, Zhu Haiqua, asserted that, "China is committed to resolving relevant disputes through negotiation and consultation with parties directly involved. This is the only right choice."[52] This statement implicitly stated China's reluctance to accept Indonesia's role as facilitator in the process of the formulation

---

48 *The Jakarta Post*, "RI Circulates Draft Code of Conduct on South China Sea," September 29, 2012.

49 Ibid.

50 C. F. Luhulima, "Can SBY End China's Dominance in the South China Sea," *The Jakarta Post*, May 5, 2014.

51 *Liputan 6*, "Menlu Retno: RI Dorong Situasi Kondusif di Laut China Selatan," June 13, 2015; Sekretariat Kabinet Indonesia, "Menlu: Tekanannya, Indonesia ingin perdamaian di kawasan Laut China Selatan terwujud," March 24, 2015.

52 *The Jakarta Post*, "Arbitration Panel OKs Jurisdiction in South China Sea Case," October 30, 2015.

of the COC in the SCS. Moreover, the response is a display of China's commitment to its minute-by-minute action and response strategy as events and developments unfold in and concerning the SCS. For Indonesia, the acceptance of the COC by all claimants is key for addressing the growing security and military tension in the region. After the issuance of the Tribunal Awards in 2015, the most immediate aim for the Indonesian government was for ASEAN and China to reach an agreement over the timeframe to finalize the COC.[53] Indonesia pushed for an agreed timeline on the COC, given the perceived slowness in reaching an agreement between ASEAN and China. In October 2015, the Director of the ASEAN Political and Security Directorate at the Indonesian Ministry of Foreign Affairs, Muhammad Chandra W. Yudha, explained that his ministry had continued to keep the momentum up in an effort to complete the COC in a timely manner.[54] He explained that, "the process continues to roll and makes significant progress for ASEAN and China to establish a code of conduct ... Without the CoC, we cannot regulate everything related to the conflict in the South China Sea."[55] According to Yudha, the Indonesian Ministry of Foreign Affairs and relevant parties have continued "to negotiate the elements and structures of COC" that deal with various instances such as "collision between vessels, search and rescue of vessels under distress, and the development of hotline communication if an incident occurs in the South China Sea."[56]

A leap forward in the COC negotiation took place in 2018. In August 2018, China and ASEAN finalized a single draft COC negotiating text, and in November 2018 the two parties reached an agreement to finalize the COC within three years, starting from 2019.[57] According to Carl Thayer, the negotiations are marked with continuing differences due to: the undefined geographic scope of the SCS; disagreement over dispute settlement mechanisms; different approaches to conflict management (self-restraint, mutual trust, and confidence-building); and the undefined legal status of the COC.[58] The negotiations have been marked with differences because the absence of geographical clarity regarding the SCS dispute. Vietnam proposed that all disputed features and overlapping maritime areas must be included

---

53 *Liputan 6*, "Menlu Retno: RI Dorong Situasi Kondusif di Laut China Selatan," June 13, 2015; Sekretariat Kabinet Indonesia, "Menlu: Tekanannya, Indonesia ingin perdamaian di kawasan Laut China Selatan terwujud," March 24, 2015.

54 *Republika*, "AIPR Cegah Campur Tangan Internasional di ASEAN," October 30, 2015.

55 Ibid.

56 Ibid.

57 Minh Quang Nguyen, "Saving the China-ASEAN South China Sea Code of Conduct," June 29, 2019, *The Diplomat*.

58 Ibid.

in the COC.[59] Indonesia, as a non-claimant state, proposed that a statement regarding the requirements for states to respect the EEZ and continental shelf of the coastal states in the SCS – in line with UNCLOS – be inserted in the COC.[60] Agreement has not been reached on any dispute settlement mechanism. Indonesia and Vietnam proposed the principles in the Treaty of Amity and Cooperation to be used as a guideline for the first stage of the dispute settlement prior to resorting to an international dispute settlement mechanism.[61] Brunei, Cambodia, China, Malaysia, and Singapore suggested that the authority to monitor the implementation of the COC be handed to the ASEAN-China Senior Officials' Meeting.[62] Vietnam proposed the establishment of a new commission led by foreign ministers of ASEAN and China.[63] The legal status of the COC has also proven to be a source of disagreement, though one might surmise that dragging out the COC is a deliberate strategy on the part of China to avoid establishing guidelines by which states should act. China refuses to join a binding COC that could challenge Beijing's claims in the SCS and possibly, if not likely, restrict its more aggressive and coercive approach to achieving is goals, whereas Vietnam seeks a legally binding COC that calls for ratification on the domestic level.[64]

In 2020, ASEAN and China entered the second year of the COC negotiation. The beginning of January 2020 was marked by a diplomatic spat between Indonesia and China in the North Natuna Sea. China's actions came at the time when the diplomatic and security cooperation between the two countries have showed significant improvement. The media reports on Sino-Indonesian relations from January 2018 to October 2019, as shown in Table 8.1, for example, made no reference to China's threatening behaviour in the SCS. The increase of China's investment reached a sum of US$240 million in Indonesia. Further, the resumption of the high-speed railway project, connecting Jakarta and Bandung, and funded by the Chinese Development Bank, had become the highlight of Sino-Indonesia relations prior to a spate of illegal fishing activities by Chinese fishers in Indonesian Natuna Sea, located in the southernmost tip of the SCS, in December 2019.[65] Following the Sino-Indonesian diplomatic row in the North Natuna Sea, Indonesia's hardening stance in the SCS dispute was observed. In her annual press statement on January 8, 2020, Marsudi asserted

59 Ibid.

60 Ibid.

61 Ibid.

62 Ibid.

63 Ibid.

64 Ibid.

65 Nabiha Shahab, "Indonesia's Natuna Challenge," *The Diplomat*, March 13, 2020.

that, "sovereignty diplomacy" was one of the ministry priorities in 2020.[66] As part of the diplomacy efforts she noted that Indonesia is increasing the intensity of maritime boundaries negotiations with Malaysia and Vietnam. These are the two countries that Indonesia share maritime boundaries with in the South China Sea. Marsudi did not reference China. However, in her speech she stressed Indonesia's sovereignty and sovereign rights in its own waters. To quote her: "Specifically, I would like to emphasise one principle regarding sovereignty and sovereign rights in Indonesian waters. That any claim, by any party, must be made in accordance with international law, including UNCLOS 1982 … Indonesia will continue to reject claims that are not recognized by international law."[67]

The growing tension in the SCS was one of the topics discussed during the first meeting of ASEAN foreign ministers in 2020. It was the first ASEAN meeting organized since Vietnam become the regional organization chair in 2020. In recent years, military standoff between China and Vietnam has also become a key feature in the two countries foreign relations. In 2019, for example, a number of Chinese vessels were deployed in a month-long standoff with Vietnamese authorities in the area adjacent to an oil block located within Vietnam's EEZ.[68] During the ASEAN Ministerial Meeting in January 2020, the Vietnamese Foreign Minister, Phạm Bình Minh, stated that all ASEAN member states voiced their concerns regarding serious incidents in the SCS.[69] He called on member states to:

> exercise self-restraint in the conduct of activities and avoid actions that may further complicate the situation … and reaffirmed that international law, including the 1982 UNCLOS, is the basis for determining sovereignty, sovereign rights and legitimate interests over maritime areas. We further reaffirmed that the 1982 UNCLOS is the overarching framework of legal order for the seas that must be respected by all countries.[70]

Although the Vietnamese Foreign Minister's statement did not explicitly mention China's misconduct in the SCS, Indonesian media insinuated that the "statement is an apparent reference to China, whose sweeping claims to

---

66 Indonesian Ministry of Foreign Affairs. "Pernyataan Pers Tahunan Menteri Luar Negeri Tahun 2020." January 8, 2020.

67 Ibid.

68 *The Jakarta Post*, "ASEAN reaffirms international law as basis for sovereignty in South China Sea," January 18, 2020.

69 Ibid.

70 Ibid.

the South China Sea were based on the so-called nine-dash line."[71] During the meeting, Marsudi emphasized Indonesia's full support of Vietnam's leadership. She reminded ASEAN member states that ASEAN needs to maintain peace and stability in the region, including in and around the SCS, and to ensure that international law, particularly the 1982 Law of the Sea Convention (LOSC) is respected by all parties with connections to the SCS. Her statement reflected Indonesia's traditional position of emphasizing ASEAN's centrality in dispute-settlement in the SCS. It also served as a message to China, a party to the 1982 LOSC, to honour its commitment.

During the ministerial meeting in January 2020, Marsudi also reiterated Indonesia's commitment for the ASEAN Outlook on Indo-Pacific cooperation by organizing infrastructure and connectivity forums in Jakarta in July 2020. Indonesia initiated the development of an ASEAN Indo-Pacific cooperation concept to diffuse the security tension in the SCS since 2013. Recognizing the challenges in the Indo-Pacific, including "the unresolved maritime disputes in the South China Sea, and the dynamics in major powers interactions in the region," Indonesia proposed an Indo-Pacific-wide treaty of friendship and cooperation.[72] According to the Indonesian former foreign minister, Natalegawa, this treaty is "a commitment by states in the region to build confidence, to solve disputes by peaceful means, and to promote a concept of security that is all encompassing; underscoring that security is a common good."[73] Indonesia began to promote the Indo-Pacific cooperation concept with ASEAN at various ASEAN meetings throughout 2018, including the ASEAN Heads of Government Summit in April 2018, the ASEAN Foreign Ministers' Meeting in August 2018, the ASEAN Senior Officials' Retreat Meeting in Jakarta in September 2018, and the ASEAN Summit in November 2018. Members of ASEAN have adopted the ASEAN Outlook on the Indo-Pacific document in June 2019 that provides details on objectives, principles, and cooperation areas that can be explored. The ASEAN Outlook on Indo-Pacific cooperation was adopted against the background of increasing power competition in the SCS, not only among claimant states, but also between China and the US. As Donald E. Weatherbee argues, the region has become an expanded theatre of US-China rivalry with Washington's promotion of a Free and Open Indo-Pacific (FOIP) and China's Belt and Road (BRI) Initiative (Weatherbee 2019b).

[71] Ibid.

[72] Indonesian Ministry of Foreign Affairs, "Profile: Dr. R. M. Marty M. Natalegawa," Buletin Komunitas ASEAN, Jakarta, Indonesia (2013).

[73] Ibid.

Maritime cooperation is the first area of cooperation mentioned in the ASEAN Indo-Pacific cooperation document. The document further noted "cooperation for peaceful settlement of dispute" as the first area of maritime cooperation.[74] An Indonesian senior official who has been involved in bilateral cooperation between Indonesia and Vietnam explained that Jakarta has encouraged Vietnam to use its leverage both as the ASEAN Chair and a United Nations Security Council (UNSC) member to further developing the Indo-Pacific cooperation concept and to speak on behalf of ASEAN members regarding the cooperation initiative at international forums.[75] He further argued that the development of the ASEAN Indo-Pacific cooperation will provide Vietnam with opportunities to advocate a cooperation agreement that can help both Vietnam and ASEAN member countries to protect their maritime rights and interests.[76]

In order to secure its maritime rights and interests in areas adjacent to the SCS, Indonesia has combined its diplomatic strategies with security and military measures. After the Arbitral Tribunal issued the award on jurisdiction in 2015, Indonesia began to put in place a number of new security measures in its territory close to the SCS.[77] The new measures include all components of the country's Armed Forces including the Navy, Air Force, and Army. The Indonesian Navy sent seven of its warships to Natuna at the beginning of November 2015 to bolster its naval presence in the area.[78]

The Indonesian Air Force has intensified its patrols and put in place resources, including Hawk and F-16 fighter jets, to carry out its task.[79] The Indonesian patrol operation to monitor Indonesian maritime borders close to SCS has involved jet fighters from three air bases: Kalimantan, Halim, and Pekanbaru.[80] The Commandant of Roesdin Nurjadi Air Base in Pekanbaru, Marsma TNI Henri Alfiandi, explained that this operation aimed to generate a "deterrent effect to conflicting parties in South China Sea."[81] He pointed out the need for Indonesia to increase its "presence," given the growing tensions in the SCS, to secure the country's territory without getting further involved or taking side in the dispute.[82]

74 See ASEAN, "ASEAN Outlook on the Indo-Pacific," June 2019.

75 Interview with an Indonesian senior official (Hanoi, November 5, 2019).

76 Interview with an Indonesian senior official (Hanoi, November 5, 2019).

77 The discussion about Indonesia's security and military measures in the Natuna Sea following the tribunal award on jurisdiction in 2015 is drawn from Febrica, 2016.

78 *Banjarmasin Post*, "Kirim 7 Kapal Perang ke Natuna, Ini Alasan TNI," November 9, 2015.

79 *Liputan 6*, "Konflik Laut China Selatan TNI Rajin Patroli Perbatasan," November 9, 2015.

80 Ibid.

81 Ibid.

82 Ibid.

The Indonesian Army, Military Resort Command 031, Wirabima Riau, has prepared and trained Indonesian army personnel as part of the country's rapid reaction forces, in anticipation of conflict escalation in SCS, although no actual numbers have been released.[83] Wirabima Riau Commandant, Brigjen TNI Nurendi, confirmed that, "the rapid reaction forces have been established. They are still training until now, all of them are ready to be deployed to face any worst possibility ... if physical contact or war takes place."[84] Despite the presence of war-like preparations, Nurendi stressed that Indonesia is not taking part or adopting a side in the SCS. The rapid reaction forces will be deployed from Riau only to defend the archipelago.[85]

Despite increasing military activities in Indonesian territory bordering the SCS, the Head of the Navy Information Department, Laksma M. Zainudin, denied that the reason underpinning the deployment of warships and the increased frequency of air patrols in the area is the growing tensions in the region. Rather, as Zainudin stated, these activities "are only part of routine operations ... to secure Natuna waters. Especially, [since] illegal fishing often happens in [waters surrounding] Natuna."[86] The Air Force Commandant of Roesdin Nurjadi Air Base in Pekanbaru, Alfiandi, and the Army Wirabima Riau Commandant, Nurendi, however, have stated that the security measures are taken to increase Indonesia's military presence in its borders with SCS, guard the country's territorial integrity, and defend Natuna – the country's outer island in the region – if war occurs.[87]

The military standoff between Indonesian and China maritime authorities over Chinese fishers' illegal fishing activities in North Natuna Sea in December 2019 to January 2020 has led Indonesia to further extend its military presence in the area. On January 4, 2020, the Indonesian Navy (Naval Fleet Command 1) and Air Force (Air Force Command 1) units in the vicinity of Natuna were placed under combat-ready status. The Indonesian Armed Forces have put in place eight naval vessels, one maritime surveillance aircraft, and one air force Boeing airplane to patrol Indonesian boundaries in the SCS. The Indonesian Coordinating Minister for Maritime Affairs, Luhut Binsar Panjaitan, announced in January 2020 that Indonesia would purchase an ocean-going vessel of 138–140 metres in length to strengthen the Indonesian Maritime Security Board patrol operation in the North Natuna

83 *Liputan 6*, "Prajurit TNI AD Dilatih Antisipasi Konflik Laut China Selatan," November 10, 2015.

84 Ibid.

85 Ibid.

86 *Banjarmasin Post*, "Kirim 7 Kapal Perang ke Natuna, Ini Alasan TNI," November 9, 2015.

87 *Liputan 6*, "Prajurit TNI AD Dilatih Antisipasi Konflik Laut China Selatan," November 10, 2015.

Sea.[88] He also explained his ministry's plan to further equip the Indonesian Coast Guard and to develop a naval base in addition to the Ministry of Fishery's Coast Guard unit base in Natuna.[89]

As part of the Indonesian government plan to modernize its weapons system, the Indonesian Minister of Defence, Prabowo Subianto, met with Russian Minister of Defence, Sergey Shoygu, in Moscow on January 29, 2020 to discuss the government's plan to purchase 11 SU-35 fighter jets from Russia.[90] Indonesia is also planning to purchase 48 Dassault Rafale fighter jets, four Scorpène-class submarines, and a corvette navy ship from France.[91] French Ambassador to Indonesia, Olivier Chambard, confirmed that the Indonesian Minister of Defence had conducted an initial stage of negotiation regarding the plan with his French counterparts during his visit to Paris on January 11–13, 2020.[92] However, despite Indonesia having put in place all these security measures to improve its defence system in its North Natuna Sea, Indonesia has continued to prioritize a peaceful solution to resolve conflicts in the region, even though it has undertaken significant moves to strengthen its military position and readiness. The Indonesian military has consistently framed military operations in the North Natuna Sea as part of its routine operation to prevent any provocation, but also to be ready to respond with force if the need were to arise. A senior military officer, Mayjen TNI Sisriadi, stated on January 9, 2020 that, "[w]e are still securing the area [North Natuna Sea]. I will repeat that again, the Indonesian Armed Forces (TNI) will continue to carry out its routine operation, that operation is routine. Perhaps in terms of intensity we will see what happens in the field."[93]

Conclusion

This chapter has presented an examination of Indonesia's official position with respect to the maritime dispute in the SCS and diplomatic and security

88 *CNN Indonesia*, "China Ngotot Punya Hak dan Kedaulatan di Laut Natuna," January 4, 2020; *CNN Indonesia*, "Jokowi soal Kapal China di Natuna: Tak Ada Kompromi," January 4 2020.

89 Ibid.

90 *CNBC*, "Blak-blakan, Alasan Prabowo Beli Senjata Militer Baru buat RI," February 2, 2020.

91 *CNN Indonesia*, "Prancis Buka Suara soal Rencana Prabowo Beli 48 Jet Tempur," January 24, 2020.

92 Ibid.

93 Detik, "TNI: Kapal Nelayan China Keluar dari ZEE Usai Kunjungan Jokowi ke Natuna," January 9, 2020.

measures that the Indonesian government has taken to protect its rights and interests. As part of Indonesia's official position in the SCS, the government has consistently emphasized four points. First, Indonesia is a non-claimant state in the overall dispute. Indonesia does not claim any territory or maritime features in the SCS. Second, Indonesia does not acknowledge China's "nine-dash line" as a basis of its territorial claims in the SCS. From Indonesia's perspective, the country has no shared boundaries with China in the SCS. Indonesia only has shared maritime boundaries in the SCS region with Malaysia and Vietnam. Third, Indonesia has consistently sought to advance a peaceful resolution to the SCS dispute in spite of being the target of China's aggressive and coercive measures involving the presence of Chinese military warships. Indonesia continues to emphasize the centrality of ASEAN in finding a peaceful settlement and to dissolve the ever-growing tension in the SCS.

Indonesia views itself as a neutral third party and an active peacebroker in finding a peaceful solution to the dispute. However, in recent years, a range of policies implemented by China in the SCS, including those that resulted in the presence of nuclear submarines and warships, and the establishment of an airstrip in the areas suitable for military use, has raised the Indonesian government's concern exponentially. Moreover, a number of incidents that have taken place between 2010 and 2020 have resulted in several major diplomatic spats between Indonesia and China. These include multiple clashes between Indonesian maritime authorities and their Chinese counterparts over the practice of illegal fishing in the Indonesian North Natuna Sea in 2010, 2013, 2016, late 2019 until early 2020, and the inclusion of part of Indonesia's Natuna Sea in China's territorial map in 2016. Responding to China's growing aggressiveness in the SCS, Indonesia has continued to push for the finalization of the COC, which has entered its second year of negotiation. At the same time, Indonesia has also increased its policy collaboration with Vietnam, encouraging Vietnam to use its leverage as the current chair of ASEAN and also an UNSC member to promote the ASEAN Outlook on Indo-Pacific cooperation and explore further areas of maritime cooperation required to find a peaceful settlement.

Lastly, Indonesia has put a number of security and military measures in place to secure its maritime rights and interests in the SCS. Foremost, the country has increased its military presence in the Natuna Sea, since the tribunal announced that it has jurisdiction over the *Philippines v. China* arbitration case in 2015. The recent military standoff between Indonesia and China in the North Natuna Sea from December to January 2020 has further contributed to Indonesia extending its military presence in the area. Against this backdrop, Indonesia has planned to modernize its military services' weapon systems by purchasing a number of jet fighters, submarines, and a naval ships from other countries. However, despite undertaking these measures, Indonesia – as an armed and ready, wary warrior – has consistently reiterated its position as a non-claimant state and prioritized finding a peaceful and diplomatic solution over the evolving and multifaceted conflict in the SCS.

References

Arsana, Andi. "Is China a Neighbour to Indonesia?" *The Jakarta Post*, August 8, 2011. https://www.thejakartapost.com/news/2011/08/08/is-china-a-neighbor-indonesia.html

ASEAN. "Terms of Reference of the ASEAN-China Joint Working Group on the Implementation of the Declaration on the Conduct of Parties in the South China Sea," May 14, 2012. https://asean.org/?static_post=terms-of-reference-of-the-asean-china-joint-working-group-on-the-implementation-of-the-declaration-on-the-conduct-of-parties-in-the-south-china-sea.

ASEAN. "ASEAN Outlook on the Indo-Pacific." June 2019. https://asean.org/storage/2019/06/ASEAN-Outlook-on-the-Indo-Pacific_FINAL_22062019.pdf

Ba, Alice D. "China and ASEAN: Renavigating Relations for a 21st-Century Asia." *Asian Survey* 43, no. 4 (2003), 622–47.

Banjarmasin Post. "Kirim 7 Kapal Perang ke Natuna, Ini Alasan TNI." November 9, 2015. http://banjarmasin.tribunnews.com/2015/11/09/kirim-7-kapal-perang-ke-natuna-ini-alasan-tni

Baviera, Aileen. "Preventing War, Building a Rules-Based Order: Challenges Facing the ASEAN Political–Security Community." ASEAN@50 4, Building ASEAN Community: Political-Security and Socio-Cultural Reflections. https://www.eria.org/ASEAN_at_50_4A.0_Baviera_final.pdf.

Borchers, Henning. "ASEAN's Environmental Challenges and Nontraditional Security Cooperation: Towards a Regional Peacekeeping Force?." *ASEAS – Austrian Journal of South-East Asian Studies* 7, no. 1 (2014), 5–20. https://www.ssoar.info/ssoar/bitstream/handle/document/40164/ssoar-aseas-2014-1-borchers-ASEANs_environmental_challenges_and_non-traditional.pdf?sequence=1&isAllowed=y&lnkname=ssoar-aseas-2014-1-borchers-ASEANs_environmental_challenges_and_non-traditional.pdf

CNBC. "Blak-blakan, Alasan Prabowo Beli Senjata Militer Baru buat RI." February 2, 2020. https://www.cnbcindonesia.com/news/20200202095927-4-134528/blak-blakan-alasan-prabowo-beli-senjata-militer-baru-buat-ri

CNN Indonesia. "China Ngotot Punya Hak dan Kedaulatan di Laut Natuna." January 4, 2020. https://www.cnnindonesia.com/internasional/20200103194528-113-462273/china-ngotot-punya-hak-dan-kedaulatan-di-laut-natuna

CNN Indonesia. "Jokowi soal Kapal China di Natuna: Tak Ada Kompromi." January 4, 2020. https://www.cnnindonesia.com/nasional/20200104125555-20-462354/jokowi-soal-kapal-china-di-natuna-tak-ada-kompromi

CNN Indonesia. "Prancis Buka Suara soal Rencana Prabowo Beli 48 Jet Tempur." January 24, 2020. https://www.cnnindonesia.com/internasional/20200123165421-106-468083/prancis-buka-suara-soal-rencana-prabowo-beli-48-jet-tempur

Connelly, Aaron J. "Sovereignty and the Sea: President Joko Widodo's Foreign Policy Challenges." *Contemporary Southeast Asia* 37, no. 1 (2015), 1–28. https://www.lowyinstitute.org/publications/sovereignty-and-sea-president-joko-widodos-foreign-policy-challenges

Detik. "TNI: Kapal Nelayan China Keluar dari ZEE Usai Kunjungan Jokowi ke Natuna," January 9, 2020. https://news.detik.com/berita/d-4852606/tni-kapal-nelayan-china-keluar-dari-zee-usai-kunjungan-jokowi-ke-natuna

Emmers, Ralf. "Indonesia's Role in ASEAN: A Case of Incomplete and Sectorial Leadership." *The Pacific Review* 27, no. 4 (2014), 543–62.

Febrica, Senia. "Indonesia's Diplomatic and Security Responses," in *South China Sea Lawfare: Legal Perspectives and International Responses to the Philippines v. China Arbitration Case*. Taipei: South China Sea Think Tank and Taiwan Center for Security Studies, 2016, 101–110.

Febrica, Senia. "Philippines v. China Arbitration Case: Indonesia's Diplomatic and Security Responses," in Fu-Kuo Liu and Jonathan Spangler (eds), *South China Sea Lawfare: Legal Perspectives and International Responses to the Philippines v. China Arbitration Case*. Taiwan: South China Sea Think Tank and Taiwan Center for Security Studies, 2016, 101–110.

Febrica, Senia. *Maritime Security and Indonesia: Cooperation, Interests and Strategies*. Abingdon, Routledge, 2017.

Febrica, Senia, and Suzie Sudarman. "Indonesia's Perception of China's Leadership in Southeast Asia." Presentation paper for the Joint East Asian Studies Conference in September 2016 at SOAS, University of London, United Kingdom.

Febrica, Senia and Suzie Sudarman. "Analysing Indonesian Media and Government Representation of China," *British Journal of Chinese Studies* 8, no. 2 (2018), 89–119.

Hao, Zheng. "Could China-US Tensions in the South China Sea Escalate Into a Hot War?," *Think China*, July 29, 2020. https://www.thinkchina.sg/could-china-us-tensions-south-china-sea-escalate-hot-war

Indonesian Ministry of Foreign Affairs. "Profile: Dr. R. M. Marty M. Natalegawa." Buletin Komunitas ASEAN, Jakarta, Indonesia, 2013.

Indonesian Ministry of Foreign Affairs. "Pernyataan Pers Tahunan Menteri Luar Negeri Tahun 2020," January 8, 2020. https://kemlu.go.id/portal/id/read/946/pidato/pernyataan-pers-tahunan-menteri-luar-negeri-ri-tahun-2020/

Indonesian Presidential Office. "Indonesia Sebagai Poros Maritim Dunia," November 13, 2015. http://www.presidenri.go.id/maritim/indonesia-sebagai-poros-maritim-dunia.html

Jensen, Fergus and Bernadette Christina Munthe. "Indonesia Says it Feels Peace Efforts on South China Sea 'Sabotaged.'" *Reuters*, March 31, 2016. https://br.reuters.com/article/us-indonesia-southchinasea-idUSKCN0WN0B6

Khemakorn, Pakjuta. "Sustainable Management of Pelagic Fisheries in the South China Sea Region," United Nations, New York, United States, November 2006. https://www.un.org/depts/los/nippon/unnff_programme_home/fellows_pages/fellows_papers/khemakorn_0607_thailand.pdf

Kompas. "17 Agustus Nanti, Menteri Susi Siap Tenggelamkan 71 Kapal." August 1, 2016. https://money.kompas.com/read/2016/08/01/132454526/17.agustus.nanti.menteri.susi.siap.tenggelamkan.71.kapal

Kompas. "Luhut: RI Tidak Perlu Tanggapi Protes China soal Penembakan Kapal di Natuna." June 20, 2016. https://kupang.kompas.com/read/2016/06/20/21034511/luhut.ri.tidak.perlu.tanggapi.protes.china.soal.penembakan.kapal.di.natuna

Kompas. "Menteri Susi Heran China Protes Penamaan Laut Natuna Utara," July 18, 2017. https://nasional.kompas.com/read/2017/07/18/11063771/menteri-susi-heran-china-protes-penamaan-laut-natuna-utara

Liputan 6. "Konflik Laut China Selatan TNI Rajin Patroli Perbatasan," November 9, 2015. http://news.liputan6.com/read/2361406/konflik-laut-china-selatan-tni-rajin-patroli-perbatasan

Liputan 6. "Menlu Retno: RI Dorong Situasi Kondusif di Laut China Selatan." June 13, 2015. http://news.liputan6.com/read/2251337/menlu-retno-ri-dorong-situasi-kondusif-di-laut-china-selatan

Liputan 6. "Prajurit TNI AD Dilatih Antisipasi Konflik Laut China Selatan." November 10, 2015. http://news.liputan6.com/read/2362396/prajurit-tni-ad-dilatih-antisipasi-konflik-laut-china-selatan?ref=yfp

Luhulima, C. P. F. "Can SBY End China's dominance in the South China Sea." *The Jakarta Post*, May 5, 2014. http://www.thejakartapost.com/news/2014/05/05/can-sby-end-china-s-dominance-south-china-sea.html#sthash.9cN0vJ6K.dpuf

Mastro, Oliana Skylar. "Military Confrontation in the South China Sea." Contingency Planning Memorandum No. 36, Council on Foreign Relations, New York, United States, May 21, 2020. https://www.cfr.org/report/military-confrontation-south-china-sea

Minemura, Kenji. "INTERVIEW/John Mearsheimer: US-China Rift Runs Real Risk of Escalating into a Nuclear War." *The Asahi Shimbun*, August 17, 2020. http://www.asahi.com/ajw/articles/13629071

Nguyễn, Hồng Thao. "The 2002 Declaration on the Conduct of Parties in the South China Sea: A Note." *Ocean Development & International Law* 34, no. 3–4 (2002), 279–85.

Nguyen, Minh Quang. "Saving the China-ASEAN South China Sea Code of Conduct," *The Diplomat*, June 29, 2019. https://thediplomat.com/2019/06/saving-the-china-asean-south-china-sea-code-of-conduct/

Parameswaran, Prashanth. "Why Did Indonesia Just Rename Its Part of the South China Sea?," *The Diplomat*, July 17, 2017. https://thediplomat.com/2017/07/why-did-indonesia-just-rename-its-part-of-the-south-china-sea/

Perlez, Jane. "Alarm as China Issues Rules for Disputed Area." *The New York Times*, December 2, 2012. http://www.nytimes.com/2012/12/02/world/asia/alarm-as-china-issues-rules-for-disputed-sea.html?_r=0

Permanent Court of Arbitration. "Arbitration between the Republic of the Philippines and the People's Republic of China: Tribunal Renders Award Jurisdiction and Admissibility; Will Hold Further Hearings," PCA Case No. 2013-19, October 29, 2015. https://www.pcacases.com/pcadocs/PH-CN%20-%2020160712%20-%20Award.pdf

Pitlo, Lucio Blanco. "Fishing Wars: Competition for South China Sea's Fishery Resources," Center for Security Studies, ETH Zürich, Switzerland, July 10, 2013. http://isnblog.ethz.ch/security/fishing-wars-competition-for-south-china-seas-fishery-resources

Republika. "AIPR Cegah Campur Tangan Internasional di ASEAN," October 30, 2015. http://www.republika.co.id/berita/koran/internasional-koran/15/10/30/nx0zxy1-aipr-cegah-campur-tangan-internasional-di-asean

Reuters. "Asserting Sovereignty, Indonesia Renames Part of South China Sea." July 14, 2017. https://www.reuters.com/article/us-indonesia-politics-map/asserting-sovereignty-indonesia-renames-part-of-south-china-sea-idUSKBN19Z0YQ

Robles, Jr., Alfredo C. *Endangered Species and Fragile Ecosystems in the South China Sea: The Philippines v. China Arbitration*. London: Palgrave Macmillan, 2020.

Sekretariat Kabinet Indonesia. "Menlu: Tekanannya, Indonesia ingin perdamaian di Kawasan Laut China Selatan terwujud," March 24, 2015. http://setkab.go.id/menlu-tekanannya-indonesia-ingin-perdamaian-di-kawasan-laut-china-selatan-terwujud/

Shahab, Nabiha. "Indonesia's Natuna Challenge." *The Diplomat*, March 13, 2020. https://thediplomat.com/2020/03/indonesias-natuna-challenge/

Smith, Stephen and Hugo Seymour. "Australia Looks to Indonesia in an Era of Uncertainty," *The Jakarta Post*, August 19, 2019. https://www.thejakartapost.com/academia/2019/08/19/australia-looks-to-indonesia-in-an-era-of-uncertainty.html

Song, Yann-huei. "The South China Sea Workshop Process and Taiwan's Participation," *Ocean Development & International Law* 41, no. 3 (2010), 253–69.

Suryadinata, Leo. "What Does Indonesia's Renaming of Part of the South China Sea Signify?," ISEAS – Yusof Ishak Institute, Singapore, August 18, 2017. https://www.iseas.edu.sg/images/pdf/ISEAS_Perspective_2017_64.pdf

The Guardian. "Beijing Rejects Tribunal's Ruling in South China Sea Case," July 12, 2016. https://www.theguardian.com/world/2016/jul/12/philippines-wins-south-china-sea-case-against-china

The Jakarta Post. "RI Circulates Draft Code of Conduct on South China Sea," September 29, 2012. http://www.thejakartapost.com/news/2012/09/29/ri-circulates-draft-code-conduct-south-china-sea.html#sthash.E1KsiHFb.dpu

The Jakarta Post. "Arbitration Panel OKs Jurisdiction in South China Sea Case," October 30, 2015. http://www.thejakartapost.com/news/2015/10/30/arbitration-panel-oks-jurisdiction-south-china-sea-case.html-0#sthash.i5rSDKcP.dpuf

The Jakarta Post. "Indonesia Protests against China in South China Sea Fishing Dispute." March 21, 2016. http://www.thejakartapost.com/news/2016/03/21/indonesia-protests-against-china-south-china-sea-fishing-dispute.html

The Jakarta Post. "US Envoy Reaffirms Religious Tolerance amid Trump Ban," February 8, 2017.

The Jakarta Post. "ASEAN reaffirms international law as basis for sovereignty in South China Sea," January 18, 2020. https://www.thejakartapost.com/seasia/2020/01/18/asean-reaffirms-international-law-as-basis-for-sovereignty-in-south-china-sea.html

The Jakarta Post. "Indonesia lodges strong protest against China for trespassing, poaching in Natunas," January 1, 2020. https://www.thejakartapost.com/news/2020/01/01/indonesia-lodges-strong-protestagainst-china-for-trespassing-poaching-in-natunas.html

Tomotaka, Shoji. "ASEAN Security Community: An Initiative for Peace and Stability." *NIDS Security Reports* 3, no. 4 (2008), Tokyo, Japan: The National Institute for Defence Studies, 17–34. http://www.nids.mod.go.jp/english/publication/kiyo/pdf/2008/bulletin_e2008_3.pdf

Weatherbee, Donald E. *ASEAN's Half Century: A Political History of the Association of Southeast Asian Nations.* Lanham: Rowman & Littlefield, 2019a.

Weatherbee, Donald E. "Indonesia, ASEAN, and the Indo-Pacific Cooperation Concept," *Perspectives*, Issue 2019, No. 47, ISEAS Yusof Ishak Institute, Singapore, June 7, 2019b.
https://www.iseas.edu.sg/images/pdf/ISEAS_Perspective_2019_47.pdf

9

The South China Sea Dispute: Regional Integration, Status Ad Quem, and Singapore's Position

Hui-Yi Katherine Tseng

Introduction

Some years have passed since the South China Sea (SCS) Arbitral Tribunal Award was issued in 2016.[1] The atmosphere now is very different from the days when the region had been plagued by occasional maritime skirmishes and standoffs. Regional leaders are busy talking about economic integration and measures to boost inter-state and intra-regional trade exchanges, with a language characterized by development, stability, and common destiny. Yet, the contention of freedom of navigation and shadows of great-power wrestling have stirred up regional waters, sending a palpable reminder that the danger of inadvertent conflicts is that they may easily lapse into a serious, whole-scale confrontation. This has given the SCS issue an opportune redefinition, particularly in a context of seeing the irrepressible tensions escalating between China and the US. That intensification of the SCS

[1] See, Herbert Smith Freehills, "Final Award Published in the South China Sea Arbitration," Public International Law Notes, July 20, 2016, https://hsfnotes.com/publicinternationallaw/2016/07/20/final-award-published-in-the-south-china-sea-arbitration/#:~:text=On%2012%20July%202016%2C%20the,Sea%20(%22UNCLOS%22).&text=The%20Tribunal%20found%20in%20favour,the%20main%20points%20in%20issue

issue can be deemed a process integral to China's development, and to the entailed tensions between China as a rising power and the US as an existential extra-regional power. In other words, the SCS issue, in and of itself, should always be considered in a broader context, seeing the competition of agenda-setting power between China and the US. Therefore, territorial disputes in the maritime forefront are a prelude to this great-power wrestling in the macro aspect, and a reflection of the dual dilemma encountering regional claimants and countries in a micro sense.[2] It is from this regionalization-regionalism perspective[3] that how Singapore currently views the SCS issue should be evaluated.

This chapter addresses the SCS issue in the context of consistently advancing regional integration in Southeast Asia. In particular, Singapore's efforts and postures in steering the simmering SCS issue through this advancing regional integration under the shadow of intensifying great-power wrestling and regional terrorist attacks will be studied. In this vein, this chapter intends to view the SCS issue as an integral part of the reconfiguration of a transnational order in Southeast Asia, discussions of which can only be comprehensive when various aspects are factored into the deliberation. Up to the present day, it is fair to argue that this transnational order (and re-ordering) is mainly economic-oriented, while regionalization has been a major push force.

Regional integration in Southeast Asia: the promising economic aspect

Amid the shadow of the Sino-US trade war[4] and thriving right-wing nationalistic sentiments, the prospect of economic growth in the Association of Southeast Asian Nations (ASEAN) is expected to remain resilient, with a steady growth in the coming years. The statistics show that with a rate of 5.3 per cent in 2017, growth is forecast at 5.2 per cent for the year 2018–19, driven by private consumption, strong investments particularly in public infrastructure, and robust exports.[5] In terms of trade and investment,

[2] Donald E. Weatherbee, *ASEAN's Half Century: A Political History of the Association of Southeast Asian Nations* (Lanham: Rowman & Littlefield, 2019), Chapter 10; Anders Corr, *Great Powers, Grand Strategies: The New Game in the South China Sea* (Annapolis: Naval Institute Press, 2018).

[3] Alexius Pereira, "Singapore's Regionalization Strategy," *Journal of Asia Pacific Economy* 10, no. 3 (2005): 380–96.

[4] Dorcas Wong and Alexander Chipman Koty, "The US-China Trade War: A Timeline," *China Briefing*, August 25, 2020, https://www.china-briefing.com/news/the-us-china-trade-war-a-timeline/

[5] Asian Development Bank. *Asian Development Outlook 2018*, 2018.

there are uneven developments. The trend of trade-recovery is developing, while inflows of foreign direct investment from major trading partners are lower in 2017 than previous years. The European Union (EU) remains the largest source of external investment, accounting for 23 per cent of the total investment amount (US$25.4 billion, out of US$110.4 billion).[6] China continues to the largest trading partner to the region, with total bilateral merchandise trade valued at US$436.8 billion (17.1 per cent).[7] Meanwhile, ASEAN's linkages in foreign direct investment continue to strengthen.

The debates: status quo and status ad quem

Contextual development aside, economic potential and regional development in Southeast Asia attracts further scholarly attention, particularly in how to theorize the ASEAN case by applying existing intellectual theses. Among the voluminous efforts, the concept of "ASEAN centrality" is respected as a guiding principle for further regional integration, and has been pushed forward consciously after it was first used in the joint statement of ASEAN Economic Ministers (AEM) in 2006 in the context of ASEAN's external economic relationship. In terms of how "ASEAN centrality" has been enabled and practised in inter-regional and extra-regional politics, most of the research pays attention to the extent to which ASEAN centrality is effective and can be appropriated in the regional material domain formed by interest-based power politics. For example, Archarya and Kuroyanagi[8] examine ASEAN's intrinsic factors pertinent to historical records to manage its intra-polities disputes and produce stability and peace in Southeast Asia and external conditions, where great powers cancel each other out, thereby accepting ASEAN's lead in forming mechanisms for broad consultation as contributing to mutual checking and constraint.

To some extent, this ASEAN centrality, and the evolution pattern of regionalism unique to Southeast Asia, are mutually implicating upon each other, while shedding light on the stalled progress of regional integration politics in other parts of Asia. Beeson[9] contends that, while exerting

6 ASEAN Secretariat. "ASEAN Economic Integration Brief," no. 3 (June 2018), https://asean.org/asean-releases-third-issue-economic-integration-brief/

7 Ibid.

8 Amitav Acharya, "Advancing the Study of Asian and Comparative Regionalism," *International Relations of the Asia-Pacific* 15, no.3 (April 2015): 559–64; Yoneji Kuroyanagi, "ASEAN chusin-sei no kensho [Evaluating ASEAN centrality]," *Kaigai Jijo* 63, no. 4 (2015): 2–17.

9 Mark Beeson, "Living with Giants: ASEAN and the Evolution of Asian Regionalism," *TRaNS: Trans-Regional and -National Studies of Southeast Asia* 1, no. 2 (July 2013): 303–22.

an ideational and political influence in forming regional institutional architectures, ASEAN still faces daunting challenges in preserving its centrality in the rapidly evolving regional affairs. This can largely be attributed to the several neighbouring countries entering into intensifying competition, and the growing pressures from the emergence of other large-scale regional organizations. The Asia Infrastructure and Investment Bank (AIIB) is one vivid example. Similarly, Hermawan[10] also discusses rising regional organizations that may pose threats to ASEAN by referring to AIIB. Hermawan warns that the credibility and centrality of ASEAN may be at stake in the face of a developing giant regional bank. Further, the still brewing frictions in the SCS, wrought from oil exploration and land reclamation, would only overshadow regional cooperation and embarrass ASEAN, because of its apparent vulnerability in the front of a powerful and resourceful China. Hermawan also makes a recommendation, one that has been the source of criticism from western scholars, that a united position is needed among ASEAN members in the face of other major powers, so that the institutional framework of ASEAN could be strengthened, while making the prospect of a closely integrated community realistic and pragmatic.[11]

The debates highlight the gap between ASEAN's status quo and ASEAN as a status ad quem, namely, ASEAN as an object and as a course of action. In other words, ASEAN, as a closely-knit community with well-established institutional structure and strengthened rule, seems aspirational, as ASEAN centrality is, at present, a phenomenon that is socially constructed and therefore, politically contested.[12] The contestation lies in the reality characterized by the gap between the collaborative political efforts of states to form a regional organization (regionalism), and the actions driven by economic activities dispersed in various fields, including multi-national corporations and private enterprises (regionalization).[13]

10 Yulius Purwadi Hermawan, "China's Dual Neighborhood Diplomacy and Indonesia's New Pragmatic Leadership: How Can ASEAN Preserve Its Centrality in a New Challenging Dynamic?," *Georgetown Journal of Asian Affairs* 2, no. 1 (Spring/Summer 2015): 31–40.

11 Ibid.

12 Donald E. Weatherbee, *ASEAN's Half Century: A Political History of the Association of Southeast Asian Nations* (Lanham: Rowman & Littlefield, 2019), Chapter 10; Anders Corr, *Great Powers, Grand Strategies: The New Game in the South China Sea* (Annapolis: Naval Institute Press, 2018).

13 Mark Beeson and Troy Lee-Brown, "The Future of Asia Regionalism: Not What it Used to Be?," *Asia & The Pacific Policy Studies* 4, no. 2 (February 2017): 195–206.

Regionalism and regionalization

In Southeast Asia, efforts in concretizing regionalism, namely, the self-conscious attempt to create politically defined and organized regions, lie mainly in the security scenario. The still brewing SCS issue serves as one vivid example of the efforts of regionalism, in terms of strengthening and prioritizing ASEAN centrality in any decisions made by respective member states. Further, the realization of ASEAN centrality in the SCS scenario can only be meaningfully achieved when other criteria are upheld, namely a rule-of-law order at both regional and international level, and dispute settlement via a compound of peaceful means. In this sense, challenges encountering ASEAN in preserving and advancing this centrality concept lie in both internal and external aspects. Internally, member states would need to strike a balance between national and regional interests: the former cannot be deemed legitimate when being pursued at the cost of the latter. Some regional leaders may be of constructive help in facilitating this interest-balancing act, as shown in the Yudhoyono regime (2004–14) in Indonesia.

Externally, ASEAN would need to defend this centrality position in the face of powerful external actors, or in the wake of events that would cast profound impacts on the international community, and the region as well. Recent trade tensions between China and the US can be counted as an example of this external aspect. Further, the grand cross-regional plan vigorously promoted by China, the Belt and Road Initiative (BRI), serves as another example of a critical event. For these external events, ASEAN spares no efforts in defending and solidifying ASEAN centrality via its emphasis on a rule-of-law system, the concept of equitable and reciprocal treatment, dispute settlement via peaceful means, and pragmatic flexibility. When reflecting these concepts in realistic practice, the position that ASEAN supports BRI, on the premise that BRI is to enhance and supplement the infrastructure and connectivity plan under ASEAN's initiative, is reasoned and reasonable.[14]

The efforts to push further a regional organization aimed at supra-national issues, which requires the delegation of sovereign authority from member states, are cautious and slow-paced. However, integrating actions driven by economic activities across the region – whereby regionalization is being pursued without political calculations as dominant concerns – are thriving and evolving. Nevertheless, there are new developments that may influence

[14] This position of ASEAN in China's BRI initiatives is reiterated in several occasions, one latest is by Tommy Koh, Ambassador-at-Large at Singapore's Ministry of Foreign Affairs, in 13th China-Singapore Forum (November 28, 2018).

this regionalization process in, mainly, the economic aspect, despite a more consolidated region-wide consensus and a more definite outlook that benefits all regional members and extra-regional stakeholders.

It is a global reality that economic development has been influenced by a fusion of top-down and bottom-up forces. The top-down forces are vividly characterized by the rising trade tensions between China and the US, the consciousness and measures holding the banner of protectionism, and the gradual politicization of trade issues. This last criterion may be embodied and exacerbated by the resurging prominence of geopolitics, within which the rising China could be counted as driving further regional dynamisms. Meanwhile, the bottom-up forces cannot be easily neglected. Technology changes that impact the supply and value chain, and the shifting paradigm of public opinions toward a beneficial globalization are two vivid examples of the forces emanating from the bottom level, which could allegedly change the nature and form of economic cooperation.[15]

In this context, it is strongly advocated that ASEAN should take an active posture in resisting protectionism and defending multilateralism. This latter advocate can be deemed, arguably, a reinterpretation of the insistence of ASEAN centrality in the face of critical, external events, in which ASEAN would insist on maintaining good terms with external great powers, while not taking sides with specific positions in any occasion. Again, this would only be possible when certain criteria are observed and honoured in consistent practices, whereby ASEAN centrality could be strengthened and reified via re-interpretation and re-projection of these practices. In this sense, it can be gleaned that the crux of further deepened integration in ASEAN lies in the understanding and riding on the tide that regionalism and regionalization are actually mutually implicating upon on another.

Singapore's one-year chair position

Singapore has taken over the Chair of ASEAN for the year 2017–18.[16] Singapore is well prepared and determined to tap on this one-year chairmanship to assert Singaporean influence in the evolving ASEAN agenda, despite the relatively short term, the routine nature of intra-institutional rotation, and the sacrosanct notion of ASEAN centrality.

[15] See, Giles Mohan, "Dislocating Globalisation: Power, Politics and Global Change," *Geography* 85, no. 2 (April 2000): 121–33.

[16] Lynn Kuok, "Singapore Sounds an Optimistic Note but Eyes Tough Year Ahead as ASEAN Chair," Brookings Op-Ed. February 22, 2018. https://www.brookings.edu/opinions/singapore-sounds-an-optimistic-note-but-eyes-tough-year-ahead-as-asean-chair/.

Beginning in 2018, Singapore announced, in a foreign minister meeting in early February, the Singaporean theme which underlines its one-year chairmanship. Comprising two dimensions, the "resilience" aims at strengthening ASEAN member states' ability to withstand crisis, while the "innovation" is set to increase regional integration and connectivity in such areas as digital technologies. It seems a fair observation that the city-state, judging its inherent conditions and realistic limits, has projected handling this opportunity by focusing on rule consolidation, concept renovation, and respatialization of the region via technology innovation.

To facilitate these, Singapore has proposed several initiatives, including the ASEAN Smart Cities Network and the ASEAN Leaders' Statement on Cybersecurity Cooperation. Other efforts are the negotiations to finalize the Regional Comprehensive Economic Partnership (RCEP), the Model ASEAN Extradition Treaty (MAET), and the adoption of the ASEAN Single Window. All such are part of ongoing efforts to boost integration and community building within ASEAN.

Based on these previous achievements, Singapore has projected delivering on five key thrusts during its one-year chair position,[17] namely: promoting innovation and e-commerce; improving trade facilitation; deepening services and investment integration; cultivating a conducive regulatory environment; and progressing ASEAN's external relations. These measures are to position ASEAN as a region for seamless economic activity and growing opportunities, especially in e-commerce and the digital economy.

Apparently, Singapore has dedicated efforts to infrastructure building and establishing institutions to equip the region with the required institutional capacity that would help facilitate further integration. By avoiding addressing issues closely intertwined with regional leadership, Singapore thus shuns the tough task, as the Chair-turned-leader, during this one-year chair service, while accomplishing the enhancement of institutional capacity which is urgently needed if regional integration is to develop consistently and effectively. In this sense, how the Singaporean efforts in facilitating further regionalization will help catalyse and consolidate the political wills required for the sophistication of regionalism in ASEAN remains to be seen. For now, the message is clear that the one-year Singapore chair position reifies again the significance of "ASEAN centrality," to which all members, including Singapore, should dedicate their own and integral contributions.

---

[17] Termsak, Chalermpalanupap, "Singapore as the ASEAN Chair: Responsibilities and Legacies," *ASEAN Focus* 23, no. 4 (July 2018), 14–15. https://www.iseas.edu.sg/images/pdf/ASEANFocusIssue4.pdf.

Singapore on the regional maritime agenda

The SCS issue has centred on the maritime security issues in the region, in which continuity and change have remoulded the contour of the political manoeuvring in the negotiation forum. China's strategy in the SCS issue undoubtedly influences others, which has manifested a dynamic continuum that could be prescribed with two key constraints.

First, it shows explicit objection to legally binding instruments, which would bind both ASEAN and China, with the concern that its leverage in both policy making and action would be undermined. This has sensationally conflicted regional countries' as well as Singapore's preference to the approach that stresses multilateralism and rule of law in the SCS scenario.

Second, the occupation and reclamation of islets in the SCS have continued, despite diplomatic engagement and international attention. China and Vietnam are two claimants with an extensive history of reclamation activities and competition in exploiting maritime resources. With Vietnam assuming the ASEAN Chairmanship in 2020, at the time of writing it remains to be seen how it will steer the COC negotiation through the water of rising Sino-US trade wars and developing protectionism sentiments in national and local communities. Singapore would, again, have recourse to its hedging practice between the US and China, while prioritizing ASEAN as a main actor.

Continuity aside, there are changes which vividly echo the changing posture in China's self-projection in global affairs, and its evolving SCS policy.[18] The former has seen a shift from a low-profile posture in Deng Xiaoping's era, "to hide and bide," to Xi Jinping's calling for the realization and rejuvenation of the Chinese nation. The latter could be better embodied in the influences generated on ASEAN countries, for example, the undermining of ASEAN unity, the postures of becoming assertive, and the increasing economic statecraft for geopolitical gains. For Singapore, these trigger worrying alarms against the increasing Chinese influences and the correspondingly shrinking leverages it has in trade, as well as other aspects, such as the statecraft of governance and social stability. Nevertheless, Singapore would not object fiercely to the efforts of economic integration between China and ASEAN. With the understanding that ASEAN's economic success has been underpinned by its openness to trade and investment, and a rules-based order and functioning multilateral system with the US and EU at the centre, Singapore has shown great flexibility and adaptiveness to the reality of China's increasing economic heft and developing influences in Southeast Asia.

---

[18] Irene Chan, "Reversing China's Belt-And-Road Initiative – Singapore's Response to The BRI and its Quest for Relevance," *East Asia* 36, no. 3 (2019): 185–204.

It is fair to say that Singapore has become a leader in crafting and leading the threads of regional maritime cooperation.[19] This is particularly the case in the context of varying maritime enforcement capacity in the region. It is also clear that Singapore would dedicate itself further to preserve the multilateralism enshrined in the ASEAN mechanism, while upholding the rules-based value shared by the international community. Meanwhile, Singapore would spare no efforts in advancing its cooperation with China in various aspects, like trade, technology and innovation, and business entrepreneurship. Amid the intensifying Sino-US rivalry, this trend is likely to continue, despite the alteration and fine-tuning of the tactics.

Just like its regional fellow countries, hedging between regional and extra-regional powers has been one core principle in Singapore's practices and deployment of its external relations. It is not surprising that Singapore would not want to be caught in any countervailing coalition, led by the US or otherwise, against China. A clear demonstration reifying this Singaporean inclination is in an interview with the *Washington Post* in September 2019. Singapore does not deem itself to have permanent friends in the US and China; it only pursues pro-US and pro-China policies when such policies are judged to be in the country's interests.

Yet, it is unlikely that Singapore can avoid making a stark choice indefinitely, in the face of Sino-US confrontation that is becoming acute. The still-evolving SCS issues serve a reminder to remain vigilant.

Singapore and the South China Sea dispute

In the context of intensifying trade tensions between two great powers and the evolving regionalization progress, regional countries, including Singapore, are left fewer options, in terms of the SCS issue, to which many have adopted an evasive posture, while betting on the multilateral forum to carve out a solution acceptable to both claimants and stakeholder countries.[20] Indeed, the ongoing formal negotiations over the proposed COC in the SCS can serve as a constraining factor on the actions of various parties, including claimant and non-claimant states, especially the two big powers.[21] It would not be in anybody's interest to sour the dialogue atmospherics,

19 Mateusz Chatys, "Relations between Singapore and The People's Republic of China in the Light of Donald Trump's New Southeast Asia Policy," *International Studies, Interdisciplinary Political and Cultural Journal* 23, no. 1 (2019): 133–48.

20 Jane Chan, "Singapore and the South China Sea: Being an Effective Coordinator and Honest Broker," *Asia Policy* 21, no. 1 (2016): 41–6.

21 Lay Hwee Yeo, "Singapore's Policy in The Asia-Pacific: ASEAN and Open Regionalism," *Baltic Journal of European Studies* 9, no. 2 (2019): 20–39.

Table 9.1: Issues that attract ASEAN attention

	2017	2018	2019
Indonesia	Terrorism	Terrorism	Terrorism
Malaysia	Terrorism		Great-power wrestling
The Philippines	Terrorism	Terrorism	Great-power wrestling
Singapore	Trade protectionism	Great-power wrestling	Great-power wrestling
Vietnam	North Korean nuclear issue		Great-power wrestling

Source: Compiled by the author, by screening the statements of state representatives in various multilateral forums

particularly when some notable progress has been achieved, with the promulgation of first a draft framework in 2017 and the adoption of a Single Draft Negotiating Text in 2018. Yet, is this what regional countries have at hand to tackle the SCS issue? In this aspect, there emerges a trend that seems to forebode a new direction among regional countries regarding the development of the SCS issue. Could it offer a silver lining to the seemingly intractable SCS issue?

Besides the multilateral forum, regional countries seem to reposit the SCS issue in the broader context of mushrooming terrorist attacks in the region. This can be demonstrated in the record of regional countries' statements in multilateral forums in past years. See Table 9.1 for the summary of regional countries' stances.

However, what is entailed in this repostulation of the SCS issue, in the scenario of thriving terrorist attacks in the region, requires meticulous consideration. Several issues are raised. First, in company with thriving threats of terrorist attacks in the region, it can be expected that regional countries may invest further in the scaling of military preparation for the immediate terrorist threat. However, for the past several years, there have already been prevailing speculations, regarding the militarization of great power and regional countries in scaling up their military capabilities, while intensifying military presence in certain occasions that connote symbolic implications. On these accounts, it is worth the effort to seriously consider a commonly accepted definition of "militarization," while spelling out what other actions should not be taken by claimant states in the SCS.

Second, as shown in Table 9.1, great-power wrestling has prevailed among regional countries' discourses, which thus drives regional countries to pool regional issues thereunder in the course of deliberations. To repostulate the SCS issue in the lens of great-power wrestling, this would make ASEAN even more passive in future negotiations with China, while a tacit agreement to an overtly cautious approach can well be expected. One example is how regional countries respond to the Indo-Pacific strategic plan proposed by the US, which can shed light on the regional countries' position on the SCS issue.

Indonesia and Singapore serve two contrasting examples in this aspect. Indonesia has been proactive, in terms of its efforts in riding on the momentum of the Indo-Pacific strategy to fuel the development of its maritime policy. The more exclusive and immediate economic benefits aside, Jakarta has further aimed at enhancing its status as a regional power and a country with active global engagement. On the contrary, Singapore has been extremely cautious, hoping to maintain the greatest extent of strategic ambiguity and flexibility in policy implementation in shaping its discourses and position to the Indo-Pacific strategy plan.[22] Further, Singapore also expresses its concerns in the multilateral forum, implying that Singapore also views the strategic ambiguous position one best option for ASEAN, in a near future where confrontations among regional, extra-regional great powers are expected to intensify. Yet, while ASEAN is a community characterized by the co-existence of states and plurality of their interests, it would not be surprising to see the overriding of national interests upon the community ones, which is particularly the case when clashes/skirmishes break out and add fuel to the developing rivalry in the SCS.

Challenges ahead

It is apparent that establishing a political organization, as efforts of concretizing regionalism, is a challenging undertaking at the best of times. It would particularly be the case where politics and economics have been deeply integrated, and where their interactions continue to shape the environment in which cooperation at the regional level takes place under the shadow of political considerations.[23] At a juncture when the international order is ruptured by self-centred great powers, and the original rules and principles overshadowed by unilateral calculations and prioritized national interests, ASEAN has made clear to the world how the efforts of regional integration

[22] Mateusz Chatys, "Relations between Singapore and The People's Republic of China in the Light of Donald Trump's New Southeast Asia Policy," *International Studies, Interdisciplinary Political and Cultural Journal* 23, no. 1 (2019): 133–48.

[23] Hui-Chin Lai, "Singapore Model and Mainland China Model in Terms of GDP Development," *Advances in Politics and Economics* 1, no. 2 (2018): 91.

so far have been dearly valued by regional members, and should be respected by regional, as well as extra-regional powers and countries. ASEAN's efforts, in terms of the political and economic aspects, to strengthen and consolidate ASEAN centrality are gaining prevailing recognition, both regionally and internationally.[24] For this, lessons from other cases of regional integration like the EU may be helpful reference points. The cultural factor may point out a direction worth further consideration and deliberation.[25]

It is observed that both Indonesia and Malaysia seem to lose patience, while hardening their stances as to Chinese claims. Yet, it remains to be seen how the overall dynamic will play out in the near future, with the smattering of different perspectives and priorities increasingly contributing to an uncertain situation that needs to be traversed with caution. In this sense, a careful balance is vividly demonstrated between assertion of power and tactful diplomacy that has been observed among actors on all sides, as armed conflict is not desirable for any party involved. For claimant states in the region, it is unconvincing to claim of conciliation, but a fluid situation, while the jury is still out.[26]

Yet, without hesitation, one could claim that the SCS issue confronts this ASEAN centrality as conceptually an ideal and substantially a policy position, with realistic challenges. In a region with a history of colonization, inter-state and intra-state conflicts, and lingering memories of bullying by regional powers, the essence characterizing ASEAN centrality, plurality, and tolerance, may turn out to be, inadvertently, the Achilles heel of the advancement of regional integration, and of a regional community that shares the consciousness of a common destiny. The region is still aching, because of the polarization wrought by the SCS Arbitral Tribunal, which could become further entrenched due to the regression of democracy in several regional countries. In the face of a self-willed US administration and a China empowered by an unprecedentedly strong state mechanism, how ASEAN could handle the Sino-US trade war, and the confrontations collaterally triggered in various non-trade fronts, would be of critical importance to ASEAN's next steps. Being practical is a regional legacy that has been touted consistently by ASEAN countries, including Singapore. Yet, there is always

---

24 Lay Hwee Yeo, "Singapore's Policy in The Asia-Pacific: ASEAN and Open Regionalism," *Baltic Journal of European Studies* 9, no. 2 (2019): 20–39.

25 Hong Liu and Ting-Yan Wang. "China and the 'Singapore Model:' Perspectives from Mid-Level Cadres and Implications for Transnational Knowledge Transfer," *The China Quarterly* 236 (2018): 988–1011.

26 Xiangning Wu, "Continuity and Change, China-Singapore Relations Under the Framework of China's 21st Century Maritime Silk Road Initiative," *Asian Education and Development Studies* 10, no. 1 (2020): 147–59.

the moment when practical considerations and development prospects pale in front of the aspiring great nation expectation.

References

Acharya, Amitav. "Advancing the Study of Asian and Comparative Regionalism." *International Relations of the Asia-Pacific* 15, no. 3 (April 2015): 559–64.

ASEAN Secretariat. "ASEAN Economic Integration Brief." no. 3 (June 2018). https://asean.org/asean-releases-third-issue-economic-integration-brief/

Asian Development Bank. *Asian Development Outlook 2018*. 2018.

Beeson, Mark. "Living with Giants: ASEAN and the Evolution of Asian Regionalism." *TRaNS: Trans-Regional and -National Studies of Southeast Asia* 1, no. 2 (July 2013): 303–22.

Beeson, Mark and Lee-Brown, Troy. "The Future of Asia Regionalism: Not What It Used to Be?" *Asia & the Pacific Policy Studies* 4, no. 2 (February 2017): 195–206.

Chalermpalanupap, Termsak. "Singapore as the ASEAN Chair: Responsibilities and Legacies." *ASEAN Focus* 23, no. 4 (July 2018), 14–15. https://www.iseas.edu.sg/images/pdf/ASEANFocusIssue4.pdf

Chan, Irene. "Reversing China's Belt-And-Road Initiative – Singapore's Response to the BRI and Its Quest for Relevance." *East Asia* 36, no. 3 (2019): 185–204.

Chan, Jane. "Singapore and the South China Sea: Being an Effective Coordinator and Honest Broker." *Asia Policy* 21, no. 1 (2016): 41–6.

Chatys, Mateusz. "Relations between Singapore and the People's Republic of China in the Light of Donald Trump's New Southeast Asia Policy." *International Studies, Interdisciplinary Political and Cultural Journal* 23, no. 1 (2019): 133–48.

Corr, Anders. *Great Powers, Grand Strategies: The New Game in the South China Sea*. Annapolis: Naval Institute Press, 2018.

Freehills, Herbert Smith. "Final Award Published in the South China Sea Arbitration." *Public International Law Notes*, July 20, 2016, https://hsfnotes.com/publicinternationallaw/2016/07/20/final-award-published-in-the-south-china-sea-arbitration/#:~:text=On%2012%20July%202016%2C%20the,Sea%20(%22UNCLOS%22).&text=The%20Tribunal%20found%20in%20favour,the%20main%20points%20in%20issue

Hermawan, Yulius Purwadi. "China's Dual Neighborhood Diplomacy and Indonesia's New Pragmatic Leadership: How Can ASEAN Preserve Its Centrality in a New Challenging Dynamic?." *Georgetown Journal of Asian Affairs* 2, no. 1 (Spring/Summer 2015): 31–40.

Koh, Tommy. 13th China-Singapore Forum, November 27–28, 2018. http://en.nanhai.org.cn/index/info/content/cid/20/id/6341.html

Kuok, Lynn. "Singapore Sounds an Optimistic Note but Eyes Tough Year Ahead as ASEAN Chair." Brookings Op-Ed. February 22, 2018. https://www.brookings.edu/opinions/singapore-sounds-an-optimistic-note-but-eyes-tough-year-ahead-as-asean-chair/

Kuroyanagi, Yoneji. "ASEAN chusin-sei no kensho [Evaluating ASEAN centrality]." *Kaigai Jijo* 63, no. 4 (2015): 2–17.

Lai, Hui-Chin. "Singapore Model and Mainland China Model in Terms of GDP Development." *Advances in Politics and Economics* 1, no. 2 (2018): 91.

Liu, Hong, and Ting-Yan Wang. "China and the 'Singapore Model': Perspectives from Mid-Level Cadres and Implications for Transnational Knowledge Transfer." *The China Quarterly* 236 (2018): 988–1011.

Mohan, Giles. "Dislocating Globalisation: Power, Politics and Global Change." *Geography* 85, no. 2 (April 2000): 121–133.

Pereira, Alexius. "Singapore's Regionalization Strategy." *Journal of Asia Pacific Economy* 10, no. 3 (2005): 380–96.

Weatherbee, Donald E. *ASEAN's Half Century: A Political History of the Association of Southeast Asian Nations*. Lanham: Rowman & Littlefield, 2019: Chapter 10.

Wong, Dorcas and Koty, Alexander Chipman. "The US-China Trade War: A Timeline." China Briefing, August 25, 2020, https://www.china-briefing.com/news/the-us-china-trade-war-a-timeline/

Wu, Xiangning. "Continuity and Change, China-Singapore Relations Under the Framework of China's 21st Century Maritime Silk Road Initiative." *Asian Education and Development Studies* 10, no. 1 (2020): 147–59.

Yeo, Lay Hwee. "Singapore's Policy in the Asia-Pacific: ASEAN and Open Regionalism." *Baltic Journal of European Studies* 9, no. 2 (2019): 20–39.

10

Cambodia's South China Sea Policy: From ASEAN Aligned to Echoing Chinese Clientism

Veasna Var

Introduction

The South China Sea has once again become a flashpoint for conflict between China and some ASEAN states, particularly the Philippines and Vietnam. It has also strained relations between China and the United States (US). China's recent position of growing more assertive in advancing its claims has raised tensions and risked the militarization of competing claims by other states including the US and its allies. The diplomatic impasse between China and the ASEAN claimant states, as well as within ASEAN has, furthermore, made the situation less predictable. Worse still, taking advantage of a world distracted by the current coronavirus (COVID-19) global pandemic, China took new and bolder actions, as evidenced through its declaration of the establishment of two new administrative districts in the Paracel and Spratly Islands.[1]

China's growing assertiveness in the South China Sea has put ASEAN states, other actors, and Cambodia in a challenging strategic situation, seeking to balance with China and the US to further their strategic interests. Cambodia has decided to adopt a different policy approach from its ASEAN member states regarding China and the US. Some other states in the region chose to have engaged in a balanced strategy (that is, hedging or neutral) with both

[1] Maria Angela, "China's South China Sea Moves Raise Concerns," *The ASEAN Post*, May 1, 2020.

superpowers in order to gain benefits from both sides: economic interests from China and security interests from the US. In contrast, Cambodia has pursued a strategy of bandwagoning towards China to accrue economic interests.[2]

Among the strategic challenges facing Cambodia, balancing between ASEAN, the West, and China on the contentious issue of the South China Sea is and continues to be the most significant to their foreign policy in the 21st century. Since 2012, the South China Sea has re-emerged as the most significant and challenging foreign policy dilemma for Cambodia.[3] As a non-claimant state, the South China Sea is not of direct concern for Cambodia. However, it holds great relevance to Cambodia as a member of ASEAN and as a nation that is a significant beneficiary of Chinese aid and investment.[4] While ASEAN has always been a cornerstone of Cambodia's foreign policy, the country has been accused of siding with China at the expense of ASEAN, and hence damaging the unity of ASEAN.[5]

Drawing particularly upon interviews, observations and investigations, this chapter examines Cambodia's approach to the territorial disputes in the SCS. Under Prime Minister Hun Sen, Cambodia's approach to the SCS dispute has moved from that of an active player in efforts to find a peaceful solution to the broader disputes, to one of jumping on the Chinese bandwagon, designed to protect and promote its own national interests, especially since Cambodia's second period as Chair of ASEAN. The shift in the Cambodian position has been driven by economic interests from China.[6] The foreign policy approach that Cambodia has pursued to align with China on the issue of the South China Sea presents both opportunities and challenges. Cambodia's bandwagoning with China for accruing economic benefits has played a fundamental role in not only the country's economic development but also the legitimacy and survival of the Hun Sen regime. The major

2 See for example, Vibhanshu Shekhar, "Asean's Response to the Rise of China: Deploying a Hedging Strategy," *China Report* 48, no. 3 (2012).

3 Sovinda Po and Veasna Var, "Cambodia's South China Sea Dilemma between China and Asean," *IPP Review*, May, 3, 2017.

4 Veasna Var, "Cambodia Looks for Middle Ground in the South China Sea," *East Asia Forum*, June 20, 2015.

5 Sukmawani Bela Pertiwi, "Is Asean Unity in Danger from the South China Sea?," *The Diplomat*, August 3, 2016.

6 Sigfrido Burgos and Sophal Ear, "China's Strategic Interests in Cambodia: Influence and Resources " *Asian Survey* 50, no. 3 (2010); Sigfrido Burgos Cáceres and Sophal Ear, *The Hungry Dragon: How China's Quest for Resources Is Reshaping the World* (New York: Routledge, 2013); Terence Chong, "The Politics Behind Cambodia's Embrace of China," *Yusof Ishak Institute* 59, no. 2017 (August 2, 2017); Chheang Vannarith, "Cambodia Embraces China's Belt and Road Initiative," *ISEAS Yusof Ishak Institute* 48, no. 2017 (July 6, 2017).

drawback of this approach is the negative impact of Cambodia's foreign policy within ASEAN and relations with western powers, which are also the cornerstone of Cambodia's foreign and development policy.[7] This chapter explores the reasons why this approach has already had a negative impact on regional stability, and why it may undermine Cambodia's long-term interests.

The latter half of this chapter will proceed by dividing the discussion into four sections: the overview of Cambodia-China relations with the focus on the confluence of interests, Cambodia's policy to the SCS disputes, its determinants and implications, and conclusion.

Overview of Cambodia-China relations: confluence of interests

China played a historically prominent role in Cambodia's foreign relations after the country attained independence from France in late 1953. Sino-Cambodian relations have centred on the evolution of geostrategic and geopolitical factors. Despite some complications, including China support for the genocidal Khmer Rouge regime and involvement in the Cambodian civil wars, these relations have reflected a reciprocal diplomatic style with an increase in flexibility and opportunities.[8] The legacy of China-Cambodia relations, led either by Sihanouk or other Cambodian leaders including the current Cambodian leader Hun Sen, is to view China as a key protector and friend in need of Cambodia in its relations with two large and powerful neighbours – Vietnam and Thailand – as well as its relations with the Western powers.[9] This was evident, for example, when in 1993 Sihanouk stated that China is "the cause of our survival because of a balance of menaces between China and hostile Vietnamese and Thai troops who want to kill Cambodia … the influence of France and United States may come and go, but China was a constant factor."[10]

---

7 Heng Sarith, "Cambodia's Foreign Policy Grand Strategy," *The Diplomat*, September 11, 2014; Veasna Var, "Holding Balance between Two Superpowers: Cambodia's Strategic Choices for Foreign and Development Policy," *Eurasia Review*, July 27, 2016; "Cambodia: Between China and the United States," *The Diplomat*, May 20, 2015.

8 Cáceres and Ear; Sophal Ear, "The China–Cambodia–Us Nexus," in *New Dynamics in Us-China Relations: Contending for the Asia Pacific*, ed. Mingjiang Li and Kalyan M. Kemburi (New York: Routledge, 2015); Burgos and Ear.

9 Chong; Heng Pheakdey, "Cambodia–China Relations: A Positive-Sum Game?," *Journal of Current Southeast Asian Affairs*, no. 2 (2012).

10 Quoted in Carlyle A. Thayer, "China's Relations with Laos and Cambodia," in *China's Internal and External Relations and the Lessons for Korea and Asia*, ed. Jung-Ho Bae and Jae H. Ku (Seoul: Korean Institute for National Unification (KINU), 2013).

Similarly, after Hun Sen's consolidation of power in a 1997 coup which resulted in the imposition of Western economic sanctions, and when Hun Sen's government was isolated by the Western powers,[11] Hun Sen jumped onto China's bandwagon and praised China's generosity by stating:

> Although some international community members have not yet clearly understood the real situation in Cambodia, a number of friendly countries have maintained their just and fair stance on the Cambodian issue. Among them, the PRC, which has firmly adhered to the principle of peaceful coexistence, continues to respect the Kingdom of Cambodia's independence and sovereignty and does not interfere in Cambodian internal affairs.[12]

Although rooted in an air of mistrust, since the 1990s, the two countries have buried their past and are embracing each other to further their national interests. While China sees Cambodia in an important strategic location to advance national interests and influence in the region, Cambodia also sees China's rise and influence as an opportunity for urgently required economic development and political support.[13] As a result, over the last decade or so, bilateral ties between Cambodia and China have experienced significant growth, across the realms of political, economic, and defence cooperation.[14]

The relationship between the countries is largely based on shared convergent interests in dealing with economic, security, and strategic challenges. Cambodia's geographical and economic landscapes have allowed Cambodia-China bilateral relations to take a vital position in Beijing's foreign policy.[15] Cambodia is important geopolitically for the interests of China because the country holds a very important strategic location in mainland Southeast Asia as well as being a member of the Association of Southeast Asian Nations (ASEAN). In addition to its strategic importance, Cambodia offers economic opportunity to China as a provider of natural resources and as a market for Chinese goods.[16]

---

[11] For example see, "Cambodia–United States Relations," in *Cambodia: Progress and Challenges since 1991*, ed. Sothirak Pou, Geoff Wade, and Mark Hong (Singapore Institute of Southeast Asian Studies, 2012); "US Rapprochement with Laos and Cambodia," *Contemporary Southeast Asia* 32, no. 3 (2010).

[12] Paul Marks, "China's Cambodia Strategy," *Parameters* 30, no. 3 (2000).

[13] Thayer, "China's Relations with Laos and Cambodia."

[14] Veasna Var, "Reform of the Royal Cambodian Armed Forces Organization to Meet the Challenges of the 21st Century," *The Korean Journal of Defense Analysis* 28, no. 2 (2016).

[15] Thayer, "China's Relations with Laos and Cambodia."

[16] Pheakdey.

The two countries solidified their bilateral ties as a Comprehensive Partnership for Cooperation in April 2006, and this was upgraded to a Comprehensive Strategic Partnership of Cooperation in 2010. This was a significant milestone in the deep and comprehensive cooperation between the two nations. In recent years, relations between China and Cambodia have grown to a new peak.[17]

By embracing China, Cambodia received significant aid, and trade and investment, in addition to substantial military aid.[18] Since 1992, China has provided Cambodia with considerable development aid of approximately US$200 million annually and has disbursed around US$3 billion in concessional loans and grants.[19] With Chinese development aid and loans, Cambodia has built ten bridges and more than 2,000 kilometres of road.[20] As of February 2017, China had disbursed around US$4.2 billion of aid in both grants and soft loans to fund physical infrastructure, agriculture, education, and social development to Cambodia.[21] As for bilateral trade, the two countries have increased this dramatically from year to year.[22] While bilateral trade in 2015 was about US$4.4 billion, in 2016 trade increased to around US$4.8 billion, with exports from Cambodia accounting for US$830 million and imports from China US$3.9 billion.[23] According to data from the Cambodian Ministry of Commerce, bilateral trade between the two countries is expected to reach US$6 billion by 2020.[24]

China has also become the largest investor in Cambodia with more than US$10 billion in cumulative investments and more than 400 investment projects.[25] The main fields of China's investment in Cambodia include agriculture, mining, physical infrastructure projects, hydropower dams, and

---

17 Veasna Var, "Belt and Road Initiative: Opportunities for Cambodia's Development?," *IPP Review* August 2, 2017; "China's Influence in Cambodia," *Khmer Times*, June 29, 2016.

18 Touch Siphat, "Patterns and Impacts of Chinese Assistance in Cambodia," in *Impact of China's Rise on the Mekong Region*, ed. Yos Santasombat (New York: Palgrave Macmillan, 2015).

19 Var, "China's Influence in Cambodia."

20 Ramesh Thakur and Carlyle A. Thayer, *The Soviet Union as an Asian Pacific Power: Implications of Gorbachev's 1986 Vladivostok Initiative* (Boulder and London: Westview Press, 1987).

21 May Kunmakara, "PM Backs China's Key Role," *Khmer Times*, April 12, 2017.

22 See for example, Alvin Cheng Hin Lim, "Cambodia Joins the 'Belt and Road'," *IPP Review*, October 14, 2016.

23 Kunmakara.

24 "China Urges Cambodia to Use Yuan in Bilateral Trade," *The Straights Times*, February 6, 2018.

25 Prashanth Parameswaran, "China and Cambodia: With Friends Like These ...," *China Brief* 13, no. 1 (2013).

garment production. Moreover, under Chinese President Xi Jinping's Belt and Road Initiative (BRI) (also known as One Belt, One Road [OBOR]), which he put forward in 2013, Cambodia would be expected to gain enormous economic benefits in infrastructure development – ports, roads, and railways that connect Cambodia to the region.[26]

China's growing economic clout in Cambodia has also led to growing military ties.[27] China has emerged as Cambodia's most significant military partner, providing considerable military training as well as engaging in joint naval and military exercises.[28] China's defence cooperation with Cambodia has also significantly strengthened since the 1990s. China has provided a considerable amount of military assistance to the Royal Cambodian Armed Force's (RCAF) professional and capability development.[29] In recent years, China has significantly increased military cooperation with the RCAF by providing loans and military equipment including trucks, helicopters, and aircraft, built military training and medical facilities, and donated uniforms to the Royal Cambodian Armed Forces. For example, China lent Cambodia US$195 million to purchase Chinese-made Zhishenji-9 twin-engine light-utility helicopters as well as sponsored training for 25 pilots and mechanics in 2013.[30]

Beijing has also actively engaged in military exercises with the kingdom's military. For example, a naval exercise occurred in late February 2016, and an army exercise codenamed "Dragon Gold" occurred in mid-December 2016. These military exercises were seen as signalling the closest ties between the two militaries since the Khmer Rouge was in power. Clearly, during a period in which the RCAF is committed to a long-term process of reform and force structure review, the strong defence ties between Beijing and Phnom Penh have considerably contributed to the strengthening of the Cambodian national defence sector.[31] However, there has been growing concern over the quality and the professionalism of the RCAF, as human

[26] Var, "Belt and Road Initiative: Opportunities for Cambodia's Development?."

[27] Michael Raska and Richard A. Bitzinger, "Strategic Contours of China's Arms Transfers," *Strategic Studies Quarterly* Spring (2020): 107.

[28] Prashanth Parameswaran, "What Did the 2020 China-Cambodia Golden Dragon Military Exercise Actually Achieve?," *The Diplomat*, April 1, 2020.

[29] Alvin Cheng Hin Lim, "Sino-Cambodian Relations: Recent Economic and Military Cooperation – Analysis." *Eurasia Review*, June 30, 2015.

[30] Neou Vannarin, "Cambodia Strengthens Military Ties with China," *Voice of America News*, July 25, 2015.

[31] Veasna Var and Sovinda Po, "Cambodia Looks to China Rather Than the Us," *Australian Institute of International Affairs*, March 20, 2017.

rights and democratic development is not Beijing's main focus in its military aid and training.[32]

The emergence of China as Cambodia's most significant military benefactor has reflected Cambodia's growing dependence on China that aligns with shifts in Cambodia's foreign policy. Increasing development of military ties between China and Cambodia has put a significant strain on Cambodia relations with Western powers. This issue has much broader implications for maritime security, peace, stability, and security in the region at a time of the US' and China's growing geopolitical rivalry.[33] Some commentators are seeing Cambodia as a battleground of a new Cold War between China and the US.[34] Cambodia's recent decision to suspend or postpone important military exercises with the US and Australia is one of the prime examples of China's growing influence over Cambodia. The recent and routine high-level official military visits, accompanied with aid packages, are widely seen to be at the expense of the US and other key defence partners, such as Australia. As a report to the US Congress points out, "China's defence relationship with Cambodia is growing at the expense of the U.S. and regional interests."[35]

As for China's opportunities, facing trust deficit and with few allies in the region since 1992, opportunistic China sees Cambodia as a strategic state, playing a very important role for China's exertion of influence in the region.[36] As one analyst rightly put it, "having a strong ally in Cambodia means China occupying a central position on Indochina."[37] China's relationship with Cambodia is motivated by, first and foremost, political and core interest support and, secondarily, commercial interests.[38] With economic influence from Beijing, Cambodia offers China political support on a number of regional and international issues, including the SCS dispute. These issues will

[32] Var, "Reform of the Royal Cambodian Armed Forces Organization to Meet the Challenges of the 21st Century."

[33] Var and Po; David Hutt, "Us, China Tensions Put Cambodia in Potential Peril," *Asia Times*, June 6, 2019.

[34] David Hutt and Shawn W. Crispin, "Cambodia at the Center of a New Cold War," *Asia Times*, November 15, 2018.

[35] Carolyn Bartholomew and Dennis C. Shea, "2017 Report to Congress of the US-China Economic and Security Review Commision, Executive Summary and Recommendations," (Washington, DC: US-China Economic and Security Review Commission, 2017).

[36] Vannarith Chheang, "The Political Economy of Chinese Investment in Cambodia," *Yusof Ishak Institute* 2017, no. 16 (2017).

[37] David Koh, "Chinese Investments in Cambodia: View of Chinese Soft Power from the Ground Up," (Phnom Penh: CICP, 2016).

[38] See for example, John D. Ciorciari, "A Chinese Model for Patron–Client Relations? The Sino-Cambodian Partnership," *International Relations of the Asia-Pacific* 15, no. 2 (2014).

be discussed in more detail in the later section. With commercial interests, Cambodia offers China preferential access to its economy, land, and natural resources.[39] In interviews with independent social and political analysts, some interviewees characterized Sino-Cambodia relations as: "Both countries need each other's support. Cambodia embraces China for economic benefits, while China needs Cambodia for political and strategic support."[40]

Cambodia's South China Sea approach

Cambodia's role in ASEAN and as 2002 ASEAN Chair

Since ASEAN's inception in 1999, the regional grouping has always been a cornerstone of Cambodia's foreign policy.[41] In his statement, Prime Minister Hun Sen stressed the importance of ASEAN in the country's foreign policy, stating that, "ASEAN has become a core of Cambodia's foreign policy which reflects the country's political and socio-economic development, including regional reintegration and international cooperation."[42] Some analysts explain that the conviction of Cambodia to join ASEAN came because ASEAN "has helped promote Cambodia's national prestige and interests."[43] Former Prime Minister and Minister of Foreign Affairs and International Cooperation, Hor Namhong, explained that: "ASEAN will bring us more investment, more commercial exchange. ASEAN as a whole will be a very big market for Cambodian products."[44]

The grouping would provide the kingdom with international platforms to raise its profile in the international arena, promote Cambodia's "political security and outward stability," and bring economic benefits, as well as protecting Cambodia's independence and sovereignty.[45] Cambodian

[39] Pheakdey.

[40] The author's interview with independent social and political analysts in Phnom Penh in 2017.

[41] Pich Charadine, "Cambodia within ASEAN: Twenty-Years in the Making," (Phnom Penh: Konrad-AdenauerStiftung (KAS) and Cambodian Institute for Cooperation and Peace (CICP), March 2020; Cheunboran Chanborey, "The South China Sea and ASEAN Unity: A Cambodian Perspective," *Cambodian Institute for Strategic Studies (CISS)*, September 5, 2016.

[42] Ben Sokhean, "What It Means for Cambodia to Be an ASEAN Member State," *Khmer Times*, April 30, 2019.

[43] Chheang Vannarith, "Cambodia, ASEAN: 19 Years On," *Khmer Times*, May 4, 2018.

[44] Quoted in Chheang Vannarith, "Cambodia, ASEAN: 19 Years On," *Khmer Times*, May 4, 2018

[45] Cheunboran Chanborey, "Cambodia's Strategic China Alignment," *The Diplomat*, July 8, 2015.

Prime Minister Hun Sen stated in early 2012 that as a Chair of ASEAN, "Cambodia would fulfil its leadership role responsibly and would work to neutrally moderate and mediate all regional and international issues."[46] In this context, Cambodia's first role as ASEAN Chair in 2002 is viewed as independent and neutral.[47] As a small state in the region, major powers and international institutions play a crucial part in the survival and security of the country.[48] As evidence, two years after joining the regional grouping, Cambodia joined hands with Laos and Vietnam to issue a joint statement opposing any outside intervention in the newly independent territory of East Timor (now Timor-Leste).

As a non-claimant state, Cambodia follows a neutral policy on SCS disputes, which is in accordance with its pragmatic foreign policy principles as articulated in its Constitution and national interests. The most significant development for Cambodia's employing of this policy occurred when the small kingdom took up the ASEAN Chair in 2002 in Phnom Penh. As ASEAN Chair, Cambodia triumphed in bringing China and the ASEAN member states into an agreement to adopt a legally non-binding Declaration on the Conduct (DOC) of Parties in the SCS. Although the DOC mechanism cannot be used to completely settle the territorial disputes in the SCS, it has at least played an important part in refraining China and ASEAN claimant states from using military means to resolve their maritime disputes. This DOC made it possible for ASEAN and China to adopt another document, namely the Guidelines for the Implementation of the Declaration of Conduct in 2011. In short, during this period, Cambodia's major strategic objective was viewed as contributing to the peaceful resolution of the SCS dispute which served the national interests of its regional grouping as well as that of China.

Cambodia's 2012 ASEAN Chairmanship and beyond

Since its 2002 ASEAN Chair, Cambodia's policy towards the SCS issue has significantly shifted. Since 2012, Cambodia has employed a policy of siding with China to accrue its own economic benefit. Excessive dependence on China has placed Cambodian foreign policy firmly under China's influence. While China's economic assistance may boost Cambodia's

46 Chheang Vannarith, "Results, Expectations, and Challenges for Cambodia's 2012 ASEAN Chairmanship," *Asia Pacific Bulletin*, no. 183 (October 25, 2012).

47 The author's interview with Cambodian political analysts in Phnom Penh in 2017.

48 Sorpong Peou, "Cambodia: From Isolation to Involvement in Regional Community Building," in *Regional Community Building in East Asia: Countries in Focus*, ed. Lee Lai To and Zarina Othman (New York: Routledge, 2017).

economic development to a certain extent and enable Cambodia to maintain sovereignty and pursue an independent foreign policy on the international stage, Cambodia's current foreign policy is seen as serving Beijing's broader geopolitical and strategic interests.[49] Beside Cambodia's staunchest support of the "One China" policy and other policies in favour of China's interests, the most noteworthy single event demonstrating the considerable influence of China towards Cambodia's foreign policy was in 2012 when Cambodia assumed the role of ASEAN Chair and hosted a number of ASEAN ministerial meetings such as ASEAN summits, the ASEAN+3 Summit and the East Asia Summit.[50]

The year 2012 marked an important turning point in Cambodia-China relations under the comprehensive strategic partnership, when China successfully exerted its influence over Cambodia for furthering China's strategic interests. Cambodia is seen as a strong supporter of China's "core national interests" in the SCS dispute. This resulted in ASEAN's failure to issue a unified Joint Communiqué following its 45th Annual Ministerial Meeting in Phnom Penh in July 2012.[51] It was the first time in the history of the group there was no communiqué as Cambodia had arguably declined to play the Chair's customary role of seeking agreement among the ten ASEAN members. Carl Thayer illustrates how Cambodia played China's zero-sum game on the dispute in the South China Sea:

> Cambodia played the role of spoiler at the forty-fifth ASEAN Ministerial Meeting (AMM) … Hun Sen complied with China's wishes and Cambodia deleted references to the South China Sea from the formal ASEAN summit agenda. This did not stop other ASEAN members, such as the Philippines and Vietnam from raising South China Sea issues. Cambodia, as ASEAN chair, intervened twice to support China's position. First, Cambodia supported a Chinese proposal for an Expert Persons Group to be set up consisting of twenty members, ten each from ASEAN and ten from China. Cambodia also supported China's early inclusion in ASEAN discussions on a code of conduct for the South China Sea. Cambodia was rebuffed on both proposals due to a lack of consensus.[52]

---

49 See for example, Burgos and Ear.

50 Po and Var.

51 Carlyle A. Thayer, "ASEAN's Code of Conduct in the South China Sea: A Litmus Test for Community-Building?," *The Asia-Pacific Journal* 10, no. 34 (2012).

52 "ASEAN's Code of Conduct in the South China Sea: A Litmus Test for Community-Building?."

A number of ASEAN members and some major powers pointed the finger at Cambodia for rejecting a proposal by the Philippines and Vietnam that mentioned their territorial disputes with China in the unified statement.[53] As a result, Cambodia was criticized by its closer ally, Vietnam, by other ASEAN members, and by the international community for lacking an independent foreign policy.[54] Known as the Phnom Penh fiasco, this incident undermined Prime Minister Hun Sen's commitment to play a neutral leadership role in setting regional related issues, and his pledge that, "Cambodia would fulfil its leadership role responsibly and would work to neutrally moderate and mediate all regional and international issues."[55]

Cambodia faced another significant challenge with respect to China's influence at the 49th ASEAN Summit in Vientiane, Laos, in September 2016. Cambodia was once again portrayed as a "thorn" inside the regional bloc, and there was more friction over issuing a Joint Communiqué on the South China Sea. While some ASEAN members lean toward China, only Cambodia was put in the spotlight. Cambodia again was accused of refusing to include any mention of the Arbitral Tribunal's ruling in the document. Although the Joint Communiqué was issued, as Adam Leong Kok Wey points out, it was seen as "too soft," and it "failed to explicitly denounce China's assertive actions in the South China Sea."[56] Cambodia was seen as responsible for preventing ASEAN from issuing a common position to confront China. Therefore, some analysts argued that Cambodia's siding with China on the South China Sea issue at the expense of ASEAN, the cornerstone of Cambodia's foreign policy,[57] undermined ASEAN unity. Some critics, quoted by the media, criticized Cambodia for damaging ASEAN unity by contending that: "Cambodia is not even a claimant, so its wielding of a veto in the consensus-based bloc on behalf of a non-member patron country can be seen as fundamentally undermining ASEAN's founding principle of strict non-interference in its member-countries' affairs."[58]

The issues of the South China Sea and ASEAN unity have become a point of diplomatic friction between Cambodia and some other ASEAN states, in particular the claimant states of Vietnam and the Philippines, and

---

53 Peou, 49.

54 Kheang Un, "Cambodia in 2012: Beyond the Crossroads?," *Asian Survey* 53, no. 1 (2013).

55 Vannarith, "Results, Expectations, and Challenges for Cambodia's 2012 ASEAN Chairmanship."

56 Adam Leong Kok Wey, "Is the South China Sea Fracturing ASEAN?," *East Asia Forum*, August 25, 2016.

57 Chanborey, "The South China Sea and ASEAN Unity: A Cambodian Perspective."

58 "Cambodia Is Killing the ASEAN Dream," *The Nations*, August 17, 2016.

between Cambodia and Western countries.[59] Cambodia's foreign policy of leaning toward China at the expense of ASEAN's unity has led to some observers and commentators sensationally painting Cambodia in a negative manner, with headlines such as "Cambodia is killing the ASEAN dream" and "Cambodia is ASEAN's maverick."[60] One ASEAN diplomat bluntly described Cambodia's rejection of any mention of China in the section on the South China Sea this way: "Cambodia is unbelievable. It is blocking any phrase about the [Hague] arbitration and about [China's] 'militarization' of the South China Sea. The effect of these developments on ASEAN credibility cannot be understated."[61]

Despite there being no existing provision in the ASEAN Charter concerning the dismissal or withdrawal of a member state, some observers have gone even further and suggested dismissing Cambodia from the regional grouping so that ASEAN can move forward on the South China Sea. For example, Singapore's ambassador-at-large Bilahari Kausikan proposed Cambodia's expulsion from ASEAN in a comment on his Facebook page.[62]

Cambodia is evidently under China's enormous political and economic influence; it has no choice but to side with China over the South China Sea dispute.[63] This became apparent when China announced a further US$600 million aid package to Cambodia almost immediately after the Arbitral Tribunal verdict. Moreover, a week after the meeting in Laos, China continued its powerful economic diplomacy by expressing a commitment to financing a Cambodian request for a 12-storey office building for the Country's National Assembly.[64]

The critics attacked China's assertive behaviour in the SCS and the Chinese rejection of the Arbitral Tribunal ruling and connected these to the Chinese influence on Cambodia. Such claims are extant because during President Xi Jinping's visit to Cambodia in 2016 several deals were viewed

---

59 Koichi Sato, "The Rise of China's Impact on ASEAN Conference Diplomacy: A Study of Conflict in the South China Sea," *Journal of Contemporary East Asia Studies* 2, no. 2 (2013); Tomotaka Shoji, "Vietnam, ASEAN, and the South China Sea: Unity or Diverseness?," *NIDS Journal of Defense and Security* 13 (2012).

60 "Cambodia Is Killing the ASEAN Dream."; Kavi Chongkittavorn, "Cambodia Remains ASEAN's Maverick," *The Nation*, July 18, 2016.

61 Simon Webb and Manuel Mogato, "ASEAN in Discord Ahead of Meeting with Top China, US Diplomats," *Reuters*, July 23, 2016.

62 Puy Kea, "Why Cambodia Is Portrayed as the Thorn in ASEAN's Side," *Kyoto News*, July 26, 2016.

63 Pheakdey; Chong. The author interviewed Cambodian political analysts and international scholars in Phnom Penh in 2017.

64 Veasna Var, "Security Issues and Challenges for Cambodia: Domestic and Regional," *The Korean Journal of Defense Analysis* 29, no. 2 (2017).

as China's rewarding Cambodia for its compliance, especially in the SCS dispute. Moreover, President Xi offered US$148 million in aid for economic cooperation, cancelled US$89 million of Cambodia's debt, and pledged an additional US$14 million in military aid.[65]

Determinants and implications of Cambodia's South China Sea policy

Cambodia's SCS policy is determined by its strategic interests and in alignment with its foreign policy of siding with China, which is deeply influenced mainly by economic factors. This factor is playing a crucial role in the legitimacy and the survival of Hun Sen's ruling Cambodian People's Party (CPP) government. A variety of analysts and scholars have claimed other factors – such as the kingdom's perceived threat from its more powerful neighbours, Vietnam and Thailand, and the kingdom's mistrust of ASEAN's ability to guarantee its security against threats from these bigger neighbours – make a case for driving Cambodia's foreign policy towards China and the South China Sea dispute.[66] These claims seem to have some validity. However, they appear to overlook the political reality in Cambodia. One of the major strategic objectives of the current Hun Sen/CPP government is Hun Sen and his elites' consolidation of power.[67]

Hun Sen's recent drift from democracy, as recently evidenced in the government's unprecedented crackdown on the country's major opposition party, the Cambodia National Rescue Party (CNRP), independent media, and civil society, illustrates the fundamental fear of losing power or regime change. It seems to be clear in the eyes of CPP elites that playing the democratic game may not help secure Hun Sen and his government to remain in power.[68] However, Hun Sen's recent political move has met with mounting pressures from the international community and Western powers: the US

[65] Prak Chan Thul, "Chinese President Xi Jinping Visits Loyal Friend Cambodia," *Reuters*, October 13, 2016.

[66] See for example, Sovinda Po and Christopher B. Primiano, "An 'Ironclad Friend': Explaining Cambodia's Bandwagoning Policy Towards China," *Journal of Current Southeast Asian Affairs* (2020); Chanborey Cheunboran, "Cambodia-China Relations: What Do Cambodia's Past Strategic Directions Tell Us?," in *Cambodia's Foreign Relations in Regional and Global Context*, ed. Sok Udom Deth, Suon Sun, and Serkan Bulut (Phnom Penh: Konrad-Adenauer-Stiftung 2017).

[67] Carlyle A. Thayer, "Cambodia: The Cambodian People's Party Consolidates Power," *Southeast Asian Affairs* (2009). The author interviewed with Cambodian political analysts in mid-2017.

[68] The author interviewed some senior government officials and independence political analysts in mid-2017.

imposed some sanctions (that is, visa restriction) aiming at Cambodia's high-ranking government officials, and the European Union has already partially withdrawn its Everything But Arms (EBA) trade preferences.[69]

Growing external pressure creates significant negative impacts on Cambodia's economic growth and development trajectory and are a source of heightening domestic grievance.[70] As a result, these challenges could present a risk to Hun Sen's power if his government is unable to maintain the momentum of development and economic progress.[71] As economic development is a cornerstone to the legitimacy and political survival of Hun Sen's government, Hun Sen has no other better option but is compelled to embrace with China to secure economic interests.[72] When asked about Hun Sen's current manoeuvring in embracing with and so accepting towards China almost exclusively, most interviewees expressed the same views that, "the reason is easy to understand, and everyone knows this. Hun Sen wants to remain in power forever, so only China can save his consolidation of power."[73]

It remains to be seen whether Beijing's continued support of the Cambodian government is a sustainable policy. It is worthwhile noting that Cambodia-China relations are based on the convergence of interests or reciprocity of the relations: Cambodia is in desperate need of China for economic benefits and China is in need of Cambodia for geostrategic and geopolitical interests. In an op-ed on "Kingdom Should Be Wary of EBA Loss," the authors caution about Cambodia's pursuance of the foreign policy of putting all its eggs in one basket with China, that:

> Hun Sen may think he has China's Xi Jinping to turn to for help, especially in time of economic or legitimacy crisis; however, Hun Sen should not forget that China supports Cambodia because the two countries are in a reciprocal relationship. The reciprocity of their patron-client relations depends on mutual interests and therefore it cannot be guaranteed that China would not abandon Cambodia in time of desperate need.[74]

---

[69] The European Commission, "Commission Decides to Partially Withdraw Cambodia's Preferential Access to the Eu Market," news release, February 12, 2020.

[70] The author interviewed some senior government officials and independence political analysts in mid-2017. See also, Chheang.

[71] The author interviewed Cambodian political analysts in mid-2017.

[72] The author interview both Cambodia's official government and political analysts.

[73] The author interviewed some senior government officials and independence political analysts in mid-2017.

[74] Kimkong Heng and Veasna Var, "Kingdom Should Be Wary of EBA Loss," *Phnom Penh Post*, March 25, 2019.

Beijing's economic engagement has brought significant benefits to Cambodia's socio-economic development and boosted economic development. At the same time, the Chinese development approach has considerable social, political, and environmental impacts on Cambodia. It remains to be seen if China's economic aid and investment projects that are not focused on governance and democracy could help achieve Cambodia's sustainable development, one that can raise Cambodia from a low-income to high-income country. It seems clear that, in the relationship between China and Cambodia, the two countries are far more interested in short-term economic and political gain over long-term democratic development. With the main focus on infrastructure development and less focus on good governance and reform, as pronounced in Cambodia's Rectangular Strategy as the core pillars of Cambodia's development strategy, whether or not China's economic influence can help the small kingdom realizes its development strategy is still a question for discussion.

The recent phenomenon of bilateral ties between China and Cambodia has raised significant concern over the legitimacy of China's ambitions in the region, as obvious evidence points to growing Chinese assertiveness in the South China Sea. A reported agreement between China and Cambodia to build a strategic outpost on the Gulf of Thailand has attracted heavy criticism from the US and other Western countries.[75] Although Cambodia's Hun Sen swiftly dismissed the report as "fake news," saying that "No such thing could happen because hosting foreign military bases is against the Cambodian constitution,"[76] it still has been unconvinced of the denial given China's strategic ambition and assertiveness in the region and its existing overseas bases, such as in Djibouti and Sri Lanka, Hambantota.[77] The report about the potential military facilities, whether true or not, has irritated US-Cambodia relationships and has also undermined the small kingdom's foreign policy in the international arena. In a letter sent to the Cambodian government, former US Vice President Mike Pence raised his government's concern over an alleged Chinese naval base in Cambodia's Koh Kong province.[78] The US State Department in its statement encouraged Cambodia to decline such an arrangement, stating that the kingdom had a "constitutional

[75] Jeremy Page, Gordon Lubold, and Rob Taylor, "Deal for Naval Outpost in Cambodia Furthers China's Quest for Military Network," *The Wall Street Journal*, July 22, 2019.

[76] Pete Schroeder, David Brunnstrom, and Prak Chan Thul, "Cambodia Denies Deal to Allow Armed Chinese Forces at Its Naval Base," *Reuters*, July 22, 2019.

[77] Leah Dreyfuss and Mara Karlin, "All That Xi Wants: China Attempts to Ace Bases Overseas," (Washington, DC: Brookings Institution, September 2019).

[78] Niem Chheng, "'No Need to Violate Constitution' with 'Base,' PM to Tell US' Pence," *The Phnom Penh Post*, November 20, 2018.

commitment to its people to pursue an independent foreign policy."[79] The statement placed emphasis on the impact of foreign military in Cambodia on ASEAN's coherence and centrality: "We are concerned that any steps by the Cambodian government to invite a foreign military presence in Cambodia would threaten the coherence and centrality of the Association of Southeast Asian Nations in coordinating regional developments, and disturb peace and stability in Southeast Asia."[80] If the Chinese military facilities in Cambodia turn out to be true, according to experts it would enable China to project its military power deep into Southeast Asia.[81] It will also have direct implications on the wider balance of power in Southeast Asia and the Asia-Pacific.[82] Because of its geopolitical location, the presence of the Chinese naval outpost in Cambodia could provide China with capabilities of air, land, and sea to the eastern Gulf of Thailand. Access to Cambodia would therefore provide China with options to address its disputes in the South China Sea with Vietnam, Taiwan, the Philippines, and Malaysia, especially to secure its claim on the Spratly Islands and its natural resources. In the case of conflict, China may need Cambodian naval facilities as a strategic, sea-accessible location from which to launch a timely response.[83] From the operational and tactical perspectives, as one analyst put, "[i]f warplanes were to launch from Dara Sakor airport, they would be able to strike targets in Vietnam, Singapore, and Thailand."[84]

Conclusion

This chapter has explored Cambodia's policy towards China and its claims over the South China Sea since 2002, when Cambodia became the first ASEAN Chair. It has highlighted the fact that, under Hun Sen, Cambodia's South China Sea policy is inconsistent, moving from a flexible, pragmatic foreign policy that was seen an independent and neutral stance that will not risk upsetting China, Vietnam, the Philippines, or ASEAN as a whole in 2002, to embrace China with a foreign policy primarily focused on reaping Cambodia's own economic interests. By embracing China, the

79 Quoted in Schroeder, Brunnstrom, and Thul.

80 Quoted in "Cambodia Denies Deal to Allow Chinese Forces at Its Naval Base," *Aljazeera*, July 22, 2019.

81 Charles Edel, "Hiding in Plain Sight: Chinese Expansion in Southeast Asia," *War on the Rocks*, May 9, 2019. The author interviewed political and military analysts.

82 Page, Lubold, and Taylor; Prashanth Parameswaran, "Why a New China Naval Outpost in Cambodia Would Matter," *The Diplomat*, July 23, 2019.

83 Burgos and Ear, 615; Edel.

84 Hannah Elten, "Chinese Naval Base in Cambodia," *Global Risk Insights*, October 6, 2019.

kingdom received significant political backing, development aid, and loans and investment from the Asian giant. At the same time, Cambodia helped China to achieve its national interests and regional expansion, as can be seen in the South China Sea dispute when Cambodia as a Chair of ASEAN in 2012, sided with China in blocking the group joint statement condemning China's growing assertiveness in the South China Sea. Cambodia's policy towards the South China Sea since 2012 has undermined ASEAN's unity and centrality as well as undermined Cambodia's face on the international stage. Cambodia's policy of bandwagoning with China has negatively affected regional security and stability.

Cambodia's approach to the SCS dispute has been determined by economic consideration. This consideration is vitally important to Hun Sen's CPP government, given his government and himself are in a time of economic and government legitimacy crisis. However, it is unlikely that the help from China to restore Hun Sen's economy and his legitimacy will be sustained in the long term. Hun Sen's policy of accommodating China met with significant backlashes in terms of its foreign, development, and domestic policy as well as a range of important regional implications.

As growing pressure and uncertainty from domestic politics and the international community, especially the US and the EU, still continue to unfold, Cambodia under Hun Sen can be expected to adopt a policy of further embracing China and remaining apt to jump on the Chinese bandwagon without reservation for economic benefits and regime survival.

References

Angela, Maria. "China's South China Sea Moves Raise Concerns." *The ASEAN Post*, May 1, 2020. https://theaseanpost.com/article/chinas-south-china-sea-moves-raise-concerns

Bartholomew, Carolyn and Dennis C. Shea. "2017 Report to Congress of the US-China Economic and Security Review Commission, Executive Summary and Recommendations." Washington, DC: US-China Economic and Security Review Commission, 2017.

Burgos, Sigfrido and Sophal Ear. "China's Strategic Interests in Cambodia: Influence and Resources." *Asian Survey* 50, no. 3 (2010): 615–39.

Cáceres, Sigfrido Burgos and Sophal Ear. *The Hungry Dragon: How China's Quest for Resources Is Reshaping the World*. New York: Routledge, 2013.

"Cambodia Denies Deal to Allow Chinese Forces at Its Naval Base." *Al Jazeera*, July 22, 2019. https://www.aljazeera.com/news/2019/7/22/cambodia-denies-deal-to-allow-chinese-forces-at-its-naval-base

"Cambodia Is Killing the ASEAN Dream." *The Nations*, August 17, 2016. https://khmercircle.blogspot.com/2016/08/cambodia-is-killing-asean-dream.html

Chanborey, Cheunboran. "Cambodia's Strategic China Alignment." *The Diplomat*, July 8, 2015. https://thediplomat.com/2015/07/cambodias-strategic-china-alignment/

Chanborey, Cheunboran. "The South China Sea and ASEAN Unity: A Cambodian Perspective." *Cambodian Institute for Strategic Studies (CISS)*, September 5, 2016. http://repository.unpar.ac.id/bitstream/handle/123456789/6465/Cover%20-%20Bab1%20-%203314037sc-p.pdf?sequence=1&isAllowed=y

Charadine, Pich. "Cambodia within ASEAN: Twenty-Years in the Making." Phnom Penh: Konrad-AdenauerStiftung (KAS) and Cambodian Institute for Cooperation and Peace (CICP), March 2020. https://www.kas.de/documents/264850/8437634/20-03-04+Cambodia+and+ASEAN.pdf/7df3f55d-4770-e4bd-9495-0ec8c814d8e7?version=1.0&t=1587355678563

Cheunboran, Chanborey. "Cambodia-China Relations: What Do Cambodia's Past Strategic Directions Tell Us?" in *Cambodia's Foreign Relations in Regional and Global Context*, edited by Sok Udom Deth, Suon Sun and Serkan Bulut, 227–48. Phnom Penh: Konrad-Adenauer-Stiftung, 2017, Chapter 12.

Chheang, Vannarith. "The Political Economy of Chinese Investment in Cambodia." ISEAS – Yusof Ishak Institute, Singapore, 2017. https://www.iseas.edu.sg/images/pdf/TRS16_17.pdf

Chheng, Niem. "'No Need to Violate Constitution' with 'Base,' PM to Tell US' Pence." *The Phnom Penh Post*, November 20, 2018. https://www.phnompenhpost.com/national-politics/no-need-violate-constitution-base-pm-tell-us-pence

"China Urges Cambodia to Use Yuan in Bilateral Trade." *The Straits Times*, February 6, 2018. https://www.straitstimes.com/asia/se-asia/china-urges-cambodia-to-use-yuan-in-bilateral-trade

Chong, Terence. "The Politics Behind Cambodia's Embrace of China." ISEAS – Yusof Ishak Institute, Singapore, August 2, 2017. https://www.iseas.edu.sg/images/pdf/ISEAS_Perspective_2017_59.pdf

Chongkittavorn, Kavi. "Cambodia Remains ASEAN's Maverick." *The Nation*, July 18, 2016. http://www.nationmultimedia.com/opinion/Cambodia-remains-Aseans-maverick-30290816.html?utm_source=Daily+News+on+the+Southeast+Asian+Region+-+18+July+2016&utm_campaign=Daily+news+alert_20160718&utm_medium=email

Ciorciari, John D. "A Chinese Model for Patron–Client Relations? The Sino-Cambodian Partnership." *International Relations of the Asia-Pacific* 15, no. 2 (2014): 245–78.

Dreyfuss, Leah and Mara Karlin. "All That Xi Wants: China Attempts to Ace Bases Overseas." Washington, DC: Brookings Institution, September 2019. https://www.brookings.edu/research/all-that-xi-wants-china-attempts-to-ace-bases-overseas/

European Commission. "Commission Decides to Partially Withdraw Cambodia's Preferential Access to the EU Market." February 12, 2020. https://trade.ec.europa.eu/doclib/press/index.cfm?id=2113

Ear, Sophal. "The China–Cambodia–Us Nexus" in *New Dynamics in Us-China Relations: Contending for the Asia Pacific*, edited by Mingjiang Li and Kalyan M. Kemburi, New York: Routledge, 2015, 283–4.

Edel, Charles. "Hiding in Plain Sight: Chinese Expansion in Southeast Asia." *War on the Rocks*, May 9, 2019. https://warontherocks.com/2019/05/hiding-in-plain-sight-chinese-expansion-in-southeast-asia/

Elten, Hannah. "Chinese Naval Base in Cambodia." *Global Risk Insights*, October 6, 2019. https://globalriskinsights.com/2019/10/chinese-naval-base-in-cambodia/

Heng, Kimkong and Veasna Var. "Kingdom Should Be Wary of EBA Loss." *The Phnom Penh Post*, March 25, 2019. https://www.phnompenhpost.com/opinion/kingdom-should-be-wary-eba-loss.

Hutt, David. "US, China Tensions Put Cambodia in Potential Peril." *Asia Times*, June 6, 2019. https://asiatimes.com/2019/06/us-china-tensions-put-cambodia-in-potential-peril/

Hutt, David and Shawn W. Crispin. "Cambodia at the Center of a New Cold War." *Asia Times*, November 15, 2018. https://asiatimes.com/2018/11/cambodia-at-the-center-of-a-new-cold-war/

Kea, Puy. "Why Cambodia Is Portrayed as the Thorn in ASEAN's Side." *Kyoto News*, July 26, 2016. https://news.abs-cbn.com/overseas/07/26/16/why-cambodia-is-portrayed-as-the-thorn-in-aseans-side

Koh, David. "Chinese Investments in Cambodia: View of Chinese Soft Power from the Ground Up." Phnom Penh: CICP, 2016, 79–89. http://www.cicp.org.kh/userfiles/file/Publications/Selected%20CICP%20Publications%202016.pdf

Kunmakara, May. "PM Backs China's Key Role." *Khmer Times*, April 12, 2017. https://www.khmertimeskh.com/15902/pm-backs-chinas-key-role/

Lim, Alvin Cheng Hin. "Sino-Cambodian Relations: Recent Economic and Military Cooperation – Analysis." *Eurasia Review*, June 30, 2015. https://www.eurasiareview.com/30062015-sino-cambodian-relations-recent-economic-and-military-cooperation-analysis/

Lim, Alvin Cheng Hin. "Cambodia Joins the Belt and Road." *IPP Review*, October 14, 2016. https://ippreview.com/index.php/Blog/single/id/255.html

Marks, Paul. "China's Cambodia Strategy." *Parameters* 30, no. 3, 2000: 92–108. https://press.armywarcollege.edu/cgi/viewcontent.cgi?article=1993&context=parameters.

Page, Jeremy, Gordon Lubold, and Rob Taylor. "Deal for Naval Outpost in Cambodia Furthers China's Quest for Military Network." *The Wall Street Journal*, July 22, 2019. https://www.wsj.com/articles/secret-deal-for-chinese-naval-outpost-in-cambodia-raises-u-s-fears-of-beijings-ambitions-11563732482

Parameswaran, Prashanth. "China and Cambodia: With Friends Like These ...," *China Brief* 13, no. 1, 2013. https://jamestown.org/program/china-and-cambodia-with-friends-like-these/

Parameswaran, Prashanth. "Why a New China Naval Outpost in Cambodia Would Matter." *The Diplomat*, July 23, 2019. https://thediplomat.com/2019/07/why-a-new-china-naval-outpost-in-cambodia-would-matter/

Parameswaran, Prashanth. "What Did the 2020 China-Cambodia Golden Dragon Military Exercise Actually Achieve?" *The Diplomat*, April 1, 2020. https://thediplomat.com/2020/04/what-did-the-2020-china-cambodia-golden-dragon-military-exercise-actually-achieve/.

Peou, Sorpong. "Cambodia: From Isolation to Involvement in Regional Community Building" in *Regional Community Building in East Asia: Countries in Focus*, edited by Lee Lai To and Zarina Othman, New York: Routledge, 2017, 33–56.

Pertiwi, Sukmawani Bela. "Is ASEAN Unity in Danger from the South China Sea?" *The Diplomat*, August 3, 2016. https://thediplomat.com/2016/08/is-asean-unity-in-danger-from-the-south-china-sea/

Pheakdey, Heng. "Cambodia–China Relations: A Positive- Sum Game?." *Journal of Current Southeast Asian Affairs* no. 2 (2012): 57–85.

Po, Sovinda, and Christopher B. Primiano. "An 'Ironclad Friend:' Explaining Cambodia's Bandwagoning Policy Towards China." *Journal of Current Southeast Asian Affairs* (2020): 1–21.

Po, Sovinda and Veasna Var. "Cambodia's South China Sea Dilemma between China and ASEAN." *IPP Review*, May, 3, 2017. https://ippreview.com/index.php/Blog/amp/id/425

Raska, Michael and Richard A. Bitzinger. "Strategic Contours of China's Arms Transfers." *Strategic Studies Quarterly* 14, no. 1 (Spring 2020): 91–116.

Sarith, Heng. "Cambodia's Foreign Policy Grand Strategy." *The Diplomat*, September 11, 2014. https://thediplomat.com/2014/09/cambodias-foreign-policy-grand-strategy/

Sato, Koichi. "The Rise of China's Impact on ASEAN Conference Diplomacy: A Study of Conflict in the South China Sea." *Journal of Contemporary East Asia Studies* 2, no. 2 (2013): 95–110.

Schroeder, Pete, David Brunnstrom, and Prak Chan Thul. "Cambodia Denies Deal to Allow Armed Chinese Forces at Its Naval Base." *Reuters*, July 22, 2019. https://www.britishherald.com/cambodia-denies-deal-to-allow-armed-chinese-forces-at-its-naval-base/

Shekhar, Vibhanshu. "ASEAN's Response to the Rise of China: Deploying a Hedging Strategy." *China Report* 48, no. 3 (2012): 253–68.

Shoji, Tomotaka. "Vietnam, ASEAN, and the South China Sea: Unity or Diverseness?." *NIDS Journal of Defense and Security* 13 (2012): 1–20.

Siphat, Touch. "Patterns and Impacts of Chinese Assistance in Cambodia" in *Impact of China's Rise on the Mekong Region*, Yos Santasombat (ed). New York: Palgrave Macmillan, 2015, 195–225.

Sokhean, Ben. "What It Means for Cambodia to Be an ASEAN Member State." *Khmer Times*, April 30, 2019. https://www.khmertimeskh.com/599143/what-it-means-for-cambodia-to-be-an-asean-member-state/.

Thakur, Ramesh and Carlyle A. Thayer. *The Soviet Union as an Asian Pacific Power: Implications of Gorbachev's 1986 Vladivostok Initiative.* Boulder and London: Westview Press, 1987.

Thayer, Carlyle A. "ASEAN's Code of Conduct in the South China Sea: A Litmus Test for Community-Building?." *The Asia-Pacific Journal* 10, no. 34 (2012): 1–23.

Thayer, Carlyle A. "Cambodia-United States Relations" in Sothirak Pou, Geoff Wade, and Mark Hong (eds), *Cambodia: Progress and Challenges Since 1991.* Singapore Institute of Southeast Asian Studies, 2012, 124–35.

Thayer, Carlyle A. "Cambodia: The Cambodian People's Party Consolidates Power." *Southeast Asian Affairs* (2009): 85–101.

Thayer, Carlyle A. "China's Relations with Laos and Cambodia" in Jung-Ho Bae and Jae H. Ku (eds), *China's Internal and External Relations and the Lessons for Korea and Asia.* Seoul: Korean Institute for National Unification, 2013, 189–249.

Thayer, Carlyle A. "US Rapprochement with Laos and Cambodia." *Contemporary Southeast Asia* 32, no. 3 (2010): 442–59.

Thul, Prak Chan. "Chinese President Xi Jinping Visits Loyal Friend Cambodia." *Reuters*, October 13, 2016. https://www.reuters.com/article/us-china-cambodia/chinese-president-xi-jinping-visits-loyal-friend-cambodia-idUSKCN12D0NV

Un, Kheang. "Cambodia in 2012: Beyond the Crossroads?." *Asian Survey* 53, no. 1 (2013): 142–9.

Vannarith, Chheang. "Cambodia, ASEAN: 19 Years On." *Khmer Times*, May 4, 2018. https://www.khmertimeskh.com/486435/cambodia-asean-19-years-on/

Vannarin, Neou. "Cambodia Strengthens Military Ties with China." *Voice of America News*, July 25, 2015. https://learningenglish.voanews.com/a/cambodia-strengthens-military-ties-with-china/2875873.html

Vannarith, Chheang. "Cambodia Embraces China's Belt and Road Initiative." Singapore: ISEAS – Yusof Ishak Institute 2017, no. 48, July 6, 2017. https://www.iseas.edu.sg/wp-content/uploads/pdfs/ISEAS_Perspective_2017_48.pdf

Vannarith, Chheang. "Results, Expectations, and Challenges for Cambodia's 2012 Asean Chairmanship." *Asia Pacific Bulletin*, no. 183, October 25, 2012. https://www.eastwestcenter.org/publications/results-expectations-and-challenges-cambodias-2012-asean-chairmanship.

Var, Veasna. "Belt and Road Initiative: Opportunities for Cambodia's Development?" *IPP Review*, August 2, 2017. https://ippreview.com/index.php/Blog/amp/id/519

Var, Veasna. "Cambodia Looks for Middle Ground in the South China Sea." *East Asia Forum*, June 20, 2015. https://www.eastasiaforum.org/2015/06/20/cambodia-looks-for-middle-ground-in-the-south-china-sea/

Var, Veasna. "Cambodia: Between China and the United States." *The Diplomat*, May 20, 2015. https://thediplomat.com/2015/05/cambodia-between-china-and-the-united-states/

Var, Veasna. "China's Influence in Cambodia." *Khmer Times*, June 29, 2016. https://www.khmertimeskh.com/25255/chinas-influence-in-cambodia/

Var, Veasna. "Holding Balance between Two Superpowers: Cambodia's Strategic Choices for Foreign and Development Policy." *Eurasia Review*, July 27, 2016. https://www.eurasiareview.com/27072016-holding-balance-between-two-superpowers-cambodias-strategic-choices-for-foreign-and-development-policy-analysis/

Var, Veasna. "Reform of the Royal Cambodian Armed Forces Organization to Meet the Challenges of the 21st Century." *The Korean Journal of Defense Analysis* 28, no. 2 (2016): 249–75.

Var, Veasna. "Security Issues and Challenges for Cambodia: Domestic and Regional." *The Korean Journal of Defense Analysis* 29, no. 2 (2017).

Var, Veasna and Sovinda Po. "Cambodia Looks to China Rather Than the US." *Australian Institute of International Affairs*, March 20, 2017. https://www.internationalaffairs.org.au/australianoutlook/cambodia-looks-to-china-ahead-us/

Webb, Simon, and Manuel Mogato. "Asean in Discord Ahead of Meeting with Top China, US Diplomats." *Reuters*, July 23, 2016. https://br.reuters.com/article/us-southchinasea-ruling-asean-idUSKCN1030KU.

Wey, Adam Leong Kok. "Is the South China Sea Fracturing ASEAN?" *East Asia Forum*, August 25, 2016. https://www.eastasiaforum.org/2016/08/25/is-the-south-china-sea-fracturing-asean/

11

ASEAN's Involvement in the South China Sea Disputes: The Economics-Security Conundrum

Mingjiang Li and YingHui Lee

Introduction

It is important to note that the South China Sea (SCS) disputes are multi-dimensional and ASEAN is selectively involved in some aspects of these dimensions. There are at least four major dimensions that one can observe in the disputes. Setting the stage for the volume, Joshua Hastey and Scott N. Romaniuk, and then Romaniuk and Tobias Burgers address the major pillars of conflict and geostrategic interest in the SCS in this volume's introductory chapters. The first dimension is about territorial sovereignty disputes among claimant parties over various land features in the South China Sea. ASEAN has stated explicitly that it does not intend to get involved in determining whose sovereignty claim is more legitimate. The second dimension has to do with the maritime area claims and maritime rights claims by the disputant parties. Although ASEAN has made it clear that it does not want to be an arbiter for maritime boundary demarcations, many of its statements do suggest that ASEAN attempts to uphold certain principles on how a claimant should legally and legitimately claim maritime zones and rights, for instance by constantly referring to the United Nations Convention for the Law of the Sea (UNCLOS) in its numerous statements.

The third dimension pertaining to the maintenance of peace and security in the SCS includes many elements. Examples include proposing rules and norms to regulate various parties' policies, urging all claimant parties to observe the overall status quo, keeping dialogue channels open, forging maritime cooperation, strengthening confidence-building measures, and even fostering limited preventive diplomacy. It is in the third dimension that ASEAN, together with China, has played the most salient role. The fourth dimension of the SCS disputes concerns the role of other external powers, especially the United States (US), in the disputes. ASEAN cannot dictate or significantly influence other major powers' actions in the South China Sea disputes. ASEAN has, however, tacitly encouraged other powers to play an intervening role, and at the same time attempted to tamp down the escalations that these external players' actions may cause in the SCS.

ASEAN's security management role in the disputes has been shaped by four main factors. First, the regional grouping's self-claimed institutional responsibility for maintaining regional peace and stability has made it inevitable that it has to be proactive in the disputes, otherwise its credibility of acting as a regional multilateral security platform would be severely undermined. Second, ASEAN leaders have to overcome the challenge of different and sometimes conflicting interests of its member states in the SCS disputes. Third, ASEAN's operational principles and characteristics, in particular the so-called ASEAN Way, have had a noticeable bearing on its involvement in the disputes. Fourth, the whole region's geopolitical relations with other major powers, particularly China and the US, have also been a main determinant for the grouping's approaches to the SCS issue.

This chapter analyses ASEAN's involvement in the SCS security management. We will trace the evolution of ASEAN's intervention in the disputes and account for ASEAN's achievements and failures. The remainder of this chapter discusses the divisions within ASEAN which prevented a unified ASEAN response to the SCS and highlights the implications for ASEAN centrality within the fast-evolving regional security architecture. The most daunting challenge for ASEAN is an economics-security conundrum that the group may continue to face in the future. Largely because of growing economic dependence on China, ASEAN and some of its member states just cannot adopt any confrontational posture toward Beijing. The growing economic structural constraints will continue to limit ASEAN's role in the SCS. We also suggest that geopolitical rivalry among the major players is likely to intensify in the SCS, partly because of the growing limitations for ASEAN's role in managing security in the region.

ASEAN's intervention in managing security in the South China Sea

Any discussion about ASEAN's participation in the SCS disputes will have to centre on ASEAN-China interactions on this matter. China attracts the most attention and criticism for its actions in the SCS due to the sheer scope of its claim, and its growing military assertiveness and naval presence in regional waters. A fundamental objective for ASEAN is to persuade Beijing to refrain from taking unilateral actions that would destabilize the status quo and to respect various legal principles and norms in handling the disputes. It should be pointed out that other claimant parties have also been engaged in various activities that help expand their presence and achieve economic benefits in the disputed areas of the SCS, but ASEAN has seldom taken any collective action against its member states. Conflicts between ASEAN claimant states are usually managed bilaterally by these countries themselves.

The SCS conflict began to be an issue for the ASEAN as an organization in the early 1990s. In its first public display of the importance of the SCS for peace and stability in the region, ASEAN issued a declaration in July 1992 urging "all parties concerned" to exercise restraint in order to create "a positive climate for the eventual resolution of all disputes."[1] This declaration came after China and Vietnam, which has yet to join ASEAN, clashed over oil exploration activities in the South China Sea. The SCS continued to be mentioned in various Joint Communiqués for the ASEAN Ministerial Meetings from 1992 to 1994.

However, these declarations did not seem to have any major effect. In fact, Chinese activities in the semi-enclosed body of water intensified over the next two years, and by mid-1994 China had started occupying the Mischief Reef, which was also claimed by the Philippines. China's move was regarded as a significant turning point in the conflict as, up until this point, the actual conflict was predominantly a China-Vietnam conflict. The Mischief Reef incident marked the first time China occupied a feature claimed by an ASEAN member state. It was at this point that ASEAN began taking on a more interventionist posture in the disputes in response to the Philippine lobby for ASEAN member states to adopt a Code of Conduct (COC) to limit Chinese expansion in the South China Sea. In subsequent years, discussion for a COC with China became a central task for ASEAN in the security management in the SCS. The call for "claimants to address the issue in various bilateral and multilateral fora"[2] in the 1995 Joint Communiqué of the 28th ASEAN Ministerial Meeting clearly demonstrated ASEAN's changing approach toward the SCS: the dispute can no longer be settled bilaterally between China and the individual Southeast Asian claimants; a unified multilateral ASEAN response has become necessary for conflict management. The ASEAN Regional Forum (ARF) also expressed concerns over developments in the SCS for the first time in 1995.

1 *1992 ASEAN Declaration on the South China Sea.*

2 *1995 Joint Communique of the 28th ASEAN Ministerial Meeting.*

Nevertheless, it soon became clear that any hopes for a united ASEAN response to the SCS disputes was destined to face many challenges. The Philippines had pushed for an ASEAN draft COC before the document was presented to China for further negotiations. However, the reconciliation of various positions and interests of the various ASEAN countries proved a daunting task: ASEAN took more than five years to formulate its version of the draft COC. In the meantime, China had produced its own version of the draft. Finally, in March 2000, both sides agreed to exchange drafts and combine the two versions into a final agreed text.

Unfortunately, by 2002, it became clear that a binding COC was not achievable in the short term and a compromise was made in November for an interim, non-binding Declaration on the Conduct of Parties (DOC) in the SCS to be signed between the ASEAN member states and China. The document referred to certain fundamental principles for all parties to observe in the SCS, for instance the legal requirements of the UNCLOS. It called for the exercise of self-restraint of all parties. All signatory parties pledged to resolve the disputes in a peaceful manner. The DOC was also meant as a confidence-building mechanism. The document suggested that parties concerned should engage in maritime cooperation related to environmental protection, scientific research, navigation safety and communication, search and rescue operation, and transnational crime prevention. Perhaps most importantly, the DOC laid the foundation for follow-up negotiations and the eventual signing of a COC.[3] The DOC signified ASEAN's success in presenting itself as a legitimate and accepted player in the eyes of China and other external powers in the security management of the SCS.

Analysts have different assessments regarding the efficacy of the DOC. Some believed that the document has largely been a failure. They noted that almost no claimant party strictly abided by the policy suggestions that were stipulated in the DOC. Not many maritime cooperation or confidence-building measures were conducted in subsequent years. The DOC did not result in any significant growth of trust among the claimant countries. They also noted that the DOC did not prevent various maritime disputes from taking place. Other observers, who were slightly more positive in their evaluation of the DOC, argued that the DOC might have played a role in maintaining the overall peace and stability in the remaining years of the 2000s. The document at least served as a moral constraint for all claimant parties. The DOC, to a certain extent, also enabled China, the Philippines, and Vietnam to work together on a joint seismic study project from 2005 to 2008. The DOC continued to serve as a reference point in numerous

[3] ASEAN, "Declaration on the Conduct of Parties in the South China Sea."

ASEAN-China joint statements and other policy documents in the following years. These pundits argued that some of the dialogue mechanisms that were established under the DOC process proved to be useful, for instance the ASEAN-China Senior Officials' Meeting (SOM) that was set up to oversee the implementation of the DOC and a joint working group that was supposed to handle the specifics.

Regardless of the different assessments of the DOC's efficacy, ASEAN at this point appeared united in its dealings and negotiations with China. In ASEAN's draft Guidelines for the Implementation of the DOC tabled at the first meeting of the Joint ASEAN-China Working Group to implement the DOC, ASEAN called for intra-ASEAN consultations prior to negotiations with China. China quickly objected to the provision for intra-ASEAN consultation and this provision for intra-ASEAN consultation prior to meeting with China remained the main issue of debate for another six years. In October 2009, Xue Hanqin, China's former ambassador to ASEAN, noted that the dispute is between China and individual South China Sea coastal states – not an issue between China and ASEAN. Therefore, she said that the Chinese government wanted to resolve territorial disputes through bilateral negotiations.[4] The final Guidelines for the Implementation of the DOC were adopted in July 2011. The final result of the negotiation was a victory for China with ASEAN dropping its insistence on prior consultations.[5] This episode highlighted a crucial Chinese strategy in its dealings with ASEAN – a divide and rule tactic to weaken ASEAN solidarity in the SCS negotiations.

Stark evidence of the success of the Chinese strategy came during the 45th ASEAN Ministerial Meeting in July 2012, when ASEAN failed to issue a Joint Communiqué for the first time since its formation in 1967, due to the member states' lack of consensus regarding the inclusion of two issues in the document: first, the Philippines' objections to Chinese deployment of paramilitary vessels to Scarborough Shoal (see, Rommel C. Banlaoi, Chapter 6); second, Vietnam's objections to Chinese leasing of oil blocks within Vietnam's exclusive economic zone (see, Đỗ Thanh Hải and Nguyễn Thùy Linh, Chapter 5). Cambodia, in its position as ASEAN Chair, objected to the inclusion of both statements on the grounds that ASEAN joint statements should exclude bilateral issues.

A blame-game quickly ensued, with both sides blaming each other for the embarrassing episode. The Philippines and Vietnam accused Cambodia of working under China's tutelage and helping to advance the interest of a non-ASEAN member. Cambodia, on the other hand, accused the

---

4 Chosun Ilbo Online, "Beijing: South China Sea."

5 *2011 Guidelines.*

Philippines and Vietnam of hijacking the ASEAN agenda to advance their respective national interests. In the end, the shuttle diplomacy of the then-Indonesian foreign minister Marty Natalegawa enabled ASEAN to issue the Six-Point Principles on the SCS on July 20, 2012. Later in November that same year, Cambodian Secretary of State for the Ministry of Foreign Affairs Kao Kim Hourn claimed that, "ASEAN leaders decided that they will not internationalize the South China Sea from now on" and that, "they will focus entirely within the current existing ASEAN-China mechanism"[6] – a view quickly refuted by Philippine foreign minister Albert Del Rosario.[7]

In 2013, Brunei as ASEAN Chair proposed that ASEAN and China adopt a dual-track approach to the South China Sea issue and Beijing supported Brunei's proposal. Under the dual-track approach, issues pertaining to territorial and maritime disputes would be left to the claimant countries to deal with, while the ASEAN-China mechanisms would focus on the security management of the South China Sea. Apparently, this approach was supposed to more clearly define ASEAN's role in managing the security of the South China Sea, but not all ASEAN countries seemed to be explicitly supportive of this formula. Other ASEAN claimant states may have wanted to deliberately maintain the ambiguity of ASEAN's role in the disputes should they need to resort to ASEAN as a policy avenue to exert pressure on Beijing.

The July 2012 Phnomh Penh fiasco was not the only instance when internal ASEAN divisions had led to ASEAN's indecision. Between June 13 and 14, 2016, ASEAN encountered the same experience at the ASEAN-China Special Foreign Ministers' Meeting in the city of Yuxi in China's southwestern Yunnan province. Before the meeting, ASEAN countries initially agreed to issue an ASEAN joint statement with clear and strong language to suggest that the SCS disputes were undermining ASEAN-China relations. Beijing, with the support of Cambodia and Laos, put pressure on ASEAN officials and successfully dissuaded ASEAN from releasing the document.[8]

Another example is ASEAN's response to the result of a Philippines-initiated legal action against China. During the Aquino III era, the Philippines brought a legal case to an Arbitral Tribunal created under the UNCLOS. In February 2016, the US and ASEAN convened a special summit in Sunnylands. The ASEAN-US joint statement emphasized the importance of "full respect for legal and diplomatic processes without resorting to the threat or use of force." This statement was an American effort to get ASEAN to support a position that the Tribunal's verdict would be binding on China and the

---

6 Kong, "No 'Internationalization."

7 Yap, "No ASEAN Unity."

8 Prashanth Parameswaran, "After China Meeting."

Philippines.[9] The Tribunal made a ruling in July 2016. When ASEAN foreign ministers were discussing ASEAN's response to the verdict, Cambodia opposed the Philippines and Vietnam for wanting the ASEAN Joint Communiqué to refer to the ruling and the need for parties to respect international law.[10] In the end, the ASEAN foreign ministers' statement did not include any mention of the ruling.

On the issue of China's massive land reclamation in the Spratlys, ASEAN was also divided in its response at the 26th ASEAN Summit in Malaysia in April 2015. After the meeting, ASEAN stated that China's island building had "eroded trust and confidence and may undermine peace, security and stability." While Vietnam and the Philippines attempted to push ASEAN to issue even more critical statements on China, other ASEAN member states opted for more moderate stances. Cambodia, as usual, lent support to China through proposing apparently neutral and independent positions. Even Indonesia and Thailand supported the Chair's emphasis on the importance of economic cooperation and diplomatic engagement with China.[11]

In the past few years, ASEAN and Chinese officials have focused their talks on the draft COC. A single draft of the COC was proposed in August 2018. ASEAN states and China agreed to finalize the COC in three years from 2019. Experts have identified four major difficulties the follow-up COC negotiations would encounter: the ambiguity of the geographic scope of the disputes; differences over dispute settlement mechanisms; different approaches to conflict management (self-restraint, mutual trust, and confidence building); and the unclear legal status of the COC.[12] It is still not entirely clear when a COC could be reached and how effective such a policy document could be in regulating the security interactions of various parties in the SCS.

Explaining divisions within ASEAN: an economics-security conundrum

Most discussions on the SCS issues appear to oversimplify the issue – often limiting discussions of the conflict to the China-ASEAN conflict. However, the sovereignty disputes basically involve only four out of the ten members of ASEAN – Brunei, Malaysia, the Philippines, and Vietnam. Although China is generally seen as a potential source of threat to smaller Southeast Asian nations due to the enormous asymmetry in both economic and military power, the

9 Ibid.
10 Mogato, Martina, and Blanchard, "ASEAN Deadlocked."
11 Var, "Cambodia Looks."
12 Nguyen, "Saving the China-ASEAN."

ten ASEAN members are divided in their perceptions of China. One major reason is that claimant countries and non-claimant countries naturally have very different stakes on the issue. The ASEAN Way of working through consultations and consensus means that all ten member states – claimant and non-claimants alike – have an equal say on ASEAN's position and response vis-à-vis China in the SCS. Claimant countries are naturally guided by their individual sovereignty claims; non-claimant countries are primarily interested in maintaining not only peace and stability in the region, but also positive relations with major powers, including the major claimant country China.

China has been able to exploit this disparity within ASEAN to its advantage to undermine ASEAN solidarity on the SCS issue. Given that China is the largest and fastest growing economy in the region, economic ties with China are inevitably a serious consideration for all ASEAN countries, especially non-claimants, in the formulation of their SCS policy. As the example of Cambodia in 2012 shows, the use of economic "carrots" by China can successfully drive a wedge between ASEAN countries on the SCS issue. In the words of Cambodian Prime Minister Hun Sen, "Cambodia's strong economic growth in past years owes a great deal to Chinese investment and steady technical and financial assistance."[13] In 2012, Chinese foreign direct investment (FDI) in Cambodia accounted for 20.69 per cent of total investment capital in the country, making it the single largest source of FDI into the country.[14] Beijing's use of "carrots" to entice Phnom Penh to support its policies over the South China Sea was apparent in the run up to the ASEAN meetings, when it became clear that there was a widening difference between China and some ASEAN claimants on the SCS issue. In the days preceding the 20th ASEAN Summit in Phnom Penh in April 2012, Chinese President Hu Jintao made a state visit to Cambodia. In the first head of state visit to Cambodia since 2000, Hu pledged US$70 million in aid (US$40 million in grants, US$30 million in loans and diplomatic complements) to the kingdom,[15] with a US$20 million military aid deal signed in May[16] and a US$430 million loan to be signed in June of the same year,[17] and renewed talk of a US$17 billion bilateral trade target by 2017 in exchange for Cambodian support for China's position on the SCS dispute.[18] The prospects of economic benefits for supporting Beijing's stance on the issue explains Phnom Penh's pro-China stance in the SCS.

[13] Emerging Frontiers, "China's Aid Contributes Greatly to Cambodia's Economic Growth."

[14] Council for the Development of Cambodia, "Investment Trend."

[15] *Straits Times*, "China Pledges $800m."

[16] *Voice of America*, "China Offers $20 Million."

[17] *Phnom Penh Post*, "Cambodia Takes $430m."

[18] Thul, "Hu Wants Cambodia."

The asymmetric economic prowess equips Beijing with substantial economic leverage over smaller ASEAN countries – an advantage China has on various occasions exploited to coerce or bribe individual ASEAN countries to do its bidding on the SCS. In particular, non-claimant countries with no direct sovereignty claims and national interests in the SCS are especially susceptible to such forms of coercive economic diplomacy. The degree of dependency on Chinese foreign direct investment shapes the attitude of ASEAN countries toward Beijing. For all ASEAN countries, including claimants, China is an important economic partner. Bilateral trade between China and ASEAN has increased rapidly since the 1990s: from US$8 billion in 1991 to US$362.85 billion in 2011, and to US$514.8 billion in 2017.[19] In particular, an overall increase in trade dependency on China, compared to a decade ago, is also evident. For instance, China rose from being Singapore's fourth export destination in 2006 to Singapore's top export partner in 2015, accounting for 13.76 per cent of the island-state's total exports.[20] Similarly, China rose from fourth to third spot in Indonesia's trading partner over a ten-year period to reach 10.01 per cent in 2015; and moved up two spots to become Vietnam's second largest export partner from 2006 to 2015.[21] China is now one of the top five trading partners for eight out of the ten ASEAN member states.

China's growing economic role complicates the ongoing SCS disputes for the economies of claimant countries' and for other ASEAN economies. The growing asymmetry in trade relations has prompted concerns over the possibility of China's ability to use economic sanctions or economic coercion to advance its political agenda in the SCS. Beijing's willingness (or ability) to put political pressure on ASEAN or on its smaller ASEAN neighbours through the use of economic coercion was exemplified during the standoff with the Philippines over the Scarborough Shoal in April 2012. China's decision to quarantine banana imports from the Philippines a month after the standoff was perceived by the Philippines as a direct response to the standoff, despite the denial of the Chinese government.[22] With exports to China accounting for 16 per cent of the Philippines total banana exports, the 2012 quarantine restrictions resulted in an economic loss of approximately one billion PHP for the Philippine economy.[23]

---

19 CGTN, "China-ASEAN in Numbers."

20 World Bank, "Export Partner Share."

21 Ibid.

22 Glaser, "China's Coercive Economic Diplomacy."

23 *Asia Sentinel*, "The China-Philippine Banana War."

Table 11.1: China's outward foreign direct investment flow to ASEAN, 2013–17

2013	2014	2015	2016	2017
6 165.21	6 811.74	6 571.77	9 609.60	13 700.59

Source: ASEAN Statistics Data Portal

More significantly, Chinese investment in ASEAN has increased at a tremendous pace, especially since the introduction of the Belt and Road Initiative (BRI) by China's President Xi Jinping in 2013. Chinese FDI in ASEAN more than doubled over a span of only five years, rising from US$6165.21 million in 2013 to US$13700.59 million in 2017 (see Table 11.1). Considering the huge infrastructure gap in Southeast Asia, this increase is especially significant. The Asian Development Bank's latest projections show that, from 2016 to 2030, Asia would need to invest US$1.7 trillion annually to maintain its current trajectory of growth.[24] In particular, US$8.4 trillion investment is needed for developing transport infrastructure, including seaports and airports.[25] However, a huge infrastructure gap persists as the region has currently invested only an estimated US$881 billion in infrastructure.[26] Multilateral development banks have contributed only an estimated 2.5 per cent of infrastructure investments required in Asia's developing countries.[27]

The BRI provides crucial funds for infrastructure development in many ASEAN countries. Table 11.2 shows the breakdown of Chinese FDI in individual ASEAN countries in 2017. Chinese FDI accounts for a significant proportion of total FDI inflow into Cambodia and Laos, and other capital-scarce countries.

China's economic leverage is not limited to non-claimant countries. For example, Philippine President Rodrigo Duterte decided to shelve the 2016 Arbitral Tribunal ruling in the Philippine's favour in exchange for stronger economic cooperation with China. Trade deals amounting to US$13.5 billion was announced during Duterte's visit to China in October 2016 immediately after Duterte's decision.[28]

[24] Asian Development Bank, *Meeting Asia Infrastructure Needs*, 11.

[25] Ibid.

[26] Ibid.

[27] Ibid.

[28] BBC, "Duterte in China."

Table 11.2: China's outward foreign direct investment flow to ASEAN by country, 2017 (US$ in millions)

Brunei	71.36
Cambodia	744.24
Indonesia	1682.25
Laos	1219.95
Malaysia	1722.14
Myanmar	428.18
Philippines	108.84
Singapore	6319.9
Thailand	1057.59
Vietnam	764.4

Source: Statistica (2020)

China's economic might is a fact that every country in Southeast Asia has to come to terms with. There are huge economic benefits to be reaped from the Belt and Road Initiative; therefore, ASEAN countries cannot risk being left out. Beijing knows this well and has mastered the skill of pitting ASEAN countries against one another. Singapore, the only ASEAN state that openly called for China to respect the Arbitral Tribunal ruling, faced a strong backlash from China in the form of detention of Singapore's Terrex vehicles in Hong Kong and exclusion of Singapore's Prime Minister Lee Hsien Loong from the inaugural Belt and Road Summit.

The differing level of economic development and dependency on the Chinese economy determines individual ASEAN countries' preferences on ASEAN's dealings with China and underscores intra-ASEAN division over the SCS issue. Each ASEAN member's approach to the SCS is ultimately influenced by its national interest, and determined by comparing the benefits of ASEAN unity and multilateral cooperation with the benefits of enhanced economic benefits from China. The former benefits can often only be seen in the long term; in contrast, the latter are evident in the short term. This contrast presents a dilemma for many ASEAN countries. Their ability to maintain their grip on power is highly dependent on successful economic development, as explained by Calmer Johnson's concept of the developmental state in East Asia.[29]

[29] Calmer Johnson. *MITI and the Japanese Miracle.*

The susceptibility of ASEAN countries to Chinese economic statecraft is determined by the country's threat perception of China. Member states' perception of "China threat" is influenced by the presence of competing sovereignty claims and by member states' accessibility to partners other than China. This is a clear source of division for ASEAN as only four of its ten members face Chinese threat to their sovereignty in the SCS. In the midst of Western pressure and sanctions, the authoritarian governments in several ASEAN countries also drew closer to China. In 1999, for instance, government of Cambodia received US$200 million in interest-free loans and US$18.3 million in foreign assistance guarantees from China, in one of the largest aid packages China has ever given to any government since Beijing assumed the role of a foreign aid donor.[30] Unconditional Chinese aid, unlike aid coming from Western donors, is highly welcomed in Cambodia. According to a senior officer at the Cambodian Rehabilitation and Development Board of the Council for the Development of Cambodia, "[i]n terms of ownership, China respects the receiving countries in terms of how the money should be used. China listens to the receiving countries' needs and allows them to use the money without any conditions."[31] Cambodian Prime Minister Hun Sen has also on more than one occasion endorsed Chinese aid to Cambodia: "They are all without conditions."[32]

In contrast, major Western donors such as the US have periodically threatened to cut aid to the impoverished kingdom whenever demands for reforms are not met. For instance, the US threatened to cut aid to Cambodia in 2013 following accusations of unfair elections. As a country highly dependent on foreign aid and yet wary of Western conditionality, China offers "unconditional" ("no-strings-attached") aid which is of vital importance to Cambodia.[33] China has also demonstrated support for Cambodia in face of Western sanctions. For instance, in response to US threats to cut aid in 2013, Prime Minister Hun Sen remarked that "[l]ast time the U.S. cut our aid, they were going to give us 100 old trucks. The Chinese saw this and gave us 257 trucks."[34] For countries such as Cambodia, China acts as a cushion for Cambodia against Western sanctions and interference in Cambodian politics and hence Beijing is an ally that they do not want to antagonize. The same could be said of Philippine President Duterte's

[30] Long, "Sino-Cambodia Relations."

[31] Heng, "Cambodia-China Relations," 64.

[32] Prime Minister Cabinet Office, *Cambodia New Vision*.

[33] Pheakdey, "Cambodia-China Relations: A Positive-Sum Game?"

[34] Wong, "Cambodia's Hun Sen."

increased cosiness with China as a result of increased criticism of its war against drugs.[35]

While the political and economic diversity within ASEAN is apparent, this diversity is insufficient to explain ASEAN's inability for united action on the SCS. Ultimately, ASEAN's inability to act multilaterally can be traced to its institutional setup. The principle of consensus decision making has been a cornerstone of ASEAN since its formation. While this principle has helped to build trust between ASEAN member states in ASEAN's formative years, it has also led to problems when members' interests conflict and strategic calculations differ, as in the case of the SCS dispute. The problem is also likely exacerbated by the expansion of ASEAN member states, as increasing membership led to greater diversity and growing complexity in collective decision making. According to Australian scholar Christopher Roberts, ASEAN "incapacity was not only complicated by intra-ASEAN divisions over their contradictory claims, but was also compounded by ASEAN membership expansion."[36] His statement effectively implied that ASEAN expansion through the addition of countries with different policy preferences would have a significant impact on ASEAN solidarity on the SCS disputes.

Conclusion

The analysis in this chapter shows that ASEAN has been playing an active role in the security management of the SCS. ASEAN, as a regional grouping, has attempted to maintain the overall status quo in the disputes, prevent escalation of tensions and conflicts, improve mutual trust and confidence between regional claimant states and China, and promote rules and norms to strengthen peace and stability in the region. One can argue that ASEAN has been at least partially successful in all these respects. It is also clear that ASEAN faces significant challenges in the security management of the SCS. The most significant challenge is the lack of solidarity among its members due to different interests among the ASEAN states in the disputes and China's influence in Southeast Asia, particularly Beijing's economic power. Almost all ASEAN countries face the challenge of balancing their regional security interests in the region with their economic ties with China. This economics-security conundrum has generated the divisions among ASEAN countries over the SCS issue.

Divisions within ASEAN have given China the opportunity to use a delay tactic to deal with the SCS disputes. A divided ASEAN and delay in

35 BBC, "Profile: Duterte."

36 Roberts and Collinson, "The Role of ASEAN," 34–9.

adopting a binding COC provided China with the opportunity to strengthen its maritime claims in the SCS through the reclamation and building of artificial islands on its occupied features.

Divisions within ASEAN also heighten the risk of the SCS becoming a battlefield for great-power rivalry and strategic competition between China and the US. Located at the geostrategic crossroad between the Indian Ocean and the Pacific Ocean, the SCS has attracted the interest of major powers in the Southeast Asian region. The importance of the SCS for international maritime transit naturally means that the ongoing conflicts are of concern to external powers such as the US. The US in particular has sought to challenge China's excessive maritime claims through its Freedom of Navigation Operations (FONOPs) through the SCS. Other powers – including Britain, Japan, and France – have also sought to elevate the SCS dispute to an issue of international concern. For instance, during the meeting of the foreign ministers of the Group of Seven Nations (G7) in April 2016, a joint statement was issued expressing the opposition to coercive and provocative actions that could change the status quo in the SCS. While China has opposed the "interference of external powers" in the SCS, some ASEAN countries have welcomed the involvement of external powers to balance the influence of China in the SCS. They recognized that the economic and military disparity implies that no individual ASEAN country can challenge China.

However, US involvement in the SCS can turn the region into the ground for geostrategic competition between the US and China. Washington views Beijing as a revisionist power and strategic competitor in the maritime domain. Washington alleges that Beijing is challenging the current rules-based order and undermining US influence and leadership in the region. ASEAN's inability to play a central role in the SCS as a result of intra-ASEAN divisions could limit ASEAN's role in the South China Sea and also in the emerging Indo-Pacific construct. Disunity on the SCS issue could risk the marginalization of ASEAN by regional security architecture and the erosion of ASEAN centrality. ASEAN centrality risks being reduced to mere lip-service if ASEAN fails to prove its utility to great power in the evolving geopolitical landscape. In a 2007 article, David Martin Jones and Michael L. R. Smith retorted that ASEAN was making process but not progress toward an East Asian Regional Order.[37] The slow progress toward East Asian regionalism is a result of a complex number of factors; one important factor was the deadlock between ASEAN claimants and China over disputes in the SCS.

[37] Jones and Smith, "Making Process," 148–84.

The inability of ASEAN as an organization to reach internal consensus on the issue and effectively mediate between China and ASEAN claimants casts serious doubts on ASEAN's credibility and leadership ability in handling regional issues. Ian Storey, for instance, pointed out that the breakdown of ASEAN unity over the issue during the 45th ASEAN Ministerial Meeting (AMM) in July 2012 had damaged ASEAN's credibility in East Asia.[38] This sentiment is echoed by Singapore's Foreign Minister K. Shanmugam, who stated that ASEAN's inability to handle the issue ruined its image in the region.[39] As the major political conflict involves ASEAN and a larger regional power (China in this case), ASEAN's ability to manage the SCS conflict and induce cooperation from China can be seen as the litmus test of ASEAN's ability to forge consensus on difficult political issues and lead the larger process of East Asian integration in the shadows of much larger regional powers. In essence, disunity over the SCS issue has cast serious doubts over the ability of ASEAN "to socialize the [East Asian] region with the same norms and values that have proved successful in Southeast Asia."[40] Given the importance of ASEAN leadership and centrality to the success of East Asian regionalism because of the strong historical animosities and mistrust between the three Northeast Asian countries,[41] the failure of ASEAN in managing the SCS will also have serious implications for the future of regionalism in East Asia.[42]

References

ASEAN. *1992 ASEAN Declaration on the South China Sea.*

ASEAN. *1995 Joint Communiqué of the 28th ASEAN Ministerial Meeting.*

ASEAN. "Declaration on the Conduct of Parties in the South China Sea." October 17, 2012. https://asean.org/?static_post=declaration-on-the-conduct-of-parties-in-the-south-china-sea-2

"ASEAN by Source Country." February 15, 2020. https://data.aseanstats.org/fdi-by-hosts-and-sources

ASEAN and China. *2011 Guidelines for the Implementation of the Declaration of Conduct on the South China Sea*

Asia Sentinel. "The China-Philippine Banana War." June 7, 2012. https://www.asiasentinel.com/p/the-china-philippine-banana-war

38 Storey, "China Pushes."

39 *Ministry of Foreign Affairs Singapore*, "Transcript Of Minister."

40 Smith, "ASEAN's Ninth Summit," 432.

41 Hund, "ASEAN Plus Three," 383–417; Malik, "The East Asian Summit," 207–11.

42 Buszynski, "ASEAN's New Challenges," 555–77.

Asian Development Bank. *Meeting Asia Infrastructure Needs.* Manila: Asian Development Bank, 2017.

BBC. "Duterte in China: Xi Lauds 'Milestone' Duterte Visit." October 20, 2016. https://www.bbc.com/news/world-asia-37700409

BBC. "Profile: Duterte the controversial 'strongman' of the Philippines." May 22, 2019. https://www.bbc.com/news/world-36659258

Buszynski, Leszek. "ASEAN's New Challenges." *Pacific Affairs* 70, no. 4 (1997): 555–77.

CGTN. "China-ASEAN in Numbers: Trade Ties." September 11, 2018. https://news.cgtn.com/news/3d3d414e3145544d7a457a6333566d54/share_p.html

Chosun Ilbo Online. "Beijing: South China Sea Territorial Disputes Not on ASEAN Agenda." October 22, 2009. OSC Transcribed Text via World News Connection (Dialog File Number 985 Accession Number 288650010).

Council for the Development of Cambodia. "Investment Trend." February 15, 2020. http://www.cambodiainvestment.gov.kh/why-invest-in-cambodia/investment-enviroment/investment-trend.html

Emerging Frontiers. "China's Aid Contributes Greatly to Cambodia's Economic Growth." February 2, 2012. http://www.emergingfrontiers.com/2012/02/02/chinas-aid-contributes-greatly-to-cambodias-economic-growth/

Glaser, Bonnie, "China's Coercive Economic Diplomacy." *The Diplomat*, July 25, 2012. http://thediplomat.com/2012/07/chinas-coercive-economic-diplomacy/

Heng, Pheakdey. "Cambodia-China Relations: A Positive-Sum Game?" *Journal of Current Southeast Asian Affairs* 31, no. 2 (2012): 64.

Hund, Markus. "ASEAN Plus Three: Towards a New Age of Pan-East Asian Regionalism? A Skeptic's Appraisal." *Pacific Review* 16, no. 3 (2003): 383–417.

Johnson, Chalmer. *MITI and the Japanese Miracle: The Growth of Industrial Policy, 1925–1975.* California: Stanford University Press, 1982.

Jones, David and Michael Smith, "Making Process, Not Progress: ASEAN and the Evolving East Asian Regional Order." *International Security* 32, no. 1 (2007): 148–84.

Kong, Sothanarith. "No 'Internationalization' of the South China Sea, ASEAN Leaders Say." *Voice of America Cambodia*, November 19, 2012. https://www.voacambodia.com/a/no-internationalization-of-the-south-china-sea-asean-leaders-say/1548612.html

Long, Kosal. "Sino-Cambodia Relations." *CICP Working Paper* 28 (July 2009). http://cicp.org.kh/userfiles/file/Working%20Paper/CICP%20Working%20Paper%20No%2028_%20Sino%20Cambodia%20Relations%20by%20Long%20Kosal.pdf

Malik, Mohan. "The East Asian Summit." *Australian Journal of International Affairs* 60, no. 2 (2006): 207–11.

Ministry of Foreign Affairs Singapore. "Transcript Of Minister For Foreign Affairs K Shanmugam's Reply to The Parliamentary Questions." August 13, 2012. http://www.mfa.gov.sg/content/mfa/overseasmission/shanghai/press_statements_speeches/2012/201208/press_20120815.html

Mogato, Manuel, Michael Martina, and Ben Blanchard. "ASEAN Deadlocked on South China Sea, Cambodia blocks statement." *Reuters*, July 25, 2016. https://www.reuters.com/article/us-southchinasea-ruling-asean/asean-deadlocked-on-south-china-sea-cambodia-blocks-statement-idUSKCN1050F6

Nguyen, Minh Quang. "Saving the China-ASEAN South China Sea Code of Conduct." *The Diplomat*, June 29, 2019. https://thediplomat.com/2019/06/saving-the-china-asean-south-china-sea-code-of-conduct/

Parameswaran, Prashanth. "After China Meeting, ASEAN Must Heed Early South China Sea Warning." *PacNet* #52, June 24, 2016. https://www.pacforum.org/analysis/pacnet-52-after-china-meeting-asean-must-heed-early-south-china-sea-warning

Pheakdey, Heng. "Cambodia-China Relations: A Positive-Sum Game?" *Journal of Current Southeast Asian Affairs* 2 (2012): 57–85.

Phnom Penh Post. "Cambodia Takes $430m China Loan." June 14, 2012. www.phnompenhpost.com/index.php/2012061456790/Business/cambodia-takes-430m-china-loan.htm

Prime Minister Cabinet Office. *Cambodia New Vision #139*, 2009. www.cnv.org.kh/cnv_html_pdf/cnv_139_sep_09.pdf

Reuy, Rann. "Cambodia Takes $430m China Loan." *Phnom Penh Post*, June 14, 2012. https://www.phnompenhpost.com/business/cambodia-takes-430m-china-loan

Roberts, Christopher and Gary Collinson. "The Role of ASEAN." In *The South China Sea and Australia's Regional Security Environment*, edited by Leszek Buszynski and Christopher Roberts, 34–9. Canberra: Australian National University, National Security College, 2013.

Smith, Anthony. "ASEAN's Ninth Summit: Solidifying Regional Cohesion, Advancing External Linkages." *Contemporary Southeast Asia* 26, no. 3 (2004): 432.

Statistica. "China's Outward FDI Flows to ASEAN in 2017, by Country." February 15, 2020. https://www.statista.com/statistics/722607/china-outward-fdi-flows-to-asean-by-country/.

Storey, Ian. "China Pushes on the South China Sea, ASEAN Unity Collapses." *China Brief* 12, no. 15 (August 2012). https://jamestown.org/program/china-pushes-on-the-south-china-sea-asean-unity-collapses/

Straits Times. "China Pledges $800m in Aid to Cambodia." January 23, 2019. https://www.straitstimes.com/asia/se-asia/china-pledges-800m-in-aid-to-cambodia

Thul, Prak Chan, "Hu Wants Cambodia Help on China Sea Dispute, Pledges Aid." *Reuters*, March 31, 2012. http://www.reuters.com/article/2012/03/31/us-cambodia-china-idUSBRE82U04Y20120331

Var, Veasna. "Cambodia Looks for Middle Ground in the South China Sea." *East Asia Forum*, June 20, 2015.

Voice of America. "China Offers $20 Million in Military Aid ahead of ASEAN Meeting." May 29, 2012. www.voanews.com/khmer-english / news/politics/China-Offers-20-Million-in-Military-Aid-Ahead-of-Asean-Meeting-155432515.html

Wong, Chun Han. "Cambodia's Hun Sen Slams US Threats over Aid." *Wall Street Journal*, August 3, 2013. http://blogs.wsj.com/searealtime/2013/08/03/cambodias-hun-sen-slams-u-s-threats-over-aid/

World Bank. "Export Partner Share." World Integrated Trade Solution. https://wits.worldbank.org/CountryProfile/en/Country/by-country/StartYear/LTST/EndYear/LTST/TradeFlow/Export/Partner/WLD/Indicator/XPRT-PRTNR-SHR

Yap, D. J. "No ASEAN Unity in Sea Row with China." *Philippine Daily Inquirer*, November 20, 2012. https://globalnation.inquirer.net/56974/philippines-says-no-asean-unity-over-china-row

PART III

Quadrilateral Security Dialogue States

12

The United States and the South China Sea Question

John Callahan

> The United States has no territorial claim in the South China Sea and does not take a position on the sovereignty of any of the geographic features in the SCS, but has urged that disputes be settled without coercion and on the basis of international law.[1]

Introduction

The United States (US) has been a presence in East Asia since the early part of the 19th century. Over the decades that role grew, until, by 1945, Washington found itself the dominant power in the region. Since that time, regional powers have risen and fallen, but the US remains a critical player in the region. This chapter focuses on the importance of the South China Sea (SCS) to the US, and the evolution of its attitudes and actions toward the region. America's intentions in the SCS have changed little since the 19th century. Washington seeks to keep the peace, keep trade flowing through the region, prevent the rise of a dominant power in the region, and preserve its own freedom of action in the region, primarily through ensuring Freedom of the Seas. The rise of the People's Republic of China (PRC) since 1948 has

[1] Congressional Research Service. *South China Sea Disputes: Background and US Policy*. Washington DC, February 23, 2017. 1.

proven to be the primary challenge to US objectives.[2] Since 1948, Beijing has sought to expand its power and influence in any way that it could. With the massive growth of its economy, particularly since the 1980s, the PRC has become increasingly ambitious and belligerent in its actions in the SCS. Over that same period, US responses have become increasingly strident. This chapter will discuss US efforts in the region, focusing on the history of US involvement and the changing nature of US positions and responses to events in the region, particularly during the presidencies of Barack Obama and Donald Trump.

The US in the South China Sea up to 1945

American activity in the Western Pacific and the SCS began shortly after the founding of the Republic. As early as 1784, the first American merchant ship, the *SS Empress of China*, arrived in the region.[3] Growing trade with China eventually drove the US in its westward expansion across the Pacific Ocean in the 19th century, culminating with the acquisition of the Philippines and other islands following the successful war with Spain in 1898.

But the acquisition of the Philippines was far from the first US interaction with the SCS area. In 1819, the Monroe administration deployed a sailing frigate, *USS Congress*, to the region to protect US shipping from the depredations of pirates, and in 1831 directly intervened in Sumatra after Malay pirates attacked the *SS Friendship*, prompting a direct US response. The *USS Potomac* attacked the pirate settlement of Quallah Battoo and thoroughly defeated the pirates, warning them that further piracy would be met with increasing force. This bought half a decade's respite before further piracy occurred, but was followed by a recurrence of pirate attacks and swift, brutal retaliation from US Naval Forces through the period leading up to the American Civil War in 1861. These actions are critical in understanding the US' role in the region. Much like its first major interaction with the Middle East, which resulted in the famous Barbary Pirate Wars of the first decade of the 19th century, the US' first interaction with Southeast Asia and the SCS was one of using naval forces to attempt to compel what were essentially economic decisions on a region.

2 Joshua Hastey and Scott N. Romaniuk, in their opening chapter, draw attention to China's efforts to assertively realize their strategic ambitions under the guise of "peaceful development" and humanitarian interests.

3 In this chapter, "SS" will be used to preface the names of merchant ships, while "USS" will indicate military vessels.

1945 to the end of the Cold War

Of course, actually owning territory along the SCS increased the US' role in the region substantially, and US victory in the Second World War placed it as a dominant power in the region. Of note in that war is the role that the US played in East Asia, keeping allied focus on China and its war against the Japanese when America's European allies pressed for a "Germany First" strategy.[4] But US dominance would not be easy to maintain, since the victory of 1945 also unleashed two major forces, decolonization and communism, into the region. As early as 1947, China, which was at the time still wracked by civil war, released a map outlining its claims in the SCS. The map, which delineated the area with eleven "dashes" became the model for later expansionist claims after the communist victory in the Civil War in 1949. Furthermore, the map itself, which received little notice outside of China, became a part of an oft-repeated legalese construct used by both the PRC and Russia. Since no one disputed the map, Beijing claimed that that was the equivalent of acquiescence.[5] This was further reinforced when the 1951 San Francisco Peace Treaty failed to definitively address the status of the Spratly Islands, which had been occupied by the Japanese through 1945, but which were unclaimed after the Japanese defeat in the Second World War.[6]

The SCS region returned to prominence for the US during the Vietnam War, which took place along its western littoral, with the sea itself serving as a mostly secure base from which the US could launch air and naval strikes against North Vietnam. The end of that war by the mid 1970s meant that Washington's sea and air dominance of the region would no longer be absolute, and Vietnam opened itself to Soviet naval and air basing, ensuring that the Cold War would continue to divide the region through the 1980s. In 1974, conflict between the PRC and South Vietnam over the Paracel Islands ended with the US urging the combatants themselves to negotiate a de-escalation. In the end, the PRC ended up with the Paracel chain, as Đỗ Thanh Hải and Nguyễn Thùy Linh discuss in Chapter 5. This choice is clearly linked to the relationship Richard Nixon and Henry Kissinger had developed with the PRC as part of their successful effort to split the

4 Coker, Christopher. *The Improbable War: China, the United States and the Logic of Great Power Conflict*. London: C. Hurst and Company, 2015. 37.

5 Hussein, Kamrul. The UNCLOS and the US China Hegemonic Competition over the South China Sea. *Journal of East Asia and International Law*, Volume 1, 2013. 115.

6 James, Donald M. Between Declaration and Dreams: China, US Foreign Policy, and Southeast Asia. *Policy*, Volume July, No. 1, Autumn 2018. 46.

communist bloc. The late 1980s and early 1990s brought significant blows to the US position in the region, when the PRC went on to seize the Spratly Islands in 1988. The end of the Cold War also brought a further blow to the US in the region, when Washington was asked to remove its forces and bases from the Philippines in 1991. That action, in a single stroke, reversed the power order in the region, placing the PRC as the leading local military power in the region, and making the US an external player, albeit a very powerful one.[7]

Growing action: 1991 to 2001

The end of the Cold War, with the collapse of the Soviet Union, left America once more unchallenged across most of the world. However, the rise of China as an economic and increasingly military power meant that it would grow, by the 2000s, to replace the Soviet Union as a major competitor and threat to American interests, most specifically in the sea areas off its own coast. As a result, tensions between the US and its allies on the one hand and China on the other, with third parties thrown in for good measure, have been on the rise, although the US encouraged China's early economic rise, going so far as to endorse Chinese entry into the World Trade Organization (WTO) in 2001. For the first decade of the 21st century, the US sought to keep clear of economics, while maintaining the regional balance of power. Unfortunately, allowing one while attempting to deny the other seems to be increasingly untenable, with military and economic responses becoming more and more intertwined.

1995 was the year in which the US first took a public stance on issues in the SCS. Prompted by the PRC's occupation of Mischief Reef in late 1994, the Clinton administration announced the principles that have largely remained in place until the present day. They include: peaceful resolution of disputes; peace and stability; preservation of Freedom of Navigation (FON); neutrality on the question of sovereignty; and rejection of acts in violation of the 1982 United Nations Convention on the Law of the Sea (UNCLOS).[8] The UNCLOS defined national rights related to use of continental shelves, internal waters, territorial waters, archipelagic waters, contiguous zones, and, critically, exclusive economic zones (EEZs). At the time of writing, 167 countries had signed the UNCLOS, but the US, while

---

7 Fisher, Richard D. *China's Military Modernization: Building for Regional and Global Reach. Stanford: Stanford University Press*, 2010. 127.

8 Daily Press Briefing, US Department of State, May 10, 1995, http://dosfan.lib.uic.edu/ERC/briefing/daily_ briefings/1995/9505/950510db.html

acknowledging and abiding by nearly all of its provisions, rejects the EEZ provisions, which allow for aspects of sovereignty out to a distance of 200 nautical miles (compared to territorial waters, which extend 12 nautical miles from recognized land features).

The first recent confrontation between the US and the PRC took place in April 2001, in the opening months of the presidency of George W. Bush. When a Chinese fighter collided with and forced down a US intelligence gathering aircraft off the coast of Hainan Island, the Chinese held the US aircrew for ten days. The aircraft itself was retained on Hainan for a greater period, long enough to extract its intelligence gathering and surveillance equipment.[9] A further air intercept issue took place over a decade later, with a Chinese fighter intercepting an American surveillance aircraft 135 miles east of Hainan in August 2014.[10]

Differing or conflicting motivations: the US and China

The SCS is a critical economic zone for the US, with an estimated US$1.2 trillion in US-bound trade passing through the region each year.[11] The imposition of EEZs and the establishment of sovereign space in such a vital sea lane is only part of the problem. PRC militarization of the region, which has advanced hand in hand with the sovereignty issue, constitutes a clear threat to US interest, particularly with the installation of air and sea denial weaponry, in the form of missile systems, on the various PRC-occupied geographic features in the SCS.[12]

According to a recent Congressional Report, PRC bases in the SCS endanger many US capabilities. These include, but are not limited to, the ability to: intervene militarily in any future crisis between the PRC and Taiwan; fulfil US treaty objectives with regional partners, including Japan, the Philippines, and South Korea (the report also discussed the Senkaku Islands which are occupied by Japan but claimed by the PRC); operate US Forces in the Western Pacific to secure regional security; and prevent the rise of China as a regional hegemonic military power.[13]

---

9 Allison, Graham. *Destined for War: Can America and China Escape Thucydides Trap?* New York, Mariner Books, 2017. 159.

10 Nguyen, Phuong. Deciphering the Shift in America's South China Sea Policy. *Contemporary South East Asia*, Vol. 38, No. 3, 2016, pp 389–421. 393.

11 Nguyen. 392.

12 Ibid. 396.

13 Congressional Research Service. *China's actions in the South and East China Seas: Implications for US Interests – Background and Issues for Congress*. Washington, DC, January 31, 2019.

In the case of the SCS, the US is acting as a status quo maritime power, putting as its primary aim the maintenance of open and free trade access and shipping lanes, which in turn means the enforcement of Freedom of Navigation (FON) in the area. According to Christopher Coker, "[t]he United States is a status quo power whose instincts, though they may often lead to a war or conflict, are not necessarily belligerent. The same does not apply in the case of China."[14]

Like Germany in the era before the First World War, the development of a robust modern navy by the PRC has a distinctive nationalist element, in which a large navy features significantly in self-identification as a great power, regardless of whether such a force is actually necessary to fulfil political objectives. In Chapter 1 of this volume, Joshua Hastey and Scott N. Romaniuk call the PRC a "revisionist power," and this description is certainly shared by US observers.

The US, acting as the dominant naval power in the region, has, on numerous occasions, mass-deployed naval assets in China's claimed waters. President Truman deployed the US 7th Fleet, the naval force assigned to the Western Pacific, into the Strait of Taiwan in June, 1950, following the PRC seizure of Hainan Island from the Republic of China.[15] During the Vietnam War, the SCS was the platform from which the same fleet launched shore bombardment and air support missions against North Vietnam.

US focus on the "global war on terror" (GWOT) and radical Islam was a significant factor in how it dealt with issues in the SCS from the late 1990s onward, and especially after the 9/11 terrorist attacks. This did not necessarily put it in good stead with many of the actors bordering the SCS, particularly Indonesia and Malaysia, which are Muslim-dominated, and has at times damaged the US position with the Philippines. This is notwithstanding massive humanitarian aid assistance following the winter 2004–5 tsunami (Indonesia) and the 2015 typhoon Damyan (Philippines).[16]

American exceptionalism, and its fundamental denial of the legitimacy of the Chinese ("communist") government, also stands as a potential barrier to successful negotiations between the two countries.[17] This fact, combined with what John Ruggie calls "Exemptionalism," actively avoids the restrictions of the rules it attempts to enforce on others, to create resistance

14 Coker. 6.

15 Cole, Bernard. *The Great Wall at Sea*, Second Edition. Annapolis, Naval Institute Press, 2010. 8.

16 Fisher, Richard. *China's Military Modernization: Building for Regional and Global Reach*. Stanford: Stanford Security Studies, 2008. 60.

17 Coker. 33.

to US efforts to act as a mediator or police power, especially when it does so unilaterally.[18]

A piece of the exceptionalism puzzle is Washington's continuing refusal to ratify UNCLOS in spite of its general policy of following the rules of the treaty.[19] President Obama used this as a political tool against his Republican opposition, claiming that signing would influence the PRC, and support for joining the treaty did not rise in the Trump presidency. Opponents of US accession note that China is unlikely to follow the tenets of the treaty in the SCS, whether or not the US joins.[20] They further note that joining might expose the US to criticism, and even lawsuits, due to environmental provisions of the treaty.[21] UNCLOS is interpreted by the US and the majority of signatories as giving naturally formed land features that can sustain human habitation and remain above high tide a 200km exclusive economic zone (EEZ) while smaller natural features can only maintain a 12km territorial sea status.[22] The US has an explicit global interest in denying the right of regional powers to enforce EEZs. If every country on earth enforced EEZs in adjoining waters, over 40 per cent of all of the world's seas would be claimed, including vital sea lanes and indeed entire strategic sea areas such as the Persian Gulf and the Baltic Sea. As a status quo maritime power, setting the precedent of EEZ recognition can therefore clearly be seen as against American interests.[23]

American exceptionalism is fundamentally opposed to the Chinese version. This is not only the case in their respective interpretations of governance and liberty, but in the parlance of political discourse. The US fundamentally believes that civilization is democracy and Western values, in other words, the "American way." At times, the US has conflated its own expansion with the expansion of civilization. This is in contrast to China, which has expected others to emulate its civilization, but without actively seeking to spread anything but an acknowledgement of Chinese power.[24]

US problem-solving approaches are also quite different from those of China, and emphasize timely accomplishment of discrete tasks rather than a

[18] Ruggie, John Gerard. American Exceptionalism, Exemptionalism, and Global Governance, in Michael Ignatieff (ed.) *American Exceptionalism and Human Rights*, Princeton, NJ, Princeton University Press. 2005. 305; and Coker. 46.

[19] Gallo, William. Why Hasn't the US Signed the Law of the Sea Treaty? June 6, 2016.

[20] Ibid.

[21] Ibid.

[22] Congressional Research Service, February 23, 2017. 2.

[23] Nguyen. 394.

[24] Allison. 144.

longer term, more measured approach. The Chinese attitude that, "[t]here is nothing new under the sun" belies this approach, while simply watching the evening news provides ample evidence of the US approach, where every crisis seems to be newly hatched.[25]

The PRC has exerted pressure on all of its neighbours, pressing territorial claims against Japan over the Senkaku Islands and of course denying the right to independence of Taiwan. But its most interesting actions have taken place in the South China Sea region. Perhaps the SCS is China's most vital Sea Line of Communication (SLOC), since it lies between the Straits of Malacca, through which trade flows west from Asia. But it is also critical as a potential provider of oil, one of the numerous ingredients of modern industry that it does not hold domestically. The Chinese solution to the issue of securing both the SLOC and the oil is to claim it as part of Chinese territory.

That said, the PRC is not the only claimant to the various island groups, such as the Spratlys and Paracels, which dot the SCS. Each neighbour presses its own claims, leaving Washington with several dilemmas, creating fears in Washington that the PRC is attempting to dominate the SCS militarily and economically, contravening long-standing efforts to prevent the rise of a hegemonic power in the area.[26]

The US-Philippines relationship is a central one in understanding Washington's role in the SCS situation. In 1951, Washington signed the Philippines Mutual Defense Treaty, a part of its system of bilateral alliances in the region. While pledging to defend Philippine territoriality, Washington's interpretation of the treaty has been consistent in not including territories that were claimed by Manila after the treaty's signature. In 2013, the Philippines asked the Arbitral Tribunal to arbitrate Chinese actions, which it felt violated its rights under UNCLOS. In July 2016, the Arbitral Tribunal reaffirmed the stance of the US and others, stipulating that China's claims in the region were essentially groundless, and violated Philippine sovereign rights. This has become the go-to US position in spite of general apathy toward the findings by the Philippine administration since President Rodrigo Duterte took office in 2016.[27] In effect, the Philippines under Duterte is pursing what Rommel C. Banlaoi (see Chapter 6) calls a hedging policy toward both the US and China in this book's chapter on Manila's current policies.

---

[25] Allison. 145.

[26] Congressional Research Service, February 23, 2017. 1.

[27] Congressional Research Service, February 23, 2017. 2.

Growing response: the Obama administration, 2008–17

Following the general increase in tensions in the region in the late 2000s, in 2011 the Obama administration added four additional tenets to the US stance. Articulated by Secretary of State Clinton on July 23, 2010, the new additions included: resolution of disputes without coercion; adherence to the democratic principles put forth in a 2002 Declaration on the Conduct of Parties between the PRC and ASEAN; support for the drafting of a full Code of Conduct (COC); and the position that sovereignty claims should only be based on the legitimacy of claims to land."[28] Of note was the fact that Secretary Clinton herself gave the press statement. To that point, she was the most senior US official to have commented on the SCS situation.[29]

2012 saw a further clarification of the US stance after the PRC escalated the situation in the SCS by establishing a prefectural level city, Sansha, on Woody Island, while engaging in an open confrontation with the Philippines on the Scarborough Shoal. While not invoking the alliance, Washington did broker talks between Beijing and Manila for the withdrawal of both sides from the Shoals while still remaining neutral on the core sovereignty issues.

In June 2013, Chinese and US representatives met in Washington DC, forming a Maritime Legal Issues Working Group to clarify each side's position on the EEZs; however, planned follow-on meetings never took place. However, in November 2014, during a state visit by PRC leader Xi Jinping, a memorandum of understanding was signed between the two parties which focused on clarifying safety measures and "rules of behaviour" for air and sea activities in the SCS, including rules for air and maritime encounters.[30]

One of the primary American goals in dealing with the PLAN and Beijing over its territorial claims is deterrence. By making increasingly clear what it will and will not consider to be aggression, Washington hopes to defuse the situation and discourage the PRC from such acts both above and below the threshold for armed conflict. The US has sought to deter the PLAN by assisting regional partners directly. Examples of this include strengthening security cooperation with partners across the region and the Pacific theatre generally, as well as direct military support. In May 2015, the Pentagon began a five-year long programme to help partners, specifically Vietnam

---

[28] "Remarks at Press Availability," July 23, 2010, http://www.state.gov/secretary/rm/2010/07/145095.htm

[29] Fravel, M. Taylor. "US Policy Towards the Disputes in the South China Sea since 1995." Singapore: S. Rajarathan School of International Relations. March 2014. 5.

[30] Nguyen. 397.

and the Philippines, to increase their capability to perform maritime patrols in disputed waters.[31]

In May 2015, US pressure on the PRC increased on the diplomatic front, with Assistant Secretary of Defense for East Asia, David Shear stating that the PRC should: "[r]educe strategic uncertainty by adjusting the nine dash line to match the provisions of the UNCLOS, renounce the establishment of a territorial sea or national airspace in the contested areas, halt reclamation projects, and sign a code of conduct on use of the SCS with ASEAN member states."[32] In other testimony, he denied the validity of the PRC's claims, stating that: "Many of the features, including those claimed by China, are submerged features. They do not generate a legal territorial claim. We reserve the right of passage in such areas."[33] Senate Foreign Relations Committee Chairman Robert Corker expressed his concern that a tactically adroit PRC could quickly establish control over the entirety of the SCS, while a US-led response, be it diplomatic or military, could take months or even years to materialize.[34]

US military forces regularly challenge the PLAN and the PRC's claims in the region, particularly through what are described "Freedom of Navigation Exercises" (FONs). Typically involving US Navy (USN) ships, the exercises normally involve approaching to within the international accepted 12 km limit of Chinese-held islands, essentially demonstrating that Washington does not recognize PRC control of the various artificial islands in the area or any right of territorial exclusivity.

A notable FON operation took place on October 27, 2015. On that date, the *USS Lassen* sailed within 12 nautical miles of various features claimed both by the PRC and several other SCS claimants without prior notice.[35] This particular FON Operation was unique, though, in what Benjamin Wagner called "unprecedented transparency."[36] Although no prior diplomatic notice of the 72-mile passage was given, the mission had been a subject of public debate for half a year prior to its execution, which also means that it was not a total surprise to any of the claiming parties, amounting to notice,

---

31 Called "Maritime Domain Awareness," or MDA. Congressional Research Service, February 23, 2017. 2.

32 Nguyen. 401.

33 US Senate Committee on Foreign Relations: Safeguarding American Interests in the East and South China Seas. Washington DC, May 2013, 2015. https://www.foreign.senate.gov/hearings/safeguarding-american-interests-in-the-east-and-south-china-seas

34 Nguyen. 405.

35 Nguyen. 409.

36 Wagner, Benjamin K. Lessons from Lassen: Plotting a Proper Course for Freedom of Navigation Operations in the South China Sea. *Journal of East Asia International Law*. 2016. 138.

at least in a de facto sense. Certainly, preventive action could have been prepared long in advance, but no action was taken.

Further FON operations took place in January 2016, when the *USS Curtis Weldon* passed within the 12 nautical mile limit of features claimed by three SCS parties. In May, the *USS William P. Lawrence* entered the limit of four claimants when it manoeuvred near Fiery Cross Reef.[37] In March 2016, President Obama seems to have delivered a verbal warning to Beijing about activities in the Scarborough Shoal, hinting that further activity might make the US reconsider its prior position on Philippine claims and their relevance to the US-Philippines Mutual Defense Treaty. Chinese activities there ceased, at least temporarily.[38] In spite of statements to the contrary, for all intents and purposes, the US never pivoted to Asia, in spite of the statements of Obama to the contrary, with around 80 per cent of National Security Council focus being on the Middle East through 2015.[39]

The Trump administration, 2017–20

The Trump administration approached the SCS issue in several ways, emphasizing competition with the PRC, and urging regional partners to take on more of the financial burden of their own defence. The President's first statement specifically addressing the SCS came on February 10, 2017. Speaking from Japan, Trump committed to "maintaining a maritime order based on international law, including freedom of navigation and overflight and other lawful uses of the sea," adding that the US and Japan "oppose any attempt to assert maritime claims through the use of intimidation, coercion, or force," and asked the "countries concerned to avoid actions that would escalate tensions in the SCS, including the militarization of outposts, and to act in accordance with international law."[40]

The "Free and Open Indo-Pacific" (FOIP) attempted to cooperate with allies in the region and to generate infrastructure development and other projects to compete with PRC-funded projects such as the Belt and Road Initiative (BRI). According to the Congressional Research Service, the Trump White House called such PRC projects "predatory" and "debt traps."[41] Eschewing the Trans Pacific Partnership (TPP), a pet project of

37 Nguyen. 409–10.

38 Nguyen. 412.

39 Allison. 7

40 Congressional Research Service, February 23, 2017. 1.

41 Congressional Research Service. *In Focus: The Asia Pacific: Challenges and Opportunities for US Policy*. Washington, December 14, 2018. 1.

the Obama administration, the administration preferred to utilize existing bilateral agreements, and unilateral tariffs, in its efforts to navigate the issues of the region.[42] Simultaneously, Washington, in some ways, was moving past its traditional "Spoke and Hub" approach to alliances in the Pacific to encourage bilateral agreements between regional partners. An example of this is Japan's provision in 2018 to the Philippines of specialized maritime patrol equipment.[43] FON exercises in the region are nothing new, however, their method of execution changed under the Trump administration. Under the Obama administration, ships entering the 12 km limit did so at high speed, without stopping, tacitly admitting that they should not be there. Since 2017, however, the exercises have been undertaken at normal cruising speeds, reinforcing the US denial of legitimate Chinese claims on the reefs and islands.[44] Then Defense Secretary James Mattis emphasized that "Freedom the Seas is Absolute," and that "we will practice in international waters and transit international waters as appropriate."[45] From May 2017 to January 2019, the USN conducted ten Freedom of Navigation Operations in the SCS.[46]

The new administration's approach to the SCS issue was reinforced by governmental doctrine publications. The administration's first National Security Strategy (NSS), released in December 2017, openly accused the PRC of violating its neighbours' sovereignty, restricting free trade, and threatening regional stability. It also decried what it called "a rapid military modernization campaign designed to limit US access to the region and provide China a freer hand there."[47] The Strategy calls for "sustained US leadership in a collective response that upholds a regional order respectful of sovereignty and independence." In Spring 2018, economics were incorporated into the US response to the PRC with the beginnings of a trade war focused on increasing US exports to China and facilitating the restoration of US domestic industries.[48]

In January 2019, the US communicated to the PRC that provocative acts by what it calls its Maritime Militia would be treated in the same fashion as those carried out by regular PLAN navy vessels. The PRC has used its

42 Ibid.

43 Ibid. 2.

44 Ali, Idrees. US destroyer challenges China's claims in the South China Sea. Reuters. August 10, 2017.

45 Congressional Research Service, February 23, 2017. 2.

46 Congressional Research Service, January 31, 2019. 88.

47 National Security Strategy of the United States of America. Washington, December 2017. 46.

48 Swanson, Anna. Trumps Trade War with China is Officially Underway. *The New York Times*, July 5, 2018.

Maritime Militia and its highly armed Coast Guard (which, unlike the American practice, has been placed under direct control of the military since 2018, making it a de facto part of the PLAN) to enforce its maritime claims.[49] This effort to enforce its will on its neighbours without using its grey hulled navy harkens back to Russia's use of "little green men" and the Wagner group to hide its direct involvement in military actions. Perhaps more important, such obfuscation hinders the ability of regional players and the US to directly counter provocative and aggressive actions.

In March 2019, Secretary of State Mike Pompeo reiterated the US commitment in meetings with Philippine President Duterte and Foreign Secretary Toedoro Locsin, confirming Admiral Richardson's January message to the PRC, assuring the Philippines that, "China's island-building and military activities in the SCS threaten your sovereignty, security and therefore economic livelihood as well as that of the United States," adding that: "Any armed attack on Philippine forces, aircraft or public vessels in the South China Sea will trigger mutual defense obligations."[50]

The US stance under Trump had two components. The first was to deter the PRC from activities which might alter the status quo balance of power in the region, while the second was to impose penalties on Beijing if it attempts to do so in a more aggressive fashion.[51] The problem with this is that Chinese power is growing significantly faster than that of the other powers in the SCS region. The implication of this is that Washington must be prepared to commit more and more of its own resources, military, diplomatic, and economic, to the region in order to bridge the gap. This fits into America's global strategy, which is based on the prevention of the rise of new regional hegemons in any part of Eurasia, and can therefore be seen holistically along with US actions against Russian revanchism in Europe.[52]

The Trump administration continued the general trend of increased resistance to PRC activity in the SCS. On May 3, 2018, the administration expressed public concern with Chinese activity in the SCS, particularly the installation of area access denial weapons in the area.[53] On May 23 of that year, US Pacific Command rescinded its invitation to the People's Liberation Army Navy (PLAN) to participate in the regional Rim of the Pacific Exercise (RIMPAC) naval exercise for that year. On November 13, National Security Advisor John Bolton stated that the US would not abide by any agreements

[49] Sevastopulo, Demetri and Hill, Kathrin. US Warns China on Aggressive Acts by Fishing Boats and Coast Guard. *The Financial Times*, April 28, 2019.

[50] Ibid.

[51] Nguyen. 390.

[52] Ibid. 391.

[53] Congressional Research Service, January 31, 2019. 37.

with the PRC that might limit passage through the region of international commercial or military vessels, adding that the US Navy would continue to exercise Freedom of Navigation in the area.[54]

Conclusion

This chapter has described US' responses and actions in the SCS, with a focus on Washington's increasingly strident responses to PRC actions in the region. In line with its role as a status quo power, US interests have focused on limiting the PRC and preserving its own freedom to act. This will certainly become increasingly difficult as the PRC continues to use its robust economy to increase its military capabilities. Combined with its growing adventurism and nationalism, it remains to be seen whether the US will continue to maintain its role as a regional balancer and military first among equals. Doing just that certainly seems to have been the objective of the Trump administration. Nothing is guaranteed in World history. There is no guarantee that the US and the PRC will clash just because Germany and the British Empire did. History need not be a trap, but it also must not be ignored.

References

Ali, Idrees. US Destroyer Challenges China's Claims in the South China Sea. *Reuters*, August 10, 2017.

Allison, Graham. *Destined for War: Can America and China Escape Thucydides Trap?* New York, Mariner Books, 2017.

Coker, Christopher. *The Improbable War: China, the United States and the Logic of Great Power Conflict*. Oxford: Oxford University Press.

Cole, Bernard. *The Great Wall at Sea*, Second Edition. Annapolis: Naval Institute Press, 2010.

Congressional Research Service. *South China Sea Disputes: Background and US Policy*. Washington, DC, February 23, 2017. 1.

Congressional Research Service. *In Focus: The Asia Pacific: Challenges and Opportunities for US Policy*. Washington, DC, December 14, 2018. 1.

Congressional Research Service. *China's Actions in the South and East China Seas: Implications for US Interests – Background and Issues for Congress*. Washington, DC, January 31, 2019.

Daily Press Briefing, US Department of State, May 10, 1995, http://dosfan.lib.uic.edu/ERC/briefing/daily_briefings/1995/9505/950510db.html

[54] Ibid. 41.

Fisher, Richard D. China's Military Modernization: Building for Regional and Global Reach. Stanford: Stanford University Press, 2010.

Fravel, M. Taylor. "US Policy Towards the Disputes in the South China Sea since 1995." Singapore: S. Rajarathan School of International Relations. March 2014.

Gallo, William. Why Hasn't the US Signed the Law of the Sea Treaty? VOA News, June 6, 2016, www.voanews.com/usa/why-hasnt-us-signed-law-sea-treaty

Hussein, Kamrul. The UNCLOS and the US China Hegemonic Competition over the South China Sea. *Journal of East Asia and International Law*, Volume 1, 2013.

James, Donald M. Between Declaration and Dreams: China, US Foreign Policy, and Southeast Asia. *Policy*, Volume July, No. 1, Autumn 2018.

National Security Strategy of the United States of America. Washington, December 2017.

Nguyen, Phuong. Deciphering the Shift in America's South China Sea Policy. *Contemporary South East Asia*, Vol. 38, No. 3, 2016, pp 389-421.

"Remarks at Press Availability," July 23, 2010, http://www.state.gov/secretary/rm/2010/07/145095.htm

Ruggie, John Gerard. American Exceptionalism, Exemptionalism, and Global Governance, in Michael Ignatieff (ed) *American Exceptionalism and Human Rights*. Princeton, NJ, Princeton University Press. 2005.

Sevastopulo, Demetri and Hill, Kathrin. US Warns China on Aggressive Acts by Fishing Boats and Coast Guard. *The Financial Times*, April 28, 2019.

US Senate Committee on Foreign Relations: Safeguarding American Interests in the East and South China Seas. Washington DC, May 2013, 2015. https://www.foreign.senate.gov/hearings/safeguarding-american-interests-in-the-east-and-south-china-seas

Wagner, Benjamin K. Lessons from Lassen: Plotting a Proper Course for Freedom of Navigation Operations in the South China Sea. *Journal of East Asia International Law*, 2016.

13

Japan's Security Interests and Strategies in the South China Sea

Masafumi Iida

Introduction

The South China Sea (SCS) has been one of the sources of instability in East Asian security for decades. Territorial sovereignty and jurisdiction over islands and reefs in the SCS are contested among the littoral countries including China, Taiwan, Vietnam, the Philippines, Malaysia, and Brunei, occasionally causing tensions and even military conflicts between the competing nations. In particular, China provoked serious confrontations by its actions for expanding control of the SCS through exercise of, and/or intimidation by, military force, as Joshua Hastey and Scott N. Romaniuk, and Romaniuk and Tobias Burgers explore in their conceptual chapters (Chapter 1 and 2). In 1974, the People's Liberation Army (PLA) of China attacked the South Vietnamese army stationing in the Paracel Islands, resulting in China's full control of the islands.[1] China occupied six reefs and rocks in the Spratly Islands by exercising military force against the Vietnamese navy in 1988.[2] In what Ian J. Storey refers to as a "creeping assertiveness," China put the

---

[1] John W. Garver, "China's Push through the South China Sea: The Interaction of Bureaucratic and National Interests," *The China Quarterly* no. 132 (December 1992), 999–1028.

[2] Larry W. Coker, Jr., "The Spratly Islands Dispute: Can ASEAN Provide the Framework for a Solution?," Strategy Research Project, US Army War College, Carlisle Barracks, PA, United States. https://www.hsdl.org/?view&did=452995

Mischief Reef under its control, replacing that of the Philippines, through mobilizing warships of the PLA Navy (PLAN) around the reef in 1995.[3]

In the late 1990s, China seemed to cease aggressive actions to expand occupation in the SCS and started to take accommodating behaviours towards the Southeast Asian nations. In 2002, China and members of the Association of Southeast Asian Nations (ASEAN) signed the Declaration on the Conduct (DOC) of Parties in the SCS, which declares parties should "resolve their territorial and jurisdictional disputes by peaceful means, without resorting to the threat or use of force."[4] The DOC gave the regional countries some expectation that Beijing would pursue benign policies, leading to lower tension in the SCS. However, China soon got back to normal to show assertive postures against the competing claimants. In 2008, Chinese patrol vessels belonging to maritime law enforcement agencies started patrol missions on a regular basis in the SCS, and repeatedly obstructed navigation of foreign fishing boats and surveillance vessels.[5] In 2012, Chinese patrol vessels confronted the Philippines' Coast Guard ships around the Scarborough Shoal and finally established control of the shoal.[6] China's renewed assertive policies raised serious regional concerns about stability in the SCS.

China also directed assertive behaviour against the United States (US) in the SCS. Two Chinese "trawlers," supported by patrol vessels and a reconnaissance ship of the PLAN, harassed the *USS Impeccable* operating off the coast of Hainan Island in 2009.[7] Such an incident might cause concern over China's actions and intentions regarding the SCS in the Obama administration. In response, Secretary of State Hillary Clinton expressed the American resolve to play a role in maintaining the existing maritime order by stating that the US "has a national interest in freedom of navigation, open

[3] Ian James Storey, "Creeping Assertiveness: China, the Philippines and the South China Sea Dispute," *Contemporary Southeast Asia* 21, no. 1 (April 1999), 95–118.

[4] ASEAN Secretariat, "Declaration on the Conduct of Parties in the South China Sea," October 17, 2012. https://asean.org/?static_post=declaration-on-the-conduct-of-parties-in-the-south-china-sea-2

[5] Ryan D. Martinson, "From Words to Actions: The Creation of the China Coast Guard," Paper prepared for the China as a "Maritime Power" Conference, July 28–29, 2015, Arlington, VA, United States.

[6] François-Xavier Bonnet, "Geopolitics of Scarborough Shoal," Les Notes de l'Irasec n°14 – Irasec's Discussion Papers #14, November 2012, L'Institut de Recherche sur l'Asie du Sud-Est Contemporaine (IRASEC), Bangkok, Thailand. https://www.irasec.com/documents/fichiers/40.pdf

[7] Raul Pedroza, "Close Encounters at Sea," *Naval War College Review* 62, no. 3 (2009), 101–11.

access to Asia's maritime commons, and respect for international law in the South China Sea" at a press conference in Hanoi where she attended the ARF Ministerial Meeting in July 2010.[8] Nonetheless, China further accelerated moves to increase its military presence by conducting massive reclamation projects to create artificial islands in the Spratly Islands in 2014, and later militarized them. China's continuous efforts to expand its control of the SCS prompted the US to regard China as a strategic rival. The National Security Strategy (NSS) issued in 2017 under the Trump administration states that China's "efforts to build and militarize outposts in the SCS endanger the free flow of trade, threaten the sovereignty of other nations, and undermine regional stability," and declares a return of "great power competition" with "revisionist" China.[9]

Persistent contention over territoriality and maritime interest among the claimant nations stimulated by China's assertive behaviours, together with intensifying strategic competition between China and the United States in the SCS, have gradually raised the levels of tension and uncertainty over security in East Asia where Japan exists. Any unstable situations, even military conflicts, in the SCS will inevitably affect the peace and prosperity of Japan; therefore, Japan has actively engaged in issues in the SCS as a legitimate stakeholder. The purpose of this chapter is to examine Japan's foreign and defence policies regarding the SCS. First, the author will discuss Japan's critical interests concerned with the SCS, which motivate the Japanese government to engage in the Sea. Second, the principles and strategies which Japan advances in the ocean including the SCS will be reviewed. And finally, some specific policies, especially in defence and security areas, which the Japanese government pursues will be examined.

Japan's interests in the South China Sea

Given its rooted ties with the Southeast Asian nations in terms of economy, culture, and history, Japan has multiple interests in the SCS. From a security point of view, Japan's important interests in the Sea consist of three elements: preventing a change of status quo by coercion; maintaining a rules-based maritime order; and upholding the military predominance of the US.

---

8 US Department of State, "Remarks at Press Availability," Hillary Rodham Clinton, Secretary of State, National Convention Centre, Hanoi, Vietnam, July 23, 2010. https://2009-2017.state.gov/secretary/20092013clinton/rm/2010/07/145095.htm

9 White House, "National Security Strategy of the United States of America," December 2017. https://www.whitehouse.gov/wp-content/uploads/2017/12/NSS-Final-12-18-2017-0905.pdf

Remarkable success in economic development provided the Chinese government with significant resources to advance massive programmes of military modernization. China has continued to increase annual defence budget for more than 20 years, which makes China the second-largest military spender in the world after the US.[10] The PLA has dramatically enhanced operational capabilities through developing and acquiring a huge amount of modern and sophisticated equipment. The PLAN has acquired many types of modern surface ships, submarines, and aircraft. Consequently, the PLAN has become the largest navy in Asia, with an emphasis on conducting military operations at increasing distances from the mainland.[11] With the growing power projection capabilities, the PLAN has steadily increased frequency and scale of its activities in the SCS. In recent years, the PLA conducted a variety of military exercises, including combined live-fire drills between surface vessels and aircraft, leading to the PLAN's enhanced presence.

Not only the PLAN but also the Chinese maritime law enforcement agencies have strengthened their operational capabilities by increasing the number of larger cutters and advancing institutional reforms. In 2013, China integrated four maritime law enforcement agencies, including the China Marine Surveillance (CMS) and the Fisheries Law Enforcement Command (FLEC), for establishing the Chinese Coast Guard (CCG) under the State Oceanic Administration.[12] Five years later, China reorganized the CCG into the People's Armed Police (PAP), part of China's armed forces over which the Central Military Commission exercises absolute control. This reorganization changed the status of the CCG from a civilian law enforcement agency to a military institution, which may facilitate closer cooperation between the CCG and the PLAN and, consequently, enhance the capabilities of the CCG to expand maritime rights and interests in China's peripheral waters.

With the growing maritime force, China has engaged in attempts to change the status quo by coercive measures in the SCS. China took over control of the Scarborough Shoal from the Philippines when the Chinese law

---

10 US Department of Defense, "Annual Report to Congress – Military and Security Developments Involving the People's Republic of China 2019," May 2, 2019, 93. https://media.defense.gov/2019/May/02/2002127082/-1/-1/1/2019_CHINA_MILITARY_POWER_REPORT.pdf

11 US Defense Intelligence Agency, "China's Military Power: Modernizing a Force to Fight and Win," January 15, 2019, 63 https://admin.govexec.com/media/gbc/docs/pdfs_edit/dod-2019-china_military_power_final.pdf

12 Nong Hong, "China's Maritime Law Enforcement Reform and its Implications on the Regional Maritime Disputes," April 15, 2015. https://amti.csis.org/chinas-maritime-law-enforcement-reform-and-its-implication-on-the-regional-maritime-disputes/

enforcement patrol vessels expelled the Philippines' Coast Guard ships after the two-month long standoff in 2012. China unilaterally started exploratory drilling by the "Haiyang Shiyou 981" oilrig in the Vietnamese-claimed waters south of the Paracel Islands in 2014. Vietnam dispatched patrol boats to protest the drilling, but China mobilized more than 100 patrol ships to counterattack them, causing serious damage to the Vietnamese ships and crews. When the Arbitral Tribunal issued the ruling, which denied the Chinese claims in the SCS including the "nine-dash line" in 2016, the PLA conducted a large-scale military exercise in order to show China's strong resolve to reject the ruling, which was predicated on the existing international law.

China attempted to alter the status quo by coercion in the East China Sea as well. The Chinese government started to claim sovereignty over the Senkaku Islands, which have been Japanese territories since 1971.[13] Since then, China has been challenging Japanese sovereignty and jurisdiction over the islands and increasing pressure on Japan. In 2008, two patrol vessels of the CMS intruded into the Japanese territorial sea of the Senkaku Islands. In September 2012, China drastically increased the number and frequency of the Chinese government ships navigating the water surrounding the Senkaku Islands so as to claim Chinese sovereignty. Recently Chinese patrol vessels have been entering Japan's Contiguous Zone almost daily, and intrude into Japan's Territorial Sea at a frequency of about three intrusions per month.[14] The PLA also plays a role in intensifying pressure on the Japanese territoriality on the Senkaku Islands. For instance, a Shang-class nuclear attack submarine and a Jiangkai II-class frigate passed into the Contiguous Zone around the Senkaku Islands in January 2018.[15]

It is evident that China applies its tactics in the SCS – changing the status quo by civilian and military force to expand control of contested territories and jurisdictions – to the case of the Senkaku Islands in the East China Sea. Any success with these coercive tactics in the SCS may prompt China to take further assertive behaviours in the East China Sea. China started regular dispatch of government vessels around the Senkaku Islands just three months later, when they succeeded in occupying the

---

[13] Shigeyoshi Ozaki, "The Senkaku Islands and Japan's Territorial Rights (Part 1)," *Review of Island Disputes*, The Sasakawa Peace Foundation (SPF), Tokyo, Japan. spf.org/islandstudies/research/a00001.html

[14] Japan Ministry of Foreign Affairs, "Trends in Chinese Government and Other Vessels in the Waters Surrounding the Senkaku Islands, and Japan's Response." https://www.mofa.go.jp/region/page23e_000021.html

[15] Japan Ministry of Defense, "Defense of Japan 2019," Ministry of Defense, Tokyo, Japan, October 2019. https://www.mod.go.jp/e/publ/w_paper/wp2019/pdf/index.html

Scarborough Shoal by patrol ships. Preventing China's attempts to change the status quo in the SCS is therefore expected to be supportive of Japan's effort to protect the Senkaku Islands from growing challenges stemming from Chinese coercive actions.

Japan is an island country surrounded by oceans. Its economy heavily depends on import of natural resources and trade in goods, most of which are carried by maritime transportation. Japan, therefore, has a vital interest in maintaining safety of sea lines of communication (SLOC) connecting Japan with trading partners all over the world. The sea lane passing through the SCS is one of the most important SLOCs for Japan. According to the Agency for Natural Resources and Energy, 92 per cent of oil and 50 per cent of natural gas imported to Japan in 2016 were shipped through the SCS.[16] Japan prioritizes safe use of the SLOC based on the existing rules, including freedom of navigation in the SCS.

Some of China's behaviour in the SCS contradicts existing norms and rules shared by the international community. Chinese patrol vessels frequently harass foreign fishing boats and government ships, which clearly infringes on the principle of freedom of navigation. The Chinese warships and military aircraft occasionally approach dangerously close to the American military vessels and planes operating in the SCS. These actions of the PLA show growing assertiveness in China's behaviours and infringement of the rules of free navigation and flight in open seas. China is also opposed to the existing rules by insisting that littoral nations have right to restrict operations of foreign warships and military aircraft within their EEZ. All of the Chinese actions and assertions opposing the existing rules-based maritime order invite Japan's concern about possible instability in the SLOC caused by China's unilateral behaviours neglecting the international maritime rules.[17] Consequently, Japan has significant interest in upholding the existing rules-based order in the SCS, with the expectation that the enhanced norms and rules discourage China from taking action that could lead to the destabilization of SLOCs in the SCS.

The existing maritime order has been shared and supported by many regional countries, contributing to stability in the SCS for decades. Meanwhile, the US has played a significant role in formulating and, to some extent, enforcing the rules with its predominant naval presence

[16] Japan Agency for Natural Resources and Energy. "Viewpoints on Resources and Energy Policies from Mid- and Long-Term Perspectives" ["中長期を見据えた資源┌燃料政策の視点について"]. January 11, 2018, 9. https://www.meti.go.jp/shingikai/enecho/shigen_nenryo/pdf/023_04_00.pdf

[17] See, Christopher W. Hughes, "Japan's 'Resentful Realism' and Balancing China's Rise," *The Chinese Journal of International Politics* 9 no. 2 (Summer 2016), 109–50.

especially since the end of the Cold War. It is strong US military presence with support from allies and partners that endorses a stable SCS relying on rules-based maritime order. However, China recently emerges as a rising military power and strives to challenge the US naval predominance in the SCS. The PLAN deploys a number of modern warships to the South Fleet, including Jin-class SSBNs and a newly commissioned aircraft carrier, the *Shandong*. China constructed military outposts in the Spratly Islands and equipped them with facilities for intelligence, surveillance and reconnaissance (ISR) missions, anti-air and anti-ship cruise missiles, and so on.[18]

China appears to intend to reduce the US military presence and achieve a new balance of power favourable to China in the SCS. Once China dominates the SCS, the PLA can project more powers into the East China Sea and the Western Pacific through the uncontested sea of sanctuary. The US Defense Department urges that China's anti-access/area denial (A2/AD) capabilities[19] are currently robust within the first island chain, but "China aims to strengthen its capabilities to extend farther into the Pacific Ocean."[20] Weakened American military presence in the SCS will invite not only more assertive Chinese behaviours aiming at changing the status quo in contravention of the rules-based order, but will also undermine the operational capabilities of the US Forces in the Asia-Pacific Ocean. The US security commitments to allies and partners, assured by the overwhelming American military predominance, have provided the foundation for stability in this region. Since the Japan-US alliance plays a critical role in maintaining Japanese security, Tokyo has significant interest in sustaining and even strengthening the US military predominance in the SCS.

Japan's strategy toward the South China Sea

The Cabinet meeting of the Shinzo Abe administration authorized and issued the first-ever official document of Japan's security strategy, the National Security Strategy (NSS), in December 2013. The NSS presents principles of Japan's security, its national interests and objectives, challenges

---

18 Asia Maritime Transparency Initiative, "An Accounting of China's Deployments in the Spratly Islands," May 9, 2018. https://amti.csis.org/accounting-chinas-deployments-spratly-islands/

19 See, Vincent Alcazar, "Crisis Management and the Anti-Access/Area Denial Problem," *Strategic Studies Quarterly* 6, no. 4 (Winter 2012), 42–70.

20 US Department of Defense, "Annual Report to Congress – Military and Security Developments Involving the People's Republic of China 2019," May 2, 2019, 54. https://media.defense.gov/2019/May/02/2002127082/-1/-1/1/2019_CHINA_MILITARY_POWER_REPORT.pdf

to national security, and what strategic approaches Japan should take.[21] It is worth examining the NSS to understand Japan's strategy towards the SCS.

The NSS states that the fundamental principle of Japan's national security is to "contribute even more proactively in securing peace, stability, and prosperity of the international community, while achieving its own security as well as peace and stability in the Asia-Pacific region."[22] As a "Proactive Contributor to Peace," Japan shows its intention of playing a major role in promoting regional and international peace and stability. The NSS defines three national interests of Japan as follows:

1. To maintain Japan's sovereignty and independence; to defend its territorial integrity; to ensure safety of its nationals; and to ensure its survival.
2. To achieve the prosperity of Japan and its nationals through economic development; and to this end, to strengthen free trade regime and ensure stable environment especially in the Asia-Pacific region.
3. To maintain and protect international order based on rules and universal values including freedom, democracy, respect for human rights, and the rule of law.

With the aim of protecting these national interests, the NSS announces the following three national security objectives:

1. To improve deterrence for ensuring survival of Japan, and to defeat a threat reaching Japan and minimize the damage.
2. To improve security environment of the Asia-Pacific region through enhancing the alliance with the United States and cooperative relations with partners.
3. To improve the global security environment and build a peaceful, stable, and prosperous international community through strengthening the international order based on universal values and rules.

Issues and situations in the SCS are focal points referred to in the NSS. The document expresses Japan's concern about the risk to free and open access to the seas, based on international maritime law including the United Nations Convention on the Law of the Sea (UNCLOS), by noting, "there have been an increasing number of cases of unilateral actions in an attempt

---

21 Japan Ministry of Foreign Affairs. "National Security Strategy (NSS)." April 6, 2016. https://www.mofa.go.jp/fp/nsp/page1we_000081.html

22 Japan Cabinet Office, "National Security Strategy" (provisional translation), December 17, 2013, 8. http://japan.kantei.go.jp/96_abe/documents/2013/__icsFiles/afieldfile/2013/12/17/NSS.pdf

to change the status quo by coercion without paying respect to existing international law." Regarding the SCS, the NSS states that disputes over sovereignty between China and other coastal nations raise anxiety about stability in the Southeast Asian region. The document also shows Japan's concern on the increasing vulnerability of SLOCs passing through the SCS due to regional conflicts, international terrorism, and piracy. The Japanese government specifically shows apprehension about China's actions which are incompatible with international maritime law by saying: "China has taken actions that can be regarded as attempts to change the status quo by coercion based on their own assertions" in maritime and aerial domains in the East China Sea and the SCS.[23] The NSS more concretely criticizes China's coercive actions including intrusion into Japan's territorial waters and airspace around the Senkaku Islands.

The NSS underscores the critical importance of the SLOC through the Indian Ocean, the Straits of Malacca, and the SCS on which Japan depends for the shipping of natural resources from the Middle East. In order to secure the SLOC, the NSS declares that Japan will provide assistance to the coastal countries alongside the sea lane in enhancing their maritime law enforcement capabilities.[24] In this regard, the ASEAN and its member countries emerge as critical partners of Japan for securing the sea lane in the SCS. The NSS indeed declares Japan's intention to support the unity of ASEAN and appreciation of their efforts in settling the disputes in accordance with rules and international law, including the endeavour to formulate a Code of Conduct (COC) with China.[25]

Following the announcement of the NSS, Japan presented its basic stance and concrete policies regarding maritime security, especially in the SCS. Prime Minister Shinzo Abe made a keynote speech at the 13th Asian Security Summit, or "Shangri-La Dialogue," hosted by the International Institute for Strategic Studies (IISS) in May 2014. In his speech entitled "Peace and prosperity in Asia, forevermore: Japan for the rule of law, Asia for the rule of law, and the rule of law for all of us," Prime Minister Abe emphasized the importance of the rule of law for achieving peace and prosperity in Asia stretching from Asia-Pacific to the Indian Ocean.[26] He said, "It's absolutely imperative that we make peace and stability, something absolutely rock-solid," and "all countries must observe international law" for realizing this. Abe,

[23] Ibid., 12.

[24] Ibid., 17.

[25] Ibid., 24.

[26] Japan Ministry of Foreign Affairs. The 13th IISS Asian Security Summit – The Shangri-La Dialogue: Keynote Address by Shinzo Abe, Prime Minister, Japan, May 30, 2014. https://www.mofa.go.jp/fp/nsp/page4e_000086.html

then, expressed Japan's intention to play a greater and more proactive role than before in promoting peace in Asia and the world under the banner of "Proactive Contribution to Peace."

Prime Minister Abe further urged that all the nations benefit from making the seas from the Indian Ocean to the Pacific Ocean open, free, and peaceful, where the rule of law is fully respected. In this context, Abe proposed the three principles of the rule of law at sea: first, states shall make and clarify their claims based on international law; second, states shall not use force or coercion in trying to drive their claims; and third, states shall seek to settle disputes by peaceful means. He praised the Philippines' efforts for solving the disputes in the SCS as being consistent with the three principles, and condemned movements for accumulating faits accomplis to change the status quo as being contrary to these principles. In line with these three principles, Abe expressed Japan's great support for the ASEAN members' efforts in ensuring maritime and aerial security and maintaining freedom of navigation and overflight. As a concrete policy for supporting efforts by the ASEAN countries, he referred to the provision of patrol vessels to the Coast Guards of the Philippines, Indonesia, and Vietnam with the aim of increasing their capabilities of law enforcement at sea. Abe also expressed Japan's intention to transfer defence equipment and technology to the ASEAN states under the renewed principles of arms transfer. The Prime Minister declared that Japan supported ASEAN members' capacity to safeguard the seas by combining options including Official Development Assistance, capacity building by the Self-Defence Forces, and defence equipment and technology cooperation.

Japan's Ministry of Defence later announced its own initiative for future defence cooperation between Japan and ASEAN, called "Vientiane Vision," at the second Japan-ASEAN Defence Ministers' Informal Meeting held in Vientiane, Lao PDR, in November 2016. Vientiane Vision reviews the evolution of Japan-ASEAN defence cooperation since the 1990s, starting from defence exchanges, through operational defence cooperation, to capacity building cooperation and multilateral cooperation such as ADMM-Plus (Asian Defence Ministers' Meeting). Appreciating this expanding defence cooperation between the two sides, the Vientiane Vision proposes to promote "ASEAN-wide" cooperation in addition to the cooperation with "individual ASEAN member states." The Vision clarifies three directions the future Japan-ASEAN defence cooperation will put focus on, as follows:

1. To consolidate the order based on the principles of international law governing peaceful conduct among states, Japan supports ASEAN efforts to uphold principles of international law, especially in the field of maritime and air space.

2. To promote maritime security which is a foundation for the regional peace and prosperity, Japan supports ASEAN efforts to build up capabilities for Intelligence, Surveillance and Reconnaissance (ISR) and Search and Rescue (SAR) at sea and air space.
3. To cope with increasingly diversifying and complex security issues, Japan supports ASEAN efforts to build up capabilities in various fields.[27]

The Vientiane Vision appears to show two major purposes for Japan to promote defence cooperation with ASEAN. First, Japan seeks to strengthen the centrality and cohesiveness of ASEAN through deepening defence cooperation with ASEAN as a whole, with a view to enhancing ASEAN's position in regards to China in their effort to maintain rule of law in the SCS. Second, Japan takes a step forward to help ASEAN to increase defence capabilities needed to monitor and check Chinese activities in the SCS. To achieve these goals, the Vientiane Vision specifies five measures: promotion of international law, capacity-building cooperation, defence equipment and technology cooperation, joint training and exercises, and human resource development and academic exchange.

After three years' implementation of the Vientiane Vision, Japan updated the Vision. Defence Minister Taro Kono announced the "Vientiane Vision 2.0" at the 5th Japan-ASEAN Defence Ministers' Informal Meeting, held in Thailand in November 2019. The Vientiane Vision 2.0 reviews the progress of defence cooperation between Japan and ASEAN both in multilateral and bilateral ways, and reaffirms further practical cooperation to support ASEAN's resilience. At the same time, the updated Vision emphasizes the concept of the "Indo-Pacific." The Vientiane Vision 2.0 illustrates ASEAN as "the hinge connecting the Indian and Pacific Oceans," and indicates the commonality between the "ASEAN Outlook on the Indo-Pacific" and Japan's vision for a "Free and Open Indo-Pacific," both upholding principles such as openness, transparency, inclusivity, and a rules-based framework.[28] With this new Vision, Japan redefines its defence cooperation with ASEAN as an important part of its strategy for ensuring a free and open Indo-Pacific.

In short, the core goal of Japan's strategy toward the SCS is to maintain a stable environment and secured sea lanes, both of which are undermined by China's attempts to change the status quo by coercion. To achieve this

---

[27] Japan Ministry of Defence, "Vientiane Vision: Japan's Defence Cooperation Initiative with ASEAN." https://www.mod.go.jp/e/press/conference/2016/11/161116_1.pdf

[28] Japan Ministry of Defence, "Updating the 'Vientiane Vision': Japan's Defence Cooperation Initiative with ASEAN." November 2019. https://www.mod.go.jp/e/d_act/exc/admm/06/vv2_en.pdf

strategic goal, Japan extends defence cooperation with the United States and ASEAN, which share an interest in upholding a rules-based maritime order. In this regard, Japan makes efforts to enhance the Japan-US alliance in order to increase operational capabilities both of the US forces and the Japan SDF in this region. Japan also steadily takes steps for promoting defence cooperation with ASEAN to support their capabilities for dealing with challenges in the SCS.

Japan's defence policies toward the South China Sea

The National Security Council and the Cabinet of Japan approved the "National Defense Program Guideline for FY2019 and beyond" in December 2018.[29] The NDPG is a "grand design" to ensure the peace and security of Japan, which clarifies the posture and the level of defence capabilities Japan will pursue.[30] As to the Japan's defence policies for maritime security, the 2018 NDPG notes that Japan will conduct bilateral activities with the US such as capacity building assistance and humanitarian assistance/disaster relief (HA/DR) in order to enhance free and open maritime order and increase Japanese and US presence in the Indo-Pacific region.[31] In addition, the 2018 NDPG insists that Japan will promote practical bilateral and multilateral cooperation with the Southeast Asian nations, including joint training, defence equipment and technology cooperation, and capacity-building assistance.[32] Accordingly, Japan's defence policies relating to the SCS consist of two pillars: to enhance bilateral cooperation with the US; and to deepen practical cooperation with ASEAN and its member states, with a view to increasing Japan's presence and involvement for upholding freedom and openness in the sea.

As a part of the first pillar, the Japan Maritime Self-Defence Force (MSDF) conducted bilateral exercises with the US Navy in the SCS. In June 2017, the MSDF largest helicopter destroyer, the *Izumo*, and another destroyer, the *Murasame*, conducted exercises with US aircraft carrier *Ronald Reagan* and other vessels in the SCS. In March 2018, MSDF helicopter destroyer

---

[29] Japan Cabinet Office. "National Defence Programme Guidelines for FY 2019 and Beyond" (provisional translation). December 18, 2018. http://www.cas.go.jp/jp/siryou/pdf/2019boueikeikaku_e.pdf

[30] Japan Ministry of Defence, "Defence of Japan 2019," Ministry of Defence, Tokyo, Japan, October 2019. https://www.mod.go.jp/e/publ/w_paper/wp2019/pdf/index.html

[31] Japan Cabinet Office. "National Defence Programme Guidelines for FY 2019 and Beyond" (provisional translation). December 18, 2018, 14. http://www.cas.go.jp/jp/siryou/pdf/2019boueikeikaku_e.pdf

[32] Ibid., 16.

Ise and US aircraft carrier the *Carl Vinson* conducted exercises in the Sea. MSDF and US Navy (USN) invited other navies to join their exercises in the South China Sea. In June 2017, MSDF, USN, the Australian Navy, and the Canadian Navy carried out multilateral exercises there. In May 2019, MSDF, USN, the Indian Navy, and the Philippines Navy conducted multilateral exercises in the SCS. These bilateral and multilateral exercises are expected to enhance the presence and inter-operational capabilities of the MSDF, USN, and other navies which share an interest in upholding existing rules and norms in the SCS.

Japan, by itself, makes efforts to strengthen its operational capabilities and presence in the SCS. In September 2018, MSDF released the announcement that their surface ships and a submarine conducted anti-submarine warfare (ASW) exercises in the SCS. Vessels of the MSDF actively make port calls to the Southeast Asian nations, including Vietnam and the Philippines. In 2017, MSDF started the Indo-Pacific Deployment (IPD) exercise in which MSDF ships visit the littoral nations of the Indo-Pacific region for enhancing relations with these navies through exercises and exchanges. In the IPD 2019, the *Izumo*, *Murasame*, and a destroyer, the *Akebono*, visited Brunei, Malaysia, the Philippines, Singapore, and Vietnam. During the IPD 2019, the Japanese vessels made port calls and conducted many types of exercises with the host countries and carried out the Ship Rider Cooperation Programme, which invited naval officers of the ASEAN countries onboard the *Izumo* for deepening mutual trust and common understanding of the international maritime law.

Regarding practical cooperation with ASEAN countries, Japan proactively pursues capacity-building assistance, joint training, and defence equipment and technology cooperation.[33] In the case of Vietnam, the "Joint Vision Statement on Japan-Vietnam Defence Cooperation"[34] was signed by the both Defence Ministers in April 2018. Japan and Vietnam signed a memorandum on the orientation of the promotion of defence industry cooperation in May 2019, which paved the way for the transfer of defence equipment and technology from Japan to Vietnam. MSDF submarine *Kuroshio* paid a goodwill visit to Cam Ranh International Port in September 2018.[35] In

[33] Japan Ministry of Defence, "Defence of Japan 2019," Ministry of Defence, Tokyo, Japan, October 2019. https://www.mod.go.jp/e/publ/w_paper/wp2019/pdf/index.html

[34] Japan Ministry of Foreign Affairs, "Japan-Viet Nam Joint Statement on the Occasion of the State Visit by the President of the Socialist Republic of Viet Nam to Japan," https://www.mofa.go.jp/files/000368992.pdf

[35] "Japanese Submarine Kuroshio Starts Visit to Vietnam," *People's Army Newspaper*, September 17, 2018. https://en.qdnd.vn/military/intl-relations-and-cooperation/japanese-submarine-kuroshio-starts-visit-to-vietnam-496959

addition, the SDF provided capacity-building assistance in the fields of air rescue, peacekeeping operations, cyber security, and submarine medicine to the Vietnamese military. Regarding the Philippines, Prime Minister Abe and President Duterte agreed on the transfer of MSDF C-90 training aircraft to the Philippines in September 2016.[36] The transfer of five C-90s to the Philippines Navy was completed in March 2018. Japan also provides training for pilots and maintenance support to the Philippines Navy.

Conclusion

Even though Japan is not a claimant country over the territorial disputes in the SCS, securing the SLOC and maintaining rules-based maritime order constitute its critical national interest, which makes Japan a legitimate stakeholder in the Sea. Since China's attempts to change the status quo by coercion pose a concern over the stability and rule of law in the SCS, Japan has gradually enhanced its efforts in preserving the status quo in the Sea under the banner of a "Free and Open Indo-Pacific" in recent years. Strengthening the Japan-US alliance, in addition to cultivating defence cooperation with ASEAN, is a major way for Japan to achieve a stable SCS based on the existing rules and norms. In this context, Japan plans to strengthen operational capabilities in the space, cyberspace, and electromagnetic spectrum for realizing cross-domain operations, which are indispensable for the SDF to enhance inter-operability with US forces.

Given the intensification of strategic competition between China and the US, the SCS will remain one of the major fields of their confrontation. Because China's actions and assertions in the sea are detrimental to Japan's security, Japan will continue to invest in enhancing its self-defence capabilities, inter-operational capabilities with US forces, and defence cooperation with the ASEAN nations as long as China takes coercive behaviour to change the status quo in the SCS.

References

Alcazar, Vincent. "Crisis Management and the Anti-Access/Area Denial Problem." *Strategic Studies Quarterly* 6, no. 4 (Winter 2012): 42–70.

ASEAN Secretariat. "Declaration on the Conduct of Parties in the South China Sea." October 17, 2012. https://asean.org/?static_post=declaration-on-the-conduct-of-parties-in-the-south-china-sea-2

[36] Japan Ministry of Defence, "Defence Equipment and Technology Transfer," Section 4. https://www.mod.go.jp/e/publ/w_paper/pdf/2017/DOJ2017_3-4-4_web.pdf

Asia Maritime Transparency Initiative. "An Accounting of China's Deployments in the Spratly Islands." May 9, 2018. https://amti.csis.org/accounting-chinas-deployments-spratly-islands/

Bonnet, François-Xavier. "Geopolitics of Scarborough Shoal," Les Notes de l'Irasec n°14 – Irasec's Discussion Papers #14, November 2012, L'Institut de Recherche sur l'Asie du Sud-Est Contemporaine (IRASEC), Bangkok, Thailand. https://www.irasec.com/documents/fichiers/40.pdf

Coker, Jr, Larry W. "The Spratly Islands Dispute: Can ASEAN Provide the Framework for a Solution?." Strategy Research Project, US Army War College, Carlisle Barracks, PA, United States. https://www.hsdl.org/?view&did=452995

Garver, John W. "China's Push through the South China Sea: The Interaction of Bureaucratic and National Interests." *The China Quarterly* no. 132 (December 1992): 999–1028.

Hong, Nong. "China's Maritime Law Enforcement Reform and Its Implications on the Regional Maritime Disputes," April 15, 2015. https://amti.csis.org/chinas-maritime-law-enforcement-reform-and-its-implication-on-the-regional-maritime-disputes/

Hughes, Christopher W. "Japan's 'Resentful Realism' and Balancing China's Rise," *The Chinese Journal of International Politics* 9 no. 2 (Summer 2016): 109–50.

Japan Agency for Natural Resources and Energy. "Viewpoints on Resources and Energy Policies from Mid- and Long-Term Perspectives" ["中長期を見据えた資源「燃料政策の視点について"]. January 11, 2018. https://www.meti.go.jp/shingikai/enecho/shigen_nenryo/pdf/023_04_00.pdf

Japan Cabinet Office. "National Security Strategy" (provisional translation). December 17, 2013. http://japan.kantei.go.jp/96_abe/documents/2013/__icsFiles/afieldfile/2013/12/17/NSS.pdf

Japan Cabinet Office. "National Defence Programme Guidelines for FY 2019 and Beyond" (provisional translation). December 18, 2018. http://www.cas.go.jp/jp/siryou/pdf/2019boueikeikaku_e.pdf

Japan Ministry of Defence. "Defence Equipment and Technology Transfer" Section 4. https://www.mod.go.jp/e/publ/w_paper/pdf/2017/DOJ2017_3-4-4_web.pdf

Japan Ministry of Defence. "Defence of Japan 2019." Ministry of Defence, Tokyo, Japan, October 2019. https://www.mod.go.jp/e/publ/w_paper/wp2019/pdf/index.html

Japan Ministry of Defence. "Updating the 'Vientiane Vision:' Japan's Defense Cooperation Initiative with ASEAN." November 2019. https://www.mod.go.jp/e/d_act/exc/admm/06/vv2_en.pdf

Japan Ministry of Defence. "Vientiane Vision: Japan's Defence Cooperation Initiative with ASEAN." https://www.mod.go.jp/e/press/conference/2016/11/161116_1.pdf

Japan Ministry of Foreign Affairs. "Japan-Viet Nam Joint Statement on the Occasion of the State Visit by the President of the Socialist Republic of Viet Nam to Japan." https://www.mofa.go.jp/files/000368992.pdf

Japan Ministry of Foreign Affairs. The 13th IISS Asian Security Summit – The Shangri-La Dialogue: Keynote Address by Shinzo Abe, Prime Minister, Japan, May 30, 2014. https://www.mofa.go.jp/fp/nsp/page4e_000086.html

Japan Ministry of Foreign Affairs. "National Security Strategy (NSS)." April 6, 2016. https://www.mofa.go.jp/fp/nsp/page1we_000081.html

Japan Ministry of Foreign Affairs. "Trends in Chinese Government and Other Vessels in the Waters Surrounding the Senkaku Islands, and Japan's Response." https://www.mofa.go.jp/region/page23e_000021.html

"Japanese Submarine Kuroshio Starts Visit to Vietnam," *People's Army Newspaper*, September 17, 2018. https://en.qdnd.vn/military/intl-relations-and-cooperation/japanese-submarine-kuroshio-starts-visit-to-vietnam-496959

Martinson, Ryan D. "From Words to Actions: The Creation of the China Coast Guard," Paper prepared for the China as a "Maritime Power" Conference, July 28–29, 2015, Arlington, VA, United States.

Ozaki, Shigeyoshi. "The Senkaku Islands and Japan's Territorial Rights (Part 1)," *Review of Island Disputes*, The Sasakawa Peace Foundation (SPF), Tokyo, Japan. https://www.spf.org/islandstudies/research/a00001.html

Raul, Pedroza. "Close Encounters at Sea." *Naval War College Review* 62, no. 3 (2009): 101–11.

Storey, Ian James. "Creeping Assertiveness: China, the Philippines and the South China Sea Dispute," *Contemporary Southeast Asia* 21, no. 1 (April 1999): 95–118.

US Defense Intelligence Agency. "China's Military Power: Modernizing a Force to Fight and Win." January 15, 2019. https://admin.govexec.com/media/gbc/docs/pdfs_edit/dod-2019-china_military_power_final.pdf

US Department of Defense. "Annual Report to Congress – Military and Security Developments Involving the People's Republic of China 2019." May 2, 2019. https://media.defense.gov/2019/May/02/2002127082/-1/-1/1/2019_CHINA_MILITARY_POWER_REPORT.pdf

US Department of State. "Remarks at Press Availability." Hillary Rodham Clinton, Secretary of State, National Convention Centre, Hanoi, Vietnam, July 23, 2010. https://2009-2017.state.gov/secretary/20092013clinton/rm/2010/07/145095.htm

White House. "National Security Strategy of the United States of America." December 2017. https://www.whitehouse.gov/wp-content/uploads/2017/12/NSS-Final-12-18-2017-0905.pdf

14

Australia's Geopolitics and the South China Sea

Leszek Buszynski

Introduction

Australia is not an active participant in the South China Sea (SCS) dispute and at first sight its distance from the area may give the impression of irrelevance. However, the dispute has consequences for Australia's geopolitics in a way that is increasingly being recognized within government and the wider security community. In essence, the notion of geopolitics relates to the impact of geographic location on security and the formulation of policy, and how governments react to and devise policies towards their immediate security environment. The United States (US) may have a very clear understanding on its global geopolitics in terms of preventing one-state dominance of critical regions such as Western Europe or the Asia-Pacific region. However, because of its historical isolation, Australia's understanding of its geopolitics has been undeveloped, though largely framed in terms of ensuring the security of its northern approaches while maintaining alliance relationships with larger powers as protection. The SCS dispute, however, has had the effect of hastening the development of that understanding of geopolitics in the various debates and discussions about Australia's security. The SCS dispute involves China, which has been Australia's major trading partner and contributor to its economic growth over the past decades. However, China's regional ambitions both in Southeast Asia and the South Pacific have evoked apprehensions. Once a country that had a limited understanding of its immediate external environment, Australia has discovered that it cannot rely on its isolation, or on its alliance relationships alone to deal with this new and increasingly complicated scenario. China's activities in the SCS have quickened Australia's understanding of its geopolitical predicament and have compelled it to adjust to an uncertain security environment, which the country has avoided for too long.

Australia's geopolitics

What is geopolitics and what impact has it had on Australia? The classical geopolitics of Mackinder, Mahan and Spykman identified how geography impacted upon policy and how it shaped the great-power rivalry of the age. Its enduring legacy in the present era is the importance of the spatial dimension in security, and how governments take into account geographic location in policy making. In this sense, geopolitics is about how geography shapes and, in some cases, determines security responses including defence policies, the disposition of forces, and their deployment. Geopolitics provides guiding principles for security which are handed down from one generation of policy makers to the next and which become expressed in security or foreign policy doctrines. Classical geopolitics identified particular zones of rivalry which were designated as spheres of influence, some of which were exclusive, while others were shared to varying degrees. In the present age, spheres of influence cannot be made exclusive while governments will identify surrounding areas in their external environment as critical or important for their security. For some small and middle powers geopolitics may entail membership of protective regional associations or multilateral institutions such as the EU. For others more insecure, it may necessitate alliance relationships with stronger powers, and for others more confident in themselves, it may mean the development of defence capability and force development to meet specific threats. Not every country has a clear understanding of its geopolitics but for those countries like Australia which are concerned about their immediate security environment, notions of geopolitics become important in the framing of defence policy and security.[1]

Indeed, Australia has had an incipient idea of its geopolitics based on the often-expressed need to ensure the security of the northern approaches in Southeast Asia, and to prevent any hostile power from controlling this area. The 1986 Dibb Report to the Minister of Defence noted that, "[a] strong stable region free from external pressures is a fundamental security interest" and that Australia should cooperate with Southeast Asian and South Pacific countries to promote a sense of shared strategic interests. For Dibb, Indonesia

[1] Leszek Buszynski, *The Geopolitics of the Western Pacific: China, Japan, and the United States* (New York: Routledge, 2019).

was a priority since the "Indonesian archipelago forms a protective barrier to Australia's northern approaches."[2] The 1987 Defence White Paper identified Australia's direct military interest as an area stretching more than "7,000 kilometres from the Cocos Islands to New Zealand and the islands of the South-West Pacific, and over 5,000 kilometres from the archipelago and island chain in the north to the Southern Ocean." It included its territories and proximate ocean areas, Indonesia, Papua New Guinea, New Zealand, and other nearby countries of the South West Pacific.[3] These themes were carried over into subsequent defence white papers which stressed that Australia's strategic interests dictated a stable and secure North and the creation of a regional order based on rules and norms that would prevent hegemony by any antagonistic or hostile power.

Two decades later the 2009 Defence White Paper for the first time noted China's rise as the "strongest Asian military power" and that "the pace, scope and structure of China's military modernisation have the potential to give its neighbours cause for concern if not carefully explained."[4] The 2013 Defence White Paper extended Australia's geopolitical interests to the Indo-Pacific and adjusted Australia's priority strategic focus to the "arc extending from India though Southeast Asia to Northeast Asia, including the sea lines of communication on which the region depends."[5] The 2016 Defence White Paper stressed that maintaining the security of "Australia's maritime approaches, offshore territories and borders is essential for Australia's national security," and that, "The geography of the archipelago to Australia's immediate north will always have particular significance to our security. Any conventional military threat to Australia is likely to approach through the archipelago."[6]

Successive defence white papers have also consistently stressed the importance of the alliance with the US, which has been regarded as the foundation of Australia's security. To ensure a stable and secure Northern region, Australia has relied on this alliance, the rationale for which dates back to the Pacific War.

---

2 Paul Dibb, "Australia needs more missiles and combat pilots," *The Canberra Times*, July 10, 2019. https://www.canberratimes.com.au/story/6254377/australia-must-review-defence-force-in-light-of-china-threat/

3 Parliament of Australia, *The Defence of Australia (1987 Defence White Paper)*, www.aph.gov.au/About_Parliament/Parliamentary_Departments/Parliamentary_Library/pubs/rp/rp1516/DefendAust/1987#_Toc427833142

4 Australian Government Department of Defence, "Defending Australia in the Asia Pacific century: Force 2030," *Defence White Paper 2009*, http://www.defence.gov.au/whitepaper/2009/docs/defence_white_paper_2009.pdf

5 Australian Government Department of Defence, *Defence White Paper 2013*, http://www.defence.gov.au/whitepaper/2013/docs/WP_2013_web.pdf

6 Australian Government Department of Defence, *Defence White Paper 2016*, http://www.defence.gov.au/WhitePaper/Docs/2016-Defence-White-Paper.pdf

The Japanese invasion and occupation of Southeast Asia during the Pacific War was a shock to the country, demonstrating its vulnerability to attack from the North and brought Australia into alliance with the US through ANZUS in 1951. As a middle power, Australian could not ensure the security of the North on its own and hoped to cement a US commitment to the defence of its area of strategic interest by contributing to America's campaigns in distant conflicts. Australia contributed troops to the Vietnam War, sharing the US' belief in the need to stop communism in the region. It also contributed troops to the US' military campaigns in Iraq and Afghanistan, expecting to strengthen the US commitment to its own security under the alliance. However, the writer Bruce Grant has claimed that "loyalty to the protector" has characterized Australian foreign policy and has stunted the development of original thinking about its strategic situation. Excessive dependence on the US has meant that Australia does not have a clear idea of what its national interests are and has an "underdeveloped sense" of a nationhood.[7] This inhibited development has spurred the movement for self-reliance over the years, particularly within Labor Party security circles, and was first reflected in the 1986 Dibb report. This report noted that geographic distance made the security of the North more important to Australia than it is to the US and that Australia should rely less on the US alliance and develop its own approach to the Northern region.[8] A middle power with vast distances to defend and a relatively small population, Australia cannot be entirely self-reliant and, though it has developed policies towards the region to give expression to that urge, Australia remains firmly committed to the US alliance.

The Australian government has stressed the importance of a rules-based regional order, one that would ensure predictability, preventing the resolution of disputes by force, and ensuring respect for international law and the UN Convention of the Law of the Sea (UNCLOS). The 2016 Defence White Paper noted that, "Australia's security and prosperity relies on a stable, rules-based global order which supports the peaceful resolution of disputes."[9] The 2017 Foreign Policy paper continued with this theme, noting that Australia would "strive to ensure international law, especially UNCLOS, is respected."[10] Defence Minister Linda Reynolds, at the Shangri-La Dialogue

---

[7] Bruce Grant, *The Crisis of Loyalty: A Study of Australian Foreign Policy* (Sydney: Angus and Robertson, 1972).

[8] Paul Dibb, *1986 Review of Australia's Defence Capabilities: Report to the Minister for Defence by Mr Paul Dibb*, www.defence.gov.au/SPI/publications/defreview/1986/Review-of-Australias-Defence-Capabilities-1986.pdf

[9] Australian Government Department of Defence, *Defence White Paper 2016*.

[10] Australian Government Department of Foreign Affairs and Trade, *Foreign Policy White Paper 2017*, www.fpwhitepaper.gov.au/foreign-policy-white-paper

in July 2019, declared that strong relationships, agreed rules and norms, and effective institutions could help to lessen and even prevent conflict in the region.[11] Most important for Australia has been promoting support for regional institutions that would build on cooperative norms and confidence-building measures to enhance security, and which would channel disputes away from conflict and towards dialogue. This means supporting ASEAN as a dialogue partner, as the regional grouping can act as a stabilizing influence for Southeast Asia. Within that grouping Indonesia assumes an important role. Though Australia has had a troubled relationship with this country, Indonesia straddles Australia's immediate security zone in the North and its security ensures Australia's security. Australia's Foreign Affairs Department has emphasized the value of the regional institutions in contributing to the security of the Asia-Pacific, and in particular the 18-member East Asia Summit (EAS) which it joined in 2005. Regarded as the premier forum for strategic dialogue in the Indo-Pacific region, the 2017 Foreign Policy paper noted that Australia would bolster its role in the EAS so that it can "positively influence the region's rules and norms." Australia's Foreign Affairs Department also pursues this aim of promoting regional norms and rules through other forums, such as the Asia-Pacific Economic Cooperation (APEC), the Asian Defence Ministers' Meeting (ADMM-Plus) and the ASEAN Regional Forum (ARF).[12]

The South China Sea

Chinese commentators have often asked why Australia should be interested in the South China Sea. The answer is not hard to find. China's behaviour in the SCS dispute acts against everything that Australia's Defence and Foreign Affairs Departments have been promoting within the region. The dispute is regarded as a test of China's relationship with the region and its future behaviour as a regional power: Would it become a regional hegemon that would disregard the rights of others while bringing the regional states into its orbit? Or would it contribute to the rules-based order and the security of Australia's northern approaches? For many years, Australian commentators gave China the benefit of the doubt and accepted the US belief, expressed by presidents from Clinton to Obama, that China would

[11] Linda Reynolds, "Shangri-La Dialogue," *Australian Government Department of Defence*, June 2, 2019, www.minister.defence.gov.au/minister/lreynolds/speeches/shangri-la-dialogue-2019

[12] Australian Government Department of Foreign Affairs and Trade, *Foreign Policy White Paper 2017*.

learn to accommodate the existing regional order, and that the good neighbour policy adopted under Jiang Zemin and Hu Jintao would ensure China's integration into that order. While that may have been the case in the past, disquieting developments under Xi Jinping have raised questions about China's intentions and its ambitions. Should China move to control the SCS and turn it into a "Chinese lake," it would be able to control the sea lanes in that area and expel the US and other external powers, including Australia. Beijing has regularly declared that it would respect freedom of navigation in the SCS but its assertive behaviour does not inspire confidence in its public pronouncements. The Australian fear is that control over the SCS would give China leverage over ASEAN and compel it to submit to Beijing's mandate, impairing the rules-based order that Australia has supported in the region.

The Chinese have called for "trust" in the relationship and have decried the attitude that Australian government and media commentators have adopted towards China. But China's moves in ejecting the Philippines from Scarborough Shoal in 2012, and using its maritime militia to harass Vietnamese, Filipino, and Indonesian fishing vessels in their respective claim areas have sounded alarm bells. When, in December 2013, China began to construct artificial islands out of the seven features it occupied in the Spratly Islands area Australian concern was heightened. China built 3,000 metre runways on three of those features, Subi, Fiery Cross and Mischief Reefs, and radar facilities, hangars for aircraft, and storage buildings on others that had observers wondering about their purpose. When Xi Jinping met President Obama in September 2015, he gave an assurance that China would not militarize the SCS.[13] Subsequently the Asia Maritime Transparency Initiative (AMTI) reported that underground tunnels, missile shelters, radars, and high-frequency antennas were constructed on the features, while missile batteries were deployed there and military transport aircraft including a H-6K bomber from Woody, or Yongxing, Island have landed there.[14] These events stimulated an "awakening" within the Australian security community in regard to China and its intentions. Xi Jinping's assurance was understood as diplomatic deceit intended to lull listeners into a false sense of complacency and an indication of what could be expected from Beijing in the future. Indeed, what trust could there be in this relationship?

---

[13] David Brunnstrom and Martina Michael, "Xi denies China turning artificial islands into military bases," *Reuters*, September 26, 2015, www.reuters.com/article/us-usa-china-pacific/xi-denies-china-turning-artificial-islands-into-military-bases-idUSKCN0RP1ZH2015092

[14] Asia Maritime Transparency 2018, "Comparing Aerial and Satellite Images of China's Spratly Outpost," February 16, 2018, amti.csis.org/comparing-aerial-satellite-images-chinas-spratly-outposts

A second event that contributed to this "awakening" was China's belligerent disavowal of the Arbitral Tribunal's ruling of July 12, 2016. Prompted by China's actions in squeezing it out of Scarborough Shoal, the Philippines in January 2013 appealed to the Arbitral Tribunal of the South China Sea to rule on the legality of China's claims. When the Tribunal ruled that China's claim, the "nine-dash line," and its insistence on historical rights, had been superseded by its membership of UNCLOS, Beijing launched into a campaign to discredit the ruling. China's attitude cut to the heart of Australia's efforts to promote a rules-based order in the region, one that would bind the great powers and prevent the resolution of disputes by force. Foreign Minister Julie Bishop told the media that China would suffer "reputational damage" if it did not recognize the ruling, which she said was "final and binding on both parties."[15] Bishop had earlier criticized China for declaring an Air Defence Identification Zone (ADIZ) over the East China Sea in November 2013, and this latest statement drew a venomous response from Beijing.[16] The opposition Labor Party's shadow minister for defence Stephen Conroy declared that China has been engaged in an "aggressive and at times bullying performance" and called upon the Australian government to act if China flouted the "international rules-based order." Conroy called upon the government to join the US in its Freedom of Navigation Operations (FONOPs) in the SCS.[17] The government could not let an opposition senator force its hand over the SCS and Conroy's remarks were disowned by both Julie Bishop and Prime Minister Malcolm Turnbull, who accused him of escalating tensions in the dispute.[18] Nonetheless, Conroy's remarks tapped the disquiet in Australia in relation to China's actions and, as the *Sydney Morning Herald* noted, Beijing's dismissive response to the Arbitral Tribunal's ruling demonstrated that Australia should uphold the rules and norms in the region because as a middle power, "Australia relies heavily on the rules-based order and has a particular interesting in making sure it's maintained."[19]

---

15 Lisa Murray, "China accuses Julie Bishop of 'undermining peace,'" *Financial Review*, July 15, 2016.

16 Lisa Murray, "Bishop stands form on China Aggression," *The Australian Financial Review*, July 13, 2016.

17 "South China Sea Dispute: Labor's Stephen Conroy calls for Australia to challenge 'bullying' China," *Sydney Morning Herald*, July 13, 2016.

18 Malcolm Farr, "Australian Senator Stephen Conroy accused inflaming tensions in the South China Sea," *news.com.au*, July 13, 2016, www.news.com.au/world/asia/australian-senator-stephen-conroy-accused-on-inflaming-tensions-in-the-south-china-sea/news-tory/c2b0515a6fe71459fff7a5d6fe60e824

19 David Wroe, "South China Sea dispute: Beijing's response shows just why we need the law," *The Sydney Morning Herald*, July 13, 2016, https://www.smh.com.au/politics/federal/south-china-sea-dispute-beijings-response-shows-just-why-we-need-the-law-20160713-gq4dhb.html

In Singapore, Defence Minister Christopher Pyne said that China was "eroding regional confidence and increasing anxiety" through its land reclamation activities in the SCS, which he called "international waters." Pyne called for closer defence cooperation with Japan, and welcomed the expansion of its defence forces and predicted that Australia and Japan would conduct more operations in the SCS.[20]

What concerned Australia was the possibility of regional disruption and instability as a result of various possible scenarios in the SCS. One scenario was Chinese action to eject Vietnam from features it had occupied, or an escalation from Vietnamese action against Chinese intrusion into its claim area. A second scenario was a clash between China and the US as the Americans proceed with their FONOPs or some unforeseen miscalculation as events spiral out of control. Some 60 per cent of Australia's trade went through the SCS, and though those trade routes could be rerouted around the SCS considerable disruption would result. Australia's energy security would be also disrupted by conflict or instability there as it imports 52 per cent of its refined petroleum from refineries in Singapore, 18 per cent from South Korea and 12 per cent from Japan. Refineries in Australia have been closing due to high costs and Australia has not maintained the required 90-day stockpile against such contingencies.[21]

The prospect of regional disorder is a cause for anxiety in Australia and, as the 2016 Defence White Paper noted, the "combination of competing territorial claims and growth in military capability has the potential to destabilize the region and threaten Australia's interests." The white paper stressed that Australia did not need take sides on competing territorial claims in the SCS but is concerned that China's land reclamations in the SCS raises tensions in the region. It declared that Australia was particularly "concerned by the unprecedented pace and scale of China's land reclamation activities," and opposed the use of artificial structures in the SCS for military purposes."[22] The 2017 Foreign Policy White Paper noted that the SCS is a "major fault line in the regional order" and that Australia called upon the claimants to clarify their claims according to UNCLOS and "reaffirmed" its position that the Arbitral Tribunals ruling was "final and binding on both parties."[23] Both

---

20 Jake Sturmer, "Christopher Pyne says China has raised regional 'anxiety' over its activities in the South China Sea," *ABC News*, January 28, 2019, www.abc.net.au/news/2019-01-28/christopher-pyne-says-china-is-raises-anxiety-in-region-over-scs/10756224

21 "Australia imports all of its oil, and there are pitfalls all over the globe," *The Conversation*, May 24, 2018, http://theconversation.com/australia-imports-almost-all-of-its-oil-and-there-are-pitfalls-all-over-the-globe-97070

22 Australian Government Department of Defence, *Defence White Paper 2016*.

23 Australian Government Department of Foreign Affairs and Trade, *Foreign Policy White Paper 2017*.

defence and foreign policy white papers opposed "the assertion of associated territorial claims and maritime rights which are not in accordance with international law, including UNCLOS." Needless to say, Australia's official position and its expressed concern for the security of the region heightened tensions with China and exacerbated Australia's dilemma of pursuing its security interests while maintaining its economic relationship with China as its major trading partner.

China presses Australia

The economic relationship with China has been the main source of Australia's growth and prosperity over the past two decades. Australia's Reserve Bank has noted that China accounts for 30 per cent of Australia's exports and around 20 per cent of its imports. Australia's exports to China are mainly primary resources, with iron ore and coal accounting for 57 per cent of the total, but China has also become the largest single export market for Australia's manufactured food items. Australia's service exports to China, comprising tourism, education, and financial services, are greater than those to the US and Britain; some 200,000 mainland Chinese students attend Australian schools and universities contributing to the growth of many university departments, business and accounting schools in particular. However, despite the growth of this economic relationship, China is not a major investor in Australia, ranking ninth with only 3 per cent of total investment, well behind the US with 30 per cent.[24] Beijing has not been beneath using this trade dependence to place pressure on the Australian government to change its position over the SCS. Editorials in Chinese state media, the *China Daily* and the *Global Times*, have regularly berated Australia, declaring that the relationship had deteriorated and calling on Australia's leaders to take measures to improve it. The Chinese Ambassador to Australia, Cheng Jingye, in June 2018 castigated Australia for its "Cold War mentality," accusing it of "bias and bigotry" which had to change if relations with China were to improve. Cheng Jingye threatened Australia with a "trade war" if did not increase "mutual trust" in the relationship.[25]

[24] Reserve Bank, "Australia's Deepening Economic Relationship with China: Opportunities and Risks; Philip Lowe Governor Address to the Australia-China Relations Institute Sydney," May 23, 2018, www.rba.gov.au/speeches/2018/pdf/sp-gov-2018-05-23.pdf

[25] Gavin Fernando, "China has threatened Australia with a trade war if 'growing lack of trust' continues," *news.com.au*, April 20, 2018, https://www.news.com.au/finance/economy/world-economy/china-has-threatened-australia-with-a-trade-war-if-growing-lack-of-trust-continues/news-story/d32f3dc0267906034af733876e6e2ef3

Beijing has attempted to exploit Australia's economic dependence and the fears of its business community by threatening a disruption of the trading relationship upon which Australia's economic growth has depended. Beijing cannot hope to detach Australia from the US alliance, but it may intimidate its leaders with the intention of socializing Australian leaders into what Beijing calls correct behaviour in this relationship. Beijing would expect Australia to stay silent over the SCS and desist from tighter security cooperation with the US or with Japan in the SCS. In this connection, a campaign orchestrated by people with links to the Chinese Communist Party has been orchestrated to control the public discourse in Australia. In terms of extent and consistency this campaign, as monitored by the journalist John Garnaut and the author Clive Hamilton, has been unprecedented for a Western democratic political system.[26] Described as a "political warfare campaign" against Australia's national security community, the Chinese have attempted to swing the business community to their side by threatening trade disruption and hoping that government would be unsettled by the prospect of economic loss to desist from its current position over the SCS.[27] Former government officials have been given lucrative positions in Chinese companies and have come out in defence of Beijing and its activities. Former Ambassador to China, Andrew Raby, publicly demanded the sacking of Julie Bishop after her comments on the SCS; Raby operates a business in Beijing and sits on the board of Chinese companies in Australia. Former Foreign Minister Bob Carr was made director of the Chinese-funded Australia-China Institute and consistently supported Beijing's policies out of a misguided sense of duty.

Former Prime Minister Paul Keating, who was appointed to the advisory council to the China Development Bank, has said that the SCS does not concern Australia, which should allow a growing power like China strategic space. He thought that Australia was taking an excessively "hawkish view" of China's rise.[28] The property developer Huang Xiangmo was a billionaire aligned with the Chinese Communist Party (CCP), who settled in Australia in 2011, though his background and source of funds was unclear. He headed the Chinese lobby group called Australia Council for the Promotion of the Peaceful Reunification of China (ACPPRC), which would approach

[26] Clive Hamilton, *Silent Invasion: China's influence in Australia* (Richmond, Victoria: Hardie Grant, 2018).

[27] Ross Babbage. "Comprehensive coercion: China's 'political warfare' campaign against Australia." *The Strategist Australian Strategic Policy Institute (ASPI)*. June 5, 2018. www.aspistrategist.org.au/chinas-cold-war-campaign-against-australia/

[28] Andrew Greene, "Former prime minister Paul Keating attacks security agencies on China stance," *ABC News*, May 6, 2019, www.abc.net.au/radio/programs/am/former-pm-paul-keating-attacks-security-agencies-on-china-stance/11081978

government agencies warning them that Australia's relations with China would be damaged if they allowed critical views of China. Huang regularly made donations to both political parties, the Liberal-National Coalition and the Labor Party. After Labor Party Senator Stephen Conroy made his speech criticizing China over the South China Sea (see earlier) Huang cancelled the donation of US$400,000 to the Labor Party that he had earlier promised. Huang did achieve a coup of sorts when in June 2016 he managed to get an unwary and naïve Labor senator to endorse China's position on the SCS. Standing next to Huang, Senator Sam Dastyari told the audience that: "The Chinese integrity of its borders is a matter for China," and that, "And the best way of maintaining that relationship (with China) is knowing when it is and isn't our place to be involved."[29] However, Huang's success was fleeting as uproar ensued. Dastyari had contradicted Labor Party policy and was obliged to resign from politics in June 2018.

A backlash against Chinese activities followed. Former Prime Minister John Howard warned that China could use its one million expats in Australia to gain influence and that Huawei could be used in cyber operations to gather intelligence.[30] Former Ambassador to China, Stephen Fitzgerald, declared that China's influence-peddling brought Australian and Chinese national interests and values into confrontation, challenging fundamental values such as "freedom of speech and the media and enquiry and the very validity of our political system."[31] In June 2018, the Australian Parliament passed the National Security Legislation Amendment (Espionage and Foreign Interference) Act 2018, which targeted foreign interference in politics. Though China was not mentioned specifically, it was understood who was the main target. The legislation required cabinet ministers, politicians and public servants and lobbyists acting on behalf of foreign governments to be listed on a public register.[32] In February 2019, the government finally banned Huawei from participating in the 5G national broadband network as a security risk. There was widespread concern that the Chinese

[29] Quentin McDermott, "Sam Dastyari defended China's policy in South China Sea in defiance of Labor policy, secret recording reveals," *ABC News*, November 29, 2017, www.abc.net.au/news/2017-11-29/sam-dastyari-secret-south-china-sea-recordings/9198044

[30] Matthew Doran, "Senate rushes through foreign interference legislation before by-elections across the country," *ABC News*, June 28, 2018, www.abc.net.au/news/2018-06-28/foreign-interference-legislation-passes/9914480

[31] Chris Uhlmann, "Chinese influence 'challenging fundamentals' of Australia, says Stephen FitzGerald," *ABC News*, September 28, 2016, www.abc.net.au/news/2016-09-28/former-australia-ambassador-to-china-warns-government-of-beijing/7885140

[32] Doran, "Senate rushes through foreign interference legislation before by-elections across the country."

telecommunications company would be required to gather and share intelligence with the CCP. The ban was a result of reports by Australian intelligence agencies that had examined Chinese activities in attempting to influence Australian policy, and gain access to all levels of government.[33] Relations with China deteriorated as a consequence, as China began to make life difficult for Australian exporters in what was described as the application of selected economic sanctions against the country. Import restrictions on Australian coal were imposed and were subject to stringent environmental tests, the same tests were not applied to Indonesian, Russian, or Mongolian coal imports, and wine imports from Australia were held up by Chinese customs agencies. This was understood as retaliation for the ban on Huawei and also Defence Minister Christopher Pyne's speech, when he castigated China over its activities in the South China Sea.[34]

Beijing's hopes of ensuring Australia's neutrality in the SCS dispute by gaining an influential position in Australian politics were doomed to fail. The business community and Australia's exporters would not be allowed to decide policy over issues that had become fundamental, nor could former politicians who had profited from their positions in Chinese companies openly defend Chinese activities in the SCS without being disowned. China's push into the SCS and its rejection of the Arbitral Tribunal's ruling disturbed Australia and created the perception of a China that would increasingly ignore the rules and norms that Australia values, and that would rely on power and force to achieve a dominant position, not only in the SCS but the Western Pacific as well. In its campaign of domestic political infiltration Beijing may have hoped that political donations and the influence of the business community would bring about a change in this view, and that Australia would ignore the SCS and its activities in the region. Beijing's failure in this effort reveals its inability to understand the role of a free press in a Western democracy and how it can expose shady backroom deals and dubious political donations to public scrutiny. Moreover, it illustrates that states have evolved certain geopolitical positions that are regarded as vital for their security and which cannot be traded for transitory business benefits.

Other issues have arisen which reveal that the SCS is not the only one that impacts upon Australia's relationship with China. China has moved into the South Pacific enlisting Papua New Guinea, Vanuatu, Fiji, Samoa, Tonga, and

---

[33] John Gapper, "Huawei a security risk too great for 5G," *The Financial Review*, February 1, 2019, https://www.ft.com/content/40e68898-23b8-11e9-8ce6-5db4543da632

[34] Michael Lelyveld, "China bans coal in political rift," *Radio Free Asia*, April 9, 2019, www.rfa.org/english/commentaries/energy_watch/china-bars-australian-coal-04292019102656.html

others to its Belt and Road Initiative. Australia's Minister for International Development and the Pacific, Concetta Fierravanti-Wells, accused China of pursuing its debt-trap diplomacy in the region by saddling these small states with huge debts.[35] Chinese developmental assistance in the South Pacific would not have aroused so much attention but for the SCS issue, which has made Australia wary of China's intentions, and China's move into the area has been viewed as an intrusion into Australia's geopolitical space. Australian Prime Minister Scott Morrison has called the South Pacific the "front and centre of Australia's strategic outlook, our foreign policy and our personnel connections."[36] Australia has sought to involve both the UK as well as France, which regards itself as a Pacific power and maintains military bases in French Polynesia and New Caledonia. When Australian Prime Minister Scott Morrison met French President Emanuel Macron in June 2018 they agreed on a closer alignment of interests in the South Pacific and cooperation in development assistance and investment. What is interesting about this new French connection is that in previous decades Australians resented the French presence in the South Pacific as colonialist, and vigorously opposed French nuclear tests there. Chinese activities, however, have brought them together.[37] Furthermore, Australian public attitudes towards Beijing were being increasingly influenced by media reports of the protest movement in Hong Kong. An editorial in the *Australian Financial Review* opined that Hong Kong will be a test case for China as to what kind of "superpower" it will be.[38]

Geopolitics and the future

Australia views China through the lens of the SCS and its perceptions have been reinforced by China's behaviour and activities in other areas, such as the South Pacific. Australians have had little experience of China and within government many had assumed that constructing a relationship with it would be similar to dealing with Singapore or Malaysia. It was assumed that China would assimilate the liberal conception of international intercourse, with

---

[35] Catherine Graue and Stephen Dziedzic, "Federal Minister Concetta Fierravanti-Wells accuses China of funding 'roads that go nowhere' in Pacific," *ABC News,* updated January 9, 2018, www.abc.net.au/news/2018-01-10/australia-hits-out-at-chinese-aid-to-pacific/9316732

[36] Greg Brown, "PM's French Pacific solution," *The Australian*, June 28, 2019.

[37] Greg Sheridan, "France welcomed as bulwark against China," *The Australian*, June 28, 2019, https://www.theaustralian.com.au/commentary/french-welcomed-as-bulwark-against-china/news-story/306383eeba9f160e2d06259ee54e80be

[38] "Hong Kong is now a test of China's future," *Australian Financial Review*, July 9, 2019, https://www.afr.com/world/asia/hong-kong-is-now-a-test-of-china-s-future-20190708-p525ax

its emphasis on multilateral institutions and international law, and would respect the geopolitical space of others. Under Xi Jinping, however, China's behaviour has been a rude awakening in the SCS and a reminder of Australia's vulnerability before a growing power that may overturn the regional order Australia has attempted to promote in its North. Beijing could have done things differently in the SCS, and had it promoted international law and norms of cooperation it would have gained the trust and respect it seeks. However, it has been distressing for Australia to learn that China works to another agenda and according to a value system that differs considerably from their own. Within Australian security circles the view is that Australia has no other option but to deny the legitimacy of Chinese claims to the SCS and that the issue is a fundamental one, and not something that it can compromise on or ignore. Head of the Australian Policy Institute Peter Jennings wrote that China presents "more risks than opportunities" and that Australia has witnessed the end of the era of "peaceful rise" that has been replaced by "an assertive, dangerously nationalistic, Leninist one party state intent on replacing the US as the region's dominant power."[39] He recommended that Australia reduce economic dependence on China and diversify its economic and business ties. Such diversification may be forced upon Australia by Beijing's resort to trade as a weapon of influence in any case.

In the past, those who searched for more self-reliance and less dependence upon the US considered the idea of positioning Australia between the US and China, or actually mediating between the two. Self-reliance in this sense meant glossing over the SCS as an issue that did not concern Australia. The most prominent spokesman of this view was Hugh White who, in 2013, argued that the US should "share power" or make way for China and that Australia should have a role in making this possible.[40] By 2019, White argued that China had disturbed the regional equilibrium and threatened US naval preponderance in the Asia-Pacific and that the US had no credible response to the China challenge. White concluded that Australia has had to develop its own defences, including a submarine and air force capability, in a maritime sea denial role against a China that attempted to project power against Australia or its neighbours. He even suggested nuclear weapons for Australia, though that has no support in government and the community.[41] Former Deputy

---

[39] Peter Jennings, "Big challenges for Australia in a changing world order," *Australian Strategic and Policy Institute,* April 27, 2019, www.aspi.org.au/opinion/big-challenges-australia-changing-world-order

[40] Hugh White, *The China Choice: Why America should share power* (Collingwood, Victoria: Black, 2013).

[41] Hugh White, "With China's swift rise as a naval power, Australia needs to rethink how it defends itself," *The Conversation*, July 2, 2019, theconversation.com/

Secretary of Defence Paul Dibb opined that China's projection of military power in the SCS was threatening to constrain Australia's ability to defend its maritime approaches; he also called for an expansion of Australia's defence capabilities to deny the northern approaches to a "well armed adversary."[42] Defence commentator Ross Babbage similarly argued for a strengthened capability, saying that Australia should offer to host a wide range of American combat and combat support units on a permanent basis.[43] As a middle power, Australia cannot match China's capabilities in the Western Pacific on its own. An expansion of the defence force would be supplemented by strengthened security relationships with regional partners, such as Japan and those in ASEAN who also feel the pressure from China and are concerned about its activities in the SCS. Increasingly, the proponents of self-reliance call for a collective regional approach to China which could also bring in Vietnam and India in what would be an Indo-Pacific strategy to provide a counterweight to China.

Conclusion

China has intruded on Australia's geopolitical space or what Australia's leaders regard as a protective zone to the north through which their sea lanes and trade flows. China's efforts to expand its presence in the SCS and to harass the ASEAN claimants have had a seminal impact upon Australian views of China. In previous years, Australians had a hopeful view of China, expecting it to adjust to the existing regional order and providing support for the region's economic growth. The SCS issue, it was thought, could be manageable in that context and China and ASEAN would come to an eventual resolution. However, China's behaviour and activities have deflated those hopes. Its actions in building military facilities on occupied features in the SCS, in contradiction to President Xi's assurance to President Obama, were seen as threatening freedom of navigation. China's dismissal of the Arbitral Tribunal's ruling cut to the core of Australia's promotion of

with-chinas-swift-rise-as-naval-power-australia-needs-to-rethink-how-it-defends-itself-119459

42 Paul Dibb, Richard Brabin-Smith and Brendan Sargeant, "Why Australia needs a radically new defence policy," *Strategic & Defence Studies Centre ANU College of Asia & the Pacific*, October 2018, http://sdsc.bellschool.anu.edu.au/sites/default/files/publications/attachments/2018-11/cog_44_web.pdf; Paul Dibb, "Australia needs more missiles and combat pilots," *The Canberra Times*, July 10, 2019.

43 Ross Babbage. "Game plan – The need to rethink our national security strategy." *Defence Connect*. June 3, 2018. www.defenceconnect.com.au/blog/4160-game-plan-the-need-to-rethink-our-national-security-strategy

a rules-based order and was a denial of everything that Australia has valued. What China would do in the SCS it may well do elsewhere. Moreover, Beijing's attempts to influence domestic politics in its favour by controlling the national discourse over the SCS has left a bitter legacy among Australian policy makers, who perceive all too clearly the values that separate them. As a Western democracy in an Asia-Pacific regional setting Australia feels the values clash keenly and cannot allow itself to accommodate Chinese power in the way Beijing expects. It will promote a strategy of self-reliance within the US alliance while reaching out to forge security partnerships within the Indo-Pacific region to bring about some kind of counterbalance to China. In this way Australia will protect its geopolitical space.

References

Asia Maritime Transparency. "Comparing aerial and satellite images of China's Spratly outpost." February 16, 2018. amti.csis.org/comparing-aerial-satellite-images-chinas-spratly-outposts

"Australia imports almost all of its oil, and there are pitfalls all over the globe." *The Conversation*. May 24, 2018. http://theconversation.com/australia-imports-almost-all-of-its-oil-and-there-are-pitfalls-all-over-the-globe-97070

Australian Government Department of Defence. "Defending Australia in the Asia Pacific century: Force 2030." *Defence White Paper 2009*. http://www.defence.gov.au/whitepaper/2009/docs/defence_white_paper_2009.pdf

Australian Government Department of Defence. "Defence White Paper 2013." http://www.defence.gov.au/whitepaper/2013/docs/WP_2013_web.pdf

Australian Government Department of Defence. "Defence White Paper 2016." http://www.defence.gov.au/WhitePaper/Docs/2016-Defence-White-Paper.pdf

Australian Government. "2017 Foreign Policy White Paper." *Department of Foreign Affairs and Trade*. www.fpwhitepaper.gov.au/foreign-policy-white-paper

"Australian Senator Stephen Conroy accused on inflaming tensions in the South China Sea." *news.com.au*. July 13, 2016. www.news.com.au/world/asia/australian-senator-stephen-conroy-accused-on-inflaming-tensions-in-the-south-china-sea/news-tory/c2b0515a6fe71459fff7a5d6fe60e824

Babbage, Ross. "Game plan – The need to rethink our national security strategy." *Defence Connect*. June 3, 2018. www.defenceconnect.com.au/blog/4160-game-plan-the-need-to-rethink-our-national-security-strategy.

Babbage, Ross. "Comprehensive coercion: China's 'political warfare' campaign against Australia." *The Strategist Australian Strategic Policy Institute (ASPI).* June 5, 2018. www.aspistrategist.org.au/chinas-cold-war-campaign-against-australia/

Brown, Greg. "PM's French Pacific solution." *The Australian.* June 28, 2019.

Brunnstrom, David, and Martina Michael. "Xi denies China turning artificial islands into military bases." *Reuters.* September 26, 2015. www.reuters.com/article/us-usa-china-pacific/xi-denies-china-turning-artificial-islands-into-military-bases-idUSKCN0RP1ZH2015092

Buszynski, Leszek. *The Geopolitics of the Western Pacific: China, Japan, and the United States.* New York: Routledge, 2019.

"China has threatened Australia with a trade war if 'growing lack of trust' continues." *news.com.au.* April 20, 2018. www.news.com.au/finance/economy/world-economy/china-has-threatened-australia-with-a-trade-war-if-growing-lack-of-trust-continues/news-story/d32f3dc026790

"Christopher Pyne says China has raised regional 'anxiety' over its activities in the South China Sea." *ABC News.* January 28, 2019. https://www.abc.net.au/news/2019-01-28/christopher-pyne-says-china-is-raises-anxiety-in-region-over-scs/10756224

Dibb, Paul. "Review of Australia's defence capabilities: Report to the Minister for Defence by Mr Paul Dibb." March 1986. www.defence.gov.au/SPI/publications/defreview/1986/Review-of-Australias-Defence-Capabilities-1986.pdf

Dibb, Paul. "Australia needs more missiles and combat pilots," *The Canberra Times.* July 10, 2019. https://www.canberratimes.com.au/story/6254377/australia-must-review-defence-force-in-light-of-china-threat/

Dibb, Paul, Richard Brabin-Smith and Brendan Sargeant. "Why Australia needs a radically new defence policy," *Strategic & Defence Studies Centre ANU College of Asia & the Pacific.* October 2018. http://sdsc.bellschool.anu.edu.au/sites/default/files/publications/attachments/2018-11/cog_44_web.pdf

Doran, Matthew. "Senate rushes through foreign interference legislation before by-elections across the country." *ABC News.* June 28, 2018. www.abc.net.au/news/2018-06-28/foreign-interference-legislation-passes/9914480

Fernando, Gavin. "China has threatened Australia with a trade war if 'growing lack of trust' continues." *news.com.au.* April 20, 2018. https://www.news.com.au/finance/economy/world-economy/china-has-threatened-australia-with-a-trade-war-if-growing-lack-of-trust-continues/news-story/d32f3dc0267906034af733876e6e2ef3

Gapper, John. "Huawei a security risk too great for 5G." *The Financial Review.* February 1, 2019. https://www.ft.com/content/40e68898-23b8-11e9-8ce6-5db4543da632

Grant, Bruce. *The Crisis of Loyalty: A Study of Australian Foreign Policy*. Sydney: Angus and Robertson, 1972.

Graue Catherine and Stephen Dziedzic. "Federal minister Concetta Fierravanti-Wells accuses China of funding 'roads that go nowhere' in Pacific." *ABC News*. Updated January 9, 2018. www.abc.net.au/news/2018-01-10/australia-hits-out-at-chinese-aid-to-pacific/9316732

Greene, Andrew. "Former prime minister Paul Keating attacks security agencies on China stance." *ABC News*. May 6, 2019. www.abc.net.au/radio/programs/am/former-pm-paul-keating-attacks-security-agencies-on-china-stance/11081978

Hamilton, Clive. *Silent Invasion: China's Influence in Australia*. Richmond, Victoria: Hardie Grant, 2018.

"Hong Kong is now a test of China's future." *Australian Financial Review*. July 9, 2019. https://www.afr.com/world/asia/hong-kong-is-now-a-test-of-china-s-future-20190708-p525ax

Jennings, Peter. "Big challenges for Australia in a changing world order." *Australian Strategic and Policy Institute*. April 27, 2019. https://www.aspi.org.au/opinion/big-challenges-australia-changing-world-order-0

"John Howard warns China could use its expats to grow influence in Australia and the region." *ABC News*. Updated June 27, 2018. www.abc.net.au/news/2018-06-28/john-howard-warns-china-could-use-expats-to-grow-power-in-region/9918114

Lelyveld, Michael. "China bans coal in political rift." *Radio Free Asia*. April 9, 2019. www.rfa.org/english/commentaries/energy_watch/china-bars-australian-coal-04292019102656.html

McDermott, Quentin. "Sam Dastyari defended China's policy in South China Sea in defiance of Labor policy, secret recording reveals." *ABC News*. November 29, 2017. www.abc.net.au/news/2017-11-29/sam-dastyari-secret-south-china-sea-recordings/9198044

Murray, L. "Bishop stands firm on China aggression." *The Australian Financial Review*. July 13, 2016.

Murray, L. "China accuses Julie Bishop of 'undermining peace,'" *Financial Review*, July 15, 2016. https://www.afr.com/politics/china-accuses-julie-bishop-of-undermining-peace-20160715-gq6cf1

Parliament of Australia. *The Defence of Australia (1987 Defence White Paper)*. www.aph.gov.au/About_Parliament/Parliamentary_Departments/Parliamentary_Library/pubs/rp/rp1516/DefendAust/1987#_Toc427833142

Reserve Bank. "Australia's deepening economic relationship with China: Opportunities and risks; Philip Lowe governor address to the Australia-China Relations Institute Sydney." May 23, 2018. www.rba.gov.au/speeches/2018/pdf/sp-gov-2018-05-23.pdf

Reynolds, Linda. "Shangri-La Dialogue," *Australian Government Department of Defence*. June 2, 2019. www.minister.defence.gov.au/minister/lreynolds/speeches/shangri-la-dialogue-2019

Sheridan, Greg. "France welcomed as bulwark against China." *The Australian*. June 28, 2019. https://www.theaustralian.com.au/commentary/french-welcomed-as-bulwark-against-china/news-story/306383eeba9f160e2d06259ee54e80be

"South China Sea dispute: Labor's Stephen Conroy calls for Australia to challenge 'bullying' China." *Sydney Morning Herald*. July 13, 2016.

Sturmer, Jake. "Christopher Pyne backs Japanese defence spending amid concerns over strike capability." *ABC News*. 23 January 23, 2019. www.abc.net.au/news/2019-01-23/christopher-pyne-japan-defence-spending-izumo-refit/10743810

Uhlmann, Chris. "Chinese influence 'challenging fundamentals' of Australia, says Stephen FitzGerald." *ABC News*. September 28, 2016. www.abc.net.au/news/2016-09-28/former-australia-ambassador-to-china-warns-government-of-beijing/7885140

White, Hugh. *The China Choice: Why America Should Share Power*. Collingwood, Victoria: Black Inc, 2013.

White, Hugh. "With China's swift rise as naval power, Australia needs to rethink how it defends itself." *The Conversation*, July 2, 2019. theconversation.com/with-chinas-swift-rise-as-naval-power-australia-needs-to-rethink-how-it-defends-itself-119459

Wroe, David. "South China Sea dispute: Beijing's response shows just why we need the law." *The Sydney Morning Herald*. July 13, 2016. https://www.smh.com.au/politics/federal/south-china-sea-dispute-beijings-response-shows-just-why-we-need-the-law-20160713-gq4dhb.html

15

India and the South China Sea Crucible: Cautious Inclinations of an Extra-Regional "Leading Power"

Sourabh Gupta

Introduction

On January 26, 2015, in New Delhi, Barack Obama became the first US president to grace India's prestigious Republic Day parade as its chief guest of honour. A day earlier, President Obama and Indian Prime Minister, Narendra Modi, had issued a *Joint Strategic Vision for the Asia-Pacific and Indian Ocean Region*. Noting that "a closer partnership between the United States (US) and India was indispensable to promoting peace, prosperity and stability" in the Indo-Pacific region, the two leaders, in their *Joint Strategic Vision*, affirmed:[1]

> the importance of safeguarding maritime security and ensuring freedom of navigation and over flight throughout the region, *especially in the South China Sea* [emphasis added] [and] ... call on all parties to avoid the threat or use of force and pursue resolution of territorial and maritime disputes through all peaceful means, in accordance with universally recognized principles of

[1] Ministry of External Affairs, Government of India. "US-India Joint Strategic Vision for the Asia-Pacific and Indian Ocean Region." January 25, 2015.

> international law, including the United Nations Convention on the Law of the Sea.

The direct reference to the South China Sea (SCS) was among the first of its kind in a heads-of-government level communiqué featuring the US and India.

A year and a half later, in the course of an address to a joint session of the US Congress, Prime Minister Modi declared that India and the US had finally shed their "hesitations of history." Peering ahead ambitiously, he averred that, "[a] strong India-U.S. partnership can anchor peace, prosperity and stability from Asia to Africa and from Indian Ocean to the Pacific. It can also help ensure security of the sea lanes of commerce and freedom of navigation on seas."[2] India and the US, in the Prime Minister's telling, shared congruent security interests across the vast Western Pacific and Indian Ocean maritime space writ large. In the years to come, New Delhi would grow into the role as a privileged partner and quasi-ally of Washington in the region, including in the critical, and contested, maritime cockpit of the Indo-Pacific – the SCS.

Barely two years later, on June 1, 2018, Prime Minister Narendra Modi was singing a different tune to the gathered audience of defence ministers, uniformed officers, and defence specialists at the prestigious Shangri-La Dialogue in Singapore. In the course of one of the great foreign policy speeches on Asia by an Indian prime minister, Modi observed that New Delhi did not envision the Indo-Pacific as:[3]

> a strategy or as a club of limited members … nor as a grouping that seeks to dominate. And by no means do we consider it as directed against any country [read: China] … [India would work] individually or in formats of three or more for a stable and peaceful region. *But our friendships are not alliances of containment* [emphasis added].

Inclusiveness, openness, and ASEAN centrality would reside at the heart of India's "Act East" policy and China was, "an important pillar of this … shared vision of an open, stable, secure and prosperous Indo-Pacific Region."[4] Prime Minister Modi thereafter went on to lay out the purposes and principles

---

2 Ministry of External Affairs, "Prime Minister's remarks at the US Congress." June 8, 2016.

3 Ministry of External Affairs, "Prime Minister's Keynote Address at Shangri-La Dialogue." June 1, 2018.

4 Ministry of External Affairs, "Keynote Address."

of India's engagement with the world to its east, many of which share an uncanny resemblance with ASEAN's own recently released "ASEAN Outlook on the Indo-Pacific." These themes were further elaborated upon in Modi's "Indo-Pacific Oceans" Initiative, unveiled a year later at the 14th East Asia Summit in Bangkok.

So, which of the two visions is New Delhi's authentic strategic vision – both for the Indo-Pacific region at large and for Maritime Southeast Asia and the SCS in particular? Will it seek to forge a "natural alliance" of democratic states along the Indo-Pacific rim, framed in conscious distinction to China and ready to intervene within the latter's core regional interests, including in the SCS? Or will it seek to articulate an open and inclusive Asian model of cooperative security that is keyed to regional tradition and historical circumstance and accommodative of China's core interests, including in the SCS?

In the vast expanse of its Indian Ocean Region (IOR) of "primary" interest, a variant of the former of the two visions is likely to prevail. The Indian and the US navies already conduct high-intensity amphibious and anti-submarine drills in these waters and New Delhi, of its own accord, has been on a veritable tear to stitch up its own sub-regional "string of pearls" of littoral ports-based access and logistics facilities, intelligence exchange, and coastal surveillance arrangements in this crucial thoroughfare. By contrast, east of Sumatra, as this chapter will argue, it is the latter vision that will prevail, with India seeking to loosely balance power within while remaining conspicuously committed to a non-Western, pluralistic model of cooperative security in East Asia and the Asia-Pacific.

The breadth of India's political, strategic, and maritime engagement with Southeast Asia and in the SCS is broad. This chapter will lay out a wide-angled view of India's maritime cooperation diplomacy and the Indian Navy's operational activities in these waters over the past decade. This breadth of activities notwithstanding, the depth of India's political and defence cooperation diplomacy, and naval engagement with its Southeast Asian counterparts remains shallow. It is instructive in this regard to note what New Delhi does *not* provide, conduct, or engage in east of Malacca, especially in the SCS – despite inherent capabilities as well as a standing invitation on the part of certain littoral states, notably Vietnam, to do considerably more. The chapter will illustrate such instances of restraint, including by drawing upon New Delhi's response to the SCS (*Philippines v. China*) Arbitral Tribunal award as a prime example. It will also draw a contrast between India's restraint east of Sumatra with its budding naval diplomacy west of Sumatra with certain Southeast Asian states (Myanmar, Thailand, Indonesia) as well as its active diplomatic and naval engagements with rim states in South Asia (Sri Lanka, Maldives) and the Southern Indian Ocean tier (Seychelles, Mauritius). The chapter will conclude by positing that, barring a paradigm-shift in the geopolitics of the SCS caused by hostile Chinese conduct or aggressive designs by Beijing in New Delhi's own Indian Ocean backyard, India's cautions inclinations will not shift markedly.

India and Maritime Southeast Asia: growing habits of cooperation

India has been a long-standing external stakeholder in Maritime Southeast Asia. Since 1988, ONGC Videsh Limited (OVL), the overseas arm of India's flagship national oil and gas company, has prospected for hydrocarbon resources in Block 06.1 in the Nam Con Son Basin off the southern Vietnamese coast. Despite periodic expressions of displeasure by Beijing – Block 06.1 resides within the "nine-dash line" as well as Vietnam's 200 nautical mile coastal limit – production continues to this day. The Indian Navy has not been shy to show its flag either. In April 2002, in the aftermath of 9/11, it provided naval escorts for high-value commercial traffic traversing the Straits of Malacca, as part of US-led Operation Enduring Freedom.[5] Since the early 2010s, the Navy has disregarded occasional strong-arm tactics by the PLAN in the SCS and continues to make regular port calls on an unexceptional basis.[6] Indeed, these port calls have been ramped up significantly over the past five years. In 2013, the Indian Navy was deployed just once to the region and paid visits to four Southeast Asian countries. By 2017, there were as many as six deployments to the region featuring visits to nine Southeast Asian countries.[7]

New Delhi's defence cooperation and naval engagement activities in Southeast Asia and the SCS can broadly be grouped under five headings.

First, are *bilateral exercises* conducted with the region's navies. India conducts bilateral maritime exercises with five Southeast Asian navies – the *Republic of Singapore Navy (RSN), the Royal Thailand Navy (RTN), the Indonesian Navy, the Myanmar Navy, and the Vietnam People's Navy.*[8]

[5] David Brewster, "India's Defense Strategy and the India-ASEAN Relationship." In *India-ASEAN Defense Relations*, edited by Ajaya Kumar Das, RSIS Monograph No. 28 (2013): 131.

[6] Collin Koh Swee Lean, "ASEAN Perspectives on Naval Cooperation with India: Singapore and Vietnam." *India Review*, 12:3 (2013): 186–206. See also, Jonah Blank et al, *Look East, Cross Black Waters: India's Interest in Southeast Asia*. Santa Monica, CA: RAND Corporation (2015): 65.

[7] Ashley E. Allison, "Increased Maritime Cooperation: India and Southeast Asia" (Thesis, Naval Postgraduate School, 2019): 3.

[8] India also participates in multilateral exercises, including under the ASEAN Defence Ministers' Meeting Plus (ADMM-Plus) umbrella, that feature a wider range of Southeast Asian navies. Since 1995, the Indian Navy has also hosted a biennial exercise called

With the exception of the Singapore-India Maritime Exercise (SIMBEX) exercises with the RSN, the other exercises are of very recent vintage and, hence, rudimentary in their sophistication. India and Indonesia conducted their inaugural naval exercise in October 2015, which was embedded within the 26th edition of their coordinated patrol (IND-INDO CORPAT), and their first stand-alone exercise, Samudra Shakti, was only conducted in November 2018. India's inaugural exercises with Vietnam and Myanmar, too, date back to just 2018. The nine-day India-Myanmar Naval Exercise (IMNEX) kicked off in March 2018, and with the Vietnam People's Navy in May 2018. By contrast, India-Singapore bilateral maritime exercises date back to 1993, and the 25th anniversary of the drills witnessed an anti-submarine warfare (ASW) component, too, featuring both sides' submarine fleets. In a sign of the evolving times, a maiden trilateral maritime exercise with the Royal Thailand Navy and the Singapore Navy was conducted in September 2019. And the hope is, in New Delhi, that Indonesia and Malaysia will accede, too, and engage with the trio at a later date, so as to ensure seamless connectivity and security along the crucial approaches to and from the western end of the Straits of Malacca.[9]

Second, are *coordinated patrols* (CORPATs) that the Indian Navy conducts with three Southeast Asia counterparts – *Indonesia, Thailand and Myanmar.* The CORPATs with the former two are of long-standing vintage – the 33rd edition of the IND-INDO CORPAT and the 28th edition of the IND-THAI CORPAT having taken place in 2019. By contrast, the CORPATs with Myanmar date back to just May 2013. The three countries with which New Delhi conducts a CORPAT share a common feature: each is a maritime neighbour with whom India enjoys a settled boundary: bilateral maritime boundary agreements having been struck with Myanmar and Thailand in 1987 and 1996 respectively; trilateral boundary agreements with Indonesia and Thailand and with Thailand and Myanmar in 1979 and 1995 respectively; and the continental shelf delimited with Indonesia in 1974 (extension in 1997) and Thailand in 1978.[10] During a CORPAT, ships and aircraft undertake coordinated patrolling on their respective sides of the maritime boundary.

MILAN at its Port Blair base in the Andaman Islands, where a wider range of Southeast Asian and Indian Ocean littoral state navies have participated. 41 countries were invited to the March 2020 edition of exercise MILAN.

9 Shishir Gupta, "India, Thailand, Singapore's trilateral naval drill this month," *Hindustan Times*, September 9, 2019.

10 Ministry of Defence - Navy, Government of India, "Ensuring Secure Seas: Indian Maritime Security Strategy," (October 2015): 22.

Next, are *port calls* as well as *port access and logistics support arrangements.* The former are as extensive as the latter are selective. Regular calls by Indian naval vessels at Southeast Asian ports strung across the entire littoral have become a key feature of New Delhi's regional naval diplomacy. Every year since 2015 has featured a double-digit number of port calls annually and, in 2017, every ASEAN coastal state was visited by the Indian Navy. On the other hand, India's port access and logistics support arrangements are confined to just two Southeast Asian countries – *Singapore and, more recently, Indonesia.* In November 2017, India and Singapore initialled a Bilateral Agreement for Navy Cooperation that facilitates India's use of the Changi Naval Base for temporary deployment and logistics support. And, in 2018, India obtained port development and access rights to the Achenese port of Sabang. The port flanks the northern end of the Straits of Malacca and is strategically positioned to serve as a logistics and re-supply node for naval operations in the Eastern Indian Ocean. Indian naval and coast guard vessels have since paid visits to the port and it is probably only a matter of time until an Indian Navy submarine berths at Sabang too.[11]

Fourth, is *military-technical training and capacity-building* that New Delhi conducts for Southeast Asian navies. Arguably, such services constitute the high point of India's defence cooperation with the region, given the robust, one-way flow of expertise performed with a quiet touch. Two countries, *Singapore and Vietnam*, have been the key recipients of such technical training and capacity-building collaboration. For Singaporean mariners, training and capacity building has, by-and-large, been folded into the SIMBEX – and the prior *Lion King* – exercises, which have featured progressively more complex anti-submarine warfare as well as replenishment-at-sea training. By contrast, the technical training and capacity building that India extends to Vietnam is a function of these countries' overlapping use of Russian-made platforms and systems. India-Vietnam technical training dates back to 2006–7 when New Delhi opted to provide professional education and training for Vietnam People's Navy (VPN) personnel in warship construction and repair. Since the early 2010s, and in the wake of Hanoi's contracted purchase of six Russian-built Kilo-class submarines, India has provided training in "comprehensive underwater combat operations" to Vietnamese crew at its submarine training school in the eastern Indian city of Visakhapatnam. The level of instruction is fairly modest, though.

---

[11] Pramit Pal Chaudhuri, "Indonesia gives India access to strategic port of Sabang," *Hindustan Times*, May 17, 2018.

The final area of maritime engagement and cooperation is in the sphere of *armaments sales, including spares. Vietnam* has overwhelmingly been the key beneficiary in this regard. India-Vietnam military-technical collaboration dates back to the mid-1990s when the two sides drafted a protocol on defence cooperation. Since then, New Delhi has intermittently transferred a variety of warship ordnance-related components to the VPN, including sonar systems, torpedo launchers, and fire-control systems. At the time of writing, India is gearing up to produce and transfer five high-speed patrol boats to the Vietnam Border Guard Force. Seven additional boats are to be produced at a shipyard in Vietnam, funded overall by a Government of India US$100 million line of credit. There are discussions, too, to enhance Hanoi's maritime remote sensing capabilities over the South China Sea. The lone other Southeast Asian recipient of a naval arms transfer is *Myanmar*. The Indian Navy is currently in the process of transferring one of its Russian-built Kilo-class submarines to the Myanmar Navy.[12]

This broad portrayal of New Delhi's defence cooperation and engagement activities in Maritime Southeast Asia lends itself to a couple of observations.

First, *Singapore, Vietnam and, to a lesser extent, Indonesia and Thailand are India's preferred regional partners*. Singapore clearly enjoys pride of place within this constellation of partnerships. If New Delhi ever decides to maintain a high-tempo, "out-of-area" presence in the South China Sea, it is Singapore – not Vietnam – that will be the key facilitator.

Second, from a functional perspective, *submarine warfare-related tasks appear to be an area of expertise and cooperation prized by New Delhi's Southeast Asian counterparts*. From underwater operations training at its submarine training school in Visakhapatnam (involving Vietnamese personnel) to the ASW component in bilateral exercises (with Singapore), to the transfer of a fully-fledged, albeit ageing, submarine (to Myanmar), India has carved out a niche in this sphere of sub-surface readiness, training, and warfare.

Third, is the *relatively recent nature of much of India's naval engagement with the region*. Ties with Singapore, Vietnam and the CORPATs aside, most of what passes for India-Southeast Asia maritime cooperation is of very recent origin – less than a half-decade old. Be it bilateral drills (with Indonesia, Myanmar, and Vietnam), the trilateral drill (with Thailand and Singapore) or the port access and logistics support facility (in Indonesia), this newness

12 It is interesting that Naypyidaw has not opted to purchase the submarine from Beijing – even as China's leading shipbuilder has initiated construction of a diesel-electric submarine for the Royal Thai Navy. See "Myanmar's Balancing Act Moves to India," *The Irrawaddy*, August 2, 2019. India had earlier transferred advanced lightweight torpedoes to the Myanmar Navy too.

of purpose is readily apparent. Its impulse can be traced to Prime Minister Modi's "Act East" policy that aims to project India as a "leading power," not just a "balancing power," whose geopolitical weight and preferences could shape strategic outcomes in the Indo-Pacific region.

This recent nature of India's regional naval engagement, in turn, points to a fourth trait – *its evolving and augmented character of late.* The scale and sophistication of India's naval engagement and maritime cooperation activities in Southeast Asia, both east and west of Sumatra, is likely to look rather different in 2025 than it does today. Already, there are hints that India is gearing up to enter the Southeast Asian arms market, beyond Vietnam, with platforms and systems that feature a high level of indigenously developed content. In 2016, an Indian shipyard was shortlisted by the Philippines Navy as its preferred bidder to construct two frigates, although the procurement has since fallen by the wayside for lack of the shipyard's wherewithal to clear post-qualification financial assessment tests.[13] More operational access and turnaround agreements are likely to follow, too, in the years ahead, including at ports that fringe the South China Sea.

Finally, and the augmented scale of India's engagement notwithstanding, *the predominant body of New Delhi's activities remains concentrated in waters west of Malacca.* Be it bilateral/trilateral maritime exercises (with the sole exception of exercises with Vietnam), coordinated patrols, or access or logistics arrangements, almost all of the expansion in the Indian Navy's operational footprint has been confined to its Eastern Indian Ocean area of "primary" interest. The measured turnaround in ties with Jakarta is particularly noteworthy. As late as the 1980s, Jakarta had been suspicious of New Delhi's "hegemonic" ambitions in the Eastern Indian Ocean, given the Indian Navy's possession of an aircraft carrier and operation of a leased Soviet nuclear-powered submarine.[14] There had been anxieties too that India's outlying Andaman and Nicobar Islands could serve as a forward-deployed platform for Soviet submarines, menacing – ironically – the port of Sabang (where India recently obtained access rights) at the northern tip of Sumatra.[15]

---

13 "DND disqualifies lowest bidder in P16-B Navy frigate project." *Philippine Star*, June 30, 2016.

14 Ristian Atriandi Supriyanto, "The Indo-Indonesian Defense Relationship: Towards a Convergent Mandala." In *India-ASEAN Defense Relations*, edited by Ajaya Kumar Das, RSIS Monograph No. 28 (2013): 206.

15 Earlier, during the 1965 India-Pakistan War, Indonesian President Sukarno had supported Islamabad and threatened to divert air and naval assets towards the Andaman and Nicobar Islands in order to distract New Delhi's focus from its western front. In the event, the actual deployments were minimal.

India and Maritime Southeast Asia: the limits of cooperation (so far)

As earlier noted, India has been a long-standing external stakeholder in the maritime affairs of Southeast Asia, including in the South China Sea. In recent years, under Modi's "Act East" policy and the zeal to project India as a "leading power" in Asia and the world, the scale of New Delhi's defence cooperation and naval engagement activities has witnessed a noticeable upswing. As important as this range of activities is, it is equally instructive to illustrate what New Delhi has *not* provided, conducted, or done – particularly with regard to the South China Sea.

First, with the exception of two recent bilateral exercises with Hanoi, *New Delhi has not conducted naval exercises with any SCS claimant state*. Given the practically non-existent level of at-sea operational cooperation with the other claimant states, it is highly unlikely that New Delhi will be initiating significant naval exercises with any one of them anytime soon in this waterway. Equally, the bilateral (with US since 1992), trilateral (with US and Japan since 2015), and quadrilateral (with US, Japan, and Australia in 2007) Malabar series exercises that India has conducted with extra regional, that is, non-Southeast Asian, states have all been held in either the Arabian Sea, the Bay of Bengal/Eastern Indian Ocean, or the Western Pacific. It is unforeseeable that New Delhi will conduct a significant maritime exercise with an extra-regional power in the SCS.[16]

Second, *the Indian Navy has never conducted a patrol, let alone a joint patrol, with another country in the South China Sea* – be it a South China Sea claimant state, an ASEAN non-littoral state, or an extra-regional power. In early 2016, just as the *Philippines v. China* arbitrators were seized in final deliberations in The Hague, then-US Pacific Command (USPACOM) chief, Harry Harris, had proposed that India join the US, Japanese, and Australian navies in conducting a joint patrol in the SCS. The proposal was met with a firm rebuff. India does not conduct joint patrols with any East or Southeast Asian country; coordinated patrols (CORPATs) with maritime neighbours constitute the limit of such patrol-related activity. On the other hand, India's desire to join the loose Malacca Strait Patrol (MSP) mechanism, entailing intelligence exchange and coordinated air (eye-in-the-sky) and sea patrols

[16] The Indian Navy did conduct an opportunistic "group sail" though in the South China Sea with a Japanese helicopter carrier, a Philippines frigate and a US Navy destroyer in May 2019. The Indian vessels were returning home after participating in China's International Fleet Review (IFR) and, thereafter, in the ADMM-Plus exercises off the coast of South Korea.

starring Indonesia, Malaysia, Singapore and Thailand, too, was shot down by Jakarta in May 2018.[17]

Third, *India has not conducted – and will never conduct – a freedom of navigation operation to challenge excessive claims in the SCS.* India's stance on foreign user state rights within exclusive maritime zones, be it military navigation-related innocent passage rights through territorial seas or active intelligence gathering as well as hydrographic surveys within EEZs, largely (although not fully) mirror China's as well as those of Southeast Asian coastal states. The Obama-Modi *Joint Vision Statement* of January 2015 regarding safeguarding freedom of navigation in the US Pacific Command (USPAC) remains a dead letter to this day. Should New Delhi be truly inclined to champion a freedom of navigation operational assertion, it could simply waive its prior notification requirement and, without protest, allow the US Navy to sail through its own territorial sea in innocent passage mode.

Fourth, *India does not seek or partake in basing arrangements east of Malacca.* In the early 2010s, Hanoi had offered to host permanent berthing facilities for Indian naval vessels at its then-new Nha Trang port. The Manmohan Singh government stayed clear of the offer. By contrast, west of Malacca, particularly in its Indian Ocean zone of "primary" interest, New Delhi has been more than inclined to construct a joint-use military base, and station uniformed personnel on the Seychelles' Assumption Island as well as upgrade facilities on Mauritius' Agalega Islands. East of Malacca, basic access, replenishment, and operational turnaround (OTR) will remain the norm.

Fifth, *India has not deployed its vessels in the SCS to defend it economic interests* in this waterway. The issue came to the fore in December 2012, when India's naval chief aggressively asserted that the Navy was prepared to defend the national oil and gas company's offshore exploration and exploitation assets in the disputed waters of the SCS. The view was instantaneously shot down by India's national security advisor. New Delhi has not laid out an assertive doctrine of naval operations east of Sumatra and, although the Navy's most recent maritime doctrine does iterate the importance of securing India's seaborne trade and energy interests and routes, these waters for all intents and purposes will continue to remain an "out-of-area" theatre in which the Indian Navy will tread lightly.

Sixth, and finally, it is instructive as a point of contrast to highlight *the extent – not limits – of cooperative activities that India conducts in its Indian Ocean*

[17] Devirupa Mitra, "Indonesia Told India its Quest to Join Malacca Strait Patrols Isn't Feasible," *The Wire*, May 31, 2018

Region of "primary" interest. Within this water area, the Indian Navy already conducts each of the listed tasks (bilateral/trilateral exercises, coordinated patrols, port calls and access arrangements, military technical-training and capacity building, arms sales) that it engages in with Maritime Southeast Asia. Over and above these tasks, New Delhi also conducts periodic hydrographic surveys to chart the EEZ (for Mauritius) and joint EEZ surveillance and maritime domain awareness missions (with Seychelles, Mauritius, and Maldives), including coastal surveillance and long-range identification and tracking. Additionally, New Delhi maintains a tripartite maritime security framework with near-neighbours Sri Lanka and Maldives, which has involved intelligence sharing and exchange at the national security advisor (NSA) level.[18] And, at this time, modalities are also under way to establish Government of India-funded, and jointly managed, naval bases in Mauritius and Seychelles. Agreements to develop, manage, operate, and maintain these facilities have been initialled with the host nations but are currently mired in domestic opposition within their respective legislatures.[19]

India's illustrative response to the South China Sea Arbitration Award

On July 12, 2016, in a courtroom in The Hague, an Arbitral Tribunal constituted under the United Nations Convention on the Law of the Sea (UNCLOS) issued a highly anticipated, and controversial, award in the *Philippines v. China* case. Over the course of four sweeping observations, the Tribunal ruled that many of China's maritime claims, and actions in defence of those claims, in the SCS were contrary to UNCLOS and had thereby violated the Philippines' sovereign rights and freedoms.[20]

In the period leading up to the Award, the Modi government was neither diffident to articulate its firm preference for the peaceful settlement of disputes, including via third party mechanisms, nor shy to make common cause with Western powers on this point – as was evident in the Obama-Modi *Joint Strategic Vision* statement. This common cause with "Quad" partners evaporated, however, on July 12. Three points were clear in the statements released that day by Australia, Japan, and the US. Each

[18] Since 1987, India and Sri Lanka have also shared a treaty obligation by way of which Sri Lankan ports are barred from being made available to a third country for military use "in a manner prejudicial to India's interests."

[19] Suhasini Haider, "Indian project in Mauritius faces protests," *The Hindu,* October 27, 2018.

[20] Permanent Court of Arbitration, "The South China Sea Arbitration (*The Republic of Philippines v. The People's Republic of China*) case, Award of the Arbitral Tribunal," July 12, 2016.

welcomed the ruling; each insisted that the award was "final and binding" as per international law; each insisted that China was required to abide by the ruling. The Joint Statement released at their sixth Trilateral Strategic Dialogue meeting a fortnight later forcefully restated their ministers' strong support[21] "for the rule of law and called on China and the Philippines *to abide by* [emphasis added] the Arbitral Tribunal's Award of July 12 in the Philippines-China arbitration, which is *final and legally binding* [emphasis added] on both parties." The Indian statement released that day, by contrast, did not mention the "final and binding" character of the award nor peremptorily insist that China comply with the ruling. "Noting" that the tribunal had delivered its award and "observing that sea lines of communication passing through the South China Sea [were] critical for peace, stability, prosperity and development," New Delhi, rather, "*urge[d]* all parties to *show utmost respect* for the UNCLOS, which [had] establishe[d] the international legal order of the seas and oceans."[22] This more moderately toned phraseology, "show utmost respect," continued to carry the day thereafter. When Japanese Prime Minister Shinzo Abe, a minted China-antagonist at the time, visited New Delhi for the annual Japan-India summit that year, Modi bent him to his will on the semantic formulation concerning the Arbitration Award. The Joint Statement expressed their view whereby, "all parties should *show utmost respect* [emphasis added] to the UNCLOS, which establishes the international legal order of the seas and oceans."[23]

No mention of the "final and binding" character of the award or that China was duty-bound to comply (Japan's preferred language) was reproduced in the Joint Statement. To this day, New Delhi continues to maintain a recognizably discrete stance on the issue. More to the point, while the US-Japan-Australia trio continue to harp on the "importance of the July 2016 Philippines-China Arbitral Tribunal's award" and its "final and legally binding character,"[24] India has long ceased to be detained by the award. As with its rebuff to the then-USPACOM chief's call for joint patrols, New Delhi has hewed to a separate path at clutch moments in the politics and security of the SCS.

---

[21] US Department of State, "Joint Statement of the Japan-United States-Australia Trilateral Strategic Dialogue," July 25, 2016.

[22] Ministry of External Affairs, Government of India, "Statement on Award of Arbitral Tribunal on South China Sea under Annexure VII of UNCLOS," 2016 (emphasis added).

[23] Ministry of External Affairs, "India-Japan Joint Statement during the visit of Prime Minister of Japan," November 11, 2016.

[24] US Department of State, "Trilateral Strategic Dialogue Joint Ministerial Statement" August 1, 2019.

Conclusion

In his keynote address at the Shangri-La Dialogue in June 2018, Prime Minister Narendra Modi endorsed a vision of the Indo-Pacific where the major and middle powers of the region, along with Southeast Asia at its centre, serve as anchors of stability and prosperity. India would contribute to this vision in its own way. It would be an enabling power, seeking to establish a loose concert of common principles and best practices in the region's international relations such that power is exercised in a spirit of self-restraint by its dominant entities. It would be a law-abiding power, seeking to entrench respect for international law on land, air, and sea such that a new regional order can be constructed by a sense of obligation to rules rather than the assertion of power. India would be a pluralistic power, facilitating the involvement of the widest spectrum of Asia's stakeholders in the region's endeavours, including within flexible "minilateral" formats that are neither exclusive "club[s] of limited members" nor "alliances of containment." And it would be a stabilizing power, prepared to deploy its geopolitical weight to craft an equitable "balance of interests" within the fast-shifting Indo-Pacific equilibrium. A stable, rules-bound, geopolitical equilibrium in the Indo-Pacific region remains a necessary condition for India's rise. And it is within the praxis of this broader Indo-Pacific vision that India's overall policy in Maritime Southeast Asia, including in the SCS, is framed.

As this chapter has highlighted though, there is a clear hierarchy at work in the ordering of India's geopolitical and maritime interests and the means placed at the disposal to realize them, both, in Maritime Southeast Asia and the SCS as well as in the wider Indo-Pacific. From a functional standpoint, the "Indo" and the "Pacific" are not created equal within the constellation of New Delhi's interests. Some of the key tasks and cooperative activities that the Indian Navy conducts in the Indian Ocean region have no counterpart in the Pacific area (which broadly encompasses Maritime Southeast Asia). This differentiation extends within Maritime Southeast Asia too; west of Malacca, the range and depth of tasks that the Indian Navy engages in qualitatively exceeds that to its east. And this gap will only grow as New Delhi steadily goes about stitching together a panoply of maritime exercise formats, coordinated patrols, arms transfer, and port access and logistics support arrangements west of Sumatra. Particularly in the SCS, the Indian Navy's bilateral operational footprint remains light – even as it continues to be a busy user of this waterway and is more than happy to show its flag to mark its frequent presence.

From a geopolitical standpoint, the key differentiation resides in India's contrasting approaches to China's "Near Seas" and China's "Far Seas."[25] Within

[25] The "Near Seas" refers to the Bohai Gulf, Yellow Sea, East China Sea and the South China Sea. The "Far Seas" is shorthand for the two oceans – the Pacific Ocean and the Indian Ocean.

the latter, New Delhi has been forthright in conducting maritime exercises in variable geometric formats. It has not hesitated to engage in coordinated (or even joint) endeavours – be it patrols, EEZ surveillance, basing facilities, and so on, especially in the Indian Ocean region. It has not shrunk from being joined with – albeit not *within* – extra-regional alliance partners and purposes, both bilaterally and in variable formats,[26] and someday the "Quad" may even constitute a soft, blue-water balancing option in the face of China's rapidly modernizing "Far Seas" capabilities. Within the "Near Seas," on the other hand, New Delhi has been markedly circumspect in its profile and posture. It has by and large made its political presence felt in an independent capacity; sustained a toned-down set of operational tasks with the rare bilateral partner (although the defence sales relationship with Vietnam will bear close watching); cooperated with ASEAN partner states with a view to regionally building up minimum, internal self-balancing capabilities rather than overtly challenging China; steered clear of all variable geometric as well as "minilateral" endeavours featuring extra-regional players; and, on the whole, stayed sensitive to and deferential of China's "core" interests. How New Delhi pursues and preserves its hydrocarbon interests in the South China Sea, where it directly impinges on and contravenes a "core" interest, will be a useful marker of the extent to which it is willing to challenge China's resolve in this waterway.[27]

Barring a fundamental shift in the geopolitics of the SCS brought upon by disproportionate kinetic action by China against a claimant state or a confirmed Indian interest at sea or barring unfriendly designs by Beijing in New Delhi's own Indian Ocean backyard, such as militarizing its South Asian port infrastructure investments into forward basing facilities, India's cautious inclinations in Maritime Southeast Asia and the SCS will persist invariably into the future.

References

Allison, Ashley E. "Increased maritime cooperation: India and Southeast Asia." Thesis, Naval Postgraduate School, 2019. https://calhoun.nps.edu/bitstream/handle/10945/62778/19Jun_Allison_Ashley.pdf?sequence=1&isAllowed=y

---

[26] Collin Koh Swee Lean, "China-India Rivalry at Sea: Capability, trends and challenges," *Asian Security,* 15:1 (2018): 5–24.

[27] This issue has recently come to the fore once again with Beijing's browbeating of Hanoi – although not its O&G partners, India's OVL and Russia's Rosneft – to suspend exploration and exploitation at the said offshore block (Block 06.1). In the wake of the *Philippines v. China* award (which China does not recognize), the block now resides on Vietnam's legal and undisputed continental shelf. It is located in proximity though of Vanguard Bank, where Beijing and Hanoi share a contested resource development history.

Blank, Jonah, Jennifer D. P. Moroney, Angel Rabasa, and Bonny Lin. *Look East, Cross Black Waters: India's Interest in Southeast Asia*. Santa Monica, CA: RAND Corporation, 2015. https://www.rand.org/pubs/research_reports/RR1021.html

Brewster, David. "India's defense strategy and the India-ASEAN relationship." In *India-ASEAN Defense Relations*, edited by Ajaya Kumar Das, RSIS Monograph No. 28 (2013): 125–46. https://www.rsis.edu.sg/wp-content/uploads/2014/07/Monograph2813.pdf

Chaudhuri, Pramit Pal. "Indonesia gives India access to strategic port of Sabang." *Hindustan Times*, May 17, 2018. https://www.hindustantimes.com/india-news/indonesia-gives-india-access-to-strategic-port-of-sabang/story-KPXWKy7PGAHFUi0jCL26yJ.html

Gupta, Shishir. "India, Thailand, Singapore's trilateral naval drill this month." *Hindustan Times*, September 9, 2019. https://www.hindustantimes.com/india-news/india-thailand-singapore-s-trilateral-naval-drill-this-month/story-af8ndeALjyklYIJj12BgPL.html

Haider, Suhasini. "Indian project in Mauritius faces protests." *The Hindu,* October 27, 2018. https://www.thehindu.com/news/national/indian-project-in-mauritius-faces-protests/article25348528.ece

Integrated Headquarters, Ministry of Defence - Navy. "Ensuring secure seas: Indian maritime security strategy." October 2015. https://www.indiannavy.nic.in/sites/default/files/Indian_Maritime_Security_Strategy_Document_25Jan16.pdf

Irrawaddy Editorial. "Myanmar's balancing act moves to India." *The Irrawaddy*, August 2, 2019. https://www.irrawaddy.com/opinion/editorial/myanmars-balancing-act-moves-india.html.

Koh Swee Lean, Collin. "ASEAN perspectives on naval cooperation with India: Singapore and Vietnam." *India Review*, 12:3 (2013): 186–206. DOI: 10.1080/14736489.2013.821326

Koh Swee Lean, Collin. "China-India rivalry at sea: Capability, trends and challenges." *Asian Security*, 15:1 (2018): 5–24. DOI: 10.1080/14799855.2019.1539820

Ministry of External Affairs, Government of India. "US-India Joint Strategic Vision for the Asia-Pacific and Indian Ocean Region." January 25, 2015. https://www.mea.gov.in/bilateral-documents.htm?dtl/24728/USIndia_Joint_Strategic_Vision_for_the_AsiaPacific_and_Indian_Ocean_Region

Ministry of External Affairs, Government of India. "Prime Minister's remarks at the US Congress." June 8, 2016. https://www.mea.gov.in/Speeches-Statements.htm?dtl/26886/Prime_Ministers_remarks_at_the_US_Congress

Ministry of External Affairs, Government of India. "Statement on Award of Arbitral Tribunal on South China Sea under Annexure VII of UNCLOS." July 12, 2016. https://mea.gov.in/press-releases.htm?dtl/27019/Statement_on_Award_of_Arbitral_Tribunal_on_South_China_Sea_Under_Annexure_VII_of_UNCLOS

Ministry of External Affairs, Government of India. "India-Japan Joint Statement during the visit of Prime Minister of Japan." November 11, 2016. https://mea.gov.in/bilateral-documents.htm?dtl/27599/IndiaJapan_Joint_Statement_during_the_visit_of_Prime_Minister_to_Japan

Ministry of External Affairs, Government of India. "Prime Minister's Keynote Address at Shangri-La Dialogue." June 1, 2018. https://www.mea.gov.in/Speeches-Statements.htm?dtl/29943/Prime_Ministers_Keynote_Address_at_Shangri_La_Dialogue_June_01_2018

Mitra, Devirupa. "Indonesia told India its quest to join Malacca Strait patrols isn't feasible." *The Wire*, May 31, 2018. https://thewire.in/diplomacy/india-indonesia-malacca-strait-patrol

Permanent Court of Arbitration. "The South China Sea Arbitration (The Republic of Philippines v. The People's Republic of China) case, Award of the Arbitral Tribunal." July 12, 2016. https://pcacases.com/web/sendAttach/2086

Philippine Star. "DND disqualifies lowest bidder in P16-B Navy frigate project." June 30, 2016. https://www.philstar.com/headlines/2016/06/30/1598080/dnd-disqualifies-lowest-bidder-p16-b-navy-frigate-project

Supriyanto, Ristian Atriandi. "The Indo-Indonesian defense relationship: Towards a convergent mandala." In *India-ASEAN Defense Relations*, edited by Ajaya Kumar Das, RSIS Monograph No. 28 (2013): 191–217. https://www.rsis.edu.sg/wp-content/uploads/2014/07/Monograph2813.pdf

US Department of State. "Joint Statement of the Japan-United States-Australia Trilateral Strategic Dialogue." July 25, 2016. https://2009-2017.state.gov/r/pa/prs/ps/2016/07/260442.htm

US Department of State. "Trilateral Strategic Dialogue Joint Ministerial Statement." August 1, 2019. https://www.state.gov/trilateral-strategic-dialogue-joint-ministerial-statement-august-1-2019/

PART IV

Non-Claimants in Europe and Eurasia

16

Britain's Pivot to Asia: The Big Picture[1]

Ian Park and Kun-Chin Lin

Introduction

Despite being the world's fifth largest economy when measured in terms of gross domestic product (GDP),[2] having the sixth largest military budget,[3] being a nuclear power and a permanent member of the UN Security Council (UNSC), and member of, inter alia, the North Atlantic Treaty Organization (NATO) and the G7, the United Kingdom (UK) is facing a period of deep uncertainty. This uncertainty is in part borne out of "Brexit," but equally

[1] The views expressed are the authors' alone and do not represent those of the Royal Navy, UK Ministry of Defence, or UK Government. We would like to thank Iain Ritchie, Tim Reilly, and Professor Brendan Simms for their valuable advice, and Isabella Warren for editorial assistance.

[2] "World Economic Outlook Database," International Monetary Fund, July 2018, https://www.imf.org/external/pubs/ft/weo/2018/01/weodata/index.aspx

[3] "The Military Balance," International Institute for Strategic Studies, 2019, https://www.iiss.org/publications/the-military-balance/the-military-balance-2019. However, UK's defence budget was only 1.8 per cent of its GDP in 2017, much lower than those of the US and France, having seen a decline from the post-Cold War peak of 9.8 per cent;

Bob Seely and James Rogers, *Global Britain: A Twenty First Century Vision* (Henry Jackson Society, 2019), http://www.defencesynergia.co.uk/wp-content/uploads/2019/03/HJS-Global-Britain-_-A-Twenty-first-Century-Vision-Report-A4-web.pdf;

Christopher Martin, "The Attributes and Roles of Naval Forces" in *The UK as a Medium Maritime Power in the 21st Century* (Palgrave Macmillan, 2016), https://doi.org/10.1057/978-1-137-01237-1_2

significantly is borne out of a requirement, amid decreasing economic and military power, to redefine its role in the world and adapt to the changing geopolitical, economic and military landscape – a landscape that potentially has Asia as its fulcrum and Southeast Asia at its heart.[4]

The UK economy is dominated by the service sector that accounts for 80 per cent of GDP[5] and as such the UK is heavily reliant on trade to satisfy the needs of its citizens and businesses. This trade is in part facilitated by the UK's "Red Ensign"[6] merchant navy fleet, which is the tenth largest in the world,[7] and the Royal Navy, which is widely considered to be one of the top five most powerful navies,[8] yet both had been in decline until recently, numerically in terms of ship numbers and also in terms of influence.[9] This decline is not without consequence, most acutely in respect of the Royal Navy's ability to deploy globally and simultaneously to various areas of operation. This has been thrown into sharp relief by events in the summer of 2019, in which the Iranian Revolutionary Guard seized a British-flagged merchant vessel in the Arabian Gulf in retaliation for the Royal Marines detaining Iran's oil tanker *Grace 1* in Gibraltar on suspicion of violating European Union (EU) sanctions. Should the UK's engagement in South

---

[4] Statista, "The 15 Countries with the Highest Gross Domestic Product (GDP) in 2030," https://www.statista.com/statistics/271724/forecast-for-the-countries-with-the-highest-gross-domestic-product-gdp-in-2030/. Goldman Sachs predict that by 2030 China will be the largest economy in the world when measured by GDP, India third, and Japan fifth.

[5] UK Office For National Statistics, "GDP First Quarterly Estimate, UK: April to June 2019," https://www.ons.gov.uk/economy/grossdomesticproductgdp/bulletins/gdpfirstquarterlyestimateuk/apriltojune2019

[6] UK Department for Transport, "Shipping Fleet Statistics 2018," March 13, 2019, https://assets.publishing.service.gov.uk/government/uploads/system/uploads/attachment_data/file/785497/shipping-fleet-statistics-2018.pdf. The Red Ensign Group is the collective title for the shipping registers of the UK, the Crown Dependencies, and the Overseas Territories. Registration with the Red Ensign Group provides vessels with the support of British consular services worldwide, and British Royal Navy protection.

[7] Ibid.

[8] Kyle Mizokami, "The Five Most-Powerful Navies on the Planet," *The National Interest*, June 6, 2014, https://nationalinterest.org/feature/the-five-most-powerful-navies-the-planet-10610

[9] UK Department for Transport, "Shipping Fleet Statistics"; David Axe, "The Decline of the Royal Navy, *The Maritime Executive*, 2016, https://www.maritime-executive.com/editorials/the-decline-of-the-royal-navy; Niall McCarthy, "The UK's Shrinking Navy," January 1, 2018, https://www.statista.com/chart/12747/the-uks-shrinking-navy/. There has been a slight upward growth in personnel numbers since 2017 and hull numbers to meet uncertainty over Brexit and protection of UK water; Tony Radakin, "First Sea Lord Speech to Defence and Security Equipment International, Royal Navy News," September 11, 2019, https://www.royalnavy.mod.uk/news-and-latest-activity/news/2019/september/11/190911-1sl-speech-dsei

China Sea (SCS) be seen in the same vein of defending international rules and norms? At the same time, emerging threats in multiple maritime theatres are further exposing the Royal Navy's resource constraints.

The UK has a global trading and diplomatic presence with 134 embassies or consulates worldwide including all the states with maritime claims in the SCS, yet its military deployments in the SCS and diplomatic messaging, specifically with respect to Hong Kong, have met with significant opprobrium from the PRC (China) and strongly worded statements "not to interfere."[10] Officials and media in China have accused the UK misguided intentions when it comes to meddling in regional affairs and for displaying ineffectual intervention in the form of freedom of navigation (FON) missions. They have warned of an increase in the likelihood of armed conflict at sea and harms to bilateral ties, meaning Beijing would be justified in threatening the UK in an effort to curtail lucrative and increasingly important investment and trade deals.[11]

Acknowledging the UK's need to expand its horizons post-Brexit, while at the same time maintaining cordial and mutually beneficial relationships with its neighbours in Europe and allies across the Atlantic, it is essential that a coherent policy in respect of the SCS is developed and implemented. This policy must, of course, recognize the UK's historical links to the region and allies therein, and have a political, economic, and military dimension.

With respect to the SCS region, the UK had a sovereign presence in Singapore until 1959 and Hong Kong until July 1, 1997, and during the colonial era occupied Penang Island, Malacca, and Myanmar. The UK's historic presence in the region continues through close diplomatic and military ties. Militarily, since 1971 the UK has been a member of the Five Power Defence Arrangements (FPDA) with Australia, New Zealand, Singapore, and Malaysia, that facilitates defence cooperation between the states, albeit does not contain a mutual defence obligation. Southeast Asia is the UK's third largest market for defence exports and the focus of considerable military engagement in the form of military deployments, exercises, knowledge exchange, and military-diplomatic effort. The UK's economic relationship with Southeast Asia is not, of course, limited to defence exports.

China, Japan, Hong Kong, and South Korea are all top-15 trading partners with the UK, and Southeast Asia is the UK's third largest non-EU export market. Significantly, in 2018, the UK had a trade surplus with Hong Kong

---

10 "Hong Kong Protests: UK Should Not Interfere, Says Chinese Ambassador," BBC, August 15, 2019, https://www.bbc.co.uk/news/uk-49356495

11 Chen Xiangmiao, "Why Is the UK Expanding Its Military Presence in the South China Sea?" China-US Focus, January 15, 2019, https://www.chinausfocus.com/peace-security/why-is-the-uk-expanding-its-military-presence-in-the-south-china-sea-.

(US$7.4 billion), Singapore (US$4.8 billion), and South Korea (US$2.4 billion), but a trade deficit of US$35.3 billion with China, although UK exports to China increased 6.9 per cent that year.[12] According to the law firm Baker McKenzie, the UK received more Chinese investment than any other country in Europe and North America in 2018 at US$4.94 billion.[13] Economic complementarity has fostered stability and goodwill in Britain's bilateral diplomatic and commercial ties to Asian countries. Why then, would British leaders risk the material gains of interdependence?

Defining the British national interest

The UK sees itself as a global power and, since the Brexit vote on June 23, 2016 to leave the European Union, has championed the term "Global Britain" to capture and reflect the desire of the UK to "deliver on its global ambition."[14] More specifically, the government considers that: "Global Britain is about reinvesting in our relationships, championing the rules-based international order and demonstrating that the UK is open, outward-looking and confident on the world stage."[15] The "Global Britain" initiative undoubtedly recognizes the requirement to look well beyond the EU and North America in terms of future trading relationships, but appears to lack any specific or tangible aims or metrics by which initiatives could be undertaken or effects measured. The UK National Security Review of March 2018 stated:

> as global Britain, we are reinvesting in our relationships around the world. We are championing the rules-based system, which has served our interests as a global trading nation and is of vital importance as geopolitics becomes more contested … The rules-based system we helped to develop has enabled global cooperation to protect shared fundamental values of respect for human dignity, human rights, freedom, democracy and equality

[12] Daniel Workman, "United Kingdom's Top Trading Partners," World's Top Exports, http://www.worldstopexports.com/united-kingdoms-top-import-partners/

[13] Baker McKenzie, "Chinese FDI into North America and Europe in 2018 Falls 73% to Six-Year Low of $30 Billion," January 14, 2019, https://www.bakermckenzie.com/en/newsroom/2019/01/chinese-fdi

[14] UK Government, "Global Britain: Delivering on Our International Ambition," June 13, 2018, https://www.gov.uk/government/collections/global-britain-delivering-on-our-international-ambition

[15] Ibid.

> … we are committed to upholding and renewing the rules-based international system.[16]

On any construction the "championing of the rules-based international system" is one of the central pillars of the "Global Britain" initiative and also presents one of its greatest challenges. Despite numerous references to the significance of a rules-based international order or system both by UK government ministers[17] and the leaders of the G20 in a joint communiqué in 2018,[18] the term is ill-defined and beguilingly difficult to measure or determine. But more significantly if it is taken, within the context of the SCS, to mean a desire to uphold the provisions of the United Nations Convention on the Law of the Sea (UNCLOS) through "freedom of navigation operations," then this will inevitably lead to confrontation with China. What form this confrontation may take in the future remains to be seen.

Recognizing that the cornerstone of the UK government's post-Brexit narrative is captured in the "Global Britain" initiative, it is problematic that it lacks specificity in terms of any tangible aims or objectives. In terms of the UK's bilateral relations, the "pivot to Asia" since 2010 has been uneven with unconvincing results to show. Former UK Prime Minister David Cameron and Chancellor George Osborne pursued China quite openly, but under Prime Minister Theresa May a divergence in diplomatic approach had emerged in which the UK has been more actively investing in relations with Vietnam, Japan, and Korea, while showing some cooling off toward China – partly reflecting harder stances on China taken by Europeans and Americans, and partly due to Britain's reduced appeal as an investment destination in face of uncertainties of Brexit politics.[19]

From a neorealist perspective, the UK does not face any imminent threat of survival from the PRC and therefore should have weak traditional security reasons for reacting to Chinese and other powers' sovereignty and territorial contentions in the SCS. Yet strong securitization arguments have been made for the UK's national security interest in defending a rules-based

---

16 UK Government, *National Security Capability Review*, Cabinet Office, March 2018, https://assets.publishing.service.gov.uk/government/uploads/system/uploads/attachment_data/file/705347/6.4391_CO_National-Security-Review_web.pdf

17 UK Government, "Global Britain."

18 G20 Argentina, "Building Consensus for Fair and Sustainable Development," 2018, http://templatelab.com/buenos-aires-leaders-declaration/

19 Tim Reilly and Kun-Chin Lin, "The Russian Variable in Post-Brexit UK Foreign Relations with China, the US and EU," *Asia Dialogue*, March 3, 2017, https://theasiadialogue.com/2017/03/03/the-russian-variable-in-post-brexit-uk-foreign-relations-with-china-the-us-and-eu/

international order in the SCS. One could argue that the militarization of the SCS with interventions from Australia, Japan, and the US has created a highly charged climate of distrust and hostility between Chinese and US and other naval forces, increasing the likelihood of an unforeseen escalation that could have adverse global repercussions undermining Britain's strategic and commercial interests. Hence the UK's FON missions in the SCS represent a preventive measure – preventing not the rise of Chinese maritime power (that is, containment during the Cold War), but managing its destabilizing effects to avoid any disruption to the accessibility of sea lanes on which British trade and communications depend.

The strongest case for national security and policy recommendations for "championing the rules-based international order" action to support Royal Navy "freedom of navigation" patrols in the SCS have not come from Whitehall, but from major think tanks in London, including the Royal United Services Institute (RUSI) and the Henry Jackson Society (HJS).[20] Their advocacy of an active British presence in the SCS points to a core problem: some of the options that present are binary and do not allow for a situation where all of the UK's military allies, trading partners, and investors can be satisfied. As an illustration, specifically with respect to the SCS, if the UK continues to conduct "freedom of navigation" patrols with Royal Navy warships in the areas around the Spratly or Paracel Islands this would undoubtedly attract significant criticism from China, and potentially adverse economic consequences. Yet, to fail to do so would deeply undermine the UK's purported championing of the rules-based international order and undoubtedly attract significant criticism from allies, most notably the US. It is in this vein that the situation in the SCS and the UK's role in it must be considered. Moreover, and as the Henry Jackson Society suggests, the "Global Britain" initiative could provide an opportunity to strengthen its global role and position, but this will require a re-engineering of government to provide greater strategic direction.[21] John Hemmings of CSIS and HJS has recommended the formulation of a grand strategy, the creation of a National Security Council to oversee it, domestic political management including for the prospect of a loss of British lives, and budget increases for military modernization.[22]

---

[20] John Hemmings, "Charting Britain's Moves in the South China Sea," 2018, https://rusi.org/commentary/charting-britain%E2%80%99s-moves-south-china-sea; John Hemmings and James Rogers, "The South China Sea: Why It Matters to 'Global Britain,'" (Henry Jackson Society, 2019), https://henryjacksonsociety.org/publications/the-south-china-sea-why-it-matters-to-global-britain/

[21] Seely and Rogers, "Global Britain."

[22] Hemmings, "Charting Britain's Moves in the South China Sea."

Critics have recognized the daunting challenges of British power projection in Asia, in terms of domestic politics and generating impact. Rear Admiral James Goldrick of the Royal Australian Navy stated:

> [The UK's] armed forces have gone far past the point at which their capabilities are aligned with rhetoric of this sort ... The promised deployments may be a valuable signal of British interest, but single- or even two-ship efforts run the risk of appearing as tokenism in an environment in which both resolve and military weight are increasingly important ... Britain should be focusing its armed forces on Europe and its surrounding seas where such a concentration of effort can more readily provide the necessary military weight – and be sustained.[23]

In a November 1, 2018 debate on "South China Sea: Royal Navy Deployment" at the House of the Lords, UK politicians grappled with the implications of a potential security-commercial trade-off.[24] At best one could argue that the long-term interest of securing sea lanes offset the short-term economic threats from China, and seek solace in the fact that the Chinese track record does not strongly suggest actions matching the rhetoric in foreign diplomacy.[25] If a UK naval presence in the SCS is in fact ineffective, as the Chinese have claimed, there is no compelling reason for the Chinese to jeopardize a thriving relationship beyond firing off a few rounds of stern warnings.

A related but independent goal for the UK in the SCS is Britain's long-standing obligation to several Asian states. Senior British diplomat Sir Eyre Crowe wrote an influential memorandum in 1907, arguing that British naval power should be deployed to protect smaller nations and guarantee their

---

23 James Goldrick, "The Limits of Global Britain," *The Lowy Interpreter,* December 5, 2017, https://www.lowyinstitute.org/the-interpreter/limits-global-britain; Sam Bateman has made a parallel critique of US FONOPs in SCS, "The Risks of US Freedom of Navigation Operations in the South China Sea," *East Asia Forum*, June 1, 2015; Sam Bateman, "US FONOPs: Game On Again in the South China Sea," *The Interpreter*, May 26, 2017, https://www.lowyinstitute.org/the-interpreter/us-fonop-game-back-south-china-sea

24 Hansard, "South China Sea: Royal Navy Deployment," UK Parliament, November 1, 2018, https://hansard.parliament.uk/lords/2018-11-01/debates/9AD0AA10-3AA5-4338-A8BC-E8C8097333D0/SouthChinaSeaRoyalNavyDeployment

25 Mikael Weissmann, "Chinese Foreign Policy in a Global Perspective: A Responsible Reformer 'Striving for Achievement,'" *Journal of China and International Relations*, Vol. 3, No. 1 (2015).

national independence, as well as to champion universal free trade.[26] Bew and Jones advocated a return "East of Suez" saying:

> The first priority of UK strategy in Asia must be to ensure that these alliances are maintained and, where possible, bolstered – particularly in South and Southeast Asia. A strategic stance tuned to twenty-first century realities, rather than appeals to historical sentiment, will provide a far more effective basis for utilizing Commonwealth links to India, Pakistan, Malaysia, Singapore, Australia, and New Zealand.[27]

However, as these responsibilities are now firmly in American hands in the 21st century, the UK faces pressure to fit into the US-led collective security framework even if this aims to bolster former dependents such as Singapore and Malaysia or new strategic partners such as Vietnam. When Washington DC makes a play for "offshore balancing" – that is, minimalist maintenance of sea power, as last resort force and assignment of active responsibility for balance of power to local actors – the UK, along with other American allies in the region, is expected to pick up the slack.[28] Carl Thayer highlights a side benefit of potential business opportunities for UK arms sales to regional powers upgrading their hardware to face threats of militarization, if the UK continues to showcase its advanced military technology through regular FON and joint naval exercises.[29]

UK leaders have also made an argument that European security and security in the Indo-Pacific are not mutually exclusive but increasingly interlinked. Former Prime Minister Theresa May advocated closer UK-EU

---

[26] Wu Zhengyu, "The Crowe Memorandum, the Rebalance to Asia, and Sino-US Relations," *Journal of Strategic Studies*, Vol. 39, No. 3 (2016): 389–416.

[27] John Bew and David Martin Jones, "UK Strategy in Asia: Some Starting Principles," A *Britain in the World* project policy bite, September 2017. Policy Exchange. https://policyexchange.org.uk/wp-content/uploads/2017/09/UK-Strategy-in-Asia.pdf.

[28] Randall Schweller, "Opposite but Compatible Nationalisms: A Neoclassical Realist Approach to the Future of US–China Relations," *Chinese Journal of International Politics*, Vol. 11, No. 1 (2018): 23–48. American public intellectuals have applauded British FONs in SCS, e.g. Michael Austin, "Britain is Right to Send its Navy to the South China Sea," *The Spectator*, January 21, 2019, https://blogs.spectator.co.uk/2019/01/britain-is-right-to-send-its-navy-to-the-south-china-sea/; John Holmes, "Britannia Helps Rule the Waves," *Foreign Policy*, February 20, 2018, https://foreignpolicy.com/2019/02/20/britannia-helps-rule-the-waves/

[29] Carl Thayer, "After Brexit: Global Britain Plots Course to Return to the Far East," *The Diplomat*, January 17, 2019, https://thediplomat.com/2019/01/after-brexit-global-britain-plots-course-to-return-to-the-far-east/.

security alignment post-Brexit in the 2018 Munich Security Conference.[30] Furthermore, the coordination of UK and European navies could allow a more rational distribution of forces to uphold the continent's defence and the security of the most important European maritime communication line from Suez to Shanghai.[31] Collective actions such as a "multiple hulls" programme with a FON mission as part of a bigger joint operation could alleviate the Chinese backlash.[32] Such multilateral approaches would require the UK to calibrate its support contingent on the Asian allies' demand and needs. Bew and Jones stated clearly that a return "East of Suez" as "[e]xpressions of intent to 'engage' more with the region's leading states only provide a starting point. From this point, each step towards greater involvement must come with greater consciousness of cause and effect."[33] The process of harmonizing interests could take place in various security forums in Asia, including the Five Powers Defence Arrangement, Five Eyes Intelligence Alliance, the Quadrilateral Security Dialogue, ASEAN Defence Ministers' Meetings, ASEAN Strategic Partnerships, and so on, and more broadly in the Anglosphere of Commonwealth countries (sometimes called the CANZUK movement).[34] The nesting of British interests in the broader regional context would help to justify specific actions on the SCS.

---

30 Shashank and Graham, "'Global Britain' on the Line in South China Sea," *The Interpreter,* February 22, 2018, https://www.lowyinstitute.org/the-interpreter/global-britain-line-south-china-sea; Ian Bowers, "Can the Burden Be Shared? Europe, the Sea and the Liberal Order in Asia," *Global Asia*, Vol. 13, No. 2 (2018): 102–7, http://www.globalasia.org/v13no2/focus/can-the-burden-be-shared-europe-the-sea-and-the-liberal-order-in-asia_ian-bowers; for a more fundamental analysis of European security interests in Asia see: Benjamin Schreer and Yves-Heng Lim, "Embracing the Dragon? Europe's Major Powers and the Rise of China," *Global Affairs*, Vol. 3, No. 2 (2017): 153–63.

31 Hemmings and Rogers, "The South China Sea: Why It Matters to 'Global Britain,'" January 31, 2019.

32 Hemmings, "Charting Britain's Moves in the South China Sea."

33 Ibid. Bew and Jones stated clearly that a return "East of Suez" as an "[e]xpressions of intent to 'engage' more with the region's leading states only provide a starting point. From this point, each step towards greater involvement must come with greater consciousness of cause and effect."

34 Christian Wirth, "Whose 'Freedom of Navigation'? Australia, China, the United States and the Making of Order in the 'Indo-Pacific,'" *The Pacific Review*, Vol. 32, No. 4 (2019): 475–504; Nick Bisley and Benjamin Schreer, "Australia and the Rules-Based Order in Asia of Principles and Pragmatism," *Asian Survey*, Vol. 58, No. 2 (2018): 302–19; David Scott, "Britain Returns to the Indian Ocean?" *The Round Table*, Vol. 107, No. 3: 307–16 (2018), https://doi.org/10.1080/00358533.2018.1476096; Martin, "The Attributes and Roles."

Formal discourse versus state behaviour

Notwithstanding the UK's muted response to the Arbitral Tribunal ruling in the *Philippines v. China* case in 2016 it has, since 2018, been far more active in the South China Sea region. In February 2018, the then Secretary of State for Defence, Gavin Williamson, in an interview with *The Australian* newspaper gave the first public pronouncement of the UK's policy in respect of the South China Sea. He stated that the Type 23 frigate, *HMS Sutherland*, would "be sailing through the South China Sea … and making it clear our navy has a right to do that," going on to say that it was important for the UK to "assert our values in the South China Sea."[35] Mr Williamson did not particularize or specify what amounted to "our values," but it could be inferred that this was a reference to, at least in part, the rules-based international system. This announcement was followed by *HMS Sutherland* sailing through the South China Sea in May 2018, although the Secretary of State for Defence did not confirm that *HMS Sutherland* had sailed within 12 nautical miles (the maximum extent of a state's territorial sea as stated in UNCLOS and recognized as customary international law) of a disputed maritime feature. On board *HMS Sutherland* while the ship was docked in Singapore in June 2018, following a freedom of navigation operation, Gavin Williamson reiterated that: "the reason that they [*HMS Sutherland*] are here and the reason that we are visiting is to send the strongest of signals. We believe that countries should play by the rules;" the rules he referred to clearly include UNCLOS, and he further asserted that the UK has "been sending a clear message to all that the freedom of navigation is absolutely critical."[36] It is thus clear that the UK considers freedom of navigation patrols as a mechanism to reinforce the rules-based international system by challenging actions of states, including but not limited to China, that do not conform to UNCLOS. Such action is notwithstanding the fact that, unlike the US, the UK does not have a formal freedom of navigation policy. At first glance a formal written UK freedom of navigation policy is appealing, and it is championed by the Henry Jackson Society[37] in the following terms:

---

[35] Gavin Fernando, "British Warship to Sail from Australia to South China Sea," 2018, https://www.news.com.au/world/asia/british-warship-to-sail-from-australia-to-south-china-sea/news-story/c19ae4bf66d4c341457a9f5e0fc379dc

[36] Nicola Smith, "UK Sends 'Strongest of Signals on Free Navigation in South China Sea," *The Telegraph*, June 3, 2018, https://www.telegraph.co.uk/news/2018/06/03/uk-sends-strongest-signals-free-navigation-south-china-sea/

[37] Hemmings and Rogers, *The South China Sea.*

> to dissuade the PRC from seeking to further unilaterally revise the rules-based system, the UK should adopt its own Freedom of Navigation Policy. This would empower the Royal Navy to assist British allies and partners – not least the US, Japan, the Philippines, Vietnam and the countries of the FPDA – to prevent the further erosion of the Law of the sea in the South China Sea, along with the wider rules-based system.[38]

However, the UK would be unwise to adopt a freedom of navigation policy. The reason is simple and one of limited resources. At present the Royal Navy has only 13 frigates, six destroyers, one operational amphibious landing ship and one aircraft carrier.[39] Of these, perhaps one third could be fully operational at any given time, and recognizing the UK's other enduring commitments in the Gulf, Indian Ocean, the South Atlantic, and the Caribbean, and to NATO, to protect home waters, and an ability to respond to any emerging maritime challenges, a freedom of navigation policy with respect to the SCS would risk overpromising and underdelivering. Prior to 2018, the UK had not deployed a warship to the Pacific since 2013. It is submitted that to be effective any freedom of navigation policy must be supported by a fleet capable of regular and enduring deployments to the SCS region. At present, and particularly noting the volatile maritime environment in the Arabian Gulf, it is unlikely that the Royal Navy could satisfy such demand without drastically reducing its ability to complete its other enduring commitments. The solution of course is simple – greater numbers of frigates and destroyers.

The freedom of navigation patrol by *HMS Sutherland* in the SCS is important for a number of reasons. First, it demonstrates the global reach of the Royal Navy and the willingness of the UK to enact its policy pronouncements in respect of the "rules-based international system." Second, in so doing the UK has aligned itself with, inter alia, the US, Japan, and Australia in challenging China's claims in the SCS. Third, every indication is that the route taken by *HMS Sutherland* through the SCS did not pass within 12 nautical miles of a disputed maritime feature, unlike regular US military freedom of navigation patrols in the SCS. This is particularly significant as it could be viewed as a way to assuage the concerns of the US founded on the lack of international support for its freedom of navigation policy in the SCS, while at the same time not taking

[38] Ibid.

[39] Royal Navy, "Ships: Naval Power and Prowess," 2019, https://www.royalnavy.mod.uk/the-equipment/ships

the most provocative of routes within what could potentially constitute the 12 nautical mile territorial waters of a Chinese-claimed maritime feature. Under the terms of UNCLOS, however, a warship would have a legal right to exercise the right of innocent passage through the territorial waters of any state and therefore the actions of *HMS Sutherland* could perhaps be construed as a "mild" form of freedom of navigation patrol. The actions of *HMS Sutherland* did, however, set the scene for more UK naval activity in the SCS in 2018 and 2019.

Military build-up, organization, and applications in the South China Sea

The freedom of navigation patrol conducted by *HMS Sutherland* was followed on August 31, 2018 by the 19,500-tonne amphibious landing ship, *HMS Albion*, conducting a freedom of navigation patrol within 12 nautical miles of the Paracel Islands. Unlike the patrol of *HMS Sutherland*, the patrol of *HMS Albion* could be construed as a more direct challenge to Chinese assertions in respect of the Paracel Islands given the proximity of the warship to the islands themselves. The military and diplomatic response by China was predictable and robust. *HMS Albion* was approached and challenged by a Chinese frigate and two military aircraft, although it was reported that all parties remained calm during the incident. Diplomatically, the Chinese Ministry of Foreign Affairs sent a faxed statement to Reuters in which they asserted:

> [*HMS Albion*] had entered Chinese territorial waters around the Paracel Islands on Aug. 31 without permission, and the Chinese navy had warned it to leave. The relevant actions by the British ship violated Chinese law and relevant international law, and infringed on China's sovereignty. China strongly opposes this and has lodged stern representations with the British side to express strong dissatisfaction. China strongly urges the British side to immediately stop such provocative actions, to avoid harming the broader picture of bilateral relations and regional peace and stability. China will continue to take all necessary measures to defend its sovereignty and security.[40]

[40] Tim Kelly, "Exclusive – British Navy Warship Sails Near South China Sea Islands, Angering Beijing," September 6, 2018, https://uk.reuters.com/article/uk-britain-china-southchinasea-exclusive/exclusive-british-navy-warship-sails-near-south-china-sea-islands-angering-beijing-idUKKCN1LM00V

In a further statement, a Chinese Ministry of Foreign Affairs spokesperson stated that *HMS Albion*'s transit would risk any future UK-PRC trade agreement.[41]

These statements are interesting for a number of reasons. First, irrespective of the legal classification of the Paracel Islands or issues of sovereignty, noting that China exclusively occupies the islands, but Taiwan and Vietnam also have claims of sovereignty, UNCLOS would not require the UK to request permission to transit within 12 nautical miles of the islands. Second, the actions of *HMS Albion* did not contravene UNCLOS or any international law. Third, the Chinese Ministry of Foreign Affairs has explicitly linked military actions of the UK to an area of perceived vulnerability, namely a post-Brexit UK-PRC trade deal, and, finally, the UK does not object when Chinese warships exercise their rights of innocent or transit passage in UK territorial waters.

As China's PLAN increases in size, capability, ambition and reach, it is likely that it will increase its global deployments and demonstrate its abilities as a powerful "blue water" navy. As such, it will increasingly become reliant upon UNCLOS provisions in order to, for example, exercise its rights of innocent passage through another state's territorial waters; transit passage through international straits; and conduct military exercises in the exclusive economic zone of another state. This has the potential to be problematic for China in terms of political messaging and reciprocity. On the basis of reciprocity, states against whom China takes military action in the SCS may either require that all Chinese warships request permission to transit through their waters or harass them and make diplomatic protests when they do not comply with these demands. Alternatively, and far more likely, they might expose significant duplicity on the part of China by allowing Chinese warships to freely navigate in their waters in a way in which China fails to do in the SCS. As recently as July 14, 2019 the PLA (Navy) destroyer *Xian* sailed through UK territorial waters unchallenged and unimpeded.[42]

The freedom of navigation patrol conducted by *HMS Albion* was followed in January 2019 by the Type 23 frigate *HMS Argyll* conducting joint military exercises in the SCS with the US Arleigh-Burke guided missile destroyer *USS McCampbell* and the *USNS Henry J. Kaiser* from the US 7th Fleet.[43]

---

[41] "China Slams British Navy's South China Sea Intrusion," *Global Times*, September 6, 2018, http://www.globaltimes.cn/content/1118686.shtml

[42] Royal Navy, "HMS St Albans shadows Chinese Destroyer through English Channel," July 14, 2019, https://www.royalnavy.mod.uk/news-and-latest-activity/news/2019/july/14/190714-st-albans-shadows-chinese-destroyer

[43] Royal Navy, "HMS Argyll's US Navy Link-Up in South China Sea," January 16, 2019, https://www.royalnavy.mod.uk/news-and-latest-activity/news/2019/january/16/190116-argylls-us-link-up-south-china-sea

These exercises did not take place near any disputed maritime features and as such the Chinese response was more muted and in stark contrast to both the response to the transit of *HMS Albion* and their "furious" reaction to *USS McCampbell* sailing within 12 nautical miles of the Paracel Islands a week prior to the military exercises with *HMS Argyll*.[44]

Tactics and strategies employed in relation to competing or complementary interests

The UK could be seen to be walking a tightrope in its military activities in the SCS, with mutually exclusive and incompatible demands being made by China on the one hand and long-standing allies such as the US and Australia on the other. But this discrete issue must also be viewed within the broader context of the relationship with China that includes, inter alia, the UK's response to protests in Hong Kong and the granting of elements of the 5G mobile phone network contract to Huawei. As such, policy coherence can be found to the extent that the UK has not shied away from taking a robust position with respect to citizens' rights in Hong Kong and the potential security issues that might arise through Huawei's participation in the 5G mobile phone network. What emerges therefore is some evidence of a coherent policy with regards to both China generally and the SCS specifically, in which the UK is seeking to assert the significance of the rules-based international system. Such a policy is not, however, without significant risk insofar as it might undermine the UK's future relationship with China. That said, there must also be a recognition that China is not the "only show in town" and the UK must also be willing to engage with emerging Asian economic powers such as India, Indonesia, and Vietnam, to name but three.

Impact of political, economic, and military goals, tactics, and strategies

The actions of the UK in the SCS and the policy that underpins this has not been without consequence. There has been a military response to the freedom of navigation patrols of *HMS Sutherland* and *HMS Albion* insofar as the PLAN has deployed vessels and aircraft to intercept and interact with

[44] Ben Westcott, "US, UK Hold Rare Joint Drills in the South China Sea, CNN," January 17, 2019, https://edition.cnn.com/2019/01/16/asia/uk-us-south-china-sea-intl/index.html

the British warships. Beyond the military response, and arguably more significantly, there has been a robust political response with the associated threats of adverse economic consequences for the UK. This was widely reported that, following a speech to the Royal United Services Institute in February 2019 by the then Secretary of State for Defence, Gavin Williamson, in which he stated:

> We and our allies must deter and be ready to defend ourselves. Ready to show the high price of aggressive behaviour. Ready to strengthen our resilience. And ready, where necessary, to use hard power to support our global interests. … we need to build on our established relationship with … Singapore and Malaysia in the Five Powers Defence Arrangement. With other ASEAN nations, with Japan, the Republic of Korea and India.[45]

A planned visit to China for trade talks by the then Chancellor, Philip Hammond, was cancelled.[46] The reason for the cancelled trade talks was reported to be China's irritation at Gavin Williamson's veiled reference to Chinese activity in the SCS, although the UK Treasury claimed that the trade talks were "never announced or confirmed"[47] and did not comment further. Beyond the cancellation of these trade talks China has made explicit threats that military activity by the UK in the SCS will jeopardize any future economic relationship between the UK and China.[48] It remains to be seen what specific form adverse Chinese economic action against the UK might take.

UK military activity in support of the rules-based international system

The UK's freedom of navigation operations in the SCS should not be viewed as isolated activity in pursuance of the rules-based international system. Nor should they be viewed as activity exclusively directed against Chinese

45 UK Government, "Defence in Global Britain: Defence Secretary Gavin Williamson Gave a Speech at RUSI Outlining the Future Direction of the UK Armed Force," February 11, 2019, https://www.gov.uk/government/speeches/defence-in-global-britain

46 Mattha Busby, "Hammond's Trip to China Scuppered by Williamson's 'Gunboat Diplomacy,'" *The Guardian*, February 16, 2019, https://www.theguardian.com/politics/2019/feb/16/gavin-williamson-china-warship-threat-philip-hammond

47 Ibid.

48 Global China, "China Slams British."

expansionist activity in the SCS or driven by US intervention in the region. Rather, in the past few years alone, the UK has undertaken numerous military operations that sit comfortably within the broader ambit of upholding the rules-based international system, of which military activity in the SCS is but one. Moreover, this activity has resulted in diplomatic tension, most notably with Spain, Libya, and Iran, thereby demonstrating a willingness on the part of the UK to uphold the rules-based international system despite an entirely predictable and adverse reaction by affected states. Recent examples of UK maritime activity in support of a rules-based international system include: operations in support of the UN arms embargo in respect of Libya; the seizing of the *Grace I* by Royal Marines in support of EU regulation 36/2012; counter-piracy and maritime security operations in support of the multi-national Combined Maritime Forces based in Bahrain; the conduct of conveys to ensure the safety of shipping and rights of transit passage in the Straits of Hormuz following Iranian aggression; and the patrolling of Gibraltarian territorial waters to challenge numerous Spanish incursions that do not comply with the rules of innocent passage codified within the UNCLOS.

In response to gross violations of human rights by the Libyan government against their own people, on February 26, 2011 the UN Security Council (UNSC) unanimously adopted Security Council Resolution 1970,[49] which imposed sanctions against Libya. These sanctions included an open-ended embargo on the supply of arms and military equipment to and from Libya. On June 14, 2016, the UNSC adopted Resolution 2292[50] that authorized states to inspect vessels on the high seas believed to be in violation of the arms embargo. This authorization remains extant. In support of the UN and the EU's "Operation Sophia,"[51] the UK has deployed four warships to the region to, inter alia, enforce the UN arms embargo and in turn uphold the international rules-based system.

In July 2019, 30 Royal Marine commandos boarded and seized the Iranian-owned oil tanker *Grace I* (later renamed *Adrian Darya I*) in

---

[49] United Nations Security Council, "Resolution 1970 (2011)," https://www.undocs.org/S/RES/1970%20(2011)

[50] United Nations Security Council, "Resolution 2292 (2016)," http://unscr.com/en/resolutions/doc/2292

[51] European Union, "Council Decision (CFSP) 2015/972 of 22 June 2015 Launching the European Union Military Operation in the Southern Central Mediterranean (EUNAVFOR MED)," *Official Journal of the European Union*, Vol. 16, No. 1 (2016), https://www.operationsophia.eu/wp-content/uploads/2018/03/Council-Decision-CFSP-2015972-of-22-June-2015.pdf

Gibraltarian territorial waters. The *Grace I* was carrying 2 million barrels of oil that were loaded in Iran and bound for Syria in contravention of EU Regulation 36/2012[52] that prohibits the export to Syria of, inter alia, crude oil and petroleum products. The vessel was subsequently released by a Gibraltarian court, following assurances from Iran that the oil was not bound for Syria.

Since 2001, the UK has been a constant participant in the activities of the 33-member nation Combined Maritime Forces[53] (CMF) based in Bahrain. Pursuant to upholding the rules-based international system, the CMF is a "multinational naval partnership which exists to promote security, stability and prosperity across approximately 3.2 million square miles of international waters, which encompass some of the world's most important shipping lanes."[54] More specifically, the CMF mission is to "defeat terrorism, prevent piracy, encourage regional cooperation, and promote a safe maritime environment." In order to achieve this the CMF conducts: "Maritime Security Operations, counters terrorism and narcotics smuggling in maritime areas of responsibility; works with regional and other partners to improve overall security and stability; helps strengthen regional nations' maritime capabilities and, when requested, responds to environmental and humanitarian crises."[55] Beyond the provision of numerous warships and military aircraft to CMF operations, the UK has established a permanent military base in Bahrain that serves as a physical manifestation of the UK's commitment to maritime security in the region.

Notwithstanding that it has attracted diplomatic protest by Spain, the UK has vigorously and consistently challenged Spanish incursions into Gibraltarian territorial waters that do not comply with the UNCLOS innocent passage regulations.[56] The Royal Navy's warships, permanently stationed in Gibraltar for this purpose, have taken robust action, including

---

52 European Union, "Council Regulation (EU) No 36/2012 of 18 January 2012 Concerning Restrictive Measures in View of the Situation in Syria and Repealing Regulation (EU) No 442/2011," *Official Journal of the European Union*, January 19, 2012. https://eur-lex.europa.eu/LexUriServ/LexUriServ.do?uri=OJ:L:2012:016:0001:0032:EN:PDF

53 Combined Maritime Forces (CMF), "About Combined Maritime Forces (CMF)," 2019, https://combinedmaritimeforces.com/about/

54 Ibid.

55 Ibid.

56 George Allison. "Royal Navy Chase Away Spanish Vessel from Gibraltar," *UK Defence Journal*, May 23, 2018, https://ukdefencejournal.org.uk/royal-navy-chase-away-spanish-vessel-from-gibraltar/

the firing of warning flares,[57] to prevent unlawful activity by Spanish vessels. This is clear evidence of the UK's willingness to uphold UNCLOS and in turn the rules-based international system despite the diplomatic tension that inevitably results.

Across a broad range of contemporary activity around the world it can be seen that, in the maritime domain, the UK is proactively promoting and enforcing the rules-based international system. This is both pursuant to UN and EU authorization and based upon international treaties and law, most notably UNCLOS and in concert with allies or alone. Most significantly, however, UK maritime activity often results in diplomatic tension akin to that resulting from freedom of navigation operations in the SCS. As such, and within this context, a persuasive case can be submitted that UK activity in the SCS is not just a knee-jerk reaction to Chinese expansionist activity and US intervention, but part of wide-ranging international activity underpinned by a desire to uphold the rules-based international system.

Conclusion

Like many other middle powers in Asia and elsewhere, the UK faces a dilemma of diminished foreign policy autonomy and efficacy from the new G2 contention between US and the PRC, which in the forms of unilateralism and grand bargains has diminished the role of middle powers in the renegotiation of the security rules of global order.[58] Despite the limited leeway to deviate from American preferences and severe domestic constraints, it is possible to discern some coherence and consistency in the UK's diplomatic policy towards China and military activity in the SCS. The role of the National Security Council, chaired by the Prime Minister, will approve any freedom of navigation activity in the SCS and therefore this activity ought to sit comfortably within the broader ambit of the "Global Britain" vision. The "Global Britain" vision is not, however, without difficulty given its lack of specific aims and objectives and determinable metrics. That said, the rules-based international system is a central tenet of "Global Britain" and the freedom of navigation operations undertaken by

57 George Allison, "Royal Navy Fire Warning at Spanish Vessel Near Gibraltar as It Approaches Nuclear Submarine," September 20, 2018, https://ukdefencejournal.org.uk/royal-navy-fire-warning-at-spanish-vessel-near-gibraltar-as-it-approaches-nuclear-submarine

58 Alastair Iain Johnston, "Is China a Status Quo Power?" *International Security*, Vol. 27, No. 4 (2003): 5–56.

the Royal Navy fit within this policy insofar as they challenge the activities of China and other regional states activity in the Spratly and Paracel Islands.

The conceptual debate over "status quo" and "revisionism" in describing the intentions and behaviour of states toward the regional and international order remains relevant.[59] The UK experience shows that these are not necessarily dichotomous categories – not only because the starting point and degree of change are understood differently from the vantage points of competing stakeholders, but also because each country maintains a degree of autonomy in interpreting the means-and-end to maximize its policy gains and legitimacy.[60] For UK, the "status quo" of a rules-based international order conveniently downplays the contentious maritime history and continual conflicts among the claimants, even prior to China's escalating presence in the SCS. It draws a baseline from the 2017 Arbitral Tribunal decision, by which Chinese actions are judged to be in contravention of the status quo, even as the UK has taken no position in respect of sovereignty of the maritime features in the SCS and prefers to let the US lead in spelling out the legal implications of the claimants' rights of maritime zones in the SCS.[61] The UK is "revisionist" in contributing to American and other powers' FON missions to affect the distribution of naval power in the region to restore this imagined status quo that is actually not a return to the prior state, but a new equilibrium whose stability is guaranteed by military interventions and in compliance with international law.

That said, whether the UK's freedom of navigation activities in the SCS will continue remains to be seen. Further questions would arise if FON exercises go beyond innocent passage of FON operations and if the UK gets serious about building additional naval bases in the Indo-Pacific.[62] Would these actions then indicate that the UK is willing to face the risks of confrontation and escalation vis-à-vis the Chinese, and to bear the

59 Alexander Cooley, Daniel Nexon, and Steven Ward, "Revising Order or Challenging the Balance of Military Power? An Alternative Typology of Revisionist and Status-Quo States," *Review of International Studies*, Vol. 45, No. 4 (October 2019): 689–708; Barry Buzan, "The Logic and Contradictions of 'Peaceful Rise/Development' as China's Grand Strategy," *The Chinese Journal of International Politics*, Vol. 7, No. 4 (Winter 2014): 381–420.

60 Kun-Chin Lin and Andrès Villar Gertner, *Maritime Security in the Asia-Pacific: China and the Emerging Order in the East and South China Seas* (Chatham House, 2015).

61 US Secretary of State Michael R. Pompeo, "US Position on Maritime Claims in the South China Sea," Press Statement, July 13, 2020, US Department of State, https://www.state.gov/u-s-position-on-maritime-claims-in-the-south-china-sea/

62 Henry Jones, "UK Should Establish Military Presence in South China Sea Says Report," *UK Defence Journal*, January 30, 2019, https://ukdefencejournal.org.uk/uk-should-establish-military-presence-in-south-china-sea-says-report/

bilateral diplomatic and economic costs of Chinese displeasure? Would this apparent commitment through militarization detract from alternative, legal-institutional options in defence of the rules-based regional order, including leading discussions in international legal forums on unresolved issues of innocent passage, use of force, EEZs, and so on? Would the UK's strong and clear position on international law be compromised by its use of naval power?[63] These unintended consequences would have long-term effects on the sound principle of the defence of a rules-based international order. It seems sensible that Britain should make tough decisions on a limited operationalization of its principled stance based on: (a) specific invitations of its historical partners in the Asian region; (b) an active strategic coordination of European and American navies in various maritime hotspots around the world; and (c) the level of domestic support for military modernization and the commensurate fiscal expenditure and legal and soft power investment.

References

Allison, George. "Royal Navy Chase Away Spanish Vessel from Gibraltar." *UK Defence Journal* May 23, 2018. https://ukdefencejournal.org.uk/royal-navy-chase-away-spanish-vessel-from-gibraltar/.

Allison, George. "Royal Navy Fire Warning at Spanish Vessel near Gibraltar as It Approaches Nuclear Submarine." *UK Defence Journal*, September 20, 2018. https://ukdefencejournal.org.uk/royal-navy-fire-warning-at-spanish-vessel-near-gibraltar-as-it-approaches-nuclear-submarine

Austin, Michael "Britain Is Right to Send Its Navy to the South China Sea." *The Spectator*, January 21, 2019. https://blogs.spectator.co.uk/2019/01/britain-is-right-to-send-its-navy-to-the-south-china-sea/

Axe, David. "The Decline of the Royal Navy." *The Maritime Executive*, 2016. https://www.maritime-executive.com/editorials/the-decline-of-the-royal-navy

Baker McKenzie. "Chinese FDI into North America and Europe in 2018 Falls 73% to Six-Year Low of $30 Billion." 2019. https://www.bakermckenzie.com/en/newsroom/2019/01/chinese-fdi

[63] Critical cases include: Cameron Moore, "The Arbitral Award in the Matter of the South China Sea Between the Philippines and China. What are the Implications for Freedom of Navigation and the Use of Force?" *Asia-Pacific Journal of Ocean Law and Policy*, Vol. 2, No. 1 (July 2017): 117–39, https://doi.org/10.1163/24519391-00201007; Stephen Rose, "Naval Activity in the Exclusive Economic Zone – Troubled Waters Ahead?" *Ocean Development & International Law*, Vol. 21, No. 2 (1990): 123–45, https://doi.org/10.1080/00908328909545927

Bateman, Sam. "The Risks of US Freedom of Navigation Operations in the South China Sea." *East Asia Forum*, 2015. https://www.lowyinstitute.org/the-interpreter/us-fonop-game-back-south-china-sea

Bateman, Sam. "US FONOPs: Game On Again in the South China Sea." *The Interpreter*, May 26, 2017. https://www.lowyinstitute.org/the-interpreter/us-fonop-game-back-south-china-sea

BBC News. "Hong Kong Protests: UK Should Not Interfere, Says Chinese Ambassador." August 15, 2019. https://www.bbc.co.uk/news/uk-49356495

Bisley, Nick, and Schreer, Benjamin. "Australia and the Rules-Based Order in Asia: Of Principles and Pragmatism." *Asian Survey*, Vol. 58, No. 2 (2018): 302–19.

Bowers, Ian. "Can the Burden Be Shared? Europe, the Sea and the Liberal Order in Asia." *Global Asia*, Vol. 13, No. 2 (2018): 1027. http://www.globalasia.org/v13no2/focus/can-the-burden-be-shared-europe-the-sea-and-the-liberal-order-in-asia_ian-bowers

Busby, Mattha. "Hammond's Trip to China Scuppered by Williamson's 'Gunboat Diplomacy.'" *The Guardian,* February 16, 2019. https://www.theguardian.com/politics/2019/feb/16/gavin-williamson-china-warship-threat-philip-hammond

Buzan, Barry. "The Logic and Contradictions of 'Peaceful Rise/Development' as China's Grand Strategy," *The Chinese Journal of International Politics*, Vol. 7, No. 4 (Winter 2014): 381–420.

Chen Xiangmiao. "Why Is the UK Expanding Its Military Presence in the South China Sea?" *China-US Focus*, January 15, 2019. https://www.chinausfocus.com/peace-security/why-is-the-uk-expanding-its-military-presence-in-the-south-china-sea-

Combined Maritime Forces (CMF). *About Combined Maritime Forces (CMF).* 2019. https://combinedmaritimeforces.com/about/

Cooley, Alexander, Daniel Nexon, and Steven Ward, "Revising Order or Challenging the Balance of Military Power? An Alternative Typology of Revisionist and Status-Quo States," *Review of International Studies*, Vol. 45, No. 4 (October 2019): 689–708.

European Union. "Council Decision (CFSP) 2015/972 of 22 June 2015 Launching the European Union Military Operation in the Southern Central Mediterranean (EUNAVFOR MED)." *Official Journal of The European Union*, Vol. 16, No. 1 (2016). https://www.operationsophia.eu/wp-content/uploads/2018/03/Council-Decision-CFSP-2015972-of-22-June-2015.pdf

European Union. "Council Regulation (EU) No 36/2012 of 18 January 2012 Concerning Restrictive Measures in View of the Situation in Syria and Repealing Regulation (EU) No 442/2011." *Official Journal of the European Union*, January 19, 2012. https://eur-lex.europa.eu/LexUriServ/LexUriServ.do?uri=OJ:L:2012:016:0001:0032:EN:PDF

Fernando, Gavin. "British Warship to Sail from Australia to South China Sea." News Pty, 2018. https://www.news.com.au/world/asia/british-warship-to-sail-from-australia-to-south-china-sea/news-story/c19ae4bf66d4c341457a9f5e0fc379dc

Global Times. "China Slams British Navy's South China Sea Intrusion." *Global Times*, September 6, 2018. http://www.globaltimes.cn/content/1118686.shtml

Goldrick, James. "The Limits of Global Britain." *The Lowy Interpreter*, December 5, 2017. https://www.lowyinstitute.org/the-interpreter/limits-global-britain

Hansard, Lords. "South China Sea: Royal Navy Deployment." UK Parliament, November 1, 2018. https://hansard.parliament.uk/lords/2018-11-01/debates/9AD0AA10-3AA5-4338-A8BC-E8C8097333D0/SouthChinaSeaRoyalNavyDeployment

Hemmings, John. "Charting Britain's Moves in the South China Sea." RUSI, 2018. https://rusi.org/commentary/charting-britain%E2%80%99s-moves-south-china-sea

Hemmings, John, and Rogers, James. *The South China Sea: Why It Matters to "Global Britain."* Henry Jackson Society, 2019. https://henryjacksonsociety.org/wp-content/uploads/2019/01/HJS-South-China-Sea-Report-web-1.pdf

Holmes, James R. "Britannia Helps Rule the Waves." Foreign Policy, February 20, 2019. https://foreignpolicy.com/2019/02/20/britannia-helps-rule-the-waves/

International Institute for Strategic Studies. *The Military Balance 2019*. https://www.iiss.org/publications/the-military-balance/the-military-balance-2019

International Monetary Fund. "World Economic Outlook Database." July 2018. https://www.imf.org/external/pubs/ft/weo/2018/01/weodata/index.aspx

Johnston, Alastair Iain. "Is China a Status Quo Power?" *International Security*, Vol. 27, No. 4 (2003): 5–56.

Jones, Henry. "UK Should Establish Military Presence in South China Sea, Says Report." *UK Defence Journal*, January 30, 2019. https://ukdefencejournal.org.uk/uk-should-establish-military-presence-in-south-china-sea-says-report/

Joshi, Shashank, and Graham, Euan. "'Global Britain' on the Line in South China Sea." *The Interpreter*, February 22, 2018. https://www.lowyinstitute.org/the-interpreter/global-britain-line-south-china-sea

Kelly, Tim. "Exclusive – British Navy Warship Sails near South China Sea Islands, Angering Beijing." September 6, 2018. https://uk.reuters.com/article/uk-britain-china-southchinasea-exclusive/exclusive-british-navy-warship-sails-near-south-china-sea-islands-angering-beijing-idUKKCN1LM00V

Lin, Kun-chin and Andrès Villar Gertner, *Maritime Security in the Asia-Pacific: China and the Emerging Order in the East and South China Seas* (Chatham House, 2015). https://www.chathamhouse.org/sites/default/files/field/field_document/20150731MaritimeSecurityAsiaPacificLinGertner.pdf

Martin, Christopher. "The Attributes and Roles of Naval Forces." In *The UK as a Medium Maritime Power in the 21st Century*, 21–38 (Palgrave Macmillan, 2016). https://doi.org/10.1057/978-1-137-01237-1_2

McCarthy, Niall. "The UK's Shrinking Navy." *Statista*, January 1, 2018. https://www.statista.com/chart/12747/the-uks-shrinking-navy/

Mizokami, Kyle. "The Five Most-Powerful Navies on the Planet." *The National Interest*, June 6, 2014. https://nationalinterest.org/feature/the-five-most-powerful-navies-the-planet-10610

Moore, Cameron. "The Arbitral Award in the Matter of the South China Sea between the Philippines and China: What Are the Implications for Freedom of Navigation and the Use of Force?" *Asia-Pacific Journal of Ocean Law and Policy*, Vol. 2, No. 1 (2017): 117–39. https://doi.org/10.1163/24519391-00201007

Radakin, Tony. "First Sea Lord Speech to Defence and Security Equipment International." Royal Navy, September 11, 2019. https://www.royalnavy.mod.uk/news-and-latest-activity/news/2019/september/11/190911-1sl-speech-dsei

Reilly, Tim and Lin, Kun-Chin. "The Russian Variable in Post-Brexit UK Foreign Relations with China, the US and EU." *The Asia Dialogue*, March 3, 2017. https://theasiadialogue.com/2017/03/03/the-russian-variable-in-post-brexit-uk-foreign-relations-with-china-the-us-and-eu/

Rose, Stephen. "Naval Activity in the Exclusive Economic Zone – Troubled Waters Ahead?" *Ocean Development & International Law*, Vol. 21, No. 2 (1990): 123–45. https://doi.org/10.1080/00908328909545927

Royal Navy. "HMS Argyll's US Navy Link-Up in South China Sea." January 16, 2019. https://www.royalnavy.mod.uk/news-and-latest-activity/news/2019/january/16/190116-argylls-us-link-up-south-china-sea

Royal Navy. "HMS St Albans Shadows Chinese Destroyer through English Channel." July 14, 2019. https://www.royalnavy.mod.uk/news-and-latest-activity/news/2019/july/14/190714-st-albans-shadows-chinese-destroyer

Royal Navy. "Ships: Naval Power and Prowess." 2019. https://www.royalnavy.mod.uk/the-equipment/ships

Schreer, Benjamin, and Lim, Yves-Heng. "Embracing the Dragon? Europe's Major Powers and the Rise of China." *Global Affairs*, Vol. 3, No. 2 (2017): 153–63.

Schweller, Randall. "Opposite but Compatible Nationalisms: A Neoclassical Realist Approach to the Future of US–China relations." *The Chinese Journal of International Politics*, Vol. 11, No. 1 (2018): 23–48.

Scott, David. "Britain Returns to the Indian Ocean?" *The Round Table*, Vol. 107, No. 3 (2018): 307–16. https://doi.org/10.1080/00358533.2018.1476096

Seely, Bob, and Rogers, James. *Global Britain: A Twenty First Century Vision* (Henry Jackson Society, 2019). http://www.defencesynergia.co.uk/wp-content/uploads/2019/03/HJS-Global-Britain-_-A-Twenty-first-Century-Vision-Report-A4-web.pdf

Smith, Nicola. "UK Sends 'Strongest of Signals' on Free Navigation in South China Sea." *The Telegraph*, June 3, 2018. https://www.telegraph.co.uk/news/2018/06/03/uk-sends-strongest-signals-free-navigation-south-china-sea/

Statista. "The 15 Countries with the Highest Gross Domestic Product (GDP) in 2030." https://www.statista.com/statistics/271724/forecast-for-the-countries-with-the-highest-gross-domestic-product-gdp-in-2030

Thayer, Carl. "After Brexit: Global Britain Plots Course to Return to the Far East." *The Diplomat*, January 17, 2019. https://thediplomat.com/2019/01/after-brexit-global-britain-plots-course-to-return-to-the-far-east/

UK Department for Transport, *Shipping Fleet Statistics: 2018*. https://assets.publishing.service.gov.uk/government/uploads/system/uploads/attachment_data/file/785497/shipping-fleet-statistics-2018.pdf

UK Government. "National Security Capability Review." March 2018. https://assets.publishing.service.gov.uk/government/uploads/system/uploads/attachment_data/file/705347/6.4391_CO_National-Security-Review_web.pdf

UK Government. "Global Britain: Delivering on Our International Ambition." June 13, 2018. https://www.gov.uk/government/collections/global-britain-delivering-on-our-international-ambition

UK Government. "Defence in Global Britain: Defence Secretary Gavin Williamson Gave a Speech at RUSI Outlining the Future Direction of the UK Armed Forces." February 11, 2019. https://www.gov.uk/government/speeches/defence-in-global-britain

UK Office for National Statistics. *GDP First Quarterly Estimate, UK: April to June 2019*. 2019. https://www.ons.gov.uk/economy/grossdomesticproductgdp/bulletins/gdpfirstquarterlyestimateuk/apriltojune2019

United Nations Security Council. "Resolution 1970 (2011)." https://www.undocs.org/S/RES/1970%20(2011)

United Nations Security Council. "Resolution 2292 (2016)." http://unscr.com/en/resolutions/doc/2292

US Secretary of State Michael R. Pompeo, "US Position on Maritime Claims in the South China Sea," Press Statement, July 13, 2020, US Department of State. https://www.state.gov/u-s-position-on-maritime-claims-in-the-south-china-sea/

Weissmann, Mikael. "Chinese Foreign Policy in a Global Perspective: A Responsible Reformer 'Striving for Achievement.'" *Journal of China and International Relations*, Vol. 3, No. 1 (2015): 151–66.

Westcott, Ben. "US, UK Hold Rare Joint Drills in the South China Sea." CNN, January 17, 2019. https://edition.cnn.com/2019/01/16/asia/uk-us-south-china-sea-intl/index.html

Wirth, Christian. "Whose 'Freedom of Navigation'? Australia, China, the United States and the Making of Order in the 'Indo-Pacific.'" *The Pacific Review*, Vol. 32, No. 4 (2019): 475–504. https://doi.org/10.1080/09512748.2018.1515788

Workman, Daniel. "United Kingdom's Top Trading Partners." World's Top Exports. http://www.worldstopexports.com/united-kingdoms-top-import-partners/

Wu, Zhengyu. "The Crowe Memorandum, the Rebalance to Asia, and Sino-US Relations." *Journal of Strategic Studies*, Vol. 39, No. 3 (2016): 389–416.

17

Balancing and Hedging: The Two Levels of Russia's Behaviour in the South China Sea

Alexander Korolev

Introduction

Russia's behaviour in the South China Sea (SCS) dispute is a puzzling case for international relations scholars.[1] On the surface, Russia's official approach is to persuade the rival claimants and the broader international community that Russia is an extra-regional player that has no direct stakes in the SCS and, therefore, prefers not to be involved. However, behind the façade of disengagement are large-scale energy and arms deals with the major disputants. Most puzzling are Russia's relations with China and Vietnam – the two major rival parties in the SCS and, simultaneously, Russia's closest and most important Asian partners.

Most of the existing assessments interpret Russia-China-Vietnam relations in zero-sum terms. Thus, the strengthening of the Russia-Vietnam partnership is presented as a means for Russia to contain or balance the alleged Chinese threat.[2] According to this narrative, Russia worries about overdependence

---

1 Parts of this chapter first appeared in Alexander Korolev, "Russia in the South China Sea: Balancing and Hedging," *Foreign Policy Analysis* 15.2 (2018): 263–82 and are reprinted here by permission of Oxford University Press.

2 Tony Rinna, "The China Factor in Russia-Vietnam Security Ties," *Foreign Policy Journal*, 5 January 2016, http://www.foreignpolicyjournal.com/2016/01/05/the-china-factor-in-russia-vietnam-security-ties/

upon an increasingly influential China and tries to arm or conclude economic deals with Vietnam and other actual or potential adversaries of China in the SCS and in Asia more broadly. The other side of such an interpretation is based on the evidence of a growing military entente between China and Russia and pictures Russia as siding with China at the cost of relations with other regional partners, including Vietnam, particularly after the Ukraine Crisis. According to this story, as a China-Russia strategic alignment grows, Russia is likely to snub those of its partners who are at odds with China.[3]

These interpretations are incomplete. First, they make the coexistence of the Russia-China and Russia-Vietnam strategic partnerships a sheer paradox. However, both relationships have existed and even progressed for quite some time. Second, although Russia does try to enhance cooperation with Vietnam and other regional states, its cooperation with China continues to grow, and there is no evidence of Russia intentionally trying to slow it down. Third, the Russia-Vietnam partnership should not be underestimated, because it has been growing despite and independently of Russia-China relations. In summary, cooperating with both China and its rival claimants characterizes Russia's policies in the SCS.

This chapter argues that to untangle this situation, one must "zoom out" to see the logic of both international systemic and non-systemic (regional and domestic) levels of great-power behaviour. It explains the complexity and ambivalence of Russia's behaviour toward the SCS dispute by showing that the SCS is the point of intersection of Russia's policies of "systemic balancing" and those of "regional hedging." The former is motivated by the power distribution and threat perception within the international system, and they materialize in a balancing response against the global dominance of the system leader – the United States (US). The latter is a non-system-level "insurance policy" motivated by causal forces other than the systemic power-and-threat distribution, and emerges as measures aimed at the diversification of Russia's regional links and the prevention of potential instability that can harm its economic interests in Asia Pacific. The different incentives generated by these two prongs explain the pattern of Russia's behaviour in the SCS, particularly Russia's relations with China and Vietnam.

The chapter is organized as follows. Section one outlines Moscow's official approach to the SCS dispute and policies toward both China and Vietnam. Section two examines the systemic-balancing component of Russia's

[3] Pavel K. Baev and Stein Tønnesson, "Can Russia Keep its Special Ties with Vietnam While Moving Closer and Closer to China?" *International Area Studies Review* 18, no. 3 (2015): 312–25.

behaviour toward the SCS, whereas section three explicates its hedging dimension. Section four concludes by further elaborating how the potential prevalence of balancing vis-à-vis hedging, and vice versa, can shape Russia's policies in the SCS dispute or elsewhere.

Russia's approach to the South China Sea: rhetoric and actions

At the official level, Russia has consistently been displaying a neutral "middle of the road" posture toward the SCS dispute. Moscow has never formally accepted or publicly backed any involved country's sovereignty or position over the disputed territories. Unlike the US, Russia has never publicly questioned the legitimacy of China's "nine-dash line," which in the context of growing China-US tensions can be interpreted as indirect support of China. However, in response to media speculation, Russian Foreign Ministry spokesperson Maria Zakharova stated on July 14, 2016: "[Russia] had never been a participant in the South China Sea disputes," and that, "we consider it a matter of principle not to side with any party."[4] Moscow's official rhetoric changed slightly toward being more pro-China after the July 2016 Arbitral Tribunal ruling on the SCS dispute in favour of the Philippines. However, upon closer examination, it is clear that the related official statements were carefully crafted against the legitimacy of the institution of The Hague Arbitration Court, which Moscow has its own strong reason to challenge, and do not indicate support of anyone's territorial sovereignty. As far as the SCS dispute is concerned, Moscow has been unwilling to spend political capital to support either Beijing or its rivals and has preferred to remain aloof from the SCS conundrum.

Moscow's diplomatic posture of disengagement, however, is in discord with Russia's actual behaviour in the region, particularly when it comes to relations with China and Vietnam. Russia-China relations have been developing steadily and have reached the level of "a comprehensive strategic partnership of coordination for a new era."[5] Both Moscow and Beijing emphasized that their positions on major international issues are "either similar or identical."[6] President Putin has even referred to China as Russia's

---

4 Foreign Ministry Spokesperson Maria Zakharova's briefing, Moscow, 14 July 2016, http://www.mid.ru/en/web/guest/foreign_policy/news/-/asset_publisher/cKNonkJE02Bw/content/id/2354135

5 *Xinhua News*, "China, Russia Agree to Upgrade Relations for New Era," 6 June 2019, http://www.xinhuanet.com/english/2019-06/06/c_138119879.htm

6 Vladimir Portyakov, *Vneshniaya Politika Kitaiskoi Narodnoi Respubliki v 21-m Stoletii [The PRC's Foreign Policy in the 21st Century]* (Moscow: Institute of Far Eastern Studies, 2015), 143.

"natural partner and natural ally."[7] In 2014 and 2015, China and Russia concluded historic energy deals, and on June 25, 2016, Presidents Putin and Xi signed the *Joint Declaration of the Russian Federation and the People's Republic of China*, which states that both sides should support each other "on the issues concerning each other's security, territorial integrity, sovereignty, and other core interests."[8] Simultaneously, the "Joint Sea 2016" (Russia-China joint annual naval drills) became the first drill of this kind that involved China and another country in the waters of the disputed SCS after the Hague Tribunal came up with the ruling on China's territorial claims under the "nine-dash line," and included "joint island-seizing" exercises, which were absent from the previous "Joint Seas."[9] Given the international circumstances, the very existence of these exercises has triggered speculation about Moscow unequivocally siding with China and switching toward proactive military support of China in the SCS.

At the same time, however, Russia's relations with Vietnam have been growing. In July 2012, Russia and Vietnam signed the *Joint Statement on Comprehensive Strategic Partnership Intensification*, which has elevated their bilateral relations to the status of "comprehensive strategic partnership," roughly similar in nature to the relations Russia has with China.[10] When visiting Moscow in 2012, the President of Vietnam, Trương Tấn Sang, stated, "[the] consolidation of relations of our traditional friendship and development of comprehensive strategic partnership with the Russian Federation is one of the top priorities of Vietnam's foreign policy."[11] During his visit to Hanoi in November 2013, President Putin called Vietnam "a key partner of Russia in the Asia-Pacific region."[12] Simultaneously, Russia

---

7 "Putin Confirms Plans to Meet Chinese President during APEC Summit in Beijing," *Sputnik International*, 14 October 2014, http://sputniknews.com/politics/20141014/194060827.html

8 Sovmestnoe Zayavlenie Rossiiskoi Federatcii i Kitaiskoi Narodnoi Respubliki [The China-Russia Joint Declaration of 25 June 2016], 25 June 2016, http://www.kremlin.ru/supplement/5100

9 Ankit Panda, "Chinese, Russian Navies to Hold 8 Days of Naval Exercises in the South China Sea," *The Diplomat*, 12 September 2016, http://thediplomat.com/2016/09/chinese-russian-navies-to-hold-8-days-of-naval-exercises-in-the-south-china-sea/

10 Sovmestnoy Zayavlenie ob Ykreplenii Otnoshenii Vseobiemlyschego Strategicheskogo Partnerstva Mezhdy Rossiiskoi Federaciei i Socialisticheskoi Respublikoi Vietnam [Russia-Vietnam Joint Statement on the Comprehensive Strategic Partnership Intensification], 27 July 2012, The President of Russia http://news.kremlin.ru/ref_notes/1279

11 Nghien cuu Chien luoc va Quoc te [Center for Strategic and International Studies], no. 3, 2012, Cit. 66, cited from Yevgeny Kobelev, "Twenty Years of the Russia-ASEAN Partnership," *Far Eastern Affairs* 6 (2014), 7.

12 Vitaly Kozyrev, "Russia-Vietnam Strategic Partnership: The Return of the Brotherhood in Arms?" *Russian Analytical Digest* 145 (31 March 2014), 9.

enhanced energy and military cooperation with Vietnam and increased the transfers of advanced weapons systems that enhance Vietnam's defence capabilities. In this context, the Vietnamese Defence Minister called Russia: "Vietnam's leading strategic partner in the area of military-technical cooperation."[13] In 2013, the two countries concluded a military cooperation pact that formalized Russia-Vietnam defence cooperation and established mechanisms for information exchange. At the same time, Russia has been assisting Vietnam in building a submarine base and repair dockyards at Cam Ranh Bay (a former Soviet military base in Vietnam). In November 2014, the two countries signed an agreement considerably simplifying the use of this facility by the Russian Navy and air force.[14]

Similarly to how Russia's cooperation with China can be interpreted as an indication of its support for China in the SCS dispute, Russia's policies toward Vietnam can be viewed as an indication of Moscow's support of Hanoi. To explain this pattern of Moscow's behaviour, it is useful to discern two modes of behaviour related to two different levels of great-power foreign policy – balancing and hedging – and to demonstrate how these two modes operate in the context of the SCS dispute. The moves by Russia that appear to work both in China's interests and against them can, in fact, be manifestations of parts of different strategies of balancing or hedging. The same applies to Russia's policies toward Vietnam, depending upon the degree of US involvement in the region's affairs.

Russia's systemic balancing and the South China Sea dispute

As a systemic balancer, Russia is expected to check, block, or otherwise frustrate the geopolitical projects of the strongest power in the international system – the United States. Russia is also supposed to perceive the US (the system leader) and the US-led NATO's eastward expansion as a major threat to its existence and national security. These expectations are borne out by Russia's actual attempts to challenge the US-led system in multiple ways, as demonstrated by its policies in Georgia (2008), Ukraine (2014), and Syria (since 2015); all three run counter to the system leader's interests and significantly frustrate its geopolitical projects. From this standpoint, for Russia the SCS is a part of a larger global strategy that dictates a peculiar stance on

[13] "Russia is Vietnam's Leading Strategic Partner in the Area of Military-Technical Cooperation –Defense Minister of Vietnam," *Sputnik News*, 5 August 2013, http://in.sputniknews.com/indian.ruvr.ru/news/2013_08_05/Russia-Vietnam-cooperation/

[14] "Russia, Vietnam agree on simplified Cam Ranh port entry for Russian warships," TASS, 27 November 2014.

regional disputes. The imperatives of systemic balancing push Russia to side with China (which also resists the American unipolar domination) – but only with respect to resisting American hegemony, not issues of territorial rights. This is a crucial qualification that highlights the systemic balancing component of Russia's SCS policies; Russia sides with China not because it supports the latter's territorial claims but because, and as much as, doing so aids Russia's anti-US balancing attempts.

The pressure coming from the US-dominated global system makes the Russian political elites interpret American "rebalancing to Asia" as a manifestation of Washington's desire to strengthen its international positions by means of containing China. Some view the US's activity in Asia as a preventive measure against the possibility of Asian countries gathering around China, which "promotes the alternative model of development and has a goal to reform the present international regime,"[15] which Russia supports. Other experts and diplomats argued that all aspects of US's activity in the Asia-Pacific, including the deployment of regional anti-missile defence (AMD), the revamping of military bases at Guam and Okinawa, and the increasing of military assistance to the American allies in Asia Pacific, were directed at the SCS region, in which the United States has undertaken a course of direct confrontation with China.[16] The dominant view in Russia of the developments in the SCS is permeated by concerns about the US's hegemonic policies, which strike a chord with China's assessments and reflect the expected systemic balancing logic.[17]

Some military experts even argue that: "[T]he construction of Chinese military infrastructure [in the SCS] will provide Russia with projection in the area against US Aegis systems, Navy ships, and SM-3 and Tomahawk missiles."[18] Others propose forming a permanent Russia-China joint naval operations group, supported by Russia's Tu-22M3 strategic bombers, to

[15] Sergei Mihnevich, "SShA v Aziatsko-Tihookeanskom Regione: Liderstvo Lyuboi Cenoi [USA in Asia-Pacific Region: Leadership at any Costs], http://modernpolitics.ru/2012/01/sha-v-aziatsko-tikhookeanskom-regione-liderstvo-lyubojj-cenojj/

[16] Viktor Trifonov, "Vsdtuplenie na Zajchnom Kruglom Stole 'Factor Kitaya vo Vzaimootnosheniyah RF i SShA [Presentation at the roundtable The China Factor in Russia-US relations]," *Problemu Dal'nego Vostoka [Far Eastern Affairs]*, no. 2 (2012): 101–2.

[17] Yana Leksyutina, "Obostrenie Napyazhennosti v Yuzhno-Kitaiskom More: Vzglyad iz YuVa, KNR, i SShA [Growing tensions in the South China Sea: A View from Southeast Asia, China, and the United States], *Problemy Dal'nego Vostoka [Far Eastern Affairs]*, no. 5 (2012), 39.

[18] Victor Litovkin, "Russia Could Gain from Backing China in South China Sea Disputes," Russia Beyond the Headlines, 8 September 2016, http://rbth.com/international/2016/09/08/russia-could-gain-from-backing-china-in-south-china-sea-disputes-experts_628057

contain the US-Japan coalition naval forces in the area.[19] This is a typical logic of checking and blocking the power of the hegemon as a part of the systemic anti-hegemonic balancing conceptualized in the previous section.

That Russia is involved in such balancing, rather than simply supporting China, is borne out by the fact that Moscow consistently resists the "internationalization" (that is, greater involvement of the US) of the SCS dispute but does not openly support anyone's, including China's, territorial claims. In 2016, in his interview for the Chinese, Japanese, and Mongolian media, Russian Foreign Minister, Sergei Lavrov, emphasized that, "[i]t is necessary to terminate any meddling by extra-regional countries into the negotiations taking place between the direct participants of the dispute and to stop any attempts to internationalize the issue."[20] Although one can read this as support of China, it is so only insofar as it concerns resisting the US' interference in the dispute and does not spread beyond that to the actual dispute, that is, to China's tensions with the regional disputants such as Vietnam, the Philippines, or others.

Russia's anti-US balancing can also be traced in its relations with Vietnam, which shows the strength of the imperatives of system-level factors in shaping great-power behaviour and proves the point that presenting Russia-Vietnam military cooperation purely as a measure to check China is a gross simplification. At first sight, it might appear that Russia seeking good relations with both Vietnam and China is not consistent with the logic of balancing and the balance of power. However, since systemic balancing is directed against the strongest power (which is the US, not China) or the greatest threat in the system (which for Russia is the US, not China), the baseline logic of Russia's balancing follows the principle that everything works as long as it helps Russia to contain or avert the hypothetical or actual threat coming from the US. Thus, Russia seeking cooperation with both China and Vietnam is in accord with the balancing assumption as long as it aids Russia's goals of anti-hegemonic balancing.

A case in point is the aforementioned return of Russia to Cam Ranh Bay military base in Vietnam. In accordance with the new Russia-Vietnam

---

19 Anton Mardasov, "V Kil'vatere Kovarnogo Drakona [In the Wake of a Crafty Dragon]," Svobodnaya Pressa Online [The Free Press Online], 29 July 2016, http://svpressa.ru/war21/article/153424/

20 Interview Ministra Inostrannuh Del Rossii S.V. Lavrova SMI Mongolii, Yaponii, i KNR v Preddverii Vizitov v Eti Stranu [Russian Minister of Foreign Affairs Sergei Lavrov's Interview to the Japanese, Mongolian, and Chinese Media on the Eve of Visiting These Countries], 12 April 2016, http://www.mid.ru/foreign_policy/news/-/asset_publisher/cKNonkJE02Bw/content/id/2227965

agreement, Russia could station at Cam Ranh Bay the IL-78 tanker aircraft that were used for refuelling Tu-95 nuclear strategic bombers for the resumed patrols close to Japan and the American territory of Guam. The activity of Russian bombers close to Guam triggered Washington's admonition of Hanoi in January 2015 for letting the Russians use Cam Ranh Bay which, according to Washington, raised tensions in the region.[21]

Quite tellingly, in this context, are the Russian State Duma's internal discussions of re-establishing military presence in Vietnam, which intensified after the US Chief of Staff of the Army, General Mark Milley, stated that, "[a]rmed conflict between the United States and the Russian Federation is almost guaranteed" and that, "the United States is taking all of the necessary measures to prepare for a large-scale war."[22] The Duma Parliamentarians urged that the base in Vietnam be fully restored and its military modernization accelerated, arguing that "our strategic partners [in Washington] do not understand the language of diplomacy and rattle the sabre."[23] Russia's military bases in Vietnam and Cuba, it was argued, will be an "unpleasant surprise for the American militarism."[24] According to Russia's First Deputy Chair of Federation Council Committee on Defence and Security, Franz Klinzewitsch:

> Russia undoubtedly needs military bases in Cuba and Vietnam … Let's remember that we have a dozen military bases abroad, whereas the Americans have 800–400 active and 400 frozen. And they are still saying that they are protecting their own country without threatening anyone? Why cannot Russia do the same? Look at the map! We simply have to follow the same tactics.[25]

This once again demonstrates the role of systemic balancing in Russia's strategic calculations in the region, which makes Russia's policies toward the SCS dispute complex and multi-layered.

---

21 Nhina Lee and Collin Koh Swee Lean, "Vietnam and Great Power Rivalries," *The Diplomat,* 31 March 2015, http://thediplomat.com/2015/03/vietnam-and-great-power-rivalries/

22 "Bazovue Interesu. "Zachem Rossiiskoi Armii Garnizonu na Kybe i vo V'etname? [Basic Interests. Why does the Russian Army Needs Garrisons in Cuba and Vietnam?]," *Live Journal*, 10 October 2016, http://www.livejournal.com/media/950750.html.

23 Dmitri Olizhevsky, "Zachem Rossii Bazu v Lurdese i Camrani? [Why does Russia need military bases in Lourdes and Cam Ranh?]," *Parlamentskaya Gazeta* [*The Parliament Newspaper*], 7 October 2016.

24 "Bazovue Interesu."

25 Olizhevsky, "Zachem Rossii Bazu v Lurdese i Camrani?"

Russia's regional hedging and the South China Sea dispute

In contrast to balancing, hedging involves a vast range of players, large and small, engaged in a mix of versatile day-to-day policies in various areas of state interests that are not necessarily aimed at the system leader. It is described as a set of strategies that "cultivate a middle position that forestalls or avoids having to choose one side at the obvious expense of another."[26] As such, hedging is more directly affected by non-systemic causal factors, such as situations in immediate geopolitical environments or other unit-level circumstances.

From this standpoint, it is necessary to descend from the systemic level and examine Russia's strategic motivations and patterns of behaviour unfolding at the inter-state interactional level, which is not under direct influence of system-level trends and is subject to various regional and domestic circumstances. At this level, Russia utilizes the abundant opportunities available to great powers to realize its commercial interests and to diversify its external relations in Asia, which requires maintaining a more or less cooperative environment in the region and dictates a different behaviour in the SCS.

The context and the driver of Russia's hedging behaviour in the SCS is its comprehensive socioeconomic "reorientation to Asia," which became a national development strategy and was announced as "Russia's national priority for the entire 21st century" after Putin's return to power in 2012.[27] Its main goal is to accelerate Russia's domestic socio-economic development, primarily the projects of intensive development of Siberia and the Far East, by enhancing Russia's embeddedness in the mechanisms of Asia-Pacific integration. The essence of the new strategy is to go beyond just an "energy pivot to China" and to make the development of the Far East and Siberia international, with diverse sources of labour, technology, and investments. The main long-term goal is "maximum extension and diversification of economic links," which will allow Russia to gain from globalization and exercise truly multi-vector policies.[28] In this case, the actual policy-making calculus and the dynamics of related policies prove to be driven more by non-systemic considerations of regional economic diversification rather than by intentions to block or check the power of the hegemon.

---

[26] Evelyn Goh, "Meeting the China Challenge," *Policy Studies 16*, Washington DC: East West Center, 2005, viii.

[27] Alexander Korolev, "Russia's Reorientation to Asia: Causes and Strategic Implications," *Pacific Affairs* 89.1 (2016): 53–73.

[28] Vasily Kashin, "Rossiisky Podhod k Problemam Bezopasnosti vi ATR [Russia's Approach to the Security Issues in Asia-Pacific]," Moscow Carnegie Centre, 17 June 2016, http://carnegie.ru/2016/06/17/ru-pub-63832

Moscow tries to hedge its regional economic and security bets by expanding cooperation with as many Asian countries and multilateral organizations as possible and seeks to export energy, arms, agricultural products, machinery, space technologies, and educational services to different Asian markets. Therefore, whereas from the perspective of systemic balancing China is the main, if not the only, great power Russia can align with to effectively balance the American global dominance, from the standpoint of regional hedging, Russia needs a more diverse portfolio of partners. Moreover, Moscow can even engage in regional geopolitical competition of low intensity with China and employ tactics of engagement and resistance, containment and cooperation with various Asian partners – all to avoid undesirable regional developments that can hinder the "reorientation to Asia" strategy and harm Russia's regional economic interests. This pattern of behaviour cannot be sufficiently captured and explained by the systemic theory.

In this context, although the SCS is far from the Russian borders, disputes there became a concern for Moscow, and how Russia addresses them is affected by its regional calculations related to hedging that, when intersecting with the layer of system-level balancing, leads to the inherent ambivalence of Russia's SCS policies.

Vietnam, for example, is an important partner for Russia both in its own right and as a gate to multilateral regional organizations in Southeast Asia. It is Russia's largest trade partner in Southeast Asia, with the volume of trade growing, on average, by 20 per cent annually since 2010. Even in 2015, when because of Western sanctions Russia's trade with almost all countries, including China, shrank, Russia-Vietnam trade increased by 31 per cent and reached US$3.84 billion compared with US$2.94 billion in 2014.[29] Driven by the need to diversify its energy cooperation and hedge its economic bets, Russia's Gazprom in 2012 signed a deal with the state-owned PetroVietnam on the development of two large-scale gas projects on Vietnam's continental shelf in the parts of the SCS that fall under the nine-dash line. Subsequently, Moscow and Hanoi agreed to extend this energy partnership until 2030. Of particular importance for Russia are the long-term technology-intensive cooperation projects, such as its participation in Vietnam's ten-year plan for the development of the national electrical power industry.[30] Simultaneously, Vietnam has become the first Southeast

[29] Russian Exports, National Information Portal, "Vietnamese-Russian Bilateral Trade in 2015," 6 June 2016, http://www.rusexporter.com/research/country/detail/4672/

[30] "SRV Deputy Prime Minister of Industry and Trade Hoang Trung Hai's report to a thematic seminar in Hanoi, August 2011," cited from Yevgeny Kobelev, "Twenty Years of the Russia-ASEAN Partnership," *Far Eastern Affairs*, No. 6 (2014), 8.

Asian country to sign, in July 2016, a free-trade agreement (FTA) with the Russia-led Eurasian Economic Union (EAEU). According to the EAEU's Minister of Trade, Veronika Nikishina, the new agreement serves Russia's plans to diversify its economic relations in the Asia-Pacific, particularly in the sphere of the automobile industry, because Vietnam has agreed on the industrial assembly of cars and trucks with Russian producers. In other words, the assembled vehicles will be considered manufactured in Vietnam and will have free access to the ASEAN markets.[31] This, according to some assessments, could pave the way to a Russia-ASEAN FTA.[32]

Vietnam has also been consistently helping Russia establish connections with ASEAN; it did so in 1996 by pushing the case for Russia becoming a fully-fledged ASEAN dialogue partner and subsequently pushing for Russia's participation in the East Asia Summit (EAS). The Joint Russia-Vietnam Declaration of 2006 states that: "[I]n the spirit of relations of friendship and cooperation, Russia and Vietnam express their firm resolve to further strengthen cooperation within the ASEAN-Russia Dialogue Partnership ... and to strive to render mutual assistance in the multilateral structures now operating and taking shape in the Asia-Pacific region."[33] In July 2012, in an interview with *Rossiyskaya Gazeta* [*The Russian Gazette*, a major Russian government daily newspaper], Vietnamese President Trương Tấn Sang stated that, "I clearly see a bright future for Russia-ASEAN relations ... Vietnam and all the other ASEAN members heartily welcome the deepening of cooperation with Russia," adding that, "we deem it very important to build up Russia's activity, as a weighty political player, in ASEAN-centric forums on a regular basis."[34] Hanoi played a notable role in supporting Russia's presence in the major regional economic and security institutions, including the ASEAN Regional Forum (ARF), Asia-Pacific Economic Cooperation (APEC), the East Asia Summit (EAS), and the Asia-Europe Meeting (ASEM). On April 26, 2016, Russian Defence Minister, Sergey

[31] Gleb Fedorov, "Russian automobiles to have free access to ASEAN via Vietnam EAEU minister," *Russia Beyond the Headlines*, 8 August 2016, http://rbth.com/business/2016/08/08/russian-automobiles-to-have-free-access-to-asean-via-vietnam-eaeu-minister_619053

[32] Victor Sumsky and Evgeny Kanaev, "Russia's Progress in Southeast Asia: Modest but Steady," *Russian Analytical Digest*, No. 145, 31 March 2014, 2–5.

[33] *Tikhookeanskoye obozreniye 2006–2007* [Pacific Review 2006–2007], Moscow, 2007, 172, cited from Kobelev, "Twenty Years of the Russia-ASEAN Partnership," 6.

[34] "Ot Ho Shi Mina do VTO [From Ho Chi Ming to WTO]," Interview with the Vietnamese President Trương Tấn Sang, *Rossiyskaya Gazeta*, Issue No. 5844 (171), 27 July 2012, https://rg.ru/2012/07/26/shang-poln.html

Shoygu, hosted the very first Russia-ASEAN Defence Ministers' Informal Meeting in Moscow.[35]

All of these developments facilitate the realization of Russia's goals of diversification under its "reorientation to Asia" initiative, rather than its goals of balancing against the US. They also directly bear on Russia's approach to the SCS. Russia, while at the systemic level balancing the unipole, is also interested in forging a regional environment that is conducive to tackling the existing contradictions in non-explosive ways, so as not to severely frustrate its regional economic and development goals. This requires maintaining some sort of geopolitical equilibrium in the SCS that prevents absolute preponderance, military or diplomatic, of any of the disputants. As emphasized by Victor Sumsky, Director of the ASEAN Centre at the Moscow Institute of International Affairs, the SCS disputes cause serious tensions between China and the ASEAN member states (mostly Vietnam and the Philippines), between China and ASEAN as a whole, within ASEAN, and between China and India, that is, between Russia's close, highly valued partners. Thus, Moscow "needs to think more about how to neutralize these unhappy trends," and "special relations with both Beijing and Hanoi are a resource that should not be underestimated."[36] Some Russian experts also argue that Russia should show consistency with its partnership relations with Vietnam and encourage the formation of some sort of China-Vietnam alignment.[37] In other words, Moscow must both hedge and be a hedge for others.

These calculations on Russia's part explain why the burgeoning Russia-China military cooperation and China's status of a "privileged partner" (a system-level balancing) in Russia's foreign policy coexist with Moscow's increased attempts to create a regional security system involving ASEAN and its willingness to be a strategic partner and the largest arms supplier to Vietnam (which is an element of regional hedging). They also explain the presence of Russia's energy projects on Vietnam's continental shelf. Worth noting is that, whereas Russia's arms sales to both China and Vietnam have been driven since

---

35 "On April 26, 2016 the first informal meeting of defence ministers of Russia and the ASEAN member-states took place in Moscow," Ministry of Defence of the Russian Federation, 26 April 2016, http://eng.mil.ru/en/news_page/country/more.htm?id=12083927@egNews

36 Viktor Sumsky, "Rossiya i Problemu Yuzhno-Kitaiskogo Moria [Russia and the Problems of the South China Sea]," *Govoriat Expertu MGIMO [MGIMO Experts are speaking]*, 3 May 2012, http://old.mgimo.ru/news/experts/document223482.phtml

37 Dmitry Mosyakov, "Na Grani Fola: Politika Kitaya v Yuzno-Kitaiskom More [Extremely Risk-taking: China's Behaviour in the South China Sea]," Index Bezopasnosti [Security Index], Moscow, Vol. 19, No. 4(107) (Winter 2013), 58–67, http://www.pircenter.org/articles/1593-na-grani-fola-politika-kitaya-v-yuzhnokitajskom-more

the 1990s by commercial considerations, with the intensification of the SCS dispute since 2010 they have gained a serious strategic component, providing Russia with strategic leverage in the region. Thus, whereas commercial considerations for Moscow are not unimportant, they are interlinked with the strategic side of the issue in the current regional context.

This hedging behaviour on Russia's part fails to make everyone happy, but it largely satisfies the involved parties' basic national interests. Moscow understands that, although its strategic partnership with Hanoi, which has a strong military dimension, might appear to be against China, Beijing is willing to accept it because in the existing circumstances it, in fact, serves China's interests, namely, it helps prevent the strengthening of a Hanoi-Washington alignment. Although not happy about, and in fact contained by, Moscow's large-scale arms sales to Hanoi, Beijing understands that a termination or decline of such sales and technology transfers would lead Vietnam to shift from its own policy of hedging (that is, diversifying security and military relations) to a stronger tilt toward the United States, which would close the US' containment circle around China. Thus, despite emphatically resisting the internationalization of the SCS dispute, China accepts Russia's more active involvement and the "containment" created by the Russia-Vietnam energy and military cooperation. This explains why Beijing, although pressuring American, Indian, and Malaysian energy companies not to cooperate with Vietnam in the SCS, remains largely silent about Russia's involvement in Vietnam's offshore energy projects and Moscow's transfer of arms to Hanoi.[38]

Conclusion

This chapter has presented an analysis of Russia's policies toward the SCS dispute by highlighting the two modes of great-power behaviour: system-level balancing and regional hedging. Both modes are present in Russia's behaviour. In the SCS, they intersect with each other, generating a two-level configuration. At the systemic level, the baseline of Russia's policies is characterized by a strong anti-unipolarity pursuit that permeates Russia's interactions with China and other regional players. However, at the regional level, Russia plays a complex engage-and-resist game of hedging, aimed at averting the undesirable scenarios of regional confrontation that can undermine Russia's plans to diversify its economic development and economic integration into the Asia-Pacific region. At this non-systemic level

[38] Greg Torode, "Beijing Pressure Intense in South China Sea Row," *South China Morning Post*, 23 September 2011.

of hedging, any regional state, large or small, and China and the US, can be both a partner and a rival of Russia, and these roles can switch from time to time. However, these inter-state day-to-day relationships lack system-level causal force. This lack does not make them unimportant, but simply different.

As long as the relative weights of balancing and hedging in the two-level "balancing-hedging" configuration remain unchanged, the logic of inter-state interactions and developments unfolding at one level need not override those prevailing at the other level. As long as the system permits, movement in opposite directions at different levels of foreign policy can coexist. Thus, as a phenomenon of a different level, and assuming that the SCS situation does not change, Russia-Vietnam relations can grow and prosper without challenging Russia-China relations. Vice versa, the global politics of Russia-China alignment need not necessarily trespass into the regional hedging logic of Russia-Vietnam relations. However, lifting the SCS dispute to the level of global politics involving the US and the US-China global competition sets into motion causal forces of a systemic level and makes anti-unipolarity-balancing define Russia's behaviour.

The major implication of the two-level configuration, therefore, is that for Russia, the essence of the SCS dispute and Russia's responses to it together are rather a variable than a constant. The further the SCS dispute diverges from the regional matters of sovereignty over islands and waters into the area of US-China strategic competition, the more likely Russia's policies in the region will carry the elements of anti-US system-level balancing. Contrariwise, the less the US is engaged and the more the SCS dispute remains predominantly a regional issue, the more likely Russia's policy responses in the area are to remain detached from the systemic trends of anti-US balancing and to exhibit the elements of regional non-systemic hedging aimed at creating a more balanced network of regional contacts. The more the SCS issue is concerned with US-China relations more than with ASEAN-China or Vietnam-China relations, the more support China is likely to obtain from Russia. Conversely, the more the SCS dispute is about China and smaller states in the region, the more reluctant Russia will be to side with China in the SCS. Some Russian scholars conclude that the dispute is no longer about sovereignty over lands and maritime zones of the SCS; rather, it is about whether and how much American naval activity in the region China can accept.[39] If this assessment is correct, the game of balancing is going to dominate that of hedging in Russia's policies in the region.

[39] Evgeny Kanaev, "Developing Russia's Far East and Siberia: The Interplay of National, Regional and Global Implications," in Jing Huang and Alexander Korolev, eds., *International Cooperation in the Development of Russia's Far East and Siberia* (Palgrave Macmillan, 2015), 19–38.

References

Baev, Pavel K., and Stein Tønnesson. 2015. "Can Russia Keep Its Special Ties with Vietnam While Moving Closer and Closer to China?" *International Area Studies Review* 18, no. 3: 312–25.

Fedorov, Gleb. 2016. "Russian Automobiles to Have Free Access to ASEAN via Vietnam-EAEU Minister." *Russia Beyond the Headlines*, 8 August. http://rbth.com/business/2016/08/08/russian-automobiles-to-have-free-access-to-asean-via-vietnam-eaeu-minister_619053

Goh, Evelyn. 2005. *Meeting the China Challenge: The US in Southeast Asian Regional Security Strategies*. Washington, DC: East West Center.

Kanaev, Evgeny. 2015. "Developing Russia's Far East and Siberia: The Interplay of National, Regional and Global Implications." In *International Cooperation in the Development of Russia's Far East and Siberia*, edited by Jing Huang and Alexander Korolev, 19–38. London: Palgrave MacMillan.

Kashin, Vasily. 2016a. "Rossiisky Podhod k Problemam Bezopasnosti vi ATR [Russia's Approach to the Security Issues in Asia-Pacific]." Moscow Carnegie Centre. June 17. http://carnegie.ru/2016/06/17/ru-pub-63832

Kobelev, Yevgeny. 2014. "Twenty Years of the Russia-ASEAN Partnership." *Far Eastern Affairs* 6: 1–11.

Korolev, Alexander. 2016. "Russia's Reorientation to Asia: Causes and Strategic Implications," *Pacific Affairs* 89, 1: 53–73.

Korolev, Alexander. 2016. "Systemic Balancing and Regional Hedging: China–Russia Relations," *The Chinese Journal of International Politics* 9, no. 4: 375–97.

Korolev, Alexander. 2018. "Russia in the South China Sea: Balancing and Hedging," *Foreign Policy Analysis* 15, no. 2: 263–82.

Kozyrev, Vitaly. 2014. "Russia-Vietnam Strategic Partnership: The Return of the Brotherhood in Arms?" *Russian Analytical Digest* 145 (31 March): 8–11.

Lee, Nhina and Collin Koh Swee Lean. 2015. "Vietnam and Great Power Rivalries." *The Diplomat,* March 31. http://thediplomat.com/2015/03/vietnam-and-great-power-rivalries/

Leksyutina, Yana. 2011. "Obostrenie Napyazhennosti v Yuzhno-Kitaiskom More: Vzglyad iz YuVa, KNR, i SShA [Growing tensions in the South China Sea: A View from Southeast Asia, China, and the United States]." *Problemu Dal'nego Vostoka [Far Eastern Affairs]*, no. 5: 30–41.

Litovkin, Victor. 2016. "Russia Could Gain from Backing China in South China Sea Disputes." *Russia Beyond the Headlines*, September 8. http://rbth.com/international/2016/09/08/russia-could-gain-from-backing-china-in-south-china-sea-disputes-experts_628057

Live Journal. 2016. "Bazovue Interesu. Zachem Rossiiskoi Armii Garnizonu na Kybe i vo V'etname? [Basic Interests. Why does the Russian Army Need Garrisons in Cuba and Vietnam?]." October 10. http://www.livejournal.com/media/950750.html

Mardasov, Anton. 2016. "V Kil'vatere Kovarnogo Drakona [In the Wake of a Crafty Dragon]." *Svobodnaya Pressa Online [The Free Press Online]*, July 29. http://svpressa.ru/war21/article/153424/

Mihnevich, Sergei. 2012. "SShA v Aziatsko-Tihookeanskom Regione: Liderstvo Lyuboi Cenoi [USA in Asia-Pacific Region: Leadership at any Costs]." In *God v Bolshoi Politike [A Year in Big Politics]*, edited by Konstantin Kaminsky, 6–9. Moscow: Modern Politics Russia.

MoDRF (Ministry of Defence of the Russian Federation). 2016. "On April 26, 2016 the first informal meeting of defence ministers of Russia and the ASEAN member-states took place in Moscow." http://eng.mil.ru/en/news_page/country/more.htm?id=12083927@egNews

MoFARF (Ministry of Foreign Affairs of the Russian Federation). 2016. "Interview Ministra Inostrannuh Del Rossii S. V. Lavrova SMI Mongolii, Yaponii, i KNR v Preddverii Vizitov v Eti Stranu [Russian Minister of Foreign Affairs Sergei Lavrov's Interview to the Japanese, Mongolian, and Chinese Media on the Eve of Visiting These Countries]." April 12. http://www.mid.ru/foreign_policy/news/-/asset_publisher/cKNonkJE02Bw/content/id/2227965

MoFARF. 2016. Foreign Ministry Spokesperson Maria Zakharova's Briefing. Moscow, July 14. http://www.mid.ru/en/web/guest/foreign_policy/news/-/asset_publisher/cKNonkJE02Bw/content/id/2354135

Mosyakov, Dmitry. 2013. "Na Grani Fola: Politika Kitaya v Yuzno-Kitaiskom More [Extremely Risk-taking: China's Behaviour in the South China Sea]," *Index Bezopasnosti [Security Index]*, 19, no. 4(107): 58–67.

Olizhevsky, Dmitri. 2016. "Zachem Rossii Bazu v Lurdese i Camrani? [Why does Russia need military bases in Lourdes and Cam Ranh?]." *Parlamentskaya Gazeta [The Parliament Newspaper]*, October 7.

Panda, Ankit. 2016. "Chinese, Russian Navies to Hold 8 Days of Naval Exercises in the South China Sea." *The Diplomat*, September 12. http://thediplomat.com/2016/09/chinese-russian-navies-to-hold-8-days-of-naval-exercises-in-the-south-china-sea/

Portyakov, Vladimir. 2015. *Vneshniaya Politika Kitaiskoi Narodnoi Respubliki v 21-m Stoletii [The PRC's Foreign Policy in the 21st Century]*. Moscow: Institute of Far Eastern Studies Press.

President of Russia. 2012. Russia-Vietnam Joint Statement on Intensification of Comprehensive Strategic Partnership. July 27. http://news.kremlin.ru/ref_notes/1279

President of Russia. 2016. "Sovmestnoe Zayavlenie Rossiiskoi Federatcii i Kitaiskoi Narodnoi Respubliki [The China-Russia Joint Declaration of 25 June 2016]." June 25. http://www.kremlin.ru/supplement/5100

Rinna, Tony. 2016. "The China Factor in Russia-Vietnam Security Ties." *Foreign Policy Journal*, January 5. http://www.foreignpolicyjournal.com/2016/01/05/the-china-factor-in-russia-vietnam-security-ties/

Rossiyskaya Gazeta. 2012. "Ot Ho Shi Mina do VTO [From Ho Chi Ming to WTO]," Interview with the Vietnamese President Trương Tấn Sang. Issue No. 5844 (171). July 27. https://rg.ru/2012/07/26/shang-poln.html

Russian Exports. 2016. "Vietnamese-Russian Bilateral Trade in 2015." June 6. http://www.rusexporter.com/research/country/detail/4672/

Sputnik. 2013. "Russia is Vietnam's Leading Strategic Partner in the Area of Military-Technical Cooperation – Defence Minister of Vietnam." August 5. http://in.sputniknews.com/indian.ruvr.ru/news/2013_08_05/Russia-Vietnam-cooperation/

Sputnik. 2014. "Putin Confirms Plans to Meet Chinese President during APEC Summit in Beijing." October 14. http://sputniknews.com/politics/20141014/194060827.html

Sumsky, Viktor. 2012. "Rossiya i Problemu Yuzhno-Kitaiskogo Moria [Russia and the Problems of the South China Sea]," *Govoriat Expertu MGIMO [MGIMO Experts are Speaking]*, May 3. https://mgimo.ru/about/news/experts/223482/

Sumsky, Victor and Evgeny Kanaev. 2014. "Russia's Progress in Southeast Asia: Modest but Steady." *Russian Analytical Digest* 145 (31 March): 2–5.

TASS. 2014. "Russia, Vietnam Agree on Simplified Cam Ranh Port Entry for Russian Warships." November 27.

Torode, Greg. 2011. "Beijing Pressure Intense in South China Sea Row." *South China Morning Post*, September 23. http://www.scmp.com/article/979876/beijing-pressure-intense-south-china-sea-row

Trifonov, Viktor. 2012. "Vastuplenie na Zaochnom Kruglom Stole 'Factor Kitaya vo Vzaimootnosheniyah RF i SShA [Presentation at the roundtable 'The China Factor in Russia-US Relations]." *Problemu Dal'nego Vostoka [Far Eastern Affairs]*, no. 2: 101–2.

Xinhua News, "China, Russia Agree to Upgrade Relations for New Era." 6 June 2019, http://www.xinhuanet.com/english/2019-06/06/c_138119879.htm

18

South Korea and the South China Sea: A Middle-Power Model for Practical Policies?

Sukjoon Yoon

Introduction

This chapter examines the South Korean perspective on the South China Sea (SCS). There are various entrenched disagreements between surrounding states, which dispute economic rights and legal jurisdiction, and the SCS is also the principal theatre in which the great-power games between China and the US are played out. The problems of the SCS have a wider destabilizing effect upon East Asian maritime security, and this poses strategic issues for other regional states, such as South Korea; the importance of the SCS as a trade route means that there are also global economic ramifications.

As a responsible stakeholder, South Korea is concerned that the peace and good order of the region are threatened by the intractable attitudes of the parties involved, which seem committed to irreconcilable legal and political stances, and show little interest in resolving their differences through negotiation. On the contrary, there is an ongoing process of escalation: smaller countries are building up their navies and maritime law forces, China is also expanding its capabilities, including by creating and militarizing artificial islands in the SCS, and the US is also behaving provocatively.

As a regional middle power, South Korea is advocating balanced and constructive policies, without prejudice to any country, and is seeking to mitigate tensions and de-escalate disputes, so that regional maritime security can be restored and the threat of serious physical conflicts can be reduced.

Why is a strategic perspective needed?

Underlying every issue in the SCS today is the challenge to the existing order represented by the expanding power of China, which threatens the US regional hegemony and perhaps its global dominance.[1] In response, the US has taken some provocative steps, including naval transits of the Taiwan Strait and the so-called Freedom of Navigation Operations (FONOPs) in the SCS. This action-reaction cycle between China and the US has also prompted a general urge toward naval modernization by regional states.[2]

Fortunately, there are no direct military confrontations occurring in the SCS, and in contrast to the ongoing wars of the Middle East, there are no refugees. The SCS situation is best characterized as a "grey zone" conflict or as "hybrid competition" between the parties involved.[3] Besides actual naval forces, other actors, such as coast guards and maritime militias equipped with steel-hulled fishing vessels, have also played a role in asserting national claims, resulting in a hybrid kind of warfare which is not really peace and is not quite war.[4] The Chinese Coast Guard is now one of the most powerful maritime law enforcement agency in the world and some coastal states of the Association of Southeast Asian Nations (ASEAN) are also building up their maritime law enforcement.[5]

1 See Catherine K. Lea and Michael A. McDevitt, *Maritime Security Issues in East Asia CNA Maritime Asia Project: Workshop Four* (Washington, DC: Center for Naval Analysis, 2013); Bernard D. Cole, "Island Chains and Naval Classics," *USNI Proceedings*, November 2014, 68–73; Douglas Guifoyle, UNSW Canberra Maritime Security Research Group, *Strategy and Law in the SCS Disputes, 14–15 October 2019: Workshop report* (Canberra, Australia: UNSW, October 2019); Congressional Research Service, *US-China Strategic Competition in South and East China Seas: Background and Issues for Congress* (Washington, DC: US Congress, January 28, 2020).

2 Sam Bateman, "Solving the 'Wicked Problems' of Maritime Security: Are Regional Forums up to the Task?" *Contemporary Southeast Asia*, Vol. 33, No. 1, 2011, 1–28; C. J. Jenner and Tran Trough Thuy, ed., all., *The SCS: A Crucial of Regional Cooperation or Conflict-making Sovereignty Claims?* (Cambridge, UK: Cambridge University Press, 2016); Tran Truong Thuy, John B. Welfield and Le Thuy Trang, *Building a Normative Order in the South China Sea: Evolving Disputes, Expanding Options* (Cheltenham, UK: Edward Elgar, 2019).

3 For a recent analysis of grey zone conflict see John Grady, "US Could Do More to Deter Iran Grey Zone Strategy, Exports Say," *USNI News*, April 23, 2020. http://news.usni.org/2020/04/23/u-s-couls-do-more-to-deter-iran-grey-zone-strategy-exports-say.htlm

4 Brian Smicklas, "Guard the Coast from High-end Threats," *USNI Proceedings*, February, 2019, 44–9; Lee Willet, "Cops on the Beat: IMSC Navies Shine Light on Gulf 'Grey Zone' Areas," *Jane's Navy International*, March 2020, 10–11.

5 John Grady, "Panel: US, China SCS Tensions Show No Signs of Easing," *USNI News*, July 29, 2019. http://news.usni.org/2019/07/29/panel-u-s-china-south-china-sea-tensions-show no-signs-of-easing; Anguang Zheng, "Integrating the China Coast Guard with

In addition, the ongoing COVID-19 pandemic is a novel factor impacting the maritime disputes in the SCS. The navies of the two great powers, the US and China, have been directly affected, by having to demonstrate their ability to manage this insidious threat.[6] And there has also been an indirect geostrategic effect arising from the entanglement of military, economic, and public health issues, with both countries playing the blame game and attempting to rally domestic support through conspiracy theories.

A comprehensive strategic solution is needed to restore maritime peace and stability in the SCS, taking full account of all relevant geographical, legal and economic factors.

What underlies the South China Sea disputes?

In the SCS, legal claims, economic issues, and security affairs are deeply interwoven. The fundamental struggle is between the two great powers, China and the US, but there are numerous subsidiary struggles involving other regional states, and even some more distant powers. Thus, the US Indo-Pacific Strategy has utilized the navies of Japan, Australia, New Zealand, the United Kingdom, and France in conducting FONOPs.[7] Rather than simply supporting US regional hegemony, these operations are supposedly in support of the SCS claims made by ASEAN states. Certainly these countries have very weak militaries, quite unable to withstand China's military expansionism, but their position has also been compromised by China's financial leverage. The Chinese Belt and Road Initiative (BRI) ostensibly fosters bilateral economic cooperation between China and ASEAN members, but in practice it deploys China's economic power to establish a strategic partnership that promotes Chinese interests in the SCS.[8] The Philippines and Malaysia have

the PLA Navy," in Ian Bowers and Collin Koh Swee Lean, *Grey and White Hulls: An International Analysis of the Navy-Coast Guard Nexus* (London: Palgrave, Macmillan, 2029), 23–34.

6 Carl Thayer, "Background Brief: South China Sea: China Claims It Expelled US Warship from Paracel Islands," *Thayer Consultancy*, ABN #65 648 097 123, April 29, 2020; Sam LaGrone, "SWO Boss: Insidious COVID-19 Spread on USS Kidd Shows Evolution of Navy Response to Pandemic," *USNI News*, May 6, 2020. http://news.usni.org/2020/05/06/swo-boss-insidious-covid-19-spread-on-uss-kidd-sh

7 Michael Fabey, "USN SCS FONOPS Heightens US-China Tensions," *Jane's Navy International*, July 2018, 4; Lee Willett, "Royal Navy Operations in the Asia-Pacific," *Jane's Defence Weekly*, 29 May 2019, 2–26; Frederick Kliem, "Germany in the Indo-Pacific: New Security Actor?" *RSIS Commentary*, No. 144, 18 July 2019.

8 Sukjoon Yoon, "Decoding China's Maritime Aspirations," *USNI Proceedings*, March 2017, 44–48; Li Zheng, "PLA Aims to Become Global Stabilizer in New Era," *China Daily*, August 2, 2019. http://chinadailyasia.com/article/108/76/57/1564719557931.html?newsId=90

accepted significant funds from China to develop their infrastructure, and also Indonesia to a lesser extent, but Vietnam has declined BRI funding and is standing firm on its SCS claims.[9] Indeed, Vietnam has sufficient economic strength, and Brunei has great oil wealth, which permits them a degree of independence from China, but the other members of ASEAN are essentially in China's pocket.

The natural maritime environment is also threatened, as a side effect of the SCS disputes. The protection of fishing stocks and other natural SCS resources should be best managed cooperatively, as a regional-commons, but China continues its destructive unilateral exploitation, and the resulting conflicts with other claimants further exacerbate security issues.[10]

The economies of major trading nations, notably those of South Korea and Japan, and, ironically, that of China itself, depend heavily on the freedom of navigation encoded by the United Nations Convention on the Law of the Sea (UNCLOS).[11] The SCS comprises multiple overlapping economic zones and maritime jurisdictional areas, with many narrow straits; both regional and global prosperity depends upon safeguarding navigation rights, including innocent passage and transit passage. Trading routes through the regional sea lines of communication (SLOCs) can only be kept open by the preservation of regional maritime peace and good order.[12] This is what all parties, the US included, really need from the SCS. Outdated concepts such as maritime control or command are an unfortunate legacy of great-power politics which should be transcended.

Some problems and impediments

Chinese hardliners are fond of historical parallels, seeing the SCS in terms of the Thucydides Trap, whereby war is the inevitable consequence of competition between a rising and an established great power. Germany's 1910s commercial warfare directed at Great Britain and the US, or Imperial Japan's 1930s expansion are taken as models to interpret the strategic and military competition between China and the US.[13] But is it really unavoidable

---

9 Jane Perlez, "Myanmar Attracts Attention of Beijing," *The New York Times International Edition*, July 19, 2017, 1 & 8; Hannah Beech, "We Cannot Afford This," *The New York Times International Edition*, August 23, 2018, 1 & 6; "Belt and Road Initiative Facilitates Economic Cooperation among China, ASEAN, South Asia," *China Daily*, October 10, 2018. http://www.chinadaily.com.cna201810/10/WS5bbdb127a310eff3032819e5.html

10 Jay Caputo, "A Global Fishing War Is Coming," *USNI Proceedings*, August 2017, 32–37.

11 Dale C. Rielage, "Parsing the Chinese Challenge," *USNI Proceedings*, September 2013, 58–62.

12 See Geoffrey Till, *The Changing Maritime Scene in Asia: Rising Tensions and Future Strategic Stability* (London: Palgrave Macmillan, 2015).

13 Andrew Rhodes, "Go Get Mahan's Yardstick," *USNI Proceedings*, July 2019, 19–23.

for the SCS to be a theatre of great-power competition? The US and China are competing to be regional powerbroker, but this struggle is sidelining the true interests of the region.[14]

The SCS forms a critical geographical juncture, between the Indian and Pacific Oceans. The US has dominated the Indo-Pacific for seven decades, and sees China as an unwelcome interloper, to be contained in the SCS. Of course, the US also claims to be defending and supporting weaker local states. China wants to be in charge of its own backyard, the better to manage its global network, and from a longer historical perspective, looking back to the Middle Kingdom, sees the US as the intruder.[15] China argues that its naval build-up is not directed at ASEAN members, but is merely to counter US naval forces in a maritime region which China should and will control.[16]

China and the US appear determined to make the SCS the principal theatre for a strategic competition, which would seem silly to other actors if it were not so tragic. Both countries enjoy flaunting their powerful navies, trying to intimidate one another, as well as to attract support or reduce interference from lesser powers. As part of this sabre-rattling, both are increasing aerial and underwater surveillance and reconnaissance activities.[17] Yet, the SCS, together with the East China Sea, forms an essential economic lifeline connecting Northeast and Southeast Asia, through which more than US$5 trillion in trade passes annually. With both the US and China pursuing assertive maritime strategies in the SCS, the primary concern of regional states is SLOC security to ensure free and open maritime trade.[18]

The geographical complexity of the SCS means that the provisions of the UNCLOS are ambiguous and susceptible of various interpretations. The UNCLOS has proved useful where coastal countries' have clearly defined geographical maritime jurisdictional rights and responsibilities, but China has claimed historical rights and interests which exceed the UNCLOS regime. China still dwells upon its degradation at the hands of European and Japanese empires, but until this humiliation is consigned to the history books China will never become an honest member of UNCLOS able to

[14] Jonathan G. Odom, "China's Riskfare," *USNI Proceedings*, March 2019, 21–25.

[15] Sukjoon Yoon, "The Emergence and Consolidation of a Chinese Version of the Monroe Doctrine: Implication for Korea's China Policy," *KAS Journal on Contemporary Korean Affairs*, 1/2013, 43072.

[16] See Geoffrey Till and Jane Chan, ed., all., *Naval Modernisation in South-East Asia* (London & New York: Routledge, 2014).

[17] Gabriel Dominguez, "China Greatest Long-term Strategic Threat to Region and US, says INDOPACOM Chief," *Jane's Defence Weekly*, 20 February 2019, 6.

[18] Ridzwan Rahmat, "At-Sea Security: ASEAN Adopts Regional Approach to Maritime Threats," *Jane's Navy International*, July/August 2016, 12–13.

negotiate in good faith. Moreover, China insists that the current system of US-dominated regional order must be overturned, arguing that the existing rules-based order should accommodate so-called "common destiny," which clearly refers back to the Middle Kingdom.[19] Unless China accepts that international laws are impartial and worth respecting, then there is no path forward towards a new regional order.[20]

Is China *the* problem?

Many countries are deeply concerned about Chinese intransigence in the SCS, including South Korea, Australia, India, and ASEAN members. Among the issues are the following.

First, all SCS disputes involving China are deadlocked. China simply insists on receiving special treatment, even when the other parties, the coastal states of ASEAN express their willingness to be flexible within the UNCLOS framework.[21] There has been some recent movement towards consensus, however: on August 3, 2018 China and ASEAN agreed on a draft negotiating text for a Code of Conduct (COC) to avoid any contingencies and unplanned encounters between China and ASEAN members.[22]

Second, the SCS is believed to contain vast natural resources under the seabed, and many fear that China will claim ownership of the entirety of this wealth, based on the spurious "nine-dash line" boundary which it has advocated. Although these resources have not been quantified, and their unilateral exploitation by China would be impossible to reconcile with China's pose as a responsible adherent of international law, this issue has already caused some friction, for example over licences granted by Vietnam to an Indian oil company, within their exclusive economic zone (EEZ) but with China contesting it. In contrast, those ASEAN members which China

---

[19] Bernard Cole, "Controlling Contested Waters," *USNI Proceedings*, October 2013, 48–53; Karl Wilson, "Island Serves as Belt, Road Maritime Gateway," *China Daily*, November 21, 2018. http://usa.chinadaily.com.cn/a/201811/21/WS5bf49e09a310eff303289f93.html

[20] Peter S. Goodman and Jane Perlez, "China Rules: Paving a Way to Global Power," *The New York Times International Edition*, November 18, 2018, 1 & 10.

[21] Jonathan Ward, "The Influence of Seapower upon China." *USNI Proceedings*, August 2019, 62–67; "Chinese Premier Pushes for Free Trade, South China Sea Code in Singapore Visit," *Global Times*, November 17, 2018. http://www.globaltimes.cn/content/1127725.shtml

[22] Douglas Guifoyle, UNSW Canberra Maritime Security Research Group, *Strategy and Law in the SCS Disputes, 14–15 October 2019: Workshop Report* (Canberra, Australia: UNSW, October 2019), 11–12.

has already effectively suborned are likely to follow the Philippines' decision to pursue a joint-development relationship with China.[23]

Third, throughout the process of creating four artificial islands and installing significant military facilities on them, China consistently denied any intention to militarize the SCS, and continues, even now, to blame the US for doing exactly this.[24] In response, the US conducts FONOPs, but China is clearly making a statement about its regional military prowess, especially its naval power, and the US is likewise attempting to demonstrate that China has not succeeded in excluding the US from the SCS. Some have worried that China intends to use its artificial islands to disrupt trade through the SCS. In practice, however, the geographical separation, 150 miles between the Paracel and Spratly Islands, means that a naval blockade is not feasible. Nonetheless, the militarization of the SCS, by both sides, has also stimulated a wider naval arms build-up among other regional nations.[25] Coastal states of ASEAN are acquiring advanced modern naval platforms, including submarines, frigates, and littoral ships. Some are also expanding maritime law enforcement, and some are building or refitting naval bases.

Fourth, by creating these artificial islands, China is pushing out its strategic defensive perimeter, at least symbolically, and the Chinese military has conducted Anti-Access/Area Denial (A2/AD) exercises in the SCS, but these flat-top islands are vulnerable to strong winds and rough seas, and sophisticated modern weapons and systems can be degraded by salt winds.[26] Most military analysts believe that the islands do not provide any significant competitive advantage to Chinese forces, and so they do not threaten the US military presence in East Asia.[27]

---

[23] Shannon Tiezzi, "China-Philippines Relations: Can the Rainbow Last?" *The Diplomat*, November 22, 2018. http://thediplomat.com/2018/11/china-philippines-relations-can-the-rainbow-last/; Alex Chan, "China, the Philippines Entering a Golden Era of Bilateral Ties," *China Daily*, November 21, 2018. http://africa.chinadaily.com.cn/201811/21/WS5bf4cd0da310eff30328a1ee.ntml

[24] James Holmes, "Visualize Chinese Sea Power," *USNI, Proceedings*, June 2018, 26–31.

[25] See Congressional Research Service, *US-China Strategic Competition in South and East China Seas: Background and Issues for Congress* (Washington, DC: US Congress, January 28 2020).

[26] Sukjoon Yoon, "Why Is Beijing Militarising the South China Sea?" *The Nation Thailand*, May 11, 2015. http://www.nationthailand.com/noname/30259858

[27] Ben Werner, "New Chinese Military Strategy Casts US Military in Asia as Destabilizing," *USNI News*, July 30, 2019. http//news.usni.org/2019/07/30/new-chinese-military-strategy-casts-u-s-military-in-asia-as-destablizing

The South Korean perspective on South China Sea issues

South Korea's official policy regarding the SCS comprises three principles: international law should provide the framework for resolving all disputes; freedom of navigation and freedom of overflight should be guaranteed by the appropriate international regimes and concepts, such as the UNCLOS; and all disputes should be resolved by peaceful means. Critics have argued that these principles do nothing to actually help deal with the many complex problems of the SCS, and it is certainly true that South Korea keeps a low profile on SCS issues.

Indeed, South Korea is reluctant to tread on anybody's toes, and has therefore declined to be actively involved in US-led SCS military activities, such as FONOPs, and does not even participate in the multilateral naval and coast guard operations attempting to limit North Korean sanctions-busting, specifically the illegal ship-to-ship transfer of oil from Chinese to North Korean vessels in the East China Sea.[28]

South Korea is not itself involved in any SCS disputes, nor does it claim any maritime jurisdictional rights and interests in the SCS, and it believes that the best outcome would be for China and the other regional parties to reach agreement on SCS disputes through multilateral negotiation. South Korea therefore endorses the joint statements of the annual China-ASEAN summits, the COC agreement, and the 2016 ruling by the Arbitral Tribunal regarding the disputes between China and the Philippines.[29]

South Korea is, however, concerned about the maritime security of the SCS, especially insofar as it affects freedom of navigation. Some commentators on security affairs have raised the possibility that China might blockade sea routes through the SCS, but most South Korean economists consider such fears overblown.[30] Naval analysts also worry about disruption of the sea lanes as a consequence of increasing Chinese naval power, as well as China's expanded coast guard and huge maritime militia fleets, anticipating that this will provoke military confrontations in the SCS, whether with the

[28] Edward Wong and Christoph Koettl, "How North Korea's Leader Gets his Luxury Autos," *The New York Times International Edition*, July 18, 2019, 8 & 9.

[29] "US Navy Launches Live-fire Missiles in Warning to China," *Philippines News*, March 20, 2020. https://ph.news.yahoo.com/us-navy-launches-live-fire-120546651.html?guccounter=1

[30] Sukjoon Yoon, "Some Current Issues in Korean Maritime Security and Maritime Strategy," in Geoffrey Till and Yoon Sukjoon, *Korean Maritime Strategy: Issues and Challenges* (Seoul: Korea Institute for Maritime Strategy, 2011), 151–86.

US or with other regional states, but most expect any such conflicts to be limited and temporary.[31]

Although South Korea is not involved directly in any SCS disputes, there are some similar issues resulting from the San Francisco Peace Treaty signed after the Second World War (WW2), between the US, its allies, and Japan, at which Korea was not represented. Thus, Japan disputes the Senkaku/Diaoyu Islands with China, and Korea disputes Dokdo/Takeshima with Japan. The US bears some responsibility for creating these disputes, and both have led to significant frictions, with naval forces and coast guards dispatched in support of rival claims. These legacies from WW2 play a complicating role in regional maritime security, not least because Japan and Korea continue to quarrel over historical issues, despite both having close security relations with the US.[32] South Korea, having experience of historically bogus sovereignty claims, might reasonably be expected to sympathize with ASEAN countries being bullied by China, which claims 80 per cent of the SCS through its spurious "nine-dash line;" but South Korea's relationship with China has not been impacted by such considerations.[33]

There are also some parallels with the issue of illegal, unreported, and unregulated (IUU) fishing activities. China's vast fishing fleets roam across the seas of the world, paying scant attention to legal requirements, including in the near seas around the Korean Peninsula, where China insists that the maritime boundary with South Korea in the Yellow Sea (called the West Sea in Korea) should be determined by putative historical information about fishing zones.[34] China also makes similar claims about historical fishing zones in the SCS, for example with Indonesia. Thus, ASEAN members share some comparable problems with South Korea in their maritime disputes with China: overlapping EEZs, Chinese IUU fishing activities, and China's insistence that historical factors – often fabricated from whole cloth – outweigh international treaties like the UNCLOS. South Korea

[31] Sukjoon Yoon, "A Free and Open Indo-Pacific: The South Korean Perspective," *The Diplomat*, March 21, 2019. https://thediplomat.com/2019/03/a-free-and-open-indo-pacific-the-south-korean-perspective/

[32] See Catherine K. Lea and Michael A. McDevitt, *Maritime Security Issues in East Asia CNA Maritime Asia Project: Workshop Four* (Washington, DC: Center for Naval Analysis, 2013).

[33] Sukjoon Yoon, "Is There a Best Practice for a Peaceful Resolution of the South China Sea Disputes?" *The Journal of Territorial and Maritime Studies*, Vol. 3, No. 1, Winter/Spring 2016, 123–8.

[34] Sukjoon Yoon, "An Asia-Pacific Regional Maritime Security: Moving Beyond the Turmoil," *KMI International Journal of Maritime Affairs and Fisheries*, June 2013, Vol. 5, Issue 1, 43–58.

and ASEAN should make common cause against China on issues involving maritime boundaries and delimitation, otherwise China will surely deploy its military and economic strength to claim all and everything possible from its neighbouring countries.

The current South Korean administration has launched its so-called New Southern Policy, an ambitious attempt to reduce economic and strategic reliance upon China by forging closer links with India and ASEAN members.[35] The idea is for South Korea to develop more economic and interpersonal connections with the target countries, using the slogan: People, Prosperity and Peace. But if the policy is successful, then there may be some pushback from China, which is pursuing its own economic and political initiative in Southeast Asia (and beyond) through the so-called Maritime Silk Road, one of two pillars comprising the BRI. This Chinese investment in infrastructure has been broadly welcomed by most ASEAN members, so it is unclear whether South Korean President Moon Jae-in's New Southern Policy will gain much traction.[36]

Does South Korea have a role in helping to resolve South China Sea issues?

There are opportunities for South Korea to make a more active and constructive contribution to resolving the problems of the SCS, and though the impact may be limited such efforts are well worth the attempt.

South Korea is a capable and effective middle power, well respected regionally and globally, and as a good neighbour, it should develop practical policies which address the fraught situation of the SCS.[37] The SCS is blighted by bilateral legal disputes which threaten to disrupt the whole region, and is also riven by the great-power competition between China and the US, which must be prevented from escalating into a shooting war. China is pursuing its Chinese Dream project, which is perhaps benign in its intentions, but some see it as a quest to restore the Middle Kingdom. The

---

[35] See The Office of National Security of the Republic of Korea, *The Moon Jae-In administration's National Security Strategy* (Seoul: Republic of Korea Cheong Wa Dae, November 2018), 100–1.

[36] Jun Ji-hye, "ASEAN, India key to Korea's New Southern Policy," *The Korea Times*, November 8, 2018, 4.

[37] See Sukjoon Yoon and C. J. Jenner, "Sino-American rivalry in the SCS: Is It Time to Form a Maritime Middle Power Cooperative?" C. J. Jenner and Tran Trough Thuy, ed., all., *The SCS: A Crucial of Regional Cooperation or Conflict-making Sovereignty Claims?* (Cambridge, UK: Cambridge University Press, 2016), 241–65.

US Indo-Pacific Strategy claims to promote stability and prosperity, but it seems unambiguously designed to contain China within East Asian Seas.[38]

Most weaker regional countries, and even the other middle powers – Japan, Australia, and New Zealand – have succumbed to the relentless pressure from China and the US to clearly pick sides, but South Korea has demonstrated a striking degree of autonomy and self-reliance, most notably when the Terminal High Altitude Area Defense (THAAD) system was deployed on South Korean soil in 2017, to prepare for North Korean nuclear and missile threats. The US has also recently disclosed its intention to upgrade this facility, extending its range.[39] South Korea has also taken an independent stance by declining to agree on joint statements in which the US condemns China's actions in the SCS, resisting pressure from the US, its principal security ally, just as it resisted pressure from China, its primary strategic economic partner, over THAAD. South Korea has long balanced skilfully between China and the US, and there could be no better qualified go-between to help vulnerable ASEAN countries which are currently exposed, on the one hand to Chinese militarist bullying and economic manipulation, and on the other hand to the erratic and irrational "America First" isolationism of the blunderer-in-chief, former US President Donald Trump.

President Moon's New Southern Policy targets ASEAN members (and India), hoping to facilitate regional economic growth and development involving the maritime domain, and this could prove a fruitful opportunity for regional cooperation. Both the Korea Maritime Institute and the Korea Institute of Ocean Science & Technology have developed some promising maritime projects in cooperation with ASEAN. The weaker ASEAN members could also benefit from enhanced ties with the South Korean defence industry, which is reaching out to the Philippines, Indonesia, Malaysia and Vietnam. The South Korean Coast Guards have offered crew training to ASEAN countries, and have also provided education through multi-national maritime law enforcement mechanisms, such as the North Pacific Coast Guard Forum, the Heads of Asian Coast Guard Agencies Meeting, and the Cooperation Program for Maritime Law Enforcement Agencies in Asia and Africa.[40]

---

[38] Daniel Ward, "Going to War with China? Dust off Corbett!" *USNI Proceedings*, January 2020, 56–60.

[39] For recent developments on the deployment of THAAD, see "Editorial: Necessary Step," *The Korea Herald*, February 17, 2020, 14; Shim Kyu-Seok, "Washington Mulls Upgrading, Separating THAAD," Korea JoongAng Daily, February 17, 2020, 1.

[40] Korea Coast Guard, *2019 Korea Coast Guard Annual Report* (Incheon: Headquarters of the ROK Coast Guard, 2019), 299.

South Korea is a member of numerous regional security frameworks, such as ASEAN+, the ASEAN Regional Forum, the Asia-Pacific Economic Cooperation, the East Asia Summit, and the ASEAN-ROK Dialogue Partnership (which recently held a Commemorative Summit, together with the 1st Mekong-ROK Summit). In these forums South Korea always tries to act as an honest facilitator on SCS issues by endorsing maritime cooperation. In such frameworks South Korea can exercise substantial autonomy in support of weaker powers, being beholden neither to the US nor to China, though China's insistence on bilateral negotiations with other SCS claimants limits the utility of these multilateral institutions.[41]

South Korea also provides a model for how to measure threats and manage crises, after seven decades of dealing with North Korea. In fact, President Moon has recently made significant progress, with both Koreas agreeing, in 2018, on the still evolving Permanent Peace Initiative on the Korean Peninsula, and also signing the 9/19 military agreement. South Korea has demonstrated that a carefully calibrated balance between the two great powers is the best way to maintain the current status quo on the Korean Peninsula, and this surely offers some relevant lessons to those countries embroiled in SCS disputes.[42] The Co-Chairs' Statement of the 2019 ASEAN-ROK Commemorative Summit, held November 25–26, 2019, in Busan, reaffirmed the importance of maintaining and promoting peace, security, stability, safety, and freedom of navigation in and overflight above the SCS. This was the clearest statement on SCS issues since the foundation of the ASEAN-ROK Dialogue Partnership in 1989.[43]

South Korea also has useful experience with the de-escalation of war-like crisis situations, for example in its management of the maritime provocations by North Korea in 2010, when the *ROKS Cheonan* was torpedoed and sunk in the Yellow Sea, and Yeongpyeong Island suffered an artillery bombardment.[44] And there is now a clear pattern of naval escalation in the SCS. Although FONOPs cannot reasonably be interpreted as an act of war,

---

[41] Ser Myo-ja, "Moon Hosts ASEAN Leaders on 30th Anniversary," *Korea JoongAng Daily*, November 24, 2019. http://koreajoonagangdaily.joins.com/news/article/article.aspx?aid=3070697

[42] Sukjoon Yoon, "Maritime Asia: A South Korean Perspective," Geoffrey Till, *The Changing Maritime Scene in Asia: Rising Tensions and Future Strategic Stability* (London: Palgrave Macmillan, 2015), 92–113.

[43] Lee Chi-dong, "S. Korea-ASEAN Summit to Open in Busan, Prologue to 'New Southern Policy 2,0,'" *YONHAP News*, November 25, 2020. http://en.yna.co.kr/view/AEN20191125000200315 (assessed by May 11, 2020)

[44] David E. Singer, "North Korea Thwarts Sanctions with a Surge in Web Use," *The New York Times International Edition*, February 15–16, 2020, 3.

the US Navy has recently conducted live-fire exercises in the SCS involving an Aegis-equipped cruiser and destroyer using SM-2 ship-to-air missiles: this is a clear provocation, since it looks like a war-game scenario to prepare for conflict with China. In response, on April 20, 2020, the *Liaoning* aircraft carrier combat group sailed through the Taiwan Strait, and it has also been reported that the Chinese navy's second aircraft carrier, the *Shandong*, has been deployed to the Southern Theatre Command to celebrate the 71st anniversary of the navy's founding, on April 21, 2020.[45] Meanwhile, the US Navy has been preoccupied with the COVID-19 crisis, which has seriously affected the *USS Theodore Roosevelt*, a nuclear-powered aircraft carrier, and also the Aegis-destroyer *USS Kidd*, which is part of the forward-deployed 7th Fleet.[46]

Again, despite its security alliance with the US, South Korea has been cautious about participating in provocative deployments. It declined US diplomatic requests for naval involvement in the SCS and even refused to send a destroyer to the Strait of Hormuz, where the US Navy leads the International Maritime Security Construct, which protects shipping from the depredations of Iran's Islamic Revolutionary Guard Corps.[47] The contribution made to maritime peace and good order by military restraint is consistently undervalued.

Is South Korea's COVID-19 management relevant to South China Sea issues?

Theoretical analysis of middle powers has generally been sceptical about the extent of the leverage which they can exert to influence the great power game, but in 2020 we have seen a situation where South Korea has been admired in almost every country around the world, including in China and the US, by the common people, and by many of the political leaders, for its strikingly successful response to the COVID-19 global pandemic.[48] Are there, perhaps, some lessons from this health crisis which can be usefully transferred to geopolitical crises, such as those of the SCS?

---

45 Liu Xuanzun, "Aircraft Carriers, Destroyer Prepare for Chinese Navy's 71st Anniversary," *Global Times,* April 22, 2020. http://www.globaltimes.cn/content/1186455.shtml

46 Sam LaGrone, "Navy Confirms 18 COVID-19 Cases on Deployed USS Kidd, Destroyer Heading to Port," *US Naval Institute News*, April 24, 2020. https://news.usni.org/2020/04/24/pentagon-confirms-18-covid-19-cases-on-deployed-uss-kidd-destroyer-heading-to-port

47 Tim Ripley, "Analysis: Gulf Tanker Protection Mission Takes Shape," *Jane's Defence Weekly*, 28 August 2019, 6.

48 Bill Gates, "A Global Approach to Fight COVID-19," *The Korea JoongAng Daily*, April 13, 2020, 9.

Certainly, the pandemic has already had effects far beyond the immediate sphere of health management, the most conspicuous being the concomitant economic crisis. The world is facing the worst economic downturn since the Great Depression, and even the greatest powers have lost significant influence, with the magnitude and speed of this collapse unprecedented in our modern world.[49] Regionally, China and many ASEAN members are experiencing multiple crises: in health, in their finances, and with collapsing supply chains for food and goods. ASEAN policy makers are struggling to cope with this extraordinary situation, and their efforts are without reference to or support from the great powers.[50] Thus, the Philippines decided to terminate its Visiting Forces Agreement with the US, and three ASEAN states have recently tried to push back at China's unilateral claims in the SCS.[51]

With the US and China playing a blame-game about who is responsible for the COVID-19 pandemic, the SCS has been drawn into their struggle to find strategic scapegoats.[52] In April 2020, the US sent naval cruisers and destroyers to the Paracel and Spratly Islands in the SCS for the first time, while two nuclear-powered aircraft carriers were moored at harbours in the region. The Chinese PLA Southern Theatre Command accused the US naval vessels of conducting illegal trespass into SCS waters and claimed to have expelled them. It seems probable that the US and China will continue to exploit the COVID-19 pandemic as a tool to influence regional states strategically, which will result in tactical naval operations. With other countries entirely focused on public health, South Korea is well placed to defuse this naval escalation.

COVID-19 is a novel transnational threat, which has revealed South Korea, by comparison with almost every other country, as a shining exemplar of competent, transparent, trustworthy governance.[53] Assuming that Chinese

---

[49] Michael Green, "COVID-19 and Geopolitics, Part 2," *The Korea JoongAng Daily*, April 13, 2020, 8.

[50] Chris Patten, "Dealing with China after COVID-19," *The Korea JoongAng Daily*, April 28, 2020, 9.

[51] Dzirhan Mahadzir, "US Warns China Will Gain Edge if the Philippines Ends Visiting Forces Agreement," *USNI News*, February 12, 2020. http://news.usni.org/2020/02/12/u-s-warns-china-will-gain-edge-if-the-philippines-ends-visiting-forces-agreement; Drake Long, "Three ASEAN States Push Back on Beijing in SCS," *Radio Free Asia*, April 15, 2020. http://www.globalsecurity.org/military/library/news/2020/04/mil-200415-rfa01.htm?

[52] Peter Daszak, "Welcome to the age of pandemics," *The New York Times International Edition*, February 28, 2020, 1 and 10; Thomas L. Friedman, "Trump Plays a Dangerous Safety Game," *The New York Times International Edition*, April 20, 2020, 1 and 11.

[53] Lee Ho-jeong, "Korea to Provide $400M in Foreign Aid," *Korea JoongAng Daily*, April 28, 2020, 3.

statistics are accurate, then China has managed the pandemic with ruthless authoritarian efficiency, but few outside China have felt inspired by this model, and in liberal democracies people have once again recognized the true character of China's monolithic system, which tramples even trivial popular dissent, and grabs everything it can get its hands on from its neighbours around the SCS.[54] As for the US, a health disaster vies for headlines with an economic catastrophe, and Trump has been exposed as a breathtakingly incompetent narcissist who has done the exact opposite of "Make America Great Again" by presiding over a historic decline which will surely end with the US losing its great-power status.[55] We can only hope that the process is as graceful as the decline of British power in the previous century.[56]

Not only the US, but all major Western countries have also failed miserably to contain the spread of COVID-19. Yes, there are degrees of failure: Germany was once lauded as a European success story, but as of the beginning of 2021, that country –as with the UK – was experiencing in excess of 1,000 deaths per day, the US more than 4,000 per day, and Canada more than 200 per day[57] Moreover, although there is social distancing in South Korea, there is nothing remotely resembling the lockdowns seen elsewhere, and while the economy will be impacted, this will likely be within conventional bounds to manage.[58] South Korea is clearly setting a standard which other countries aspire to emulate, and its global stature seems likely to be considerably enhanced in the post-COVID-19 era.[59] China and the US, meanwhile, are engaged in a pathetically unedifying blame-game about which is most irresponsible, and, by extension, which system of governance is superior.[60]

54 Harold James, "The Pandemic Trilemma," *The Korea JoongAng Daily*, April 13, 2020, 9.

55 "Editorial: The America We Need," *The New York Times International Edition*, April 11–12, 2020, 13; Sarah Kim, "Masks Being Sent Abroad for Korean War Veterans," *The Korea JoongAng Daily*, May 8–10, 2020, 1.

56 Keith Bradsher, "After Decades of Growth, China Falters," *The New York Times International Edition*, March 18, 2020, 7; Kara Swisher, "Will the Most Important Industry Survive Coronavirus?" *The New York Times International Edition*, March 27, 2020, 9.

57 Worldometers.info. "Coronavirus."

58 Song Min-soon, "Augmenting Trilateral Cooperation," *The Korea JoongAng Daily*, April 27, 2020, 8.

59 Choe Sang-hun, "In Contrast to China's Response, South Korea Tries Openness," *The New York Times International Edition*, February 27, 2020, 5; Lee Sung-Eun, "Can Korea Leverage Virus Fight into Leadership?," Korea JoongAng Daily, May 11, 2020, 2.

60 Cui Tiankai, "Cooperation Vital for US and China," *The New York Times International Edition*, April 7, 2020, 1 & 11; Paul Angelo and Rebecca Bill Chavez, "How China Ups Its Game in One Region," *The New York Time International Edition*, April 22, 2020, 1 & 11.

Taiwan is another party which has dealt very successfully with COVID-19. So what do South Korea and Taiwan have in common? Both societies are highly connected with technologically savvy populations; both have competent, transparent, and responsive governments which enjoy the trust of their citizens, especially in times of crisis. Both parties have relied upon effective contact tracing which collects and integrates multiple data sources, and people have calmly accepted this as necessary and appropriate, even in a free and open society, because they trust their governments. By contrast, other countries are still arguing about privacy issues. Australia and New Zealand are two other regional middle powers which have dealt well with COVID-19, and again, the governments of these countries have retained the trust of their populations.

The US and China have both treated the COVID-19 pandemic as another opportunity to play power politics in the SCS. China's stance offers little benefit to its neighbours in the near future and the US "America First" policy of recent years has progressively erodes its world leadership. Rather than working together against a global health threat, the great powers are engaged in a COVID-19 Cold War. By contrast, the South Korean COVID-19 success story provides significant international leverage to raise South Korea's profile, both during and after the pandemic. This may afford South Korea greater strategic and diplomatic influence, allowing it to function as an essential stabilizing factor in the SCS.

Conclusion

China has quite shamelessly used its infamous "nine-dash line" to justify bullying its smaller weaker neighbours, attempting to seize economic control of valuable undersea assets. It has also behaved badly in other ways, creating and militarizing artificial islands to seize strategic control of the SCS in support of its geopolitical struggle with the US. Liberal democracies now take the view that changing political boundaries by main force is no longer legal, whereas China believes it is simply restoring the historical status quo ante. But the behaviour of the US is hardly less provocative: the Chinese economy relies upon freedom of navigation through the SCS, just as much as other economies, so the US-led FONOPs seem to be more about preserving US military dominance and keeping China in its place. The US seems determined to preserve its regional maritime hegemony, whatever the consequences, but its military advantage over China is clearly declining in relative terms, and China can afford to play a long game.

The ASEAN countries, especially those coastal to the SCS, have limited options, though they are trying to achieve a little more autonomy by expanding their maritime forces. But a general arms build-up in the SCS is hardly conducive to peace and good order, and all parties should consider their common interests in preserving a stable security environment. The US and China should therefore refrain from any further sabre-rattling, and instead work together to resolve their differences within existing international legal and security protocols, and if these are inadequate then new ones should be negotiated: it does not help matters that the US has not ratified the UNCLOS.

The world is changing, and COVID-19 will surely accelerate change. Once we had high-class fashion leaders and major-label musicians, now we have "influencers" who drive global trends from their teenage bedrooms, and some are hugely commercially successful. Perhaps there is a parallel evolution of governance, in which ordinary people will choose what they like, escaping from autocracy, and ignoring corporate interests who try to buy their compliance. Before the crisis there was growing disillusionment with liberal democracies as currently established, and some were looking to the Chinese system, but this has now become less appealing.[61] Both types of governance are now being challenged by middle powers, by competent trustworthy governments, of which there are several in the region, including South Korea. The COVID-19 crisis has exposed the flaws of *both* great powers for everyone to see, and there is now an unprecedented opportunity for the middle powers to increase their influence over geopolitical developments, including the sorry situation of the SCS.

Ultimately, nothing short of a comprehensive strategic solution will suffice to restore maritime peace and stability in the SCS, taking full account of all relevant geographical, legal, and economic factors.

References

Alex Chan, "China, the Philippines Entering a Golden Era of Bilateral Ties," *China Daily*, November 21, 2018 http://africa.chinadaily.com.cn/201811/21/WS5bf4cd0da310eff30328a1ee.ntml

Andrew Rhodes, "Go Get Mahan's Yardstick," *USNI Proceedings*, July 2019, 19–23.

[61] John Grady, "Veneer of China's Charm Offensive Cracked by Vietnamese Fishing Boat Incident," *US NI News*, April 9, 2020. http://news.usni,org/2020/04/09/veneer-of-chinas-charm-offensive-cracked-by-vietnamese; Roger Cohen, "Despotism and Democracy in the Age of the Virus," *The New York Times International Edition*, April 27, 2020, 9.

Anguang Zheng, "Integrating the China Coast Guard with the PLA Navy," in Ian Bowers and Collin Koh Swee Lean, *Grey and White Hulls: An International Analysis of the Navy-Coast Guard Nexus* (London: Palgrave, Macmillan, 2029), 23–34.

"Belt and Road Initiative Facilitates Economic Cooperation among China, ASEAN, South Asia," *China Daily*, October 10, 2018. Htttp://www.chinadaily.com.cna201810/10/WS5bbdb127a310eff3032819e5.html

Ben Werner, "New Chinese Military Strategy Casts US Military in Asia as Destabilizing," USNI News, July 30, 2019. http//news.usni.org/2019/07/30/new-chinese-military-strategy-casts-u-s-military-in-asia-as-destablizing

Bernard D. Cole, "Controlling Contested Waters," *USNI Proceedings*, October 2013, 48–53.

Bernard D. Cole, "Island Chains and Naval Classics," *USNI Proceedings*, November 2014, 68–73.

Bill Gates, "A Global Approach to Fight COVID-19," *The Korea JoongAng Daily*, April 13, 2020, 9.

Brian Smicklas, "Guard the Coast from High-end Threats," *USNI Proceedings*, February, 2019, 44–49.

C. J. Jenner and Tran Trough Thuy, eds, *The SCS: A Crucial of Regional Cooperation or Conflict-making Sovereignty Claims?* (Cambridge, UK: Cambridge University Press, 2016).

Carl Thayer, "Background Brief: South China Sea: China Claims It Expelled US Warship from Paracel Islands," *Thayer Consultancy*, ABN #65 648 097 123, April 29, 2020.

Catherine K. Lea and Michael A. McDevitt, *Maritime Security Issues in East Asia CNA Maritime Asia Project: Workshop Four* (Washington, DC: Center for Naval Analysis, 2013).

"Chinese Premier Pushes for Free Trade, South China Sea Code in Singapore Visit," *Global Times*, November 17, 2018. http://www.globaltimes.cn/content/1127725.shtml

Choe Sang-hun, "In Contrast to China's Response, South Korea Tries Openness," *The New York Times International Edition*, February 27, 2020, 5.

Chris Patten, "Dealing with China after COVID-19," *The Korea JoongAng Daily*, April 28, 2020.

Congressional Research Service, *US-China Strategic Competition in South and East China Seas: Background and Issues for Congress* (Washington, DC: US Congress, January 28 2020).

Cui Tiankai, "Cooperation Vital for US and China," *The New York Times International Edition*, April 7, 2020, 1 & 11.

Dale C. Rielage, "Parsing the Chinese Challenge," *USNI Proceedings*, September 2013, 58–62.

Daniel Ward, "Going to War with China? Dust off Corbett!" *USNI Proceedings*, January 2020, 56–60.

David E. Singer, "North Korea Thwarts Sanctions with a Surge in Web Use," *The New York Times International Edition*, February 15–16, 2020.

Douglas Guifoyle, UNSW Canberra Maritime Security Research Group, *Strategy and Law in the SCS Disputes, 14–15 October 2019: Workshop Report* (Canberra, Australia: UNSW, October 2019.

Drake Long, "Three ASEAN States Push Back on Beijing in SCS," *Radio Free Asia*, April 15, 2020. http://www.globalsecurity.org/military/library/news/2020/04/mil-200415-rfa01.htm?

Dzirhan Mahadzir, "US Warns China Will Gain Edge if the Philippines Ends Visiting Forces Agreement," USNI News, February 12, 2020. http://news.usni.org/2020/02/12/u-s-warns-china-will-gain-edge-if-the-philippines-ends-visiting-forces-agreement

"Editorial: Necessary Step," *The Korea Herald*, February 17, 2020.

"Editorial: The America We Need," *The New York Times International Edition*, April 11–12, 2020.

Edward Wong and Christoph Koettl, "How North Korea's Leader Gets His Luxury Autos," *The New York Times International Edition*, July 18, 2019.

Frederick Kliem, "Germany in the Indo-Pacific: New Security Actor?," *RSIS Commentary*, No. 144, 18 July 2019.

Gabriel Dominguez, "China Greatest Long-Term Strategic Threat to Region and US, Says INDOPACOM Chief," *Jane's Defence Weekly*, 20 February 2019.

Geoffrey Till, *The Changing Maritime Scene in Asia: Rising Tensions and Future Strategic Stability* (London: Palgrave Macmillan, 2015).

Geoffrey Till and Jane Chan, ed., all., *Naval Modernisation in South-East Asia* (London & New York: Routledge, 2014).

Hannah Beech, "We Cannot Afford This," *The New York Times International Edition*, August 23, 2018.

Harold James, "The Pandemic Trilemma," *The Korea JoongAng Daily*, April 13, 2020.

James Holmes, "Visualize Chinese Sea Power," USNI, Proceedings, June 2018, 26–31.

Jane Perlez, "Myanmar Attracts Attention of Beijing," *The New York Times International Edition*, July 19, 2017, 1 & 8.

Jay Caputo, "A Global Fishing War Is Coming," *USNI Proceedings*, August 2017, 32–37.

John Grady, "Panel: US, China SCS Tensions Show No Signs of Easing," *USNI News*, July 29, 2019. http://news.usni.org/2019/07/29/panel-u-s-china-south-china-sea-tensions-show no-signs-of-easing

John Grady, "Veneer of China's Charm Offensive Cracked by Vietnamese Fishing Boat Incident," *USNI News*, April 9, 2020. http://news.usni,org/2020/04/09/veneer-of-chinas-charm-offensive-cracked-by-vietnamese

John Grady, "US Could Do More to Deter Iran Grey Zone Strategy, Exports Say," *USNI News*, April 23, 2020. https://news.usni.org/2020/04/23/u-s-could-do-more-to-deter-iran-gray-zone-strategy-experts-say

Jonathan G. Odom, "China's Riskfare," *USNI Proceedings*, March 2019, 21–25.

Jonathan Ward, "The Influence of Seapower upon China," *USNI Proceedings*, August 2019, 62–67.

Jun Ji-hye, "ASEAN, India Key to Korea's New Southern Policy," *The Korea Times*, November 8, 2018.

Kara Swisher, "Will the Most Important Industry Survive Coronavirus?" *The New York Times International Edition*, March 27, 2020.

Keith Bradsher, "After Decades of Growth, China falters," *The New York Times International Edition*, March 18, 2020, p. 7

Korea Coast Guard, *2019 Korea Coast Guard Annual Report* (Incheon: Headquarters of the ROK Coast Guard, 2019).

Lee Chi-dong, "S. Korea-ASEAN Summit to Open in Busan, Prologue to 'New Southern Policy 2,0," *YONHAP News*, November 25, 2020. http://en.yna.co.kr/view/AEN20191125000200315

Lee Ho-jeong, "Korea to Provide $400M in Foreign Aid," *Korea JoongAng Daily*, April 28, 2020.

Lee Sung-Eun, "Can Korea Leverage Virus Fight into Leadership," *The Korea JoongAng Daily*, May 11, 2020.

Lee Willett, "Royal Navy Operations in the Asia-Pacific," *Jane's Defence Weekly*, 29 May 2019, 2–26

Lee Willet, "Cops on the Beat: IMSC Navies Shine Light on Gulf 'Grey Zone' Areas," *Jane's Navy International*, March 2020, 10–11.

Li Zheng, "PLA Aims to Become Global Stabilizer in New Era," *China Daily*, August 2, 2019. http://chinadailyasia.com/article/108/76/57/1564719557931.html?newsId=90

Liu Xuanzun, "Aircraft Carriers, Destroyer Prepare for Chinese Navy's 71st Anniversary," *Global Times,* April 22, 2020. http://www.globaltimes.cn/content/1186455.shtml

Michael Fabey, "USN SCS FONOPS Heightens US-China Tensions," *Jane's Navy International*, July 2018, 4

Michael Green, "COVID-19 and Geopolitics, Part 2," *The Korea JoongAng Daily*, April 13, 2020.

Paul Angelo and Rebecca Bill Chavez, "How China Ups Its Game in One Region," *The New York Time International Edition*, April 22, 2020.

Peter Daszak, "Welcome to the Age of Pandemics," *The New York Times International Edition*, February 28, 2020, 1 and 10

Peter S. Goodman and Jane Perlez, "China Rules: Paving a Way to Global Power," *The New York Times International Edition*, November 18, 2018.

Ridzwan Rahmat, "At-Sea Security: ASEAN Adopts Regional Approach to Maritime Threats," *Jane's Navy International*, July/August 2016.

Roger Cohen, "Despotism and Democracy in the Age of the Virus," *The New York Times International Edition*, April 27, 2020.

Sam Bateman, "Solving the 'Wicked Problems' of Maritime Security: Are Regional Forums up to the Task?" *Contemporary Southeast Asia*, Vol. 33, No. 1, 2011, 1–28.

Sam LaGrone, "Navy Confirms 18 COVID-19 Cases on Deployed USS Kidd, Destroyer Heading to Port," *USNI News*, April 24, 2020. https://news.usni.org/2020/04/24/pentagon-confirms-18-covid-19-cases-on-deployed-uss-kidd-destroyer-heading-to-port

Sam LaGrone, "SWO Boss: Insidious COVID-19 Spread on USS Kidd Shows Evolution of Navy Response to Pandemic," *USNI News*, May 6, 2020. http://news.usni.org/2020/05/06/swo-boss-insidious-covid-19-spread-on-uss-kidd-sh

Sarah Kim, "Masks Being Sent Abroad for Korean War Veterans," *The Korea JoongAng Daily*, May 8–10, 2020.

Ser Myo-ja, "Moon Hosts ASEAN Leaders on 30th Anniversary," *Korea JoongAng Daily*, November 24, 2019. http://koreajoonagangdaily.joins.com/news/article/article.aspx?aid=3070697

Shannon Tiezzi, "China-Philippines Relations: Can the Rainbow Last?" *The Diplomat*, November 22, 2018. http://thediplomat.com/2018/11/china-philippines-relations-can-the-rainbow-last/

Shim Kyu-Seok, "Washington Mulls Upgrading, Separating THAAD," *Korea JoongAng Daily*, February 17, 2020.

Song Min-soon, "Augmenting Trilateral Cooperation," *The Korea JoongAng Daily*, April 27, 2020.

Sukjoon Yoon, "Some Current Issues in Korean Maritime Security and Maritime Strategy," in Geoffrey Till and Yoon Sukjoon, *Korean Maritime Strategy: Issues and Challenges* (Seoul: Korea Institute for Maritime Strategy, 2011), 151–86.

Sukjoon Yoon, "The Emergence and Consolidation of a Chinese Version of the Monroe Doctrine: Implication for Korea's China Policy," *KAS Journal on Contemporary Korean Affairs*, 1/2013.

Sukjoon Yoon, "An Asia-Pacific Regional Maritime Security: Moving Beyond the Turmoil," *KMI International Journal of Maritime Affairs and Fisheries*, June 2013, Vol. 5, Issue 1, 43–58.

Sukjoon Yoon, "Why Is Beijing Militarising the South China Sea?" *The Nation Thailand*, May 11, 2015. http://www.nationthailand.com/noname/30259858

Sukjoon Yoon, "Maritime Asia: A South Korean Perspective," in Geoffrey Till, *The Changing Maritime Scene in Asia: Rising Tensions and Future Strategic Stability* (London: Palgrave Macmillan, 2015), 92–113.

Sukjoon Yoon, "Is there a Best Practice for a Peaceful Resolution of the South China Sea Disputes?" *The Journal of Territorial and Maritime Studies*, Vol. 3, No. 1, Winter/Spring 2016, 123–8.

Sukjoon Yoon, "Decoding China's Maritime Aspirations," *USNI Proceedings*, March 2017, 44–48. https://www.usni.org/magazines/proceedings/2017/march/decoding-chinas-maritime

Sukjoon Yoon, "A Free and Open Indo-Pacific: The South Korean Perspective," *The Diplomat*, March 21, 2019. https://thediplomat.com/2019/03/a-free-and-open-indo-pacific-the-south-korean-perspective/

Sukjoon Yoon and C. J. Jenner, "Sino-American Rivalry in the SCS: Is It Time to Form a Maritime Middle Power Cooperative?" in C. J. Jenner and Tran Trough Thuy, ed., all., *The SCS: A Crucible of Regional Cooperation or Conflict-making Sovereignty Claims?* (Cambridge: Cambridge University Press, 2016), 241–65.

The Office of National Security of the Republic of Korea, *The Moon Jae-In Administration's National Security Strategy* (Seoul: Republic of Korea Cheong Wa Dae, November 2018).

Thomas L. Friedman, "Trump Plays a Dangerous Safety Game," *The New York Times International Edition*, April 20, 2020.

Tim Ripley, "Analysis: Gulf Tanker Protection Mission Takes Shape," *Jane's Defence Weekly*, 28 August 2019.

Tran Truong Thuy, "Conclusion – Tempering the South China Sea Slow Boil: Expanding Options for Evolving Disputes," in Tran Truong Thuy, John B. Welfield and Le Thuy Trang, *Building a Normative Order in the South China Sea: Evolving Disputes, Expanding Options.*

Tran Truong Thuy, John B. Welfield and Le Thuy Trang, *Building a Normative Order in the South China Sea: Evolving Disputes, Expanding Options* (Cheltenham, UK: Edward Elgar, 2019).

"US Navy Launches Live-Fire Missiles in Warning to China," *Philippines News*, March 20, 2020. https://ph.news.yahoo.com/us-navy-launches-live-fire-120546651.html?guccounter=1

Wilson, K. "Island Serves as Belt, Road Maritime Gateway," *China Daily*, November 21, 2018. http://usa.chinadaily.com.cn/a/201811/21/WS5bf49e09a310eff303289f93.html

Worldometers.info. "Coronavirus." https://www.worldometers.info/coronavirus/.

Conclusion: Looking over the Horizon – Prospects for Settlement of the South China Sea Dispute?

Gordon Houlden

This volume has provided a broad assessment by experts of the complex political and security challenges that arise from highly divergent national views on the South China Sea (SCS). But it is evident that there is no consensus among the claimant states regarding the future of the SCS, nor among external stakeholders. This volume will most certainly not be the last word on a dispute that has endured decades, and that is likely to stretch deep into the 21st century without a comprehensive settlement or resolution.

From the defeat of the Empire of Japan by the United States (US) and its wartime allies in 1945 until the 1974 expulsion of Vietnamese armed forces from the Paracels, the SCS was a peripheral international issue in a world dominated by the security challenges of the Cold War between the US and the Soviet Union. As noted by John Callahan in Chapter 12, the US Navy (USN) was largely unchallenged in the SCS waters, while China possessed only a modest coastal naval force.

The rise in Chinese economic power allowed the People's Republic of China (PRC) to devote funding to building a blue-water navy and, through massive dredging operations, to expand islets or to create islands from atolls or rocky outcrops of the sea, and to build on these features extensive naval, coast guard, and air force installations. However, as noted by Stein Tønnesson in the Foreword, none of the other SCS claimant states possess the means to compete successfully with China in terms of military capacity. Two external stakeholders – the US and Japan – have sufficient military resources to play a role in security issues related to the SCS, but only the

US possesses the means to project sufficient power into the SCS and thus to contest PRC dominance.

Future status of the South China Sea

It is difficult to imagine the disputing claimant states achieving consensus on the competing legal claims in the foreseeable future. For the top Chinese leadership, the high profile accorded to China's efforts to solidify its SCS claims, and the personal involvement of the PRC's Xi Jinping in pushing those claims makes any backing-down on China's SCS policies unlikely. Furthermore, the very prominence of Chinese claims in the Chinese state media and in the PRC educational curriculum may serve as a brake to Chinese willingness to compromise on SCS issues.

For the other claimants, the issue is also problematic. National publics tend to identify strongly with territorial issues, including maritime claims. None of the claimants possesses, or is likely to possess, the military means to resist the Chinese armed forces in the case of military conflict. Although Vietnam possesses substantial military capabilities, its navy is modest in both size and strength compared to China.

Therefore, Southeast Asian strategies cannot rely only on their limited military deterrence capacities. The improbability of these states constructing, without external assistance, a robust policy of military deterrence will likely push these claimants toward broader non-military strategies. We have already seen the Philippine's President Rodrigo Duterte move towards a closer economic and political relationship with China, abandoning his predecessor's focus on legal challenges to Beijing's Spratly claims (Rommel C. Banlaoi, Chapter 6).

With relative military weakness compared to China, and significant economic dependence on China, it is not surprising that the claimant states have explored a range of responses to Chinese power. A central challenge for the non-Chinese claimants is their lack of group cohesion. While four of the five claimants (Brunei, Malaysia, the Philippines, and Vietnam) are members of the Association of Southeast Asian Nations (ASEAN), that organization largely depends on consensus on foreign policy issues, and there are non-claimant ASEAN members who are sensitive to PRC views on the SCS, making a strong and unified ASEAN stance problematic (Mingjiang Li and YingHui Lee, Chapter 11). In the case of Taiwan, that island's lack of international recognition as a state, combined with heightened sensitivity regarding Taiwan's "status," means that Taipei's inclusion in any international discussions on the SCS is doubly difficult, and probably unachievable.

Furthermore, China, as is generally the case with other great powers, prefers to deal with smaller states on a bilateral basis, where China's clout can be brought to bear, and where China can avoid having to engage in multilateral negotiations with a grouping of ASEAN states.

The most significant factor in calculations regarding the future of the SCS disputes is the US. Without US power projection into the Western Pacific, PRC dominance of the SCS in terms of military power would almost certainly go unchallenged. While the USN has been active in the Western Pacific since the 19th century, it was during and following the Second World War that the US achieved unmatched supremacy in the Pacific, including the Western littorals of that ocean (John Callahan, Chapter 12).

Beginning in the 1980s, based on China's considerable economic growth, there has been a parallel increase in the strength of the PRC's military power and, most relevant to the SCS, a sharp increase in the power projection capacity of Chinese naval and air power.

While the qualitative aspects of US naval power in the region have not declined, there has been a relative decline in US power in the face of the steady increase in Chinese naval and air forces, bolstered by Chinese bases within the SCS, and by the growth in the number and range of Chinese missile forces as well as submarines and blue-water surface vessels. The more success China achieves in growing its military strength across the board, the greater the chance that the US will view China's presence in the SCS with suspicion.

Underlying the US force capability in the Western Pacific is not only the capacity of the US Armed Forces, but also the political will to use those naval and air forces. Would the US be prepared to go to war over the SCS? China has declared that the SCS is a "core national interest," but is the same true for the US?

While the US is the most significant external stakeholder to the SCS dispute, other regional states, in particular Japan, have a significant interest in the issue, both because of the passage of critical raw material flows (especially petroleum) through the SCS as well as the movement of Japan's maritime trade through SCS waters (Masafumi Iida, Chapter 13). Other hemispheric states, including India, Indonesia, Australia, and South Korea, have similar concerns. This is also true of a good portion of North American and European maritime trade.

As the percentage of global trade that is centred in Asia rises, both Asian states and their extra-regional partners will increasingly rely on passage through the SCS. However, it should be noted that China itself has emphasized that it has no intention of restricting the free flow of maritime trade through the SCS, and it is in China's own economic self-interest (China being the world's largest trading nation) to have ready access for its exports and imports through the SCS as well as for those of its trading partners. China's dependence on maritime trade underwrites, in principle, the Chinese need for a conflict-free SCS.

However, for the outside powers who are focused on freedom of navigation (especially the United States), or for countries who depend upon a free flow of maritime commerce through the South China Sea, the Chinese maritime claims are problematic in their scope, even in the face of Chinese statements that the PRC will not restrict commercial shipping.

For most of Chinese history, the national security focus was on external threats arising from the steppe lands to the west and north of "China proper" (Li Yang, Chapter 3). The arrival of militarily advanced navies from the West and Japan during the 19th century gradually changed that perspective. The disintegration of the Soviet Union relieved the pressure on China from Central and North Asia, and allowed a focus on the Eastern maritime approaches. It was not surprising that China, with ambitious claims in the SCS, would seek to back up these claims with expansion and militarization of both the expanded natural features as well as the artificial islands.

But China now has a navy capable of operating far from its shores. As Chinese naval power increases, and as Chinese interest in far-flung regions increases, we may see a transition from a focus on the littorals of East Asia, and from heightened sensitivity regarding the transit of foreign navies near its shores, towards a new emphasis on the ability of Chinese naval forces to operate in distant waters near the shores of other continents.

The US itself underwent this transition during the 19th century as it moved from wariness regarding the British navy near its coasts to a focus on the projection of US naval power deep into the Pacific and other oceans. While PLAN (and China's top leadership) are currently preoccupied with promoting their claims and projecting force into the SCS, that focus may gradually shift if China's upward course continues apace, and as China's global influence waxes.

China's conservative readings of parts of the United Nations Convention on the Law of the Sea (UNCLOS), in particular the Chinese view that there are restrictions on military vessels and aircraft transiting an exclusive economic zone (EEZ), are those of a coastal state with deep concerns regarding its vulnerability from a more distant adversary (Li Yang, Chapter 3). As Chinese naval vessels expand their distant overseas patrols over time, which would simply be an extension of an existing trend, we may see a gradual shift towards view more in line with the historic views of the British navy, and the current stance of the United States Navy (USN). These views of a sea-going power tend towards an expansive view of the rights of naval ships in the proximity to coastal states. Following this logic, as occurred with the US naval doctrine, China, with an expanding and far-ranging navy, may begin to place greater emphasis on the freedom of the seas for its own navy, reducing the very different perspective of a primarily coastal state.

The SCS rivalries that have complicated any resolution of competing claims in the SCS, and the parallel disputes regarding "freedom of navigation" exercises by the USN are certainly not entirely generated by the SCS dispute. If we could know the overall character of China's relations with the states in the Southeast Asia, and external to the region, we could have more confidence in assessing the risks specific to the SCS.

Sino-Vietnamese rivalry has deep roots, and this historical enmity impedes the trust that would help reach a compromise solution to overlapping claims (Đỗ Thanh Hải and Nguyễn Thùy Linh, Chapter 5). As evidence of the particular challenges related to the incompatibility of the Vietnamese and Chinese claims, it is only the rival Sino-Vietnamese claims that have generated actual naval confrontation with loss of life.

It is difficult to be optimistic about the prospects for an early resolution to the competing legal claims to the SCS in the foreseeable future. China's "nine-dash line" that determines the shape and extent of China's maritime claims in the SCS has no foundation of support in UNCLOS, although China is a signatory. However, it is difficult to imagine China moving away from this legal position, while the other claimant states do not accept either the basis for Chinese claims nor their extent, and are unlikely to abandon this stance. These bedrock divergences are unlikely to dissipate. Furthermore, it is even more difficult to imagine the circumstances where China would voluntarily abandon its claims or evacuate any of its current holdings.

Peering into the future is never easy, and when the subject – the SCS – involves multiple claimants, plus a great number of external countries with a combination of trade and strategic interests in the SCS, predicting the evolution of the mix of rival interests is especially onerous. There are factors that push towards moderation and there are factors that feed suspicion and confrontation.

Factors that feed compromise include the economic inter-dependence between the economies in the SCS region, especially between China and ASEAN member states, but also between China and the US (despite the recent sharp downturn in the bilateral relationship), and between China and trading partners Japan, Australia, and even Taiwan.

When the rival SCS claimants have sat together and negotiated the Code of Conduct (COC) or other legal constructs they are not facing off in naval confrontations. Thus, multilateral discussions, even if falling short of formal negotiations, encourage dialogue and involve a broader range of actors than simply the military and coast guard forces.

Also serving as a brake on all parties, including claimants and external actors, are the risks of military conflict. None of the regional claimants either singly or as a group could resist the Chinese military. But China has much broader interests with all of the claimants than just China's SCS claims. The claimants are important trading partners for China, and their economies are compatible with China's own domestic economy. Southeast Asia is too important to China to allow the SCS to completely dominate its bilateral relations with the claimant states.

There are two principal antagonists in the geopolitical differences over the SCS, one is the principal claimant, China, and the other is the most powerful external stakeholder, the US. The views and actions of these two great powers are clearly the most significant factors in determining the future status of the SCS, not the less powerful claimants or international law. If we could know the likely course of the bilateral relationship between China and the US, we would have a sense of the most probable future status of the SCS dispute.

The bilateral relationship between the two great Pacific Ocean rivals in mid-2020 is at a low ebb, which would point to the risk of heightened competition in the SCS, and a reduced likelihood of a reduction of tensions, or confidence-building measures. Even less likely is a broad agreement between the US and China on how to shape a bilateral or multilateral solution.

As China's claims rest principally on historic documents (particularly but not exclusively the "nine-dash line") which do not have status within UNCLOS, it is hard to imagine circumstances where the competing claims could be satisfied by the International Court of Justice to China's satisfaction. As well, with Xi Jinping having been personally associated with China's broad maritime strategy, it is unlikely that Beijing would ever accept the risks inherent in international arbitration given the domestic consequences of China losing its case.

The SCS dispute is one of the thorniest of international disputes. The very size of the SCS, the complexity of the rival claims, and the involvement of major outside powers are all complicating factors that impede any "grand bargain" that might resolve competing claims. The prospects for an early resolution appear dim, even if, most fortunately, there are restraining factors on the behaviour of all of the players.

This intent of this volume has been to provide up-to-date assessments by a wide range of academics on what may be the most complex international issues in Asia. The varying and sometimes contradictory stances of the writers conveys the broad lack of consensus on the SCS, which nonetheless should assist the readers in assessing both the current thinking of regional experts, and the prospects of successfully addressing this most complex puzzle.

Index

E

F

G